Second Edition

THE SOCIOLOGY OF MEDICINE AND ILLNESS

Richard A. Kurtz

H. Paul Chalfant

Allyn and Bacon

BOSTON   LONDON   TORONTO   SYDNEY   TOKYO   SINGAPORE

Series Editor: Karen Hanson
Series Editorial Assistant: Laurie Frankenthaler
Production Administrator: Annette Joseph
Production Coordinator: Holly Crawford
Editorial-Production Service: Laura Cleveland/WordCrafters Editorial Services, Inc.
Manufacturing Buyer: Megan Cochran
Cover Administrator: Linda K. Dickinson
Cover Designer: Suzanne Harbison

Copyright © 1991, 1984 by Allyn and Bacon
A Division of Simon & Schuster, Inc.
160 Gould Street
Needham Heights, MA 02194

This textbook is printed on
recycled, acid-free paper.

Library of Congress Cataloging-in-Publication Data

Kurtz, Richard A.
    The sociology of medicine and illness / Richard A. Kurtz, H. Paul
Chalfant. — 2nd ed.
        p.   c m.
    Includes bibliographical references.
    Includes index.
    ISBN 0-205-12813-0
    1. Social medicine.   2. Social medicine—United States.
I. Chalfant, H. Paul.   II. Title.
    [DNLM: 1. Social Medicine.   2. Sociology, Medical.   WA 31 K96s]
RA418.K86   1991
362.1—dc20
DNLM/DLC
for Library of Congress   90-14415
                                                                                                                    CIP

Printed in the United States of America

10   9   8   7   6   5   4   3   2   96   95   94   93   92

To Pat and Lois

Contents

Part II
PATIENTS, PHYSICIANS, AND MEDICAL CARE

Part IV
SPECIAL ISSUES IN MEDICINE AND ILLNESS

Preface

It is a sociological truism that cultures change. Nowhere is this better demonstrated than in the U.S. health care institution. Consequently, the health of the population and the system of caring for the ill have changed in important ways since the first edition of this book was published. To keep up with changes, and to keep the medical sociology perspective current, this book revision was necessary.

The most significant change in health in the United States since the first edition was published was the advent of acquired immune deficiency syndrome, or AIDS, as a disease of major concern. No one in the early 1980s could have predicted the powerful impact this condition would have on the nation and its health care system. Until a cure for AIDS or its underlying infection (human immunodeficiency virus, or HIV) is found, AIDS is bound to increasingly dominate worries within the society, particularly because of fears that the disease-causing virus will spill over into the heterosexual population in a major way. Epidemiological aspects of AIDS, and society's reactions to the condition, are incorporated into this second edition.

In another change, large numbers of medical professionals are leaving solo, fee-for-service practices and are joining with other health professionals in group practice, Health Maintenance Organizations, and corporate medicine. Similar changes have affected the entire health care system, especially hospitals, which are also in a transition toward a corporate structure. As an antecedent to, or a consequence of, these changes, the authority of the physician is increasingly being questioned.

At the same time, the question of whether some sort of universal health insurance system should be established in the United States has become less controversial. For the first time, both the business community and the medical profession have recognized the need for a national system and have endorsed the idea of universal health insurance coverage. The United States is at the beginning of a debate that will eventually be settled within the political system. But, given the continuing dominance of the medical profession in the health care delivery system, the politicians will not be effective without the approval of organized medicine. Therefore, from a sociological point of view, understanding the value context of the debate is important. A discussion of viewpoints and alternatives is included in this edition of the book.

While incorporating these changes, we maintained the general format of the first edition with some modifications. For one, we reduced the number of chapters from thirteen to twelve by combining the previously separate discussions of the medical profession and the medical school. This reflects our view that the practice of medicine should be discussed in the same context as the process of becoming a physician. For another, we revised our presentation of social epidemiology by eliminating discussion of some technical aspects and by adding an extensive discussion of AIDS and HIV infection. Third, the People's Republic of China was added to our discussion of the health care systems of other countries. Finally, in recognition of the growing debate about problems in the U.S. health care institution, we recast our previous evaluation of the system into a final chapter that looks at the health care system of the United States as a social problem.

During the revision process, we attempted to keep in mind the nature of our audience—those interested in how the sociological perspective is used to interpret health, illness, and the system that has been established in response to the perceived health needs of society. Our intended readers are students taking sociology courses, students taking courses in other disciplines for whom the sociological perspective would be new and enlightening, practitioners in the health occupations and professions, and social commentators interested in social aspects of this response.

Several colleagues contributed to our approach to the subject matter of the book, particularly during the early stages of writing; we are pleased to acknowledge their contributions. Among these colleagues are Carole A. Campbell, California State University, Long Beach; Pamela D. Elkind, Eastern Washington University, Cheney; Frederic W. Hafferty, University of Minnesota, Duluth; and Marilyn Schmit, Cardinal Stritch College, Milwaukee.

We once again acknowledge the contributions of Patricia Kurtz to our thinking and writing. Her friendly comments and veiled threats added immeasurably to the organization and readability of the book.

1

Basic Sociological Concepts

INTRODUCTION

Like the other social sciences, sociology has developed by first broadening its perspectives and then by refining newly emerged interests. As the discipline of sociology developed, areas of scientific concern expanded and theories and research were extended. New interests led to new subdisciplines. Many of these now have an academic following, and many have received official recognition by sociologists and practitioners of other disciplines. In this progression, the concepts of sociology were applied to the special phenomena of new interest areas. As part of the historical development process, theoretical and methodological questions were raised, additions were made to college curricula, and research was conducted focusing on phenomena of the specialized interest. Special professional journals were founded to serve as a forum for discussion and as a means for sharing research findings, special sections of devotees were created in the national association, and, inevitably, textbooks were written to collate and explain the theories and findings of the specialty.

Within this context, sociology has broadened its perspective in the direction of medical sociology. Although a precise date of initiation is difficult to pinpoint, the mid-to-late 1800s is a convenient date to identify as the beginning of the idea for such a subdiscipline, because Virchow suggested in 1851 that medicine itself is a social science, and McIntire used the term *medical sociology* in a publication in 1894. But modern medical sociology, that is, medical sociology as we now know it, developed during the 1930s, when it was recognized that sociological insights could, and should, be applied to medicine. Particularly important were a 1927 work by Stern, who discussed social factors in medical progress, and a 1935 article by Davis, who called for research in the economic and social aspects of medicine. The first research that can truly be labeled medical sociology was undertaken in the 1930s and 1940s, when several sociologists turned their attention to health and medical phenomena (Hollingshead, 1973).

Several developments led to interest in medical sociology during the late 1940s. Significant to this development was financial and social support by such funds and foundations as Milbank Memorial, Russell Sage, Commonwealth, and Carnegie (see, for example, Freeman and Levine, 1989) along with the postwar strengthening of the National Institutes of Health and the National Institute of Mental Health. Stimuli for development came from several directions at once; the most important were the initiating of professional communication between sociologists themselves, communication between social and medical scientists, and the planning and executing of research studies. Sociology departments, colleges of medicine, and schools of public health participated in these activities.

As they moved into the new area of interest, most sociologists used their traditional academic departments as bases, but others took positions in medical and public health schools. This dual entry into what, for sociologists, was a new field is best described by Straus (1957), who refers to both the sociology *of* medicine and sociology *in* medicine. The sociology *of* medicine is an interest area within the sociology departments of arts and sciences colleges. Its emphasis is on how health phenomena fit into the wider context of society as a whole, on health and the health care system as dimensions of society; its approach to understanding health phenomena is from the society to health phenomena. Given this location, the sociology *of* medicine is academic in nature. Sociology *in* medicine, in comparison, is usually an interest area in colleges of medicine, schools of public health, nursing schools, hospitals, and local health departments. Given these locations, sociology in medicine is often practical in nature, with focus on such problems as social factors in etiology, the ways society copes with medical problems, and reactions to illness; often, the approach is from health phenomena to the society. In either case, the medical sociologists' contribution is a new perspective, a different way of interpreting health phenomena. This distinction between *of* and *in* has become less relevant as medical sociology developed and its contributions became increasingly valuable (Freeman and Levine, 1989). The sociology *of* medicine now produces results applicable to medical practice, and sociology *in* medicine has contributed to the development of sociological theory.

The sociologists' approach provided new insights and helped explain how health-relevant occurrences and behavior were influenced by social factors. The new perspective accomplished two essential tasks simultaneously: It provided more meaningful interpretations of health events, and it pointed to previously neglected factors that must be recognized for health institutions to function effectively. Mechanic and Aiken (1986) suggest that the most significant contribution of the field has been research results that have affected how intelligent laypersons and decision makers conceptualize medicine and health policy.

Actually, the philosophical context for medical sociology had been around for many years. Although the idea for such a discipline was recognized by people like Virchow as far back as 1851, the approach lacked an acceptable means of providing the right type of recognition; the idea was without a base or a methodology that would command the respect of those functioning in the health enterprise. The new approach needed the acceptance and legitimation finally provided by sociologists who applied their increasingly accepted theoretical and methodological approaches to health phenomena in a context that has come to be known as the social system perspective (Mercer, 1972).

Medical sociology has grown considerably since its earliest days. According to Freeman and Levine (1989), this occurred because all areas of knowledge are significantly affected by the social milieu. Further, they note, dramatic changes in all facets of health care make the sociological perspective more relevant. Such changes include a commitment to provide all in need with appropriate health care, the changing demographics straining U.S. resources, the development of complex equipment, the increasing specialization among physicians, and rapidly increasing health care costs.

Medical sociology is similar to all other interest areas of the discipline. In sociological terminology, the family, education, the political system, and the economy are all social institutions; they are socially developed means, structures, and personnel for meeting the basic needs of the people. From the sociological perspective, the health system is a social institution developed to meet the health needs of the population. Thus, medical sociologists focus their efforts on the health institution, just as the family sociologist focuses on the family as an institution, and those in other specialties focus on other social institutions. From a broader sociological perspective, all converge, since society consists of interdependent institutions.

In addition, medical sociologists share a particular perspective and a series of particular concepts with the members of all other sociological subspecialties. They emphasize the *social* and *cultural* nature of human behavior and the social processes and structures comprising society. People are seen as sociocultural beings who have been socialized to function in their particular groups and in society as a whole. This book emphasizes the behavioral patterns of U.S. society that are particularly important to the health institution.

Sociologists offered the medical sociology perspective as an alternative, or supplement, to the tradition-bound, medically based clinical approach of medical scientists. A description of the two perspectives will help us understand the differences.

TWO APPROACHES: THE CLINICAL AND THE SOCIAL SYSTEM

Clinical Approach

In the traditional approach, clinical practitioners focus on individual pathology or abnormality. Clinicians are educated and trained to be therapists who intervene so individuals can return to a normal (that is, nonpathological) health state. Most focus their attention on the biological organism and seek physiological explanations for malfunction. They rely on measurable attributes (such as a blood count) and on judgments of what is abnormal. Illness is thus individual pathology that can be diagnosed by objective means (although the art of the clinician is recognized, and even honored); a treatment regimen can then be instituted with the intent of bringing about a cure.

Social System Approach

In contrast to the emphasis on individual pathology, the social system perspective focuses on group phenomena and on what the group has defined as normal behavior. This is a widening of horizons, for emphasis is shifted to the total health system, to its everyday functions, and to the health behavior of people in groups.

When a distinction is drawn between the two perspectives, the most significant factor is the emphasis on what is normal rather than on what is abnormal. As a corollary, therapy and intervention give way to understanding and meaning. Focus is on the social rather than the biological. In this context, illness becomes a social condition. Questions about the antecedents and consequences of disease are questions about the social environment's contributions to the disease and the social effects of the condition. Since illness has a social meaning, social explanations and consequences make sense. For example, illness is defined as being important to the patient, the patient's groups, the doctor, the hospital staff, and society as a whole. To accompany this perspective, the sociologist offers health practitioners methods that can be used to collect information about the nature and functions of the health institution.

To set the stage for an elaboration of this perspective, we present and define several sociological concepts and discuss how each helps us understand some aspects of health and illness in the United States.

SOME BASIC SOCIOLOGICAL CONCEPTS

This section reviews the sociological concepts relevant to the study of health and medicine. It is limited to the seven most significant for understanding social aspects of health and illness: (1) culture and subculture; (2) groups and categories; (3) values, norms, beliefs, knowledges, and symbols; (4) deviant behavior; (5) status and role; (6) social institutions; and (7) social stratification.

Culture and Subculture

The Concepts.   The broadest of all sociological (and anthropological, we may add) concepts is that of *culture,* which is often defined as "the way of life of a people." This definition is easily understood, but it is too general; it leaves so much of the essential nature of the concept unstated that it is inadequate for all but the most casual understanding. *Culture* does refer to the way of life of a people or a society in a general sense, but the definition as stated does not indicate that people following this pattern of living develop both material and nonmaterial products. People carry on their ways of life within social contexts, not within vacuums. And when they are acting or behaving according to their ways, they develop preferences, notions of expected behavior, beliefs, knowledges, and symbols (some of the nonmaterial elements of culture); they also produce buildings, automobiles, stethoscopes, telephones, television sets, scalpels, photocopiers, sphygmomanometers, printing presses, X-ray machines, and blackboards (some of the material aspects of culture). Both nonmaterial and material products of human behavior are part of the culture; they are shared, in different degrees and in different ways, by those following a particular way of life.

Culture is taught and learned. Sociologists refer to this teaching and learning experience as the *socialization process.* During socialization, people are taught the ways of the society and of particular groups within the society; the biological person also becomes the social person.

When teaching and learning are mentioned, the usual thought is of a school system with its organized program of classes in which teachers impart knowledge to pupils. But the school system is not the only societal unit within which culture is transmitted. Most obvious, and certainly most powerful in the early years of life, is the family unit, the social institution that overtly and covertly transmits conceptions of the society and correct behavior within it. Another significant socializing group is the peer group, where people learn from equals. Also, the mass communications media of television, movies, magazines, newspapers, and other outlets present non-material aspects of culture to the population. Other socialization agencies and experiences exist, but those mentioned are generally the most influential.

The socialization experience is not limited to children; for most people it is a lifelong process. One tends to focus on members of the younger generation because they are in the most obvious learning situation, but adult socialization is a constant of society. True, in the usual case, the adult is not as receptive to the molding and shaping processes but, especially in a culture that experiences rapid change, adult socialization is necessary for survival. As knowledge expands and as ideas are modified, those who resist changes or new situations face difficult times.

U.S. society is particularly committed to change through scientific innovation and through the development of new ideas. During the lifetime of currently living people, for example, Americans have witnessed the development and acceptance of the airplane, nuclear energy, radio, television, hand-held calculators, heart transplant techniques, birth control pills, and computers; they also have experienced women's suffrage, the civil rights movement, the women's liberation movement, and massive protests to end a war and the weapons of war. Some changes have led to a major restructuring of the way of life in the United States, and some have led only to changes in how something is perceived.

Change is constant, but it is not uniform throughout the culture. In the United States, a reward system that honors material achievement with wealth and non-material achievement with admiration contributes to uneven rates of change between the two: The advances of the nonmaterial parts of culture lag behind the material. Sociologists refer to this phenomenon as the *cultural lag*; sociologists see it as an inevitable consequence of the U.S. way of life.

When we use the term "the U.S. way of life," we do not mean to imply a homogeneity within our society, because our society is anything but culturally homogeneous. It is true that, to some degree, Americans are committed to achievement and success, activity and work, a moral orientation, humanitarianism, efficiency and practicality, progress, material comfort, equality, freedom, external conformity, science and secular rationality, nationalism and patriotism, democracy, individuality, and group superiority themes (Williams, 1970); to the values of freedom, accomplishment, hard work, responsibility, honesty, and individual success (Rokeach, 1973); and to scientific change that improves the quality of life. These broad generalizations identify mainstream features of U.S. society, but they do not show that particular groups may reject the stated preferences or behaviors, that some may not be able to take advantage of them, and that some groups may not accept them to the same degree as others. In fact, some specific groups within society may develop distinctive ways of behavior with unique or modified ways of life and may focus the socialization process for its new generation on this distinctive way of life.

Often, when cultural lag exists, people with varied belief and knowledge systems interpret a material innovation differently, react to it in unique ways, and offer their own solutions to problems it may have caused. This can lead to value conflicts. Generally, the more heterogeneous the society, the more likely it is that disagreements will occur. Because of its cultural heterogeneity and commitment to change, U.S. society is particularly vulnerable to cultural lag and to value conflicts concerning innovations.

Culture is shared, but it is not shared equally throughout society. Even while accepting most of the mainstream or dominant culture, groups may develop particular patterns that set them off as different, for example, in language, work ethic, marriage, education, or food customs. In some cases, the mainstream way of life may be rejected. Groups practicing their own particular way of life within the larger cultural context are referred to as *subcultures*. And, if a subculture actively rejects the generally accepted way of life, if its members challenge the mainstream culture, it is referred to as a *counterculture* or *contraculture*. But in the usual case, few subcultures come into opposition with the general culture; adherents simply practice their ways of behavior within the larger context. Some examples of subcultures in U.S. society are ethnic or nationality groups (e.g., Hispanic-Americans), social class groupings (e.g., the middle class), and age subcultures (e.g., adolescents).

Applying the Concepts to the Health Institution.   The culture concept indicates that the mainstream health institution of the United States is socially derived and that it reflects the values, norms, knowledges, beliefs, and symbols of the society. Consequently, no other country has a health system precisely like that of the United States, which follows from our point that no other country has a culture just like the U.S. way of life. This statement applies to all other cultures. Further, this does not suggest that the patterns of the U.S. health institution are better or worse than any other; the only intended suggestion is that the social institutions of any society have been developed as reflections of its own particular patterns of living.

Recognizing the importance of the socialization process can help us understand the health institution of the United States in several ways. On the most general level, we see that the way Americans perceive their country's health system had to be learned. This sets the background for health education in the school system and through the communication sources that reach the adult population. Health education programs can be particularly effective in disease prevention, but the prevention concept must be consistent with the overall cultural patterns of the people. Such programs may face rejection or a lack of interest and funding in a way of life that emphasizes private responsibility for one's actions and cure rather than prevention.

The subculture concept helps us to understand disease patterns and reactions to illness. For example, the food habits people acquire during socialization in a subculture affect their weight, gastrointestinal functions, and cholesterol level. Further, both the time of recognizing a disease and reactions to it can differ considerably from one subculture to another. Perceptions of signs of potential health problems, what caused a disease, what to do about it, what is known about it, and its meaning can all differ among the subcultures of society.

The concept of adult socialization also points to the character of programs designed to train health practitioners. In medical school, nursing school, and similar programs, students acquire knowledge about the specialized field. But the training consists of much more; in addition to knowledge and technique, orientations and ways of thinking and acting also are learned. In medical school, the aspiring doctor learns how to think like a doctor, how to take the authoritative status, and how to relate to others. Medical education not only focuses on the specialized knowledge and the clinical approach that characterize the physician's practice, but also on how to think and act like a doctor.

At the forefront of cultural changes in contemporary society are some that will have important consequences for the U.S. health institution. For example, rapid changes are now occurring in biology, with biomedical innovations that can have unforeseen implications for health care and the health care system. There are reports that new techniques in recombinant DNA could have major effects on controlling disease and improving life. It is not possible to predict the specific effects that such changes will have on the way of life in the United States, but it is possible to predict that, given cultural lag and the pluralistic nature of society, they will lead to different interpretations among groups and to value conflicts.

Groups and Categories

The Concepts. At times, the discipline of sociology has been characterized simplistically as the study of groups. When a definition of *group* is offered, it is frequently "two or more people who are interacting." As in the definition of culture, such a shortcut statement presents a basic message, but it provides only superficial understanding. "Two or more people who are interacting" is a good start in defining the concept since it emphasizes the essential element of social relationships among participants. But it fails to point out that these relationships occur within a social context, and that they are regulated by rules defining the expected behavior of the participants.

A point emphasized in the discussion of culture was that people are sociocultural beings who have learned to function according to the expectations held in their particular groups. Knowledge of one's own expected behavior and of the behavior of others within the group provides a certain degree of general predictability. We refer to general predictability because the human is not a machine, not a robot with mechanical and easily predictable specific behaviors. Each person's uniqueness modifies the flow of interaction within the group, but the expectations influence the actions of all participants.

In many groups, participants interact within a system of informally defined expectations (for example, "to love, honor, and cherish"). If formal regulations or expectations intrude on the interaction of informal groups, they are ignored; if formal regulations are emphasized, this may signal a movement toward dissolving the informal group. Informal groups in which those interacting have emotional commitments, strong loyalties, intimacy, and cohesive relationships are known as *primary groups*. Examples are families, friendship groups, and, often, small occupational groups within which people work in emotionally close situations. The smallest primary group most of us participate in consists of two persons, such as husband-wife or friend-friend; the largest is generally a circle of friends or a closely knit work or study group. Primary groups usually meet many of the emotional needs of participants; if they do not, the permanency of the group is threatened.

Other groups in which we interact attempt to channel our behavior with a series of formal rules and regulations, defining expected behavior in formal or organized ways; rules may be clearly specified in written documents such as contracts and organizational charts. Such associations may define group goals precisely and may list behavioral prescriptions and proscriptions for each member. Such groups are referred to as *secondary groups*. Examples are bureaucracies, a classroom of students and a professor, and a supermarket. The smallest secondary relationship for most of us is the two-person group, such as customer-clerk or doctor-patient; the largest of our secondary groups is society.

It is the nature of social life that emotional commitments and cohesiveness among some participants will arise in secondary associations. In this case, primary groups will develop within the secondary group. Primary relations and primary groups emerge even in the most rigidly organized bureaucracy. U.S. industry, especially, has learned the importance of primary relationships among workers within its bureaucratically organized structures (Roethlisberger and Dickson, 1939).

Sociologists classify people according to their group memberships because such affiliations are important for understanding behavior. But the group is by no means the only influence on behavior. Another is the individual's personality or uniqueness. Behavior also is affected by such personal characteristics as age, sex, and marital status. None of these are attributes of groups, but rather classifications of individuals with common characteristics. The key element here is not interaction between people, but common attributes that may never actually lead to any type of relationship or contact. At best, such categories of people may be seen as a *grouping*, a term often used by sociologists, demographers, and statisticians to refer to any collection of data in which the units have common characteristics. Such groupings may be referred to as social or statistical categories; they are created by the sociologist, not by people themselves.

Although categories are not groups, groups may be formed as an outgrowth of shared characteristics because people tend to come into contact with one another and to interact with others on the basis of similarities. Age peer groups are common, as are ethnic clubs, community centers, and friendship groups centered on marital status. Even as social or statistical categories, classifications help us to understand ways of life. For example, if someone is described as an elderly married female in the middle class from an old Yankee background, we can make some fairly accurate predictions about her life experiences, perceptions, and behavioral patterns. Consequently, in most sociological research concerned with behavior, social and statistical categories are used to help account for differential perceptions and actions.

People are members of many groups and can be classified into many categories, all of which are likely to have some influence on behavior. Those groups or categories the individual psychologically identifies with are referred to as *reference groups*. Reference groups have a specific influence on a person's opinions, attitudes, values, and perceptions. A distinction should be drawn between membership groups and reference groups because the difference between physical membership and psychological identification is important for most people. Many membership and reference groups are the same for most people, but some people may desire membership in groups or categories to which they do not belong. For example, a person may want to become a member of a respected club or wish to enter the ranks of the upper class. Consequently, although maintaining the point that group or category affiliations can have an important influence on an individual's behavior, we must add that groups or categories to which individuals do not belong also can influence their behavior.

Applying the Concepts to the Health Institution.   The essence of the definitions of *group* (interaction) and *social category* (common characteristics) are extremely significant to the structure and function of the health care system. To understand this statement, one must be aware that within the sociological perspective sickness is a social condition with social antecedents and consequences. The groups and categories one belongs to or refers to are, therefore, seen as having an impact on health behavior. If we had information about someone's social interactions and characteristics, we would have a basis for explaining his or her health behavior, including the antecedents and consequences of sickness.

Medical sociologists attempt to determine whether disease rates differ by social groups and categories. Thus, the social epidemiologist may cross-classify disease rates and population characteristics. If it is found that members of specific groups or categories exhibit extraordinary rates, a search for reasons may uncover social patterns associated with the high or low rate.

Often, the primary group functions as an emotional base for its members; it is one of the few places in society where people can loosen up psychologically in the intimacy of unquestioned acceptance as total human beings. An outward expression of strong emotion, rarely allowed in U.S. society, is acceptable here. For these and other reasons, if a disease is life-threatening, if it has long-term negative consequences, if it leads to much suffering, the primary group members may be difficult to manage. For example, the doctor may find it more difficult to relate to the patient's family than to the patient.

Two-person groups, such as the doctor-patient, nurse-patient, and hospital administrator-doctor, are the smallest of the secondary groups examined by the medical sociologist. The largest health institution secondary group studied by sociologists is usually the hospital, although some have studied the total health care delivery system. The total health institution in a country or in a given community may be classified as a group from some perspectives, but we prefer to look at the total system as a conglomeration of groups since little seems to bind some of these components together.

Hospitals have received much attention from sociologists, possibly because these facilities are a special type of bureaucracy. Despite many seemingly contradictory internal characteristics, the hospital does seem to get the health care job done; most current complaints about hospitals in this country are of high costs rather than of how they function or the quality of care.

Values, Norms, Beliefs, Knowledges, and Symbols

The Concepts.   Together, values, norms, beliefs, knowledges, and symbols are the essential elements of the nonmaterial dimension of culture. They define for each member of society the social preferences, ways of acting, indicators of truth, and objects that are indicative of associations and positions. These elements provide the framework for a pattern of living in routinized, unthinking ways. They provide a particular order that gives society an overall consistency that may be referred to as "the U.S. way of life," or "the Tanzanian," "Soviet," or any other "way of life." As may be expected, these dimensions tend to be consistent with one another. More than that, some can best be understood as paired concepts, as is clearly the case for values and norms.

Values are roughly equivalent to preferences. In a societal sense, the concept refers to what society's members perceive as worthwhile or desirable. They are evaluative; they are judgments couched in terms like "good" and "beautiful" and "moral" and may be applied to any aspect of life, behavior, objects, ideas, people, or events. The commitments to individualism, financial independence, and acquisition of material goods are all reflections of the U.S. value system—that is, the U.S. preference or judgmental system.

Paired with values is the sociological concept of norms or, to distinguish it from similar but unrelated concepts, social norms. The concept refers to society's rules and regulations designed to guide behavior, to indicate appropriate and inappropriate behavior, to spell out the do's and don'ts of activities. From another perspective, social norms define the expected behavior of people. Values define the ends and norms define the acceptable means of reaching these ends for the members of society.

Social norms are concerned with the full range of behavior, from polite customs such as those listed in a book of etiquette to those considered essential to the welfare of society. The range is from norms that, if violated, would result in no or very light negative group sanctions to those whose violations could result in a severe negative sanctions (for example, imprisonment or the death penalty). The former norms, referred to as *folkways*, are not perceived as having much moral significance; the latter, referred to as *mores*, have very strong moral connotations. Norms usually do not define expectations in narrow terms; they provide a range within which behavior would be acceptable, thus allowing expressions of individual uniqueness. The acceptable range may be described as the *tolerance limits* of society. These limits are much broader for folkways than for mores. Some social norms are written and some are not; if they are written with negative sanctions for deviance from the expected behavior, they are *laws*.

When the concept of subculture was discussed, a distinction was made between the mainstream, or dominant, culture and the ways of life in subcultures. To some extent, this distinction is really between mainstream values and norms and a subculture's particular rendition of these aspects of culture. Some groups may modify values and norms, if only by providing their own interpretations. And, of course, some groups are specifically organized to emphasize particular values; they may make a distinct effort to define their values so their group is distinguished from all others. Since norms are means, the behavior of group members also may differ. In almost all cases, the values are not inconsistent with the mainstream culture, and the norms are within society's tolerance limits.

Belief and knowledge cannot be distinguished from each other for many members of the society. For our purposes, we define *belief* as the information held for which no socially acceptable means of proof exist and *knowledge* as information for which means of proof do exist. In U.S. society, the validating techniques for knowledge are part of the scientific method; for other societies and for some subcultures in U.S. society, the validating methods may be tradition, religion, or philosophy. That is, one society's beliefs may be another's knowledge. Nowhere is the distinction between the two concepts clearer than in the area of religion, although economic and political systems in the contemporary world demonstrate the same phenomenon.

Finally, we come to the concept of *symbols*. Sociologists use the term in reference to acts or objects that communicate a particular message or represent something else. Words are symbols, as are a country's flag, a Rolls Royce, a business suit, a bachelor's degree, the rank of professor, a tombstone, and one's signature. There are many health-relevant symbols, including medical jargon, the doctor's medical degree (in symbolic fashion, usually hung framed on the office wall), the nurse's uniform, and the patient's gown.

Applying the Concepts to the Health Institution.   Throughout this book we will discuss the health care institution in terms of values, norms, beliefs, knowledges, and symbols, both directly and indirectly. The application of these nonmaterial aspects of culture will be most direct when we compare the health care system of the United States with the systems of other countries; it will be least direct when the material aspects of the system are discussed. Nevertheless, the examination of the structures within which the health systems function should make it evident that they have been developed as reflections of particular values, norms, beliefs, knowledges, and symbols. When discussing the health care system of the United States, we will use nonmaterial elements to describe social aspects of the health institution.

Particularly important is the belief system of the mainstream U.S. culture, which emphasizes change of a special type: change for the better. Coupled with this belief in the inherent goodness of proper change are beliefs about the ability of people to control the environment by active mastery over events. Scientific advancement is considered the most effective way to achieve desirable changes. In the biomedical area, this belief system was the reason for establishing a massive federal bureaucracy that supports scientific research to provide information needed to combat disease and preserve health. Frequently, the investment in such research has led to findings and understandings that society cannot yet implement and formulate into practical programs. The cultural lag in such a system seems constant, with an almost built-in time gap between material and nonmaterial progress. Society pays a price for this situation: We know what causes some diseases without knowing how to develop effective intervention programs.

The various values and beliefs within a society are not always consistent. On the one hand, good health is desirable; on the other, the public's belief in individualism may lead to lack of support for programs that make some health practices mandatory. This contradiction in values may partly explain why the United States has not developed a major preventive medicine program.

The doctor is in a particularly good position to benefit from the U.S. belief system about health. Physicians have taken control of the disease process and its management. They are trained to apply the findings of science, they are committed to helping people return to good health, and they have achieved in a highly admired manner. Added to this is a respected degree of education and a professional manner that rests on an assured competence. Physicians are defined as experts in the health area by a society that tends to believe that experts should be honored.

Deviant Behavior

The Concept.   Behavior that does not conform to the social norms is considered deviant. From the sociological perspective, the term *deviance* bears neither value nor moral implications. Nor does it necessarily imply intention. Any public behavior not conforming to the normative expectations of the group or society can be considered deviant.

All of us are deviant at some time, but our behavior may be accepted or purposively overlooked by the other members of society. Only if the behavior is noticeably outside the tolerance limits, and even then only under certain conditions, will the deviance be acknowledged and be negatively sanctioned. Recognizing and sanctioning are related to several factors. First, there is the relative importance of the norm or norms that are violated. Most of us have received a ticket for illegal parking; yet the fine was minor, and we were not considered criminals. On the other hand, those arrested for driving while intoxicated may receive heavy fines, driver's license revocation, a jail term, and may be considered criminals. Second is the situation in which the deviant act takes place. For example, if a person becomes intoxicated at a party and strikes another guest, the incident may be embarrassedly shrugged off and the deviant person led away as quietly as possible. Should the same person strike a fellow employee or customer at work, the behavior could lead to severe penalties, even to being dismissed from employment. Third, the characteristics of the person performing the deviant act affect social reactions. In one community in a middle-size U.S. city, a group of high school students from upper-middle-class homes thought it fun to place bombs in mail boxes and watch them explode. When they were finally caught, these teenagers were admonished and sent home to their well-to-do parents with the warning to be good from now on. Had these students been from poor homes or had they been members of a deprived group, they may have faced severe punishment.

Notice that in the discussion of each of these factors we mentioned judgment, reaction, and decisions on the part of others. Deviant behavior is social behavior. It requires not only someone acting in this manner but also members of a group making some judgment concerning the behavior. The behavior becomes deviant when others react to it.

Applying the Concept to the Health Institution.   The concept of deviant behavior has played an important part in the development of sociological conceptions of sickness. Parsons (1951) first described the status-role of the sick person as a nonintentional deviant one. Occupants of the sick status are considered deviant because they do not carry out the usual social roles. If people feel ill but ignore the feeling and continue with usual duties, they would not be considered deviant within the context of the group. But if such people seek exemptions from usual duties, the behavior is deviant because the normal roles are not being played. Deviance resulting from the sick role exemption, however, is generally excused, and individuals are treated rather than punished for their failure to fulfill normal roles.

Status and Role

The Concepts.   *Social status* is a position in a group or category, and *social role* is the expected behavior of a person occupying a status. Status is structural and role is functional; a person occupies a status and plays a role. We all occupy many statuses and play many roles at any given time. As we go from group to group throughout the day, we may change some of our statuses while maintaining others; as we move from status to status, some of our expected behaviors change and others stay the same.

During childhood socialization, we learn about positions we will be occupying in the normal course of events, about those we may be occupying, and about those we will never occupy but that are nevertheless important to us. For example, we learn our current age and sex roles; we also learn roles for the future—marital, parental, and occupational. We learn about the status and role of the president of the United States, and those of schoolteacher, nurse, doctor, police officer, secretary, and so on. Even though we will never occupy some of these statuses, many of us learn about the rights and obligations of all because, if we know the roles of others, we know how they and we are expected to respond if interaction occurs. Furthermore, some roles we learn about motivate us toward social conformity by warning us about potential conse-quences. Examples are the roles of traitor and prisoner.

Some statuses are more important than others in specific group situations. A person's sex, marital, and occupational statuses are usually salient in all contexts because they are significant to the individual at all times and have a powerful influence on behavior. We also acquire the ability to change our behavior dramati-cally as we move from one status to another—for example, the college football player as a student in the classroom and professors as parents of college students.

Social role refers to expected behavior, rather than actual behavior. The expec-tations are constant, independent of how many people actually play any particular role. Members of a society sometimes evaluate how well a person meets the expecta-tions of role performance. For some, criteria of performance quality may be objec-tive, such as the earned run average of a baseball pitcher, but for others evaluative criteria may be subjective, such as the effectiveness of the professor in the classroom.

Evaluations are rarely made for many roles, although one could theoretically refer to a "good son" or a "good garbage collector."

Applying the Concepts to the Health Institution.   Some applications of the status and role concepts to the health institution are obvious and some are not so obvious. For example, it is easy to name the statuses and roles important in the hospital: doctor, nurse, nurse aide, administrator, pharmacist, admissions clerk, maintenance worker, laboratory technician, housekeeper, insurance clerk, switchboard operator, student nurse, and patient, among others. Imagine how different the hospital would be if some of these statuses were not occupied, if the roles were not played (especially the patient status and role). Thus, an analysis of the hospital from a status and role point of view can reveal how the facility functions. Such an analysis would first examine the structural relationships between statuses and then determine their functional relationships. A comparison of expected function with actual function may be particularly enlightening. Studying one type of interactive relationship, such as power, could indicate much about the hospital as a social system.

Instead of examining an entire system, such as the hospital, the sociologist might focus on one particular status—for example, the doctor, the nurse, or the patient. Sociological studies have tended to examine the expected behavior of incumbents of such statuses, with emphasis on how behavioral expectations fit with those of other relevant positions and with the society as a whole. When particular statuses and roles are studied, the positions and expectations should be kept within their sociocultural context, for it is only within this context that they have structural and functional meaning.

Some of the more interesting studies by medical sociologists have focused on the sick role. Although it may be difficult for some people to visualize sickness as a social condition, the person who is labeled sick is expected by group members to behave in a certain way. True, the sick person may exhibit a biological condition, but this person is also supposed to exhibit a sociocultural condition.

Social Institutions

The Concept.   Social institutions are composed of society's standardized ways of handling recurring needs of the population, needs that must be met for people to carry out culturally defined activities. If these needs are not met, society as we know it will not survive. Institutions are composed of interrelated social values, norms, beliefs, roles, groups, and interactions that have been established to meet needs and to solve problems.

Theoretically, members of each society have made decisions about how the needs of people should be met, decisions that fit with the overall culture of the particular society. This has led to a wide variety of institutional patterns among the societies of the world. In all cultures, social institutions are interdependent and function within a common sociocultural context. But not all institutions are in equally strong positions to influence society or to be taken into consideration. In the western world, the religious institution once held major power, with its leaders making political and economic decisions for the entire population, decisions having strong repercussions on the family, the school system, and the health care system. Today in the West the economic institution seems the most powerful, especially given its strong tie-in with the political system, and economic decisions can strongly affect all other patterns of living, including health patterns. Meanwhile, for many segments of the population, religious aspects of life have been compartmentalized, and few religious leaders are currently powerful.

Applying the Concept to the Health Institution.   In large measure, the focus of this book is on the standardized ways of meeting the health needs of the members of society. Because of the importance to society of keeping its members healthy, the lack of a health institution is inconceivable. Consider, for example, the blow to society's daily activities if means had not been developed to meet the health needs of the population, if a large number of people could not function because of illness.

But the health institution does not function independently; it is closely tied to all other basic social institutions. Illness is not an individual affair that affects one person alone. Depending on its nature and severity, all members of the family may become involved; if the illness is serious, the repercussions on others in the family can be major. Health personnel may see only the patient, but their decisions often affect a much larger circle of people, including the entire family.

As a consequence of historical factors, the influence of the religious institution on the health institution is now diminished, although some aspects of interdependence still exist. There are still Catholic and Jewish medical schools in this country and Catholic, Jewish, and Protestant hospitals. In some western countries, a hospital nurse is still called "sister," an indication of how things once were. And religious values still surface when illness is serious enough to raise anxiety in the patient and family. At such emotional times, the family, religious, and health institutions may become closely interdependent, with representatives of the religious system playing strong roles.

The educational institution is responsible for keeping a steady flow of technically competent people available for practice in the facilities of the health institution. When performing this role, the training facilities are constantly monitored by representatives of the health and political (through government) institutions. Accreditation teams have been formed to make certain that the educational facilities are training a new generation equal to the demands of the health institution.

Although the health institution in this country basically functions as a free-enterprise economic system, the political institution maintains significant monitoring and licensing functions. Members of health occupations are licensed by the state government to practice within political boundaries, and such facilities as hospitals must obtain licenses to continue functioning. Some states have reciprocity agreements, but practitioners must be approved by the political system of any state in which they plan to practice, although the criteria for licensing are usually set by professional organizations. Additionally, most medical schools are state owned, and many hospitals are owned by local governments. Given the control of ownership, the admission quotas of most large medical schools in the United States ensure an exceedingly high proportion of state residents among their students; usually, about 85 percent of those admitted to a state medical school must be legal residents.

Finally, the economic institution is also closely tied to the health institution. Not only is health "big business" in the United States, but the society would face serious disruption if many members could not (or volitionally do not in the case of "sick-ins") fulfill expected functions. Furthermore, the health care system is exceedingly expensive to run. This important industry employs millions of workers, and total spending on health care in the United States was approximately $600 billion in 1989. Most complaints about the U.S. health institution are not concerned with the quality of the system but with its costs. At least two values lie at the root of much criticism. One holds that the health system should be guided by a humanitarian orientation, and the other that it is an economic enterprise. In any society, it is often difficult to reconcile such conflicting values.

Social Stratification

The Concept.   In most sociological studies of attitudes and lifestyles, responses are cross-classified with an index of *social stratification*. Social stratification has been found to be a pervasive and salient variable to help explain how people perceive the world and how they adjust to it. *Social stratification* refers to the hierarchical system in societies through which the social rewards (usually identified as economic advantage, prestige, and power) are unequally distributed. This structured inequality has an all-pervasive effect on the lifestyles of people, enough so that different strata or classes sharing the same extent of rewards may be classified together as a subculture. Members of the same strata or social class share the same way of life and hold similar values, norms, beliefs, knowledges, and symbols. The people of similar strata also share similar life chances, which are reflections of their level of living.

As a consequence of the U.S. commitment to a value system honoring achievement, individuality, material wealth, and mastery over one's fate, the lines separating strata are supposed to be surmountable. The beliefs and values suggest an open-class system in which people can move upward from one social class to another (downward too, but this is rarely mentioned because it contradicts a mainstream value). Sociologists disagree among themselves about how open the class system really is in the contemporary United States. Some feel that it may be more of an ideal than a reality.

Subculture members tend to associate with other members of the same stratification grouping. Sharing life experiences with members of the same subculture helps reinforce similar perceptions and viewpoints. Such differential association also means that one's full life-experience cycle tends to take place within one social class subculture.

Applying the Concept to the Health Institution.   Innumerable sociological studies have found that members of different social classes hold significantly different perceptions of symptoms, of proper actions to be taken when symptoms are recognized, and of proper responses to the disease by the health system. These differing perceptions, actions and responses influence differential morbidity and mortality rates of disease, and also health resource utilization rates. For example, recognition that a social class position is subcultural helps explain why a health program may be successful among some people and unsuccessful among others.

The social stratification concept also clarifies aspects of the doctor-patient relationship, especially when the patient is of a social class different from the doctor. Subcultural influences are significant to all aspects of the regimen the doctor suggests to the patient. And the concept explains some interaction patterns among the various statuses in the health care system.

SUMMARY

The specialty known as medical sociology provides a new perspective for interpreting health phenomena; in so doing, it has presented a social interpretation of health events and has identified previously neglected factors that help us comprehend the health institution. This new perspective emphasizes group phenomena, a broader scope of interest than individual pathology. There is a corresponding shift away from therapy toward understanding. In taking this approach, the medical sociologist has applied the following basic concepts to the health field.

Culture and Subculture. Culture is the pattern of living followed by the members of a society; it includes both the nonmaterial aspects of life and the products created as people follow their daily activities. The culture is taught to each generation, and its ways are shared by the members of society. The concept helps us understand that the health institution was socially derived and reflects society's particular patterns of living.

U.S. society is heterogeneous, with specific groupings following their own distinctive ways of behavior, ways generally consistent with the mainstream culture. Such specific groups are called subcultures. Many sociologists feel that the most important subcultures in the society as a whole are based on ethnic, social-class, and age differences. This concept is particularly important to health behavior since people in different subcultures hold different values toward, beliefs about, and knowledge about disease, health, and the health care system. These all lead to different behaviors.

Groups and Categories. A group consists of two or more people interacting within a system of social regulations that define the expected behavior of participants. Some groups are informal, and some are bound by a formally organized system of regulations. Informal groups with strong emotional commitments among members, who hold strong loyalties and feelings of cohesion, are known as primary groups. Examples are families and friendship groups. Groups organized in a system of formal rules and regulations are known as secondary groups; examples are hospitals and the doctor-patient group. Both primary and secondary groups strongly influence the behavior of people, including health behavior.

Categories are not groups but are ways of classifying people on the basis of common characteristics, for example, all people over sixty-five years of age, all middle-class people in a community, all females, and so forth. The classification is based on the sociologist's handling of data rather than on people's behavior. Such categories are important to the medical sociologist because people with common characteristics tend to have common experiences in society, and this may lead to consistency of health attitudes and behaviors.

Reference groups are those with which an individual holds a psychological identification; they may be membership groups, but a person can identify with a group without being a member. Such psychological groups can have an important influence on how a person perceives and acts within the health situation.

Values, Norms, Beliefs, Knowledges, and Symbols. These five concepts constitute the nonmaterial dimension of culture. They are the framework within which the members of society see the world in a mostly consistent framework. As a result, we can make broad generalizations about the U.S. way of life, or the Soviet way of life, or other ways of life. These are society's relatively consistent systems of preferences, expected ways of behavior, information, and representations. The nonmaterial aspects of culture make up a large share of the sociological interest in the health institution.

Deviant Behavior. This concept refers to behavior that is inconsistent with social norms and is reacted to by others. It is important in the study of health and illness because the sick status is often seen as deviant. Nevertheless, it is a type of deviance that receives approval.

Status and Role. Social status is a position in a group or category, and social role is the behavior expected of those who occupy the position. Status is structural and role is functional; we occupy a status and play a role. Health and health-related statuses and roles are important to the medical sociologist because they provide insight into how people are organized and how they function within the health system.

Social Institutions. An institution is the socially derived standardized way of meeting the needs of society's members. Thus, the societal response to health and disease is the health institution. The medical sociologist focuses on the workings of this particular institution and its relationships with several other social institutions of society. Medical sociologists also attempt to understand the health institution in the United States by examining health institutions in other societies.

Social Stratification. The social rewards of each society, such as economic advantage, prestige, and power, are not distributed equally. Categories of people sharing similar rewards are known as social classes. Members of the same class share similar lifestyles; these are social class subcultures. Members of different class subcultures act differently toward the health institution.

References

Davis, Michael M. 1935. "Wanted: Research in the economic and social aspects of medicine." *Milbank Memorial Fund Quarterly* 13 (October): 339-346.

Freeman, Howard, and Sol Levine, eds. 1989. *Handbook of Medical Sociology*. 4th ed. Englewood Cliffs, N.J.: Prentice-Hall.

Hollingshead, August B. 1973. "Medical sociology: A brief review." *Milbank Memorial Fund Quarterly* 51 (Fall):531–542.

McIntire, Charles. 1894. "The importance of the study of medical sociology." *Bulletin of the American Academy of Medicine* 1 (February): 425–434.

Mechanic, David, and Linda H. Aiken. 1986. "Social science, medicine, and health policy." In *Applications of Social Science to Clinical Medicine and Health Policy*, ed. L. H. Aiken and D. Mechanic, 1–9. New Brunswick, N.J.: Rutgers University Press.

Mercer, Jane R. 1972. "Who is normal? Two perspectives on mild mental retardation." In *Patients, Physicians and Illness*, 2nd ed., ed. E. G. Jaco, 56–75. New York: Free Press.

Parsons, Talcott. 1951. *The Social System*. New York: Free Press.

Roethlisberger, F. J., and W. J. Dickson. 1939. *Management and the Worker*. Cambridge: Harvard University Press.

Rokeach, Milton. 1973. *The Nature of Human Values*. New York: Free Press.

Stern, Bernhard J. 1927. *Social Factors in Medical Progress*. New York: Columbia University Press.

Straus, Robert. 1957. "The nature and status of medical sociology." *American Sociological Review* 22:200–204.

Virchow, Rudolf. 1851. "Die Epidemien von 1848, Essen in der Jahressitzung der Gesellschaft fur wissenschaftliche Medizin am 27 November 1848." *Archiven fur pathologische Anatomie und Physiologie und fur klinische Medizin* 3:3–12.

Williams, Robin M., Jr. 1970. *American Society*. New York: Random House.

2

Social Epidemiology: The Approach of Demography and Ecology

INTRODUCTION

There are parallels between the social science discipline of demography and the medical discipline of epidemiology. The basic parallel is in their general focus of interest: Both are concerned with the size, characteristics, and distribution of phenomena. In the case of demography, this focus is applied to the population; in epidemiology, it is applied to medical conditions. Further, scientists in both demography and epidemiology try to identify the factors that contribute to observed patterns, both look for antecedents, and both attempt to understand consequences for the present, estimate future patterns, and predict consequences. But epidemiology always takes a step that demography may not: With its roots in medicine, epidemiology is an applied discipline, whereas demography's roots in the social sciences allow it to remain on the scientific level without application. As stated by MacMahon (1981:59), "the predominant, though not exclusive, purpose of epidemiology is the understanding of the etiology of human diseases and the identification of preventive measures."

Epidemiologists often study large arrays of statistics about society and disease as they try to ascertain whether different categories or groups of people exhibit different disease rates. Note that the epidemiologist focuses on health problems in populations or groups within a population rather than on problems of individuals; this focus differentiates it from other medical specialties. If disease-rate differentials among segments of the population are found, the challenge is to explain why they exist. If the epidemiologist is socially oriented (medical epidemiologists may not be), attention is given to social or cultural factors that have contributed to differentials. For example, a social epidemiologist monitoring the data on a health condition might observe comparatively high rates of a disease among members of a particular category of people and may note a trend toward higher rates. Further study may reveal a spreading outward of the disease from an area with high rates of infection to areas of low or medium rates. Perhaps drawing the conclusion that the spread to other areas is a consequence of travel patterns, the epidemiologist might suggest confinement or quarantine, a change in the itineraries of infected individuals, or limiting travel to those who have been inoculated against the disease.

The epidemiologist is interested in identifying any factor that contributes to the distribution of disease. In general terms, this means a search of disease variations by person, time, and place. In more specific terms, MacMahon (1981:60) states that "the specific characteristics most frequently examined include:

1. Person—age, sex, and ethnic group; occupation, education, and socio-economic group; marital status and family history.
2. Time—changes over decades; seasonal variation and other cyclic variation; and short-term changes such as over days.
3. Place—country; state or district within country; urban or rural; and distribution within local community."

From one perspective, epidemiology is a dull enterprise that necessitates poring over thousands of computer printouts of descriptive data and cross-classifications. From another, the field is as exciting as a Conan Doyle story, with the epidemiologist functioning as a detective who searches for logical relationships that are buried in mountains of observations. The detective approach can be demonstrated by the story of Sir John Snow, whose insight helped stop a cholera epidemic in London in 1855 that had claimed 500 lives in a ten-day period; because of his efforts, Snow is often referred to as "the father of modern epidemiology."

Sir John was a physician, but his focus on the behavior of people took him into the realm of the social epidemiologist. When reviewing and cross-classifying available data, he searched for common factors among those who had contracted cholera. One stood out: Many victims lived in a particular area of the city, in the vicinity of Broad Street. After interviewing people in the neighborhood with a series of questions about their daily behavior, his focus narrowed to one pattern common to the victims: They had all drunk water that came from a particular well. His logical conclusion was that the cholera pathogen was coming from contaminated water in the Broad Street well. Further evidence in support of this conclusion came from the observation of some establishments in the area where cholera was not a problem, and where people did not drink from the contaminated well. The well pump was closed down, and the number of new cases of cholera in the Broad Street neighborhood declined substantially.

Snow recommended the proper action to halt the epidemic without knowing which pathogen was infecting the cholera victims; in fact, the cholera bacillus was not isolated for another twenty-eight years. He only had the observation that a particular type of behavior and a particular disease were associated, which set the background for the conclusion that an etiological agent was transmitted, whatever its nature. Knowledge of the pathogen is extremely important for the medical doctor and the medical scientist, especially for those interested in the development of prevention, control, and treatment programs. But the methods of epidemiology do not limit practitioners to diseases for which the etiology is known. Therefore, the epidemiologist does not have to wait for the discovery or isolation of causative agents to carry out studies and to recommend meaningful actions.

At about the same time as Snow's contribution, Semmelweis observed that the death rate from childbed fever (puerperal fever) was higher in those sections of the hospital where physicians came from the morgue directly into the maternity ward. Like Snow, Semmelweis was unaware of specific etiological agents, but his suggestion to doctors and students to wash their hands with chlorinated water before examining the pregnant women led to a substantial decline in the number of puerperal fever deaths (see Sigerist, 1958). Knowledge of the specific pathogen is critical to the development of vaccines, and it is critical to decisions concerning some aspects of treatment regimens; but for the development of useful prevention programs, knowledge of disease distribution and behavior patterns may be enough.

INCIDENCE AND PREVALENCE

When conducting studies on the extent and distribution of disease, the epidemiologist is concerned with both incidence, or *the number of new cases* added to a population during a specific period of time, and prevalence, or *the total number of cases* of a disease present in the population at a given time. Knowledge of incidence provides information that may be used to determine increases or decreases in the spread of a disease; knowledge of prevalence helps determine the extent of the disease. In both cases, the distribution of the condition helps identify disease patterns. Both incidence and prevalence are expressed in rates, which allows comparison among groupings, areas, and time periods. Incidence and prevalence are interrelated since the current number of people with a disease or medical condition consists of the number of cases existing yesterday, plus the cases added today (today's incidence) minus those who either no longer have the disease or are no longer in the population. An examination of this type of relationship can be used to depict the temporal history of any medical condition. This can be illustrated through a theoretical 2 x 2 table in which the four cells consist of combinations of high and low incidence and prevalence. Realizing that *high* and *low* are arbitrarily defined terms, the theoretical table may be drawn as shown in Figure 2–1. The cells can be used to describe the present pattern of a disease, or they may be used to describe the sequential pattern or history of a disease.

Taken together, the cells can be used to suggest the progression of many health conditions. Given our knowledge about the course of many diseases, the patterns depicted in Cells B and C may be interpreted as intervening positions between the prevalence-incidence patterns depicted in Cells A and D. The following four prevalence-incidence relationships are especially revealing:

1. $++ \rightarrow +- \rightarrow --: (A \rightarrow B \rightarrow D)$
2. $++ \rightarrow -+ \rightarrow --: (A \rightarrow C \rightarrow D)$
3. $-- \rightarrow +- \rightarrow ++: (D \rightarrow B \rightarrow A)$
4. $-- \rightarrow -+ \rightarrow ++: (D \rightarrow C \rightarrow A)$

Figure 2–1
The Relationship between Incidence and Prevalence

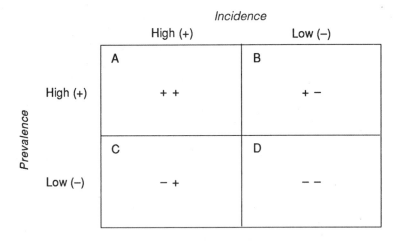

The most common transitions in the course of many diseases are presented in Patterns 1 and 4.

Pattern 1 shows the course of a disease that was once at epidemic proportions and has come under control. At one time, the condition affected a large number of individuals; many people contracted the disease and once there, few are rid of it; both incidence and prevalence rates were high, as in Cell A of Figure 2–1. Then, for some reason, the number contracting the disease declined, thus lowering the incidence rate, as portrayed in Cell B. Finally, the number afflicted with the condition also dropped, leading to low incidence and prevalence rates, as depicted in Cell D. A medical condition that has recently gone through the Pattern 1 transition is poliomyelitis. In the past, many diseases have completed this pattern, including diphtheria, scarlet fever, scurvy, cholera, and tuberculosis. Internationally, the World Health Organization has declared that the world is now free of smallpox, that is, the nations of the world have achieved a zero incidence rate. Note how the world has changed: Each of these crippling or killing diseases is an infectious disease. In western societies there has been a switch in importance from the infectious to the chronic diseases.

Pattern 4 suggests the course of a disease rising to epidemic proportions as it follows a path from low to high rates of both incidence and prevalence. Initially the condition affects few people, but this changes when a large number of new cases appear (a transition to Cell C); this is followed by an increase in the number of people afflicted with the disease, raising incidence and prevalence, which leads to high rates of each. This pattern may occur as a disease spreads, but it also may be the result of events that have little to do with true rates of incidence and prevalence. Among these are increased publicity or information campaigns, improved case-finding techniques, or an increased attempt to find all possible cases.

An example of how increased publicity and information brought about a Pattern 4 situation for a health condition is sickle cell anemia. Although a number of blacks had long had the condition, its incidence, prevalence, and consequences were poorly understood. It was only when a federal employee responded to a letter from a person seeking information concerning the condition that people began to realize how little was known about the condition. After discussions with physicians, the employee sought help from the U.S. government. As a result of the publicity, coupled with a governmental financial commitment, there was a major increase in the number of reported cases of sickle cell anemia (Kunitz, 1974).

Acquired immune deficiency syndrome, or AIDS, is in a Pattern 4 situation among young adult homosexual males and intravenous drug users. This condition went through the D to C to A transition during the 1980s: The first cases were reported early in the decade and by the late 1980s, the disease was perceived as the most serious health threat in the United States (Fineberg, 1988). When such a group-specific disease becomes prevalent, the fear among public health workers is that it may spread to the general population, with devastating consequences.

Pattern 3, in which the transition is from low to high prevalence and incidence rates by way of high prevalence and low incidence is not common; when it does occur, it is short-lived because Cell B is temporary.

A SOCIAL MODEL FOR EPIDEMIOLOGY

In the historical development of medical epidemiology, doctors interested in tracing the patterns of disease initially focused on infectious conditions. The logic of this approach was based on the germ theory, which, at one point in the history of medicine, was the primary explanation for the spread of disease. In fact, the germ theory became so powerful an explanation that it had unfortunate consequences. For example, some practitioners felt it was necessary only to trace germs to establish etiology and "the focus of epidemiology was reduced to the pursuit of specific agents, singular causes, and the means of preventing their consequences" (Susser, 1985:149). The "enormous success" of the germ theory contributed to a "maturational lag" in the development of epidemiology (Susser, 1985). New knowledge eventually revealed that this logic was based on incomplete and sometimes false information, especially as problems arose that suggested the germ theory provides only partial or even incorrect answers to many important questions about the incidence and prevalence of many diseases and is not useful at all in explaining others. For example, why do conditions like influenza appear in epidemic form only periodically, why doesn't the same exposure lead to disease among all people, and do germs account for contracting such conditions as mental illness and heart disease? The mere raising of such questions suggested that the simplistic explanation was much *too* simple.

Nevertheless, the germ theory provides an appealing explanation for disease and its patterns. One of its main attractions is that it offers a simple, easily understandable explanation of etiology. But this simplicity leads to unfortunate consequences for understanding how many diseases come about and spread. Overeager acceptance of the germ theory deflected further investigation of causes and shut off lines of inquiry that were critical to tracing the unfolding pattern of some conditions. Thus, the germ theory takes its place with some other explanations of human experience that seem to work well and are easily accepted, irrespective of whether they are valid. In this context, the germ theory is similar to the instinct theory of human behavior: Both models provide explanations that are deceptively simple, seem logical, and are often uncritically accepted. They make common sense, but they are incorrect or incomplete explanations.

As long as the epidemiological method was applied solely to the infectious diseases, its full potential for understanding disease was not being realized. At least some of the credit for freeing the discipline from its limited view must go to those social scientists who exhibited increasing interest in disease differentials among social groups. Such interest led to a major change in perspective; it introduced an epidemiology that focused on people and their social characteristics rather than on microorganisms. The focus shifted from the internal effect of disease on specific unrelated individuals to the population as a whole, the character of the environment, social groups, social categories, and interrelationships among people. This new approach is *social* epidemiology, a logical extension of medical epidemiology.

In this new perspective, whether the condition under consideration is infectious or not and whether or not it is germ-induced are not important initially. As Snow demonstrated, we can learn about some diseases by focusing on the association between differentials and social characteristics. Thus, the epidemiological perspective is broadened in important ways; the scope expands from one restricted to infectious diseases to one unlimited by any particular type of disease or medical condition. Alcoholism, schizophrenia, and even traffic accidents can now be included in the epidemiologist's areas of interest. Attention is shifted to identifying social and cultural factors within the environment that put people in contact with or shield them from particular medical conditions. For example, the dietary habits of ethnic groups now provide a clue to why members of some subcultures are subject to higher rates of gastrointestinal problems, and male circumcision is investigated as a factor associated with rates of cervical cancer.

This perspective also shifts attention from the development of disease in a specific individual to environmental factors in the social groups within which people interact. An entirely new set of clues, crucial in some cases, provides an opportunity for insights that may lead to explanations of the causes of many conditions. The monocausal germ theory approach is modified to bring into focus other possible variables that can explain the patterns of disease and health conditions. Factors such as socioeconomic status, ethnicity, diet, marriage patterns, residence type, and religious practices, and such demographic variables as age, sex, and place of residence are taken into account.

Thus, any disease or condition of medical interest is subject to the epidemiologist's skill; whether or not these are germ-related is incidental to their being the subject of investigation. The critical new observation and point of analysis and explanation is that different social groupings exhibit different rates of disease. In the search for etiology, the epidemiologist examines the sociocultural differences between those likely to contract a disease and those who seem to be protected from the condition. The question becomes: What are the risk factors that differentiate between the victims and the unaffected?

CAUSE AND EFFECT

Identification of the cause-and-effect relationship between social factors and disease is only the first step in establishing etiology. Once an association between variables has been found, the epidemiologist may face the problem of which variable in the relationship is the effect, or dependent variable, and which is the cause, or independent variable. The observation of an association means only that a relationship exists; to explain the meaning of an association, the statistics must be placed in their proper context and be interpreted. The facts *never* speak for themselves.

An illustration of the need for interpretation demonstrates the importance of the investigator's explanation: A longitudinal study found that the death rate from coronary heart disease and stroke is significantly higher among people who sleep more than ten hours a day than it is among those who sleep only seven or fewer hours a day (Kripke, Simons, Garfinkel, and Hammond, 1979). One explanation for these findings is that long hours of sleep might be a consequence of drowsiness caused by a reduced flow of blood to the brain caused by a weakened coronary system. On the other hand, the relationship could be reversed, since it might be suggested that long hours of sleep underutilize or atrophy the heart muscle, thus weakening it. Or, it is possible that both the need for long hours of sleep and the development of coronary heart disease are consequences of some other factor or factors, such as a generally rundown physical condition or poor nutrition.

In another study, an investigator of traffic accidents discovered that the fewest accidents occurred among individuals who had one or two alcoholic drinks before venturing into rush hour traffic. It might have been concluded that alcohol tends to relax drivers, making them less aggressive in their driving behavior, which led to fewer accidents. Further investigation of the association between the amount of alcohol consumed and traffic accidents, however, revealed the possibility that other significant factors were involved in the relationship. It was apparent that those who did not drink before driving and who were exhibiting the higher rate of accidents were either under eighteen or over sixty-five years of age (the high-risk age categories for accidents) and drove older automobiles that were in poor mechanical condition. Thus, it is possible that alcohol had little to do with the accident rate; age of driver and condition of automobile were intervening variables that may have been more significant in explaining the accidents.

In all research, epidemiological or other, the finding of a correlation between variables is the beginning, rather than the end, of understanding the cause-effect directional flow. Of course, there are guidelines. In the usual and desired approach of scientifically oriented disciplines, dependence and independence are established *before* the relevant data are collected; the theoretical background guides the investigator in deciding on what questions to ask. The sociological perspective indicates that social characteristics are independent variables affecting other factors; therefore, if an epidemiological study reveals a relationship between social characteristics and disease, incidence and prevalence are explained by reference to social factors. Directionality is clear: *from* the social *to* the disease.

Collecting data that reveal an association is the first empirical step toward understanding etiology. For example, the observation that people who used a particular water supply were more likely to contract cholera than those using other supplies was an initial step in understanding the source of the disease. After social epidemiologists observe a relationship, they attempt to identify the behavior that contributed to placing people into contact with (or, in some cases, shielding them from) the disease. In this manner, the epidemiological evidence sets the stage for laboratory work and for controlled, experimental investigation. For example, water can be investigated in the laboratory as the source that carries the cholera pathogen, and experiments can be devised to take account of different source or use patterns.

The general observation of an association between social characteristics and disease patterns is a finding in itself, but this means only the first question has been answered. Following this, many specific questions may be raised about the association. For example, Graham (1972), a social epidemiologist, mentions the following as possible contributory factors in a causal explanation of cancer: socioeconomic status, occupation, income, exposure to disease, general physical and mental state, hygienic environment, quality of medical attention received, extent of crowding in living conditions, nutrition, amount of sunlight received, individual complexion, number of pregnancies, breast-feeding experience, whether a hysterectomy or ovariectomy has been performed, circumcision, age of first sexual experience, frequency of sexual experience, number of sex partners, characteristics of the individuals with whom sexual relations are experienced, genetic inheritance, race, nationality background, religion, personal hygiene practices, venereal infections history, age, sex, exposure to X-rays, wine-drinking behavior, dietary customs, intervals of eating, child-care practices, marriage history, number of children borne, menstruation experience, and smoking patterns. The enterprising reader could probably think of items Graham may have overlooked.

In another source, the same author presents the epidemiological approach by constructing a model that sets the logic of the procedure (Graham, 1972); it is, generally, as follows:

1. An agent produces tissue change.
2. There is a vehicle for, or carrier of, this agent.
3. Some behavioral pattern exposes the host to the vehicle or the carrier.
4. Special characteristics of the individual lead to this exposure.

From the perspective of the social epidemiologist, the behavioral pattern of Point 3 and the special characteristics mentioned in Point 4 of the model refer to social factors. Sociologists may know little about the specific agents that change tissue (Point 1) and they may know little about the carriers of such agents (Point 2), but they can contribute to epidemiology by identifying the characteristics that expose people, groups, and categories to the agent and carrier (Points 3 and 4). Once these are identified, the search for cause can be narrowed and the patterns of the first elements mentioned in the model can be more easily understood. Sociological contributions to epidemiology, then, center on the identification of social factors related to contact with, or protection from, disease.

As indicated and emphasized, the social epidemiologist focuses on the behavior and characteristics of the individual and on the social environment. But social findings do not rule out genetic contributions to etiology. It is sometimes difficult to separate the social from the genetic because people tend to reproduce with others who are both physically and socially similar to themselves. (Reproduction patterns are socially determined, but the consequences are biological.) Consequently, the genetic pool and the social pool may be reinforcing each other, which could mean that disease-related chromosomes are being passed from one generation to another within a specific social group. A social finding might thus support, rather than rule out, a genetic explanation of etiology.

Identifying variables strongly associated with the onset of a health condition and understanding both the agents and the carriers of agents will not automatically lower disease rates. Such information provides nothing more than the opportunity to develop educational and action programs that could lead to lower rates. The success or failure of such programs is another matter entirely, one affected by community social and psychological factors that could support a program or could raise formidable barriers to implementation.

PROBLEMS OF THE
SOCIAL EPIDEMIOLOGIST

Standardization of Terms

The discussion of basic sociological concepts in Chapter 1 implied that sociologists agree on the definitions of the terms they use. Generally, this is so, but it was an optimistic implication. Actually, sociology cannot be described as a discipline in which concepts are used with precision and standardization. Within the discipline, for example, some sociologists use the term *social class* to refer to the total stratification system of a society, but others use it to refer to specific aspects, such as the economic, prestige, or power elements of society. To add to the confusion, some related terms may or may not be synonymous. For example, in reference to the stratification system of society, the term *social position* is used by some sociologists (Hollingshead and Redlich, 1958), whereas *socioeconomic status* is used by others (the U.S. Census Bureau). Eventually, sociologists may agree that *social stratification* refers to a particular phenomenon and that it should be measured by standardized criteria, but a current lack of agreement leads to many problems for the discipline and for those who try to understand and use sociological concepts and findings.

Problems of standardization are not unique to sociology. They exist in many other fields, sometimes in unexpected areas. Thus, people unfamiliar with medicine are probably unaware of the lack of term standardization in the health area. What may appear to the general public (including the sociologist) to be precise and standardized health concepts are sometimes found, on closer examination, to suffer from many of the same inadequacies as sociological concepts. Consider a situation in which two children are born at the same moment, one in Ohio and one in Illinois, after an estimated nineteen weeks of gestation. In both cases, expulsion from the mother is complete and, after separation, the children exhibit the usual life signs: breathing, heartbeat, pulsation of the umbilical cord, and movement of voluntary muscles. Within one hour after birth, each child succumbs to cyanosis and no longer exhibits signs of life. Upon examination, a physician declares each child dead. This example raises an important problem because, by official definition in Illinois, a live birth has occurred; but in Ohio, a live birth did not take place. The difference is that, in Ohio, death occurred in a situation of less than twenty weeks of gestation, which means that one of the criteria for a live birth in that state was not met. Because state definitions are not standardized, it is not possible to compare live-birth state data without first determining the specific criteria used in each.

A comparison of all state definitions of fetal death reveals that the criteria vary even more markedly than the illustration presented suggests. If only one aspect of the definition is examined—the period of gestation—it is found that a fetal death can be registered for any period of gestation in nine states. In one, such a registration can take place only if gestation is over sixteen weeks; in sixteen states, the pregnancy must have advanced to the twentieth week; in ten, the gestation period must be twenty weeks or more; in eleven, the criterion is more than twenty weeks; in two, such registration is required if the pregnancy has advanced to the fifth month; and in one state, the criterion is after the fifth month (U.S. Public Health Service, 1967).

If the problem of standardized definitions is present in such seemingly easily defined matters as life and death, imagine how much more complicated it must be in reference to conditions that are defined only with difficulty, such as alcoholism, for which there is little agreement about when overindulgence becomes alcoholism. Cases of alcoholism may be counted when an individual first encounters the legal system because of alcohol, when the person's family visits a social agency to complain about the problem, or when Alcoholics Anonymous is contacted. It is little wonder that information about the incidence and prevalence of alcoholism is unclear.

Validity and Reliability of Data

Lack of standardized definitions is only one of the research problems facing the epidemiologist. If the investigator is conducting a study that depends on the recall ability of respondents, a new series of problems emerges. For example, studies of the reliability of mothers' reports about specific aspects of the developmental histories of their children indicate that mothers' memories concerning their pregnancies and birth experiences are often in error. Poor recall reliability has been found for mothers' health during pregnancy, the duration of labor, reports of whether or not instruments were used during delivery, injuries that occurred during delivery, and the number of immediate difficulties with the newborn child. When asked to describe child-development and child-rearing practices, mothers tend to be fairly accurate in remembering information about motor development and weight, but inaccurate in remembering their children's weight after the first year, the crawling behavior of their children, illness history, whether schedule or demand feeding was used, whether the baby sucked its thumb, age of weaning, and toilet-training experiences. When a mother is incorrect in her recall, the distortion is in the direction of describing the child as close to the prevailing social norms and values. Therefore, the epidemiologist who relies on recall information may be endangering the study by using inaccurate data.

Physicians' diagnoses as written on records also present problems. Studies designed to ascertain completeness and reliability of such records point to particularly poor records. In several studies by physicians, the conclusion reached is that a fair number of doctors' diagnoses are incorrect. The interpretation of X-ray films and laboratory tests, the reading and interpreting of electrocardiograms, and comparisons of other supposedly objective and specific measures of body physiology also reveal many disagreements.

Another serious problem is the underreporting of cases. The number of reported cases may be an understatement of total incidence or prevalence. This may reflect purposive nonreporting, especially for conditions that carry social stigma (such as premarital pregnancy, mental illness, and venereal disease), unawareness of the presence of a condition, misdiagnosis, failure to keep accurate records, forgetfulness, and lack of cooperation by reporting agents.

Discussing communicable diseases, Marier (1977) notes that only a small percentage of some conditions are reported. For example, in a study of the discharge records of eleven hospitals in Washington, D.C., underreporting to the Centers for Disease Control (CDC) in Atlanta was found. Reporting rates varied by disease, with the following percentage figures indicating the unreported rates: viral hepatitis, 89;

H. influenza meningitis, 68; salmonellosis, 58; meningococcal meningitis, 50; shigellosis, 38; and tuberculosis, 37. Overall, 65 percent of the cases of communicable disease found in the hospital records were not reported to the CDC. It is reasonable to assume a similar pattern for other diseases.

A mixture of complete and incomplete data can lead to some strange findings. An article in a national alcoholism journal, for example, once reported that one midwestern U.S. city of about a quarter of a million population had the second highest rate of alcoholism in the country; this report stunned medical and social work personnel in the city. When the matter was investigated further, it was found that the city's public health officer was extremely zealous in seeing that death by cirrhosis of the liver (sometimes used to estimate the alcoholism rate) was reported on most relevant death certificates. This meant a much higher than usual reporting rate for this city than for others.

Precision of Terms

The data available to the epidemiologist are sometimes deceivingly specific and precise when, in fact, they are general and imprecise. Consider the diagnosis of epilepsy, for example. True or typical epilepsy is further specified as idiopathic epilepsy, which makes it sound even more precise. But the term *idiopathic* means that the cause is obscure or unknown, and the term *epilepsy* means only that a person experiences seizures or convulsions. In other words, what the nonmedical community accepts as a precise diagnostic term is neither precise nor a diagnosis; it is a shortcut way of describing the symptoms of a person who exhibits seizures for which the cause is not known.

For many reasons, then, the epidemiologist is often working with incomplete, imprecise, or inaccurate data. Statistical analysis of biased data may lead to invalid conclusions. One of the constant attempts of the epidemiologist is to develop techniques to collect information that reflects true incidence and prevalence. We will see in the next section of this chapter and in the next chapter how the epidemiologist has developed techniques aimed at accomplishing this end.

METHODOLOGICAL PROBLEMS ILLUSTRATED: MENTAL ILLNESS AS AN EXAMPLE

Sociologists realized that demographic methods were applicable to health conditions at about the same time they were developing theories and research aimed at understanding social life in the city. Consequently, when they plotted the distribution of such social characteristics or variables as ethnic groups, socioeconomic groupings, and crime rates in the city, some included the distribution of diseases. This set the stage for the first major social epidemiological study in the United States, which focused on the distribution of mental illness in Chicago.

Faris and Dunham Study

Faris and Dunham (1939) accepted a theoretical model that depicted U.S. cities with natural social areas distributed as concentric bands around the city center (Burgess, 1925); the inhabitants of each band were socially homogeneous in several characteristics, one of which was socioeconomic status. The theory indicated that from the city center outward, each homogeneous band was populated by residents of higher socioeconomic status, until city residential patterns gave way to the rural area. Faris and Dunham proposed a general epidemiological hypothesis of an association between socioeconomic status and mental illness, and then specified it by hypothesizing that the rate of mental illness would be found to decrease from the city center outward, just as socioeconomic status increases. On this descriptive level, then, these researchers hypothesized a negative correlation between socioeconomic status and mental illness.

To test this proposition, operational definitions of the relevant variables, in this case, residential area and mental illness, were needed; socioeconomic status already was defined because Faris and Dunham assumed that zones of residential area and socioeconomic status were equivalent. For the delineation of residential areas, the investigators accepted the theoretical concentric zone model, in which lines of delineation between zones are arbitrarily drawn. Since a gradient of socioeconomic status was hypothesized, however, precise cutoff points of this status were not needed. Given the nature of their study, Faris and Dunham found it necessary to accept the psychiatric diagnoses listed on patient records; there is little the social researcher can do to validate medical data already officially reported. Since epidemiologists often use official records, they are frequently "at the mercy" of the case-finding activities of others.

In addition to this uncontrollable problem, Faris and Dunham created some of their own in their selection of the mental illness cases included in their research: They decided to restrict their study to all Chicago residents admitted to Illinois state mental hospitals with a diagnosis of schizophrenia or manic-depressive psychosis (7,253 people) between 1922 and 1931. (To eliminate the possibility that one person could be counted twice, only first admissions were included in their data.) This decision placed a severe limitation on the research, because the investigators were not truly studying mental illness in Chicago. Rather, their data concerned people who had been institutionalized with a diagnosis of schizophrenia or manic-depressive psychosis. Sociological research has demonstrated that there are not necessarily relationships between the presence of a condition and its identification, nor between the presence of mental illness and institutionalization. Rather, both the labeling of mentally ill people and what happens to them after identification are strongly influenced by social factors (Mechanic, 1962; Sampson, Messinger, and Towne, 1962).

Despite these faults, the data on schizophrenia admissions fell precisely as Faris and Dunham had hypothesized they would, that is, the rates exhibited the predicted gradient zonal pattern. This pattern was not found for manic-depressive psychosis rates, but since schizophrenia is the most prevalent of the psychoses, the general hypothesis seemed substantiated.

Not satisfied with the descriptive observation of an association between socioeconomic status and mental illness, Faris and Dunham next asked the analytical epidemiological question of why the association existed. In attempting to explain the findings, they offered the following three ex post facto hypotheses (not intended to be mutually exclusive):

1. *The drift hypothesis.* This hypothesis suggests that when people's behavior leads to negative community reactions, they move out of their neighborhoods into areas of the city where their behavior does not lead to evident negative responses. In a way, those who do not "fit in" drift to residential areas where they feel more comfortable, perhaps because of acceptance, or perhaps because the social life in the new area allows a higher degree of anonymity. The theory holds that the move is from those areas of upper or middle socioeconomic status to the lower with, perhaps, stops between. The area that particularly attracts the drifting person, the area most suited to minimal feelings of discomfort, is the one closest to the city center, precisely where Faris and Dunham found the highest rates of schizophrenia. And, since there may have been stops along the way, the rates are lowest in the outer rings of the city (the highest socioeconomic status area) and follow an increasing pattern moving toward the city center (the lowest). From an incidence-prevalence perspective, the drift hypothesis suggests that the schizophrenia incidence rate is consistent throughout the city, while prevalence rate differentials are a consequence of drift.

2. *The social isolation or social disorganization hypothesis.* This hypothesis presents a picture quite different from that of drift. It is based on the observation that the area surrounding the central business district of the city, the one with the highest rates of schizophrenia, is also an area of high social disorganization and social isolation. Since sociologists indicate that people are products of their social experiences, the hypothesis suggests that the disorganized personality (the schizophrenic) is a product of a disorganized social life. In other words, social disorganization "causes" personal disorganization. In terms of the incidence-prevalence relationship, both are highest in the city center because more mental illness is generated in the area.

3. *The treatment hypothesis.* A person who accepts the validity of this hypothesis also must accept the view that psychiatry is successful in curing schizophrenia. The hypothesis starts with the observation that the cost of treatment for psychiatric problems is expensive and takes a long time. Therefore, professional help is available only to those who can afford the money and time, that is, only to members of the upper and middle socioeconomic status groupings. Thus, the ability to obtain psychiatric help increases from the city center outward. Therefore, the schizophrenia incidence rate is assumed to be the same across all zones; the observed prevalence rate pattern exists because members of the upper and middle socioeconomic groups enter into expensive therapy and are cured.

Which of the three hypotheses is "correct?" The data do not lend themselves to an answer to this question. It may be observed, however, that most sociologists no longer accept the premise upon which the second hypothesis is based; many urban sociologists now hold that social organization or disorganization is independent of socioeconomic status, depending on how these concepts are defined. The nature of social organization is different among social groupings, but this should not imply that one type is more organized or disorganized than any other. The third hypothesis also has its detractors since many people, lay and professional alike, do not accept the proposition that psychiatry cures mental illness; rather, many hold that the psychiatric benefit consists only of helping the mentally ill accept their problems. The drift hypothesis is perhaps the most logical, but the explanation it provides cannot stand alone—it should be accepted as part of a larger explanation of why rates vary.

Hollingshead and Redlich Study

As might be expected, the second important social epidemiological study built on the experiences of the first. This second study, published fourteen years after that of Faris and Dunham, was conducted by sociologist Hollingshead and psychiatrist Redlich, both of Yale University (Hollingshead and Redlich, 1953). Instead of dealing with specific diagnoses of mental illness, these investigators focused on the general psychiatric categories psychosis and neurosis.

To obtain their prevalence data, Hollingshead and Redlich collected information about all residents of New Haven, Connecticut, who were patients of psychiatrists and psychiatric clinics or of public and private psychiatric institutions in Connecticut and nearby states on December 1, 1950, which was declared Prevalence Day. Such an approach broadened the patient population base considerably beyond the state-mental-hospital-institutionalized cases used by Faris and Dunham. It did not broaden the sample to all cases of mental illness, however, because it dealt only with people who had been diagnosed: The prevalence count was of all patients *in treatment* by psychiatric sources on that one day. This is far different from a prevalence count of *all* people diagnosed with mental illness. Many cases are missing, including New Haven residents receiving psychiatric care from states not near Connecticut, those receiving psychiatric care in institutions or by practitioners not specifically psychiatric in nature, and those diagnosed but not in treatment on Prevalence Day.

Moving to analytic epidemiology, Hollingshead and Redlich also compared social and demographic characteristics of the "psychiatric" population with those of the "normal" population (the "normal" were residents of New Haven not under treatment on Prevalence Day) to ascertain differences. To obtain data for this comparison, the investigators selected a 5 percent representative sample of households in New Haven and collected social and demographic information that could be compared with the psychiatric population. The investigators thus undertook a psychiatric census and a control sample census in the same community on the same day.

Like Faris and Dunham, Hollingshead and Redlich hypothesized an association between socioeconomic status and mental illness. And once again, the data support the hypothesis. The investigators found that the neurosis prevalence rate was higher in the upper socioeconomic status categories, and the psychosis rate was higher in the lower socioeconomic grouping. They also observed associations between mental illness and age, sex, occupation, religion, race, nationality background, and marital experience. Further, Hollingshead and Redlich went beyond case-counting and cross-classification by focusing on three hypotheses: (1) prevalence is related to social-class structure; (2) the type of diagnosis is class-related; and, (3) treatment programs are associated with the patient's social-class position. All three propositions were supported by the data.

In criticism of the study, it should be recalled that Hollingshead and Redlich dealt only with prevalence of people in treatment for psychiatric conditions, rather than with the actual number of people with psychiatric conditions. Thus their data may constitute only a fraction of the true total number of cases (cf., the "clinical iceberg" concept; see Robinson, 1978, and Verbrugge and Ascione, 1987). From a total prevalence perspective, however, the Hollingshead and Redlich research is a major improvement over the study conducted by Faris and Dunham, who restricted their attention to first admissions to state mental hospitals. It may be concluded that the fourteen years between these two studies were important years for developing methodological ideas about studies of the social epidemiology of mental illness.

Eaton and Weil Study

At about the same time that Hollingshead and Redlich were conducting their research, another sociologist-psychiatrist team was carrying out a study that came even closer to ascertaining the total prevalence of mental illness. These investigators conducted their research in a unique community located in an area lying in both the United States and Canada, in a rural subculture that is relatively small, homogeneous, and isolated, with definite boundaries that clearly mark it off from the larger society. This study was conducted by sociologist Eaton and psychiatrist Weil (Eaton and Weil, 1953), who used as their research population the Hutterites, a religious sect community consisting of 8,542 people (in 1950) who follow a folklike life pattern of communal ownership of property and emphasis on simple living, with such modern resources as radios and motion pictures forbidden. Marriage is exclusively within the subculture. The economic activity of the community revolves around a highly mechanized agriculture, which brings the Hutterites into contact with the rest of the world for business reasons. Members at times use professional services, such as those of doctors, located outside the community. (There were no doctors within the Hutterite community itself.)

Given such a setting, a determination of the total prevalence of almost any measurable condition seems possible. To collect data on mental illness, Eaton asked residents to identify people who "behaved differently," and Weil applied the tools of his profession to either eliminate from a mental illness designation or to reach a diagnosis for all those labeled in the interview. This procedure led Eaton and Weil to believe that their study may have identified virtually all of the cases of psychosis in the subculture, past or present, under treatment or not. If this is the case, the Hutterite research comes close to ascertaining the total prevalence of the condition they were studying. This is certainly a far more accurate way to determine total prevalence than the methodologies employed by Faris and Dunham and by Hollingshead and Redlich.

As it happens, the extent of mental illness found by Eaton and Weil among the Hutterites was about the same as the prevalence observed in the other two studies.

But there are also major methodological problems with the Eaton and Weil study. Thus, people who are identified as behaving differently by members of the Hutterite community may be quite different from those identified in this way in Chicago, New Haven, or even mainstream rural America. In addition, the Hutterite study depends on the diagnostic ability of one psychiatrist, and other research has indicated that psychiatrists do not always agree with each other's diagnoses (Spitzer and Wilson, 1975).

In this case, the authors were not looking for an association between mental illness and social class. Rather, they were concerned with the question of whether the assumed simplicity of folklike living patterns shields people from mental illness, which is the other side of the hypothesis that the complexities of urban living contribute to the development of mental disorder. In discussing their data relative to this question, Eaton and Weil conclude that "in short, the Hutterite culture provides no immunity to mental disorders" (Eaton and Weil, 1953:32). Searching for other explanatory factors in the context of analytic epidemiology, the authors suggest genetic, organic, or constitutional predispositions to psychosis as possible etiological factors. But another finding of the Hutterite study is intriguing: Although the extent of mental illness seems approximately the same both in this folklike society and in urban areas, the observed pattern of specific types of illness among the Hutterites was different. Whereas schizophrenia is the most common type of psychosis reported by other investigators, among the Hutterites few cases of this condition were diagnosed. Manic-depressive reaction was the reported diagnosis for more than three-quarters of those found to be psychotic. This suggests that social and cultural factors may be significant in channeling those afflicted into specific types of mental illness.

Srole Study

In another study, Srole and his colleagues (1962) used the most common of sociological research techniques—personal interviews of a representative sample drawn from a defined population—in an attempt to collect prevalence data on mental illness. Data were collected from a sample of 1,660 adults living in New York City in 1954 by an interview team of psychologists and social workers who used an extensive field schedule composed of questions about the presence or absence of a series of psychological symptoms. The research project is known as the Midtown Manhattan Study.

Once the data were collected, each interview was summarized into a form that listed information about psychological symptoms for each respondent. The summaries were given to two psychiatrists who independently examined them, and on the basis of their number of symptoms, respondents were placed in one of the following mental health categories: well, mild, moderate, marked, severe, and incapacitated. (The last three are grouped under the term *impaired*.) If the psychiatrists' classifications disagreed about the category to which any given respondent was to be assigned, the psychiatrists met to reconcile the difference; but the two were reported to be remarkably close in their placement decisions.

As in the Faris and Dunham and the Hollingshead and Redlich studies, a strong association was found between socioeconomic status and mental health. A comparison revealed a much larger percentage of those in the highest social category classified as well and a much larger percentage of those in the lowest social class classified as impaired.

The investigators' use of standard sociological techniques to obtain data represents a major achievement for social epidemiology. Nevertheless, some problems detract from this contribution as an epidemiological study of mental illness. Intentionally or not, the focus of the study shifted. The psychiatrists did not diagnose mental illness or mental disorders; instead, they judged what may be termed "mental health." Further, assignments were based on the absence of symptoms. For example, an individual free of symptoms was designated as "well." It is disputable whether absence of symptoms alone is equivalent to mental health, just as it is questionable whether the possession of symptoms alone is an indication of mental illness. One can argue that those subjects classified as completely free of all psychological symptoms are so strange in the contemporary world that they should not have been the ones designated "well."

Nevertheless, the Midtown Manhattan Study advanced social epidemiology to a new methodological level. Unlike the Eaton and Weil information, the Midtown Manhattan data are generalizable to a large segment of the U.S. population. Furthermore, the methodology was a major advance from the Faris and Dunham and the Hollingshead and Redlich approaches to total prevalence. Viewed in conjunction with the Eaton and Weil study, which basically used an anthropological approach, we see the seeds of what social scientists can offer to epidemiology. Each study has drawbacks, but it is certainly in order to suggest that the methods of social science can be fruitfully used in the epidemiological study of mental illness or mental health.

Srole Study Update

Srole made an additional contribution to the methodology of social epidemiology by conducting a 1974 restudy of the 1954 Midtown Manhattan Study respondents (Srole, 1975). A restudy twenty years later adds an important dimension to the approach of social epidemiology. It provides the possibility for an outcome or prognosis aspect of epidemiological research, compared with the usual study, which freezes information within a particular time frame. But such a restudy opens the door to a host of additional methodological problems, with the paramount one being possible new sample nonrepresentativeness because respondents died, changed residences, and changed names. Such changes did, indeed, lead to a major decrease in the 1974 Midtown Manhattan sample size from the original 1,660 respondents to 695. Srole compared the mental health ratings of these 695 people in 1974 with their 1954 classifications and found that approximately 40 percent were classified in the same mental health category (well, mild, moderate, marked, severe, incapacitated) both times, approximately one-third rose by at least one category, and about one-quarter fell to a lower category.

Srole used a further innovation that took twenty years of additional experience into account. In 1974 he dispensed with psychiatrists' ratings of mental health, using instead computer-derived ratings based on responses to twenty-two of the questions in the 1954 field schedule; following this procedure, he recalculated the previous data in the same way and compared results with current data. This approach represents epidemiological progress also because it used subject responses instead of psychiatrists' judgments and, once cutoff-point decisions were made, sample members were classified into mental health categories by statistical means.

Dohrenwend and Dohrenwend Study

Even before Srole's 1974 restudy, Dohrenwend and Dohrenwend (1969) used twenty-two of the original Midtown Manhattan field schedule items along with fourteen from other sources in an epidemiological study of psychological disorders among people living in New York City. The Dohrenwends attempted to use epidemiological methods to test the relative contributions of environmental and genetic factors as etiological in the development of mental disorder.

The cause-effect issue is raised in a new way. Thus, if the data reveal an inverse relationship between social class and mental illness (that is, the lower the class, the higher the prevalence), does this suggest social etiology? To most social scientists the answer is yes. The Dohrenwends, however, correctly raise the question of whether the association can be explained by social selection—that is, mental illness may have contributed to low social status (cf., the drift hypothesis of Faris and Dunham discussed previously). If the latter position is taken, perhaps genetic factors can explain the association.

Like Srole and his associates (1962), Dohrenwend and Dohrenwend studied a representative sample of respondents and, as in the Midtown Manhattan restudy (Srole, 1975), they used a relatively small number of items (but not all of the same items as those used in the Srole restudy) to classify respondents into categories. Methodologically, the Dohrenwends anticipated the Midtown Manhattan restudy by several years; by combining the best of social science sampling techniques with statistical and computer-based approaches, their study made a major move toward determining total prevalence. Because of measurement problems, their data are equivocal about the environment-genetic question, but this should not detract from the methodological advances.

Holmes and Rahe Social Readjustment Rating Scale

The Dohrenwend research demonstrates the social epidemiologist's concern with the etiology of illness, and the Srole restudy demonstrates the potential of using epidemiology to ascertain change over time. Both of these interests received impetus in 1967 when Holmes and Rahe suggested that stress resulting from some social experiences can be etiological in the development of disorders. In their approach, Holmes and

Rahe (1967) developed a rating scale of forty-two items to measure a person's stressful life events; scores on this scale could be related to a person's social readjustment after the stressful event took place. This approach has had a significant impact on social epidemiology since it suggests that the discipline can predict, and account for, the incidence of some disorders.

Over the years, the Social Readjustment Rating Scale has been used extensively by social scientists. Some have suggested modifications to the original scale by deleting, changing, and adding items. For example, Dohrenwend and her colleagues (1978) presented a 102-item scale known as the Psychiatric Epidemiology Research Interview (PERI) Life Events Scale, and Tausig (1982) offered a Life Events Scale with 118 items.

If this approach offers an acceptable degree of predictability, it can change the discipline radically because the epidemiologist would be able to predict incidence, an important contribution to both preventive medicine and curative programs. Work continues in this new direction but, to date, results have not been encouraging. As Tausig (1982:52) states, "The notion that stress may be a precursor to physical and psychological conditions has high face validity, yet attempts to observe stress have generally yielded low to modest estimates of the contribution of stressful events to the appearance of some order of disturbance." Nevertheless, this is clearly a new direction for social epidemiology. (For an extensive discussion of the issues, see Dohrenwend and Dohrenwend, 1974.)

NEW PROSPECTS FOR EPIDEMIOLOGY

The success of epidemiology has led it into many new areas of activity, with prospects for further expansion as it proves its worth, especially as a tool in combatting many public-health-related diseases that result from social behavior. Thus, Glass (1986) has suggested that a broadened definition of the field includes "the application of results to the prevention and control of health problems" (p. 951). Along with this emphasis on application, epidemiology has become important in the discussion and ordering of national health priorities. So, in addition to the traditional interest in infectious and chronic diseases, today's behavior-related health problems receive proper medical and social science attention. Overall, increased emphasis on proposing epidemiologically rooted strategies for the prevention and control of medical conditions of all types has increased.

The Importance of Lifestyle

Epidemiologically based strategies have become increasingly important as epidemiological investigations continually identify specific behaviors that contribute to disease and its consequences. As stated by Hamburg (1982:399), "half of the mortality from the ten leading causes of death in the United States is strongly influenced by lifestyle. Known behavioral risk factors include cigarette smoking, excessive consumption of alcoholic beverages, use of illicit drugs, certain dietary habits, insufficient exercise, reckless driving, nonadherence to medication regimens, and maladaptive responses to social pressures." Furthermore, there is recent evidence that even the quantity and quality of social relationships are instrumental in mortality rates. Thus, sociologists House, Landis, and Umberson (1988) summarize a review of studies in this research area with the statement that "prospective studies, which control for baseline health status, consistently show increased risk of death among persons with a low quantity, and sometimes low quality, of social relationships" (540).

The pioneer epidemiological research on the contribution of lifestyle to disease incidence was carried out in Alameda County, California, in the mid-1960s (Belloc and Breslow, 1972). After identifying specific behaviors that contributed to disease in the initial study, ten years later a "longitudinal follow-up of the original 1965 cohort indicated that seven health habits were associated with subsequent favorable health status and reduced mortality. These life-style habits were: never smoking, drinking fewer than five alcoholic beverages at one sitting, maintaining desirable weight for height, sleeping 7–8 hours a night, exercising, eating breakfast regularly, and avoiding snacks" (Schoenborn and Cohen, 1986:1).

Changes in the lifestyles of Americans have been credited with the rapid decline in mortality from heart disease since the mid-1960s. In today's health-conscious society, Americans are bombarded with epidemiological information (some say "misinformation") about nutrition, excess weight, exercising, cholesterol levels, buckled seat belts, and "safe" sex. Lifestyle seems to have been singled out by the mass media as the most significant determinant in the health of the nation. While this is debatable, in today's value system, the individual's style of living has been identified as the most modifiable contributor to the etiology of many diseases. Other contributors, such as automobile and industrial pollution, are also modifiable, but this becomes a political rather than an individual matter.

New Ways of Measuring the Health of Society

Along with a new perspective have come new methods designed to measure various aspects of the health of society. For example, since 1982 the Centers for Disease Control has been publishing data about the years of potential economically productive life lost (YPLL) because of medical conditions (Glass, 1986:952). The figures are derived as follows: Arbitrarily assume that the "endpoint" of the economically productive life of workers in the United States is sixty-five years of age; a person dying at age sixty-four contributes one year to YPLL, whereas a person dying at age sixty-five or beyond adds nothing to the YPLL figure. This new statistical approach helps determine which of the causes of death are hurting the productive life of the United States most. For example, whereas unintentional injuries were ranked fourth among all causes of death in the United States in 1984, this cause ranks first in years of potential productive life lost; heart disease ranks first among causes of death, but third in YPLL. Since AIDS is mostly a young adult disease, it will soon rank very high by this measure. Hypotheses about, or the actual determination of, relative contributions to YPLL can be used to decide on priorities about how society can best utilize its resources. For example, should resources be aimed at smoking behavior, alcohol abuse, seat-belt laws, nutrition, screening programs, high blood pressure, condom use, or programs designed to curb drinking and driving?

Note the public health worker's focus on changing people's behavior. The epidemiologist is still interested in determining the prevalence and incidence of disease, but focus is also on changing the behavior of people to prevent conditions that lead to potentially avoidable disease and death. Once again, we see the importance of incorporating the social science approach into the epidemiological perspective.

SUMMARY

Social epidemiology is based on a common meeting ground of the demography of sociology and the epidemiology of medicine. In epidemiological studies, the investigator is concerned with measuring both the incidence and prevalence of a given condition. The former refers to the number of new cases added during a specified time period, and the latter refers to the total number of cases of a disease at some specified time. Obviously, these two variables are interrelated. During an epidemic, for example, both incidence and prevalence are high; after a prevention technique is developed, prevalence may remain relatively high as incidence diminishes considerably. The long-range goal of those who work in preventive medicine is the reduction of both incidence and prevalence.

The social epidemiologist monitors the incidence and prevalence of conditions to determine whether members of specific social groups or categories exhibit significantly different rates of particular diseases or conditions. If differentials are observed, an examination of the social behavior in different groups and categories can offer clues to the cause.

Although epidemiology historically has been concerned with infectious diseases, the logic of the discipline can be applied to a variety of conditions and problems. Through the use of the epidemiological approach, limitations of the germ theory of disease have been recognized, and the role of social factors in the origin, course, and outcome of disease has been brought to light. Attention is now given to identifying social factors that put individuals in contact with or shield them from health conditions. It has been found, for example, that the lifestyles and living conditions of different groups have an effect on the incidence and prevalence of many diseases.

The epidemiologist encounters several methodological problems. Among these are a lack of concept standardization, questionable validity and reliability, and underreporting. These problems plague the terminology used in both social science and health disciplines.

The first social epidemiological studies in the United States focused on the distribution of mental illness in specific localities. Prevalence studies were conducted in Chicago, New Haven, the Hutterite community, and in New York City. Each of these studies faced methodological problems in reaching its goal of determining the prevalence of mental illness, and each created problems of its own. But methodological improvements are on the horizon.

References

Belloc, N. B., and L. Breslow. 1972. "Relationship of physical health status and health practices." *Preventive Medicine* 1(3):409–421.

Burgess, Ernest W. 1925. "The growth of the city." In *The City*, ed. Robert E. Park, Ernest W. Burgess, and Roderick D. McKenzie, 47–62. Chicago: University of Chicago Press.

Dohrenwend, Barbara Snell, and Bruce P. Dohrenwend, eds. 1974. *Stressful Life Events: Their Nature and Effects*. New York: Wiley.

Dohrenwend, Barbara Snell, Larry Krasnoff, Alexander R. Ashenasy, and Bruce P. Dohrenwend. 1978. "Exemplification of a method for scaling life events: The PERI Life Events Scale." *Journal of Health and Social Behavior* 19(2):205–229.

Dohrenwend, Bruce P., and Barbara Snell Dohrenwend. 1969. *Social Status and Psychological Disorder: A Causal Inquiry*. New York: Wiley.

Eaton, Joseph W., and Robert J. Weil. 1953. "The mental health of the Hutterites." *Scientific American* 189:31–37.

Faris, Robert E. L., and H. Warren Dunham. 1939. *Mental Disorders in Urban Areas*. Chicago: University of Chicago Press.

Fineberg, H. V. 1988. "Education to prevent AIDS: Prospects and obstacles." *Science* 239(5 February):592–596.

Glass, Roger I. 1986. "New prospects for epidemiologic investigations." *Science* 234 (21 November):951–955.

Graham, Saxon. 1972. "Cancer, culture and social structure." In *Patients, Physicians and Illness*, 2nd ed., ed. E. G. Jaco, 31–40. New York: Free Press.

Hamburg, David A. 1982. "Health and behavior." *Science* 217(30 July):399.

Hollingshead, August B., and Frederick C. Redlich. 1953. "Social stratification and psychiatric disorders." *American Sociological Review* 18:163–169.

Hollingshead, A. B., and Frederick C. Redlich. 1958. *Social Class and Mental Illness: A Community Study*. New York: Wiley.

Holmes, T. H., and R. H. Rahe. 1967. "The Social Readjustment Rating Scale." *Journal of Psychosomatic Research* 11:213–218.

House, James S., Karl R. Landis, and Debra Umberson. 1988. "Social relationships and health." *Science* 241(29 July):540–545.

Kripke, D. F., R. N. Simons, L. Garfinkel, and E. C. Hammond. 1979. "Short and long sleep and sleeping pills. Is increased mortality associated?" *Archives of General Psychiatry* 36(January):103–116.

Kunitz, Stephen J. 1974. "Some notes on physiologic conditions as social problems." *Social Science and Medicine* 8(April):207–211.

MacMahon, Brian. 1981. "Epidemiologic methods." In *Preventive and Community Medicine*, 2d ed., ed. Duncan W. Clark and Brian MacMahon, 59–79. Boston: Little, Brown.

Marier, R. 1977. "The reporting of communicable diseases." *American Journal of Epidemiology* 105(June):587–590.

Mechanic, David. 1962. "Some factors in identifying and defining mental illness." *Mental Hygiene* 46:66–74.

Robinson, David. 1978. *Patients, Practitioners, and Medical Care*. 2d ed. London: William Heinemann Medical Books.

Sampson, Harold, Sheldon L. Messinger, and Robert D. Towne. 1962. "Family processes and becoming a mental patient." *American Journal of Sociology* 68:88–96.

Schoenborn, Charlotte A., and Bernice H. Cohen. 1986. "Trends in smoking, alcohol consumption, and other health practices among U.S. adults, 1977 and 1983." *Advance Data from Vital and Health Statistics*, No. 118. DHHS Pub. No. (PHS)86-1250. Public Health Service, Hyattsville, MD.

Sigerist, H. E. 1958. *The Great Doctors.* New York: Doubleday, Anchor Books.

Spitzer, R. L., and P. T. Wilson. 1975. "Nosology and the official psychiatric nomenclature." In *Comprehensive Textbook in Psychiatry II*, vol. 1., ed. A. M. Freedman, H. I. Kaplan, and B. J. Saddock, 831–835. Baltimore: Williams and Wilkins.

Srole, Leo. 1975. "Measurements and classifications in socio-psychiatric epidemiology: Midtown Manhattan Study I (1954) and Midtown Manhattan Study II (1974)." *Journal of Health and Social Behavior* 16(4):347–364.

Srole, Leo, T. S. Langer, S. T. Michael, M. K. Opler, and T. A. C. Rennie. 1962. *Mental Health in the Metropolis.* New York: McGraw-Hill.

Susser, Mervyn. 1985. "Epidemiology in the United States after World War II: The evolution of technique." *Epidemiologic Reviews* 7:147–177.

Tausig, Mark. 1982. "Measuring life events." *Journal of Health and Social Behavior* 23(1):52–64.

U.S. Public Health Service. 1967. *Fetal Deaths in the United States.* Washington, D.C.: U.S. Government Printing Office.

Verbrugge, Lois M., and Frank J. Ascione. 1987. "Exploring the iceberg: Common symptoms and how people care for them." *Medical Care* 25:539–560.

3

Some Findings of Social Epidemiology

INTRODUCTION

In the first stage of the epidemiological approach, rates are calculated by dividing the number of medical conditions observed at a particular time by the total number of people in specific social and population groupings. This results in specific rates during a specific time period, which helps answer the question of whether medical conditions are distributed differently among social and category groupings. Such an approach is referred to as *descriptive epidemiology*, since it describes occurrence variations. Descriptive epidemiology sets the background for *analytical epidemiology*, which approaches cause or etiology by focusing on why the conditions are distributed in the particular patterns observed.

The epidemiological approach can be used to chart the course and distribution of any disease or medical condition, whether communicable or noncommunicable, mental or physical, chronic or acute, curable or terminal. But since the methodology received initial impetus during the heyday of the germ theory, epidemiology started by concentrating on infectious or communicable diseases. Even today, we think of the "infectious diseases epidemiologist," although many in the discipline investigate noninfectious diseases and some focus on nondisease conditions such as traffic accidents.

THE EPIDEMIOLOGY OF SOME
MAJOR CONDITIONS

To demonstrate the epidemiological approach, this chapter will focus on the methods and findings of three medical conditions that have important social consequences. The selected conditions are hypertension, venereal or sexually transmitted diseases other than acquired immune deficiency syndrome (AIDS), and the special case of AIDS. Epidemiological findings concerning these conditions will be used as the background for a discussion of social epidemiology and the preventive medicine approach.

Hypertension

It should not be assumed that only those conditions vague in definition and unreliable in diagnosis, such as mental illness, pose methodological problems for epidemiological research. Despite apparent ease of measurement and reliability of diagnosis, hypertension, or high blood pressure, a common condition associated with other serious diseases, presents many methodological problems for the epidemiologist.

Determination of Prevalence.   The U.S. Public Health Service has estimated that approximately sixty million people in the United States have hypertensive disease (Institute of Medicine, 1988a), which marks this disease as one of the most common in the country. Since hypertension is positively associated with many other health conditions, its contribution to the health or disease status of Americans is highly significant. Stamler, Schoenberger, Shelzelle, and Stamler make the point dramatically: "Hypertensive disease is . . . one of the most important, if not *the* most important affliction producing premature sickness, disability, and death in our adult population" (1974:3).

At first glance, a determination of the prevalence of hypertension seems simple. Most people are familiar with some type of blood-pressure-measuring instrument. The most common is the sphygmomanometer, an upright board on which there are two mercury-filled tubes; attached to this is an inflatable arm band and a tube with a rubber bulb at the end that is used to pump up the band while the practitioner listens to pulse action in the arm. Recently available is a digital readout unit that works mechanically, but the sphygmomanometer is still the most commonly used instrument for measuring blood pressure. Whatever means are used, two readings are taken from the instrument: One is diastolic (blood pressure during the relaxation of the heart muscle, when the heart chambers fill with blood), and the other is systolic (during the contraction phase of the heart muscle, when the heart pumps blood into the aorta and pulmonary artery).

The simplicity of an epidemiological study of blood pressure readings rests in applying a measurement instrument to large numbers of people, since the relevant data are easily obtained by observing the mercury-filled tubes. But even here, not unlike the research on mental illness reviewed in the previous chapter, epidemiological studies stand at the mercy of definitions and measurements that may be in error. In studying hypertension, problems may arise because of instrument error (perhaps the sphygmomanometer or its calibration is inaccurate), or there may be observer error because of mental concentration problems, difficulties in pulse-hearing acuity, confusion of auditory and visual cues, misinterpretation of sound, improper rates of arm-band inflation and deflation, and misreading of the mercury as it rises and falls in the tubes (Maxwell, 1974). Any of these could account for the statement by two researchers that blood pressure readings taken by a doctor are usually higher than those taken by a nurse (Miall and Greenberg, 1987; the psychological disposition of the patient also affects the readings). Furthermore, although the World Health Organization has established a criterion figure for high blood pressure, some physicians use a lower cutoff point, which can change prevalence figures. (According to Stamler, Schoenberger, Shelzelle, and Stamler, 1974:4, lowering the cutoff point by five millimeters of mercury would increase the hypertension prevalence rate among white adults by up to 16 percent.) Also, the use of general cutoff points for the total population may be invalid; thus, Messerli (1985:35) states that "arterial pressure increases with age in westernized populations and more and more elderly patients will fulfill (arbitrarily set) criteria of being hypertensive." This means that the same blood pressure reading may indicate hypertensive disease in a young person and indicate "normal" blood pressure in an older person.

Dangers of Hypertension.   Some features of hypertensive disease make it particularly serious to those afflicted. A majority of those who have high blood pressure do not exhibit layperson-recognizable symptoms. Given its "silent" symptomology, many people first learn that they have the disease during a routine physical examination, during an examination for other health problems, or through screening programs. This means that reported prevalence rates severely understate the true extent of hypertension. It also means that large numbers of people are unaware that they have a health problem. By the time the condition is recognized, the disease may have reached an advanced stage and may be affecting the individual's general health.

This observation becomes more important because of the relationship between hypertensive disease and the increased risk of serious physical problems; even a slight elevation in blood pressure, for example, is related to premature death. Thus, pooling data from several longitudinal studies, Stamler and his associates (1974) report that over a ten-year period the heart attack mortality rate was twice as high for people with mild elevation of diastolic pressure as for those with normal blood pressure. Furthermore, these investigators report data indicating that a mild elevation of blood pressure readings among relatively young men was found to be related to a 76 percent higher death rate when they reached middle age. And, when hypertension is present with other major risk factors, the risk is additive.

Untreated hypertension can have serious consequences among older population groupings. Thus, a Veterans Administration Cooperative Study concluded that 63 percent of those over sixty years of age who had untreated hypertension will suffer a cerebral vascular accident, congestive heart failure, myocardial infarction, or a dissecting aneurysm within five years (Messerli, 1985).

Associated Demographic and Social Characteristics.   A number of demographic and social variables have been found to be associated with hypertension. Data from Stamler, Schoenberger, Shelzelle, and Stamler (1974) indicate that the hypertension prevalence rate increases with age. The rate is conspicuously higher among blacks, who tend to exhibit more severe cases. The data also show that, irrespective of age and race, the prevalence rate is much higher among men than among women. For the population between fifty-five and sixty-four years of age, the hypertension prevalence rate is 48 percent for black men, 36 percent for white men, 36 percent for black women, and 29 percent for white women. Additionally, hypertension runs in families; if both parents have the disease, the risk of their children's being afflicted is especially great. Both diet and body state are associated with hypertension. Obesity is clearly related, and body build as a youth is associated with contracting the condition in middle age. A direct relationship has been found between sodium balance and hypertension in obese patients. Cigarette smoking is also a variable related to hypertension. Another factor is occupation; for example, a study revealed that air traffic controllers exhibited high blood pressure at rates more than five times higher than the general population (Tanner, 1976).

In more general terms, Grant's (1975) review of the literature identifies three factors that appear to be significant in the presence of hypertension: family background, obesity, and personality. His statement about familial tendencies indicates a strong association: "When hypertension occurs in an adult, it may almost be taken for granted that the children will be similarly affected" (p. 61). After a discussion of the relationship between high blood pressure and obesity, Grant states that "it has been postulated that hypertension may be due, in part, to repeated psychic traumata occurring over long periods" (p. 61). But he points out that further research is necessary to test this hypothesis.

Millon and Millon (1975) include hypertension in a discussion of psychophysiologic disorders. In describing the particular type of person most likely to contract hypertension, these authors portray the individual as "forced in childhood to restrain resentments; inhibited rage; is threatened by and guilt-ridden over hostile impulses which may erupt; is a controlled, conforming and 'mature' personality; is hard-driving and conscientious; is guarded and tense; needs to control and direct anger into acceptable channels; desires to gain approval from authority" (p. 211).

Cockerham (1989) examined data indicating that nonwhites have much higher rates of hypertension than whites and offered six hypotheses to explain the differential:

1. Genetics.
2. Physical exertion. Observations show that blacks are more likely than whites to work in occupations demanding great physical exertion.
3. Associated disorders. Blacks more frequently experience diseases that lead to secondary hypertension.
4. Psychological stress. Blacks face emotional difficulties because of racial discrimination.
5. Diet.
6. Medical care. Blacks receive poorer care than whites and this results in greater morbidity and mortality.

In a study of Zulus, Scotch (1960) found a relationship between blood pressure readings and migration from the country to the city. High readings were more frequent among urban than among rural dwellers. Among city dwellers, however, high blood pressure readings were more frequent for those who had most recently migrated from the rural area. A hypothesis suggests that the differential is a consequence of the emotional strain caused by the migration experience. In a study carried out in Iran (Nadim, Amini, and Malek-Afzali, 1978), it was found once again that rural migrants to the urban area have higher blood pressure readings than people who remain in the country. The authors suggest the following hypotheses to explain the association:

Migrants may have been different from the rest of the rural population even before migrating; diet in the city is quite different from the diet in rural areas, especially from the point of view of salt intake; people in the city do much less physical activity than those in rural areas; migrants have been brought up in a completely different sociocultural situation so that, when they come to the city, stresses of city life to which they can't adapt easily lead to the increase in their level of blood pressure. (pp. 136–138)

Venereal or Sexually Transmitted
Diseases Other Than AIDS

In this age of acronyms, the abbreviation VD has been replaced by STD; that is, what were previously known as venereal diseases (VDs) are now sexually transmitted diseases (STDs). According to Cates (1986:11), the director of the Division of Sexually Transmitted Diseases in the Centers for Disease Control, the previous primary emphasis on gonorrhea and syphilis has changed; there is now an emphasis on the "numerous conditions spread through intimate human behavior." Given the prevalence of gonorrhea, syphilis, and genital herpes, however, we will focus on these three diseases in this section and will discuss the most alarming current STD disease, AIDS, in a separate section.

Determining Prevalence.   Venereal, or sexually transmitted, diseases provide a particularly important example of the underreporting problem faced by the epidemiologist. One author refers to the "vast reservoir of unreported cases" (Morton, 1976:115) of venereal disease and estimates that only about 20 percent of the cases that occur are found in official records, despite legal requirements making the reporting of all cases to health authorities mandatory. Another author (Greenberg, 1978:15) estimates the total incidence of syphilis in the United States by assuming that only one case in eight is reported in the official statistics. (An estimate of 200,000 new cases in 1976 is made on the basis of only 23,731 reported cases for the year.) More optimistically, but still recognizing severe underreporting, the Centers for Disease Control (CDC) made an estimate of the total prevalence of gonorrhea in the United States by assuming that one out of every two cases is reported: "In 1984 a total of 878,556 cases of gonorrhea were reported for both sexes, with the CDC estimating that the true number is closer to 1.8 million cases" (Metropolitan Life Insurance Company, 1986:3). If such estimates are even somewhat close to the actual situation, the number of reported cases of sexually transmitted diseases represents only the tip of the iceberg. Some authors indicate that, among the infective diseases, only the common cold has a higher prevalence today than venereal diseases (Morton, 1976; Willcox, 1975). Presently, gonorrhea is the most frequently reported infectious disease in the United States and syphilis is third. (Chicken pox is second.)

There are several reasons for such a low reporting rate. For one, many people with symptoms of venereal disease do not seek help from health agencies (World Health Organization, 1977). For another, approximately 80 percent of the sexually transmitted diseases are treated by general practitioners in private practice; many of these physicians fail to make accurate diagnoses because they lack training and because laboratory facilities are not available (Webster, 1976). Added to these technical considerations are sociological and psychological reactions to diseases such as syphilis and gonorrhea: a sense of shame and stigma, especially if the infection was thought to be transmitted by a prostitute or because of a homosexual experience; the doctor's attempt to maintain some degree of confidentiality; fear of what the symptoms mean to the individual's health; and, since some diseases respond well to treatment, the doctor's feeling that little is gained by making the disease a matter of record.

Despite weaknesses in data quality, several medical publications focus on venereal disease, and others have more than a passing interest in the condition. Many report on epidemiological studies of the disease, although they make no pretense of claiming true or total rates. The usual approach is to concentrate on studies that cross-classify reported occurrence and social variables.

Associated Demographic and Social Characteristics.   Several groups at high risk for venereal disease have been identified. Greenberg (1978:15), for example, states that almost one out of every fifteen members of the armed forces returning from World War II had syphilis. The World Health Organization (1977) lists members of the following social and statistical categories as particularly vulnerable: "the military, seafarers, immigrants, refugees, workers separated from their families, tourists and professional travelers, hotel staff, etc." (p. 17). Such a listing points toward people who are not in a normal family situation, who frequently travel out of their usual communities, and who are more likely to come into contact with prostitutes. Rapid social change may be a contributing factor among some of these people.

The social change theme is used by the World Health Organization to account for a trend away from high rates among males and low rates among females to high rates among both. Specific reasons for this change listed by the World Health Organization (1977) are rapid industrialization and urbanization, an extensive floating population in cities, greater financial independence for females, more leisure time, greater consumption of alcohol, and increases in the number of migrant workers who are either single or are separated from their families. Also, there is a relaxation of sexual norms among some social groups and categories related to new methods of contraception, the liberalization of abortion laws, and the availability of simple means of treatment for some venereal diseases. The *Statistical Bulletin* (Metropolitan Life Insurance Company, 1986) refers to "clear antecedents in the sexual revolution of the '60s and '70s" and "increasing sexual activity among adolescents" (p. 10). The young have more freedom from parental control along with greater community tolerance.

One of the more consistent trends in the spread of venereal disease is a rise in incidence among adolescents and young adults, especially among females (World Health Organization, 1977; Wiesner, Jones, and Blount, 1976; Metropolitan Life Insurance Company, 1986). Furthermore, "persons of the age group 20–24 years in males and slightly less in females are those of greatest risk" (Willcox, 1976:38). The incidence of venereal disease among young people is so high that it has been referred to as an "epidemic" (Schofield, 1978). According to Willcox (1976), "with the demands for full sex equality the double standard between the sexes has largely gone and women have their rights to experiences which may lead to the contraction of venereal disease with the men" (p. 32).

In 1970, 72 percent of all cases of gonorrhea reported were among men; in 1984, the proportion had dropped to 58 percent. Between 1970 and 1984, the rate for men stayed stable, whereas the rate among women increased by 96 percent (Metropolitan Life Insurance Company, 1986:3), although the male rate is still higher than that of the female.

Males also continue to predominate in syphilis rates. Wiesner, Jones, and Blount (1976:8) indicate that the male syphilis rate is about double that of females; however, the higher male rate may be at least partially because the symptoms of the condition are more obvious for them than for females (Morton, 1976:120), which implies that the approximately two-to-one ratio may be an exaggeration. Other evidence shows that males do have higher syphilis rates than females, partially because of one particularly high-risk grouping: homosexual males. This category is described as very high risk by the World Health Organization (1977), Greenberg (1978), Harris (1975), Willcox (1976), and Wiesner, Jones, and Blount (1976).

The World Health Organization (1977) also refers to the high rates of syphilis among male homosexuals in large cities: "It is a large proportion of male homosexuals suffering from sexually transmitted diseases, particularly primary and secondary syphilis, in capital cities or large conurbations in a number of countries" (p. 18). And Greenberg (1978) states that "syphilis is becoming more and more a disease of sexual promiscuity involving prostitution and homosexual communities" in urban areas (p. 15).

Between 1970 and 1984, physician visits for genital herpes infections increased more than sevenfold (Metropolitan Life Insurance Company, 1986:7). Women between the ages of twenty and twenty-four and men between twenty-five and twenty-nine account for most of these doctor visits. The CDC estimates an incidence in the United States of 200,000 to 500,000 cases a year, and prevalence (including asymptomatic cases) is estimated at the astonishing figure of 30 million (reported in Metropolitan Life Insurance Company, 1986:7).

The Special Case of AIDS

Particularly difficult problems of data collection, validity, and reliability are faced by epidemiologists working with data on acquired immune deficiency syndrome, the sexually transmitted disease commonly referred to as AIDS. For one thing, the viral infection and the disease occur years apart; present incidence and prevalence figures reveal infections that were acquired several years before. This means that many of those who presently have AIDS have had an opportunity to engage in a wide variety of activities while unaware of their infections. During the years after infection, for example, some may have contracted other venereal diseases, experienced other life-threatening conditions, or may have died before being identified as having AIDS; these experiences would affect the quality of data collection on the disease itself.

For another, when AIDS was finally recognized and worldwide implications of the disease were indicated, the Centers for Disease Control and the World Health Organization proposed criteria for the syndrome. The agreed-upon criteria were not useful in the developing world, however, because adequate resources to carry out the suggested definitive diagnosis were lacking. It was not until 1985 that a less precise clinical definition of AIDS was devised, one that could be used throughout the world. This is a particular example of the "standardization of terms" problem faced by the epidemiologist: It is sometimes necessary to sacrifice precision so all reporting agencies are on a standard base, and as more knowledge about a disease is obtained, the old clinical definition may be found to be inadequate. Thus, in 1987 the case definition was revised once again to include a broader spectrum of related diseases and to allow for the presumptive diagnoses of certain conditions (CDC, 1988b).

Other epidemiological problems are involved in cross-national comparisons. Thus, since the United States has a well-established national surveillance system, but many other countries do not, cases may be found in the U.S. that would not be identified in other nations. On a cross-country comparison, this could make the figures from other countries spuriously low, not because definitions vary, but because reporting systems do.

Studies of AIDS are further compounded by an emotional reaction to the disease and by value conflicts. The background to this situation is the etiology of AIDS, since the infection process forces people to consider two of U.S. society's negative social concerns and problems: homosexuality and illegal drug usage. If this is not enough to excite people, the incidence and prevalence of the disease is highest among young adult males, which means that men at an age considered by many as the "prime of life" are at particularly high risk. Furthermore, to many professionals, the disease represents a serious threat to the society as a whole: If it ever spreads to that part of the population that does not participate in infection-associated behavior, the effects of the disease can be catastrophic for the country, since a cure has not been found and death follows soon after symptoms appear. Consequently, many people, both professional and nonprofessional, consider AIDS the most serious health threat presently confronting the United States (Fineberg, 1988:592), with the Institute of Medicine (1988b:20) suggesting that, if unchecked, the current epidemic could become "a catastrophe."

The etiological agent of AIDS is the human immunodeficiency virus (HIV), which selectively infects and ultimately incapacitates an individual's immune system, making the person vulnerable to a host of infectious agents that the body can ordinarily fight off (Fauci, 1988:617). Since the body has lost its natural ability to fight pathogenic invaders, infections can now spread, leading to progressive and irreversible physiological deterioration. The most commonly occurring "opportunistic" infection is a type of pneumonia that has long been associated with immunologic deficiencies and has been found among patients undergoing therapy using immunosuppressive medications. Sixty percent of all AIDS cases reported in this country exhibit this type of pneumonia, and 57.3 percent of all AIDS deaths are attributed to it (CDC, 1989:5). In addition to rendering the person susceptible to opportunistic infections, the HIV infection has neuropsychiatric consequences that lead to a psychological problem known as AIDS dementia complex (Price et al., 1988:586).

HIV is transmitted in several ways: (1) by having sex with a person infected with the virus in which blood or semen (euphemistically referred to in the professional literature aimed at the general public as "body fluids") is passed from the infected person into the bloodstream of the partner, (2) by using needles or syringes that have been contaminated with the virus through previous use by an infected person (despite this mode of transmission, AIDS is classified as a sexually transmitted disease), (3) by being born to an infected mother (referred to as "perinatal transmission"), or (4) by receiving infected blood through transfusions (Curran et al., 1988). Since routine screening of the blood supply was instituted in the United States in 1985, transmission by the latter route has essentially been stopped (Institute of Medicine, 1988b:42–44).

It is extremely doubtful that body fluids other than blood and semen can carry the virus in high enough concentrations for infection to occur in the general population; the Institute of Medicine (1988b:172) states that "there is no evidence that the virus is transmitted in the air, by sneezing, by shaking hands, by sharing drinking glasses, by insect bites, or by living in the same household with an AIDS sufferer or an HIV-infected person." Further, in a *Journal of the American Medical Association* article, Lifson (1988) states that "there is no epidemiological evidence that contact with saliva, tears, or urine has resulted in HIV infection" (p. 1353). The Surgeon General of the United States, in a publication mailed by the government to homes throughout the nation, flatly states: "You won't get AIDS from saliva, sweat, tears, urine or a bowel movement" (U.S. Public Health Service, 1988:3). The only body fluids other than blood and semen that have been implicated as possible transmission sources are mother's breast milk and vaginal secretions. The evidence indicates that breast milk transmission occurs only from the mother to the suckling baby rather than by occupational exposure such as among health workers (CDC, 1988a:24), and that vaginal secretions are not an important means of transmission in the United States at the present time (Quinn, Mann, Curran, and Piot, 1986). Present evidence indicates that mosquitoes and possibly other insects can carry the AIDS virus, but there is no evidence that the volume or concentration can lead to transmission to humans (Booth, 1987).

Most sexual transmission in the United States has occurred among homosexual and bisexual men, especially those who participate in anal intercourse; this type of sexual contact promotes open wounds and bleeding in and around the anus, thus providing the semen-carried virus with easy entry into the bloodstream of the receptive partner. The virus also can be spread through vaginal and oral sex between a man and a woman; the significant factor is entry of the virus from an infected partner into the bloodstream of the noninfected person. People from all walks of life—male and female, young and old, rich and poor—and members of virtually all racial and ethnic groupings have contracted AIDS. But only about 4 percent of all reported AIDS cases in the United States are through heterosexual transmission, and almost all of these (83 percent) are female (Barnes, 1987:1423).

Data showing the increasing prevalence of AIDS in the United States are presented in Table 3–1. As indicated, the number has grown from less than 100 before 1981 to an estimated 40,200 in 1989. The year-by-year increase is startling, which suggests why some public health officials are alarmed about the future of the epidemic in the United States. The case-fatality death rate is also causing great concern; the condition is claiming the life of virtually every person afflicted with the disease.

About three-quarters of AIDS cases throughout the world were reported from the Americas, with the remaining one-quarter split between Africa and Europe; Asia

Table 3–1
Cases of AIDS and Case-Fatality Rates,
United States, by Year

Year	No. reported*	Case-fatality rate**
<1981	78	83.3
1981	289	92.1
1982	1,055	89.9
1983	2,882	91.2
1984	5,850	88.5
1985	10,918	86.8
1986	18,500	82.0
1987	28,100	73.2
1988	34,900	55.2
1989	40,200	33.6
Totals	142,772	61.1

*These data are provisional; all figures will undoubtedly be revised upward as reporting becomes more complete. Data prior to 1986 are reported in CDC, 1990:13; 1986 data and following years are estimates provided in a personal communication from the Statistics and Data Management Branch, Division of HIV/AIDS, CDC, May 1990.

**Estimates derived from data in CDC, 1990:13.

may be considered almost AIDS-free at this time. But even these figures are reported to be but "a fraction" of the actual number of cases in the world, since "reporting mechanisms in many of the developing nations in Africa and the Americas are hampered by an inability to carry out adequate clinical and laboratory diagnoses for various political, economic, and social reasons" (Henahan, 1988:3377). Add to this the observation that "some developed countries seem reluctant to report cases. And in some parts of the United States, such as New York and San Francisco, the caseload is so high that a kind of 'reporting fatigue' has set in" (remarks attributed to J. Mann, of the WHO, by Henahan, 1988:3377). The highest numbers of total AIDS cases in the United States have been reported for the New York, San Francisco, and Los Angeles standard metropolitan statistical areas (CDC, 1989:3).

Emerging epidemiological information indicates three broad geographic patterns in the spread of the disease. The first is that of most of the western world, in which almost all cases occur among homosexual and bisexual men and intravenous drug users; the male to female ratio is about ten or fifteen to one. A second pattern is found in Africa and some Caribbean countries, where most cases occur among heterosexuals, and there is little difference between male and female rates; given this situation, perinatal rates are relatively high. The final pattern is found in Asia, Eastern Europe, the Middle East, and most of the Pacific. Here, only a small number of cases have been reported; when they have been found, they were attributed to nonlocal conditions, such as travelers returning with the infection.

Actually, the AIDS virus has been around for several years, but for many reasons, including an incubation period measured in years, the importance of this etiological agent was not recognized for some time. Thus, "the large number of AIDS cases that are now being reported are due to the spread of HIV-1 in the 1970s before it was isolated and its pathogenesis and transmission were understood" (Piot et al., 1988:573). Unknown to the epidemiologist, an epidemic was in the making. It was first recognized in mid-1979 and came to the attention of the medical scientific community in 1982 with such article titles in professional journals as "New Disease Baffles Medical Community" (Marx, 1982). Since then, interest in the disease has become extensive.

The long incubation period of the virus points to a pernicious aspect of the disease: If HIV carriers unaware of their infection continued to engage in the behaviors that led their infection, they could have spread the virus to others, who were also unaware of their infection until the symptoms of AIDS appeared years later, and on and on. This suggests that AIDS will have consequences for the health of society for many years to come. In 1986, the U.S. Public Health Service predicted a cumulative total of 270,000 AIDS cases and 179,000 deaths due to the disease in this country by the end of 1991 (reported in Institute of Medicine, 1988b:57). And such predictions about AIDS have a way of increasing with time. Thus, it was reported by the Centers for Disease Control (1988b) that more recent predictions project a cumulative total of 365,000 diagnosed cases by the end of 1992 and a cumulative death total of 263,000. If these predictions are accurate, there will be 80,000 newly diagnosed cases and 66,000 AIDS deaths in 1992 alone; the total of 172,000 patients with the disease in that year will require medical care costing between $5 billion and $13 billion (CDC, 1988b).

The delay between the infection and the appearance of AIDS and the nature of the infection and disease put a twist on the reasoning behind usual disease identification and case listing. The Institute of Medicine publication "Confronting AIDS" states that "AIDS is the end-stage of HIV infection," and that "HIV infection itself should be considered a disease" (1988b:37). Does the epidemiologist, then, confront two medical conditions, one an infection and the other a disease? Should the epidemiologist be concerned with the incidence and prevalence of infection or with that of its end-product disease? These are not idle questions, since concentration of resources on the prevalence of one will take resources that could be used to study the other. But data on both are necessary because information about one can provide valuable information about the incidence of the other. Focus on either means concentration on special populations, particularly those at high risk, and this raises a whole series of ethical problems, with such issues as informed consent, voluntary participation, and confidentiality immediately being raised (Dickens, 1988). Despite practicing in a profession that, on the face of it, looks relatively innocuous, the epidemiologist sometimes cannot avoid becoming involved in controversial issues, value problems, and heated exchanges.

One would think that the best way to predict the prevalence of AIDS in the future would be to determine the extent of HIV infection in the society as a whole today. But the progression from the infection to the disease can take years, is not always clear and predictable, and affects people differently. For example, data from what was initially a 1978–1980 hepatitis B study of 6,700 homosexual and bisexual men in San Francisco suggest some aspects of the disease progression. In 1987 it was reported that 70 percent of these men were infected with HIV and 10 percent had AIDS (Barnes, 1987). In the same article it is predicted that, of this grouping, 15 percent will develop AIDS after 5 years of infection, 24 percent after 6 years, and 36 percent after 6.5 years. Thus, the incidence of AIDS among HIV-infected persons increases with time. At the Third International Conference on AIDS, held in 1987, James Curran of the CDC stated: "The most common question I get is, How many people in the United States are infected with HIV?" His answer: "I don't know" (reported in Barnes, 1987:1425). Most recent estimates are that 1.5 million people in the United States are infected, with about one male in thirty between the ages of twenty and fifty carrying the virus (reported in Barnes, 1987:1425); the Institute of Medicine reports that more recent estimates by the CDC place the figure at 945,000 to 1.4 million, although other sources put it between 400,000 and 2.2 million (Institute of Medicine, 1988b:50). Until an accurate study of HIV infection is conducted, predictions about prevalence must remain tentative and rough.

THE PREVENTIVE MEDICINE APPROACH

Community Medicine

The theoretical and methodological orientations that have led to the development of social epidemiology have had an important influence on the medical profession. For example, these perspectives have been the basis for the clinical specialty known as community medicine (Jonas, 1980), which is often found in the public health departments of medical schools. On a governmental level, all fifty states have departments of public health, which have the responsibility to "assure conditions in which people can be healthy" (see Byrne, 1988:1591). This medical subdiscipline has had its greatest impact in societies with health care systems that are basically preventive in orientation. Given the emphasis on curative rather than preventive medicine, the community medicine and public health approaches in the United States have not had a major impact on its general system of health care.

Practitioners of community medicine view the community as their patient. In taking this perspective, community medicine staff are concerned with the social, cultural, psychological, and biological aspects of the community that affect the occurrence of disease. Using applied epidemiology as a basic tool, these practitioners collect and analyze the background information necessary to develop and implement prevention programs (Jonas, 1980:2). To make their programs relevant, public health doctors join forces with social scientists to develop a health care system tuned to the sociocultural life of the community. Thus, just as social, psychological, and biological factors influence the incidence and prevalence of disease, so these same factors influence health care systems, especially in the area of preventive medicine.

There are, however, innumerable instances of public health prevention programs that have been unsuccessful. For example, value conflicts and other problems have prevented epidemiological studies of AIDS. And, despite clear-cut medical and social epidemiological evidence of etiology, extensive public information campaigns, restrictions on advertising, and potential prevention programs that use the best of social science knowledge, more than 50 million people in the United States continue to smoke. These failures suggest the weakness of the U.S. public health system. Thus, a panel appointed by the Institute of Medicine issued a report focused on the future of the public health system in the United States and concluded that it is "a system in disarray, weakened by poor leadership, fragmented services, and public complacency. And, without major changes, the panel sees little hope for the future" (quoted in Byrne, 1988:1591).

In their report on the future of public health, Institute of Medicine (1988a) committee members define the mission of public health in the United States as "fulfilling society's interest in assuring conditions in which people can be healthy" (p. 1). But, after completing their study, they conclude that the nation has "lost sight of its public health goals" (p. 1), "slackened our public health vigilance" (p. 2), demonstrated "lack of agreement about the public health mission" (p. 3), and created a situation of "isolation" and "suspicion" (p. 5). As a consequence, "the health of the public is unnecessarily threatened" (p. 2).

AIDS and Preventive Medicine

A current example of attempts to use the preventive medicine approach for disease control is found in public and professional reactions to AIDS. When CDC member James Curran stated that he did not know the prevalence of HIV in the United States, he followed with a statement that suggested the need for a nationwide sampling of the general population to ascertain "the precise number of people infected with the virus" (quoted in Barnes, 1987:1425). Notice that the suggestion is to sample and screen the total population, rather than to focus on homosexual men, intravenous drug users, or other high-risk population groupings. Studying a representative sample of the entire U.S. population is very costly and is rarely done, but an accurate general population sample will eliminate the problems inherent in focusing only on particular groupings, from which generalizations to the total population cannot be made. The technology for such an epidemiological screening project is at hand, but a host of value problems prevent implementation.

Screening tests are designed to determine either whether particular individuals in a population already have a condition or whether they possess characteristics that put them at high risk. These tests also can determine whether a particular person is a "carrier" who can pass the condition on to others. Often using data derived from epidemiological studies, those working toward eliminating or reducing a condition may concentrate on identifying carriers, giving special attention to people in high-risk categories. Since such screening can identify carriers of the AIDS virus (although, a one-time negative test provides no guarantee that the person is virus-free, because it may take some months for the body to develop measurable antibodies), its use sounds particularly attractive as a means of eliminating the scourge of the disease. But society does not work in such a rational way. Thus, an Institute of Medicine panel that addressed the future of public health in the United States referred to the controversy over mandatory testing for AIDS as the most recent example of a program that may be enacted or rejected for political, rather than for public health, reasons (Byrne, 1988:1591). Testing procedures for the AIDS virus became available for clinical use in 1985, but their use was immediately embroiled in legal and ethical controversy (Council on Ethical and Judicial Affairs of the AMA, 1988; Dickens, 1988).

In fact, no country has carried out an extensive epidemiological study of AIDS. In the United States, the president proposed in 1987 that immigrants, prisoners, and marriage-license applicants should undergo routine screening for AIDS, but this recommendation led to numerous protests and considerable debate. Most who voiced opposition indicated that they feared discrimination against people with AIDS in civil rights generally, and in such areas as employment and the obtaining of health and life insurance specifically. Many who oppose mandatory testing also suggest that such a program would lead to many carriers "going underground," that is, attempting to hide their condition for fear of the consequences of public exposure. Many of the public health officials who object to mandatory testing recommend containing the disease through education programs that emphasize how to prevent exposure to the virus, especially by promoting the use of condoms in all homosexual and some heterosexual relationships and the use of sterilized needles by drug users.

Barnes (1987) summarizes the present situation: "Taken together, these data on the epidemiology of AIDS show how incomplete an understanding yet exists about the disease and therefore how difficult a comprehensive national policy will be to formulate" (p. 1425). This statement also could be made about many of the United States' other socially disapproved health conditions, such as syphilis, gonorrhea, alcoholism, drug addiction, suicide, unmarried pregnancy, and mental illness. The CDC is presently moving very slowly and cautiously toward a full-scale national household seroprevalence study that will yield information about total HIV prevalence rates (Goldsmith, 1988).

Tobacco Use and Disease

A publication of the Population Information Program of Johns Hopkins University states that "the use of tobacco is one of the foremost public health problems in the world today" (*Population Reports*, 1979:1); referring to the United States, the Institute of Medicine (1988a:26) states that "smoking is the single greatest cause of premature death in this country." The failure of the public health system in this country can be demonstrated by examining the public response to the identification of the relationship emphasized in these two quotations.

Tobacco usage is associated with many diseases. For example, smoking during pregnancy is linked with low-birth-weight babies and with comparatively short fetus gestation (both are associated with health disorders, including high rates of infant mortality), higher rates of spontaneous abortion, and more frequent complications of both pregnancy and labor. Smoking during lactation also is suspect in reducing the quality of breast milk, in introducing undesirable chemicals to the infant, and possibly, in reducing the quantity of milk a mother produces. It has been found that "the lactating mother who smokes passes along more DDT to her infant than the nonsmoking mother" (*Population Reports*, 1979:20); the long-term consequences of DDT to human development are not known.

Other health problems clearly associated with tobacco use are lung cancer, heart disease, and respiratory disease. Amount of tobacco use, or intake, is apparently a significant factor in the severity of some diseases. For example, the relationship between smoking and lung cancer has been found to be dose-related; death rates due to lung cancer increase with the average number of cigarettes smoked daily.

Most of the publicity about the relationship between smoking and cancer has focused on lung cancer because the mortality rate from this disease among smokers is approximately ten times higher than among nonsmokers. In addition to lung cancer, risks of dying from cancer of the larynx, esophagus, and bladder are all between two and ten times higher for cigarette smokers than for nonsmokers; smoking contributes to as many as 100,000 deaths from cancer in the United States each year (U.S. Public Health Service data quoted in Institute of Medicine, 1988a:26). Heart disease is the major cause of death in the industrialized world; in the United States, it is the most commonly reported mortality cause, with almost ten times as many people dying from diseases of the heart as from lung cancer. The data reveal that cigarette smokers have significantly higher rates of death from coronary heart disease than do nonsmokers. The U.S. Public Health Service estimates that smoking contributes to as many as 225,000 deaths from coronary heart disease each year in this country (Institute of Medicine, 1988a:26). Here again, the finding is dose-related, that is, the risk increases with the increased number of cigarettes smoked. Thus, "cigarette smokers have a 70 percent higher death rate from all causes than nonsmokers," and "smoking is the single greatest cause of premature death in this country" (Institute of Medicine, 1988a:26).

Among the respiratory diseases, smoking-related morbidity and mortality data indicate that smokers are more likely than nonsmokers to contract bronchitis, asthma, and emphysema. Some of the data are extreme; for example, the death rate from emphysema is about twenty times higher among heavy smokers than among nonsmokers. In addition to all of these dramatic data, the Population Information Program states that "smokers have more coughs, colds, minor respiratory infections, shortness of breath, and allergy problems than nonsmokers; they take longer to recover from many respiratory conditions and also, often, from surgery. Moreover, smokers are twice as likely to develop peptic ulcers" (*Population Reports*, 1979:5). Further, the Institute of Medicine (1988a), quoting data from the U.S. Public Health Service, states that "10 million Americans suffer from debilitating chronic disease caused by smoking" (p. 27). The case against smoking seems clear.

Furthermore, there are data indicating that giving up cigarettes can remove one from high-risk death experiences. This is the conclusion in a study of nearly 60,000 British physicians, about half of whom gave up smoking. Longitudinal data show that those who stopped smoking had normal life spans, whereas those who continued to smoke died earlier. Moreover, at a time when the lung cancer death rate was increasing in Britain, it fell dramatically among the doctors who stopped smoking (Doll and Hill, 1964).

There are public policy or legislative implications of such dramatic data (see McKinlay, 1974). For example, it might be expected that a rational society would develop a plan for eliminating tobacco use, but such an expectation is tempered by consumer demand and the contributions of tobacco to the economy. In the United States, consumer spending for tobacco products amounts to billions of dollars a year and, as the tobacco lobby in Washington has pointed out, the tobacco core and supplier industries in 1987 accounted for $41 billion of the U.S. gross national product and provided 728,000 jobs, which generated $18 billion in compensation, and paid more than $20 billion in federal, state, and local taxes (Tobacco Institute, 1988). On the other hand, the annual cost in lost production from sickness, from the cost of health care, and the resulting loss of life and property totals several billion dollars. Thus, a federal study in 1985 estimated that the health care costs of smoking-related disease is between $11 and $35 billion annually and that smoking-related lost productivity costs the United States between $26.5 and $60.5 billion a year (data presented in Fielding, 1986). Furthermore, in 1988 tobacco was being produced in many developing countries in which it is a major crop that provides needed export income. The leading tobacco-leaf-producing countries in 1987, in order, were: China, United States, India, Brazil, Soviet Union, Indonesia, Turkey, Italy, Zimbabwe, Bulgaria, Greece, Burma, Japan, and Poland (Tobacco Institute, 1988).

Perhaps because of its economic contribution, no country has banned the use of tobacco. Rather, many have launched programs designed to control the advertising and use of tobacco. By 1978, at least thirty-five countries had placed restrictions on advertising tobacco products, twenty-two required health warnings on cigarette packages, twelve had placed restrictions on sales to minors, eleven had some kind of restrictions on smoking (such as in public places), and eight had initiated antismoking educational programs. Additionally, many countries have raised taxes or prices on cigarettes as a means of simultaneously generating income and discouraging smoking. In some countries, such as Britain, a graduated tax has been instituted so the highest rates are on cigarettes with the most tar.

The point is that even a clear association between specific practices and health disorders does not necessarily lead to a rational social action program geared toward the elimination of the practice. Policy decisions, after all, are consequences of values and the effectiveness of special interest groups. One of these values in each society is economic, and one of the special interest groups is the tobacco industry. The industry's representative in Washington, D.C., the Tobacco Institute, attempts to attack research that links cigarette smoking with disease; most recently the attack has been on studies that report on the danger of people's smoking to nonsmokers (Marshall, 1987).

Nor can we expect people to make rational decisions about matters concerning their health. As demonstrated in the 1920s, the legal prohibition of a substance deemed harmful to people and to society may not result in its elimination. Despite compelling evidence of negative consequences, some people want to continue smoking. And, despite a desire to stop, some have become so dependent on the practice that they cannot stop, even if they want to. A variety of means have been tried to help those in the latter category, including individual and group therapy, hypnosis, acupuncture, drug therapy, and fear arousal, all with mixed results. In the final analysis, "there is no way to accurately ascertain why people stop smoking" (National Cancer Institute, 1977:57). From a preventive medicine perspective, the most reasonable approach would be to convince people not to start in the first place.

Value Systems and the Legislation of Preventive Medicine

By the very nature of value systems, we cannot expect societies to make rational choices, especially when vested interest groups have developed effective means for influencing decision making. Consequently, the epidemiologist and the public health and preventive medicine specialist recognize that policies promoting good health are outgrowths of value and political decisions. Of course, these decisions constitute the work of politicians rather than of health personnel. This point was made by the president of the American Public Health Association, who referred to "numerous instances" in which public health information suggests one course of action while politics demands another (Bailus Walker, Jr., referred to in Byrne, 1988). A current example is public health officials who urge that condoms be used to reduce the spread of AIDS, while many in public office are reluctant to support this policy for fear their constituents would be offended.

But when a particular combination of factors occurs, a combination that awakens legislators, this country is capable of committing large sums to a disease. This was demonstrated in the campaign against poliomyelitis in the 1950s and is being demonstrated in the campaign against AIDS today: "AIDS is fast becoming the single largest program in the federal health bureaucracy" (Booth, 1988a). Thus, spending by the federal government for AIDS research and prevention exceeded the federal budget for heart disease during the 1988 fiscal year and the cancer budget in 1989; in fiscal 1988 the figure was $1.3 billion. As Booth (1988a) points out, this seems incongruous, since Congress and the administration often appear intolerant of homosexuals and drug addicts. What, then, is the driving force behind this major congressional commitment? Booth (1988a) suggests three possible factors: "compassion for the syndrome's sufferers, intense lobbying by gay activists, or fear that the human immunodeficiency virus will spread into the general population" (p. 858).

For social scientists, the best of all worlds would be if they could provide information to the preventive medicine practitioners that would bring about the changes in behavior necessary to prevent diseases such as AIDS. But, alas, this is not the case. Significant behavioral changes have taken place among high-risk AIDS populations, but it may be basic fear rather than social science that has contributed to these changes. Thus, Booth (1988b) reports that the proportion of homosexual men in San Francisco who engage in anal intercourse without a condom has decreased sharply, and many drug addicts have started to rinse their shared needles with disinfectant. But, as both Booth (1988b) and Brandt (1988) point out, social science has not yet made major contributions to the programs that brought about such changes in behavior.

SUMMARY

The first stage of epidemiological investigation involves a simple description of a disease pattern. The next step attempts to account for observed differences. The epidemiological approach can be used to chart the development of a condition and its distribution in population groupings.

Because of ease of measurement, at first glance, hypertension lends itself well to epidemiological analysis. But even here, measurement error and lack of standardization are problems. Many factors are associated with hypertensive disease, including age, sex, race, obesity, and personality.

Venereal disease demonstrates one of the major problems of the epidemiological investigation: unreported cases. It appears that the number of reported cases of sexually transmitted diseases is an understatement. Despite this weakness in the quality of data, much research on the condition has been published. Several studies have concluded that, on a worldwide basis, venereal diseases have very high incidence and prevalence rates. Among the high-risk groups are members of military units, immigrants, refugees, and workers without families. Rapid social change is also seen as a key factor. Males, particularly homosexual males, have higher risk, as do adolescents and young adults.

There are particularly difficult quality-of-data problems for epidemiologists working with AIDS. The infection and the disease occur many years apart, which affects epidemiological information about incidence and prevalence. Further, society's emotional reaction to this dreaded disease creates other problems of data collection, validity, and reliability. Particularly important is the lack of information about HIV, the virus that causes the disease.

The orientations involved in social epidemiology development have had an important influence on the medical profession. They have been the basis for the specialty known as community medicine, which views the total community as its patient. These doctors join forces with social scientists to study the community experiences affecting the antecedents and the consequences of disease. Members of these two disciplines attempt to make health care and prevention programs relevant to the social, psychological, and biological nature of the community.

Epidemiological findings lead to policy implications. It might be expected that a rational society would, for example, seek to develop epidemiological studies of AIDS and a plan for the elimination of tobacco use. A suggestion that certain groupings within society undergo a mandatory screening program for AIDS led to numerous protests and considerable debate. Data on the virus and the disease are incomplete. Calls for programs designed to decrease the consumption of tobacco because of its etiological contribution to disease have also not fared well. In the United States and other countries, spending on tobacco products is high, and the product is seen as making a major contribution to the economy. For this and other reasons, no country has placed a total ban on tobacco use. Attention primarily has been devoted to advertising campaigns aimed at convincing people to stop smoking or never to start.

References

Barnes, Deborah M. 1987. "AIDS: Statistics but few answers." *Science* 236(12 June): 1423–1425.

Booth, William. 1987. "AIDS and insects." *Science* 237(24 July):355–356.

———. 1988a. "No longer ignored, AIDS funds just keep growing." *Science* 242 (11 November):858–859.

———. 1988b. "Social engineers confront AIDS." *Science* 242(2 December): 1237–1238.

Brandt, Allan M. 1988. "The syphilis epidemic and its relation to AIDS." *Science* 239(22 January):375–380.

Byrne, Gregory. 1988. "Panel laments 'disarray' in public health system." *Science* 241(23 September):1591.

Cates, Willard, Jr. 1986. Guest Editorial: "Sexually transmitted diseases: Why such prominence?" *Statistical Bulletin* (October-December):11.

Centers for Disease Control (CDC). 1988a. "Update: Universal precautions for prevention of transmission of human immunodeficiency virus, hepatitis B virus, and other bloodborne pathogens in health-care settings." *MMWR (Morbidity and Mortality Weekly Report)* 37(24):377–382,387–388.

———. 1988b. "Quarterly report to the Domestic Policy Council on the prevalence and rate of spread of HIV and AIDS—United States." *MMWR* 37:551–554, 549.

———. 1989. AIDS Weekly Surveillance Report—United States. January 2.

———. 1990. HIV/AIDS Surveillance Report. May:1–18.

Cockerham, William C. 1989. *Medical Sociology*. 2nd ed. Englewood Cliffs, N.J.: Prentice-Hall.

Council on Ethical and Judicial Affairs, American Medical Association. 1988. "Ethical issues involved in the growing AIDS crisis." *Journal of the American Medical Association* 259(9):1360–1361.

Curran, J. W., H. W. Jaffe, A. M. Hardy, W. M. Morgan, R. M. Selik, and J. Dondero. 1988. "Epidemiology of HIV infection and AIDS in the United States." *Science* 239(5 February):610–616.

Dickens, Bernard M. 1988. "Legal limits of AIDS confidentiality." *Journal of the American Medical Association* 259(23):3449–3451.

Doll, R., and A. B. Hill. 1964. "Mortality in relation to smoking: Ten years' observations of British doctors." *British Medical Journal* 1(5395):1399–1410 and (5396):1460–1467.

Fauci, A. S. 1988. "The human immunodeficiency virus: Infectivity and mechanisms of pathogenesis." *Science* 239(5 February):617–622.

Fielding, Jonathon E. 1986. "Editorial: Banning worksite smoking." *American Journal of Public Health* 76–78:957–959.

Fineberg, H. V. 1988. "Education to prevent AIDS: Prospects and obstacles." *Science* 239(5 February):592–596.

Goldsmith, Marsha F. 1988. "HIV prevalence data mount, patterns seen emerging by the end of this year." *Journal of the American Medical Association* 260(13):1829–1830.

Grant, Murray. 1975. *Handbook of Community Health*. Philadelphia: Lea and Febiger.

Greenberg, R. N. 1978. "Syphilis: Review and overview." *Clinical Medicine* (July):14–22.

Harris, J. R. W. 1975. "Epidemiological and social aspects." In *Recent Advances in Sexually Transmitted Diseases*, ed. R. S. Morton and J. R. W. Harris, 91–96. London: Churchill Livingston.

Henahan, John F. 1988. "AIDS' economic, political aspects become as global as medical problem." *Journal of the American Medical Association* 259(23):3377–3378.

Institute of Medicine. 1988a. *The Future of Public Health*. Washington, D.C.: National Academy Press.

———. 1988b. *Confronting AIDS: Update 1988*. Washington, D.C.: National Academy Press.

Jonas, Steven. 1980. "The Need for Preventive and Community Medicine Faculty in Schools of Medicine." Mimeographed. Hyattsville, Md.: Office of Graduate Medical Education, Health Resources Administration, U.S. Public Health Service.

Lifson, Alan R. 1988. "Do alternative modes for transmission of human immunodeficiency virus exist?" *Journal of the American Medical Association* 259(9):1353–1356.

McKinlay, John B. 1974. "A case for refocusing upstream: The political economy of illness." In *Proceedings of American Heart Association Conference*, 7–17. Seattle, Washington, June 17–19.

Marshall, Eliot. 1987. "Tobacco science wars." *Science* 236(17 April):250–251.

Marx, Jean L. 1982. "New disease baffles medical community." *Science* 217(13 August):618–621.

Maxwell, Morton H. 1974. "A functional approach to screening." In *The Hypertension Handbook*, 43–62. West Point, Pa.: Merck Sharp and Dohme.

Messerli, F. H. 1985. "Essential hypertension in the elderly." *Triangle: Sandoz Journal of Medical Science* 24(1/2):35–47.

Metropolitan Life Insurance Company. 1986. "Sexually transmitted diseases in the United States." *Statistical Bulletin* (October–December):3–10.

Miall, W. E., and G. Greenberg. 1987. *Mild Hypertension: Is There Pressure to Treat?* New York: Cambridge University Press.

Millon, Theodore, and Renee Millon. 1975. "Psychophysiologic disorders." In *Medical Behavioral Science*, ed. Theodore Millon, 206–220. Philadelphia: W. B. Saunders.

Morton, Barbara M. 1976. *VD: A Guide for Nurses and Counsellors*. Boston: Little, Brown.

Nadim, A., H. Amini, and H. Malek-Afzali. 1978. "Blood pressure and urban migration in Iran." *International Journal of Epidemiology* 7(June):131–138.

National Cancer Institute. 1977. *The Smoking Digest*. Bethesda, Md.: Public Health Service, National Institutes of Health.

Piot, P., F. A. Plummer, F. S. Mhalu, J.-L. Lamboray, J. Chin, and J. M. Mann. 1988. "AIDS: An international perspective." *Science* 239(5 February):573–579.

Population Reports. 1979. "Tobacco—hazards to health and human reproduction." Population Information Program, Series L, No. 1. Baltimore, Md.: Johns Hopkins University.

Price, R. W., B. Brew, J. Sidtis, M. Rosenblum, A. C. Scheck, and P. Cleary. 1988. "The brain in AIDS: Central nervous system HIV-1 infection and AIDS dementia complex." *Science* 239(5 February):586–592.

Quinn, T. C., J. M. Mann, J. W. Curran, and P. Piot. 1986. "AIDS in Africa: An epidemiological paradigm." *Science* 234 (21 November):955–963.

Schofield, C. B. S. 1978. *Sexually Transmitted Diseases*. 3rd ed. Edinburgh: Churchill Livingston.

Scotch, Norman A. 1960. "A preliminary report of the relations of sociocultural factors of hypertension among the Zulu." *Annals of the New York Academy of Science* 86:1000–1009.

Stamler, Jeremiah, James A. Schoenberger, Richard B. Shelzelle, and Rose Stamler. 1974. "The problem and the challenge." Pp. 3-31 in *The Hypertension Handbook*. West Point, Pa.: Merck Sharp and Dohme.

Tanner, Ogden. 1976. *Stress*. New York: Time-Life Books.

Tobacco Institute. 1988. *Tobacco Industry Profile, 1988*. Washington, D.C.: Author.

U.S. Public Health Service. 1988. "Understanding AIDS." Washington, D.C.: U.S. Government Printing Office.

Webster, B. 1976. "The medical manpower situation in the United States in relation to the sexually transmitted diseases." *British Journal of Venereal Disease* 52:94–96.

Wiesner, P. J., O. G. Jones, and J. H. Blount. 1976. "The situation in the United States." In *Sexually Transmitted Diseases*, ed. R. D. Catterall and C. S. Nicol, 5–13. London: Academic Press.

Willcox, R. R. 1975. "International aspects of the venereal diseases and non-venereal treponematoses." *Clinical Obstetrics and Gynecology* 18:207–222.

———. 1976. "Society and high-risk groups." In *Sexually Transmitted Diseases*, ed. R. D. Catterall and C. S. Nicol, 31–50. London: Academic Press.

World Health Organization. 1977. *Social and Health Aspects of Sexually Transmitted Diseases*. Public Health Papers No. 65. Geneva: World Health Organization.

4

Illness Behavior and Becoming a Patient

INTRODUCTION

For most people, the concept of sickness refers to a physical disorder that results in changes in the body and its organs. We assume that we can readily recognize these changes. We also believe that healers can take action to relieve discomfort, arrest the progress of the disorder, and suggest actions that will lead to its amelioration or elimination. When sickness occurs, the ultimate goal is to eliminate the sick state and make certain the person is returned to normal activities.

This view of sickness is realistic in terms of life experiences but, to the sociologist, it is a far too limited perception of disease and illness. From the sociological perspective, sickness is much more than the biochemical phenomenon portrayed in the previous paragraph; it is also a social and psychological condition that affects the sick and those close to them. A woman interviewed in a study of health and illness in a small community makes the same point in a different way (Koos, 1954:30):

> *I wish I really knew what you meant about being sick. Sometimes I felt so bad I could curl up and die, but had to go on because the kids had to be taken care of and besides, we didn't have any money to spend for a doctor. How could I be sick? How do you know when you're sick, anyway? Some people can go to bed most any time with anything, but most of us can't be sick, even when we need to be.*

To this woman, being a sick person was not solely a biochemical or physical matter. It involved how she felt and the objective symptoms of the disease but also included responsibilities she could not forgo, permission from others to give up her normal tasks, and the money to pay for care. If this woman could "curl up and die" but did not, should she be considered sick?

When is a person actually sick? Consider, for example, a health survey focused on locating women with cancer of the breast (Robinson, 1978). Some of the women suspected they had the condition but had done nothing about it. Others found out as a result of the survey. Some reacted to having the condition by undergoing treatment immediately, but others rejected any kind of treatment. Some women told their families; others kept the condition a secret. Each woman had the physiological condition and could, therefore, be described as having a physical disorder. But is the physiological condition sufficient to say that sickness exists? What is necessary before we are able to say that these women are sick from the social point of view?

There is no simple answer to this question. The findings of health surveys show that only a small proportion of the population is totally free from some physical disorder at any given time. The existence of a condition is not necessarily related to whether it will receive medical attention. In assessing the amount of illness in a society, we are faced with what has been referred to as the "clinical iceberg" (Robinson, 1978) or the "iceberg of morbidity" (Verbrugge and Ascione, 1987); like a real iceberg, the true prevalence of illness is not the amount we can see, for most lies below the surface. Beneath the reported cases of illness are many that are not officially recognized as such, because they are not treated, are treated outside the official health care system, or are not listed on official records for some other reason.

As Gochman (1988) points out, sickness is socially constructed. Sickness as a social condition reflects social perceptions taught during the socialization process. These perceptions rest more on a selection of signs and what is considered "scientific" knowledge than on some absolute recognition of bodily functioning (Goode, 1989).

The perception of sickness as a social condition has led sociologists to make four related observations. First, sickness represents a particular position or status in the group; like all social statuses, certain patterns of behavior are expected of incumbents. Second, several social factors affect the decision to seek the sick status and the timing of the decision. Third, rules concerning entry into the position are socially defined; particularly, there are socially agreed upon means for obtaining entry approval. Finally, occupancy of the sick status implies giving up some personal autonomy to social control agents.

SICKNESS AS A STATUS-ROLE

Recognizing sickness as a social condition means that a person occupying the status is expected to play the sick role. We can gain insight into health behavior by understanding the nature of the sick role. Parsons (1951) stimulated much discussion about and research on the sick role with a model in which he detailed the socially expected behavior of sick-status incumbents. The model is not useful as a description of social behavior for all conditions accepted as sicknesses by society. It is most adequate for acute, nonimpaired, and physical medical conditions, that is, conditions most people believe are readily relieved and are eventually cured by medical intervention. The model is not appropriate for describing chronic diseases, illnesses that result in physical disabilities, mental impairments, and conditions that do not respond well to treatment.

Four Expectations of the Sick Position

Four specific expectations associated with the sick position were presented in the model; two are rights of the sick person and two are obligations. Clearly, the four are interrelated. For convenience, however, we will discuss them separately.

Excused from Social Responsibility. The first dimension of the sick role discussed by Parsons is the right to be excused from usual social responsibilities; recognized and legitimate incumbency in the status allows the person to be excused from many ordinary and usual tasks. For example, the student who is sick can receive permission to miss class, even when an examination is scheduled. In the world of work, employers allow those who are accepted as sick to be absent from their usual duties. The exemption may be general, including most physical, social, psychological, and economic activities, or it may be restricted to rather specific aspects of behavior. A school child may be excused from gym class, for instance, but not be allowed to miss school altogether.

The extent of the exemption depends on the type and severity of the illness. Thus, a person with pneumonia usually will be excused from almost all usual social responsibilities. Ordinarily, he or she will require complete bed rest for some time and few, if any, work, family, or scholastic activities. But a cold, even if severe, will allow far fewer exemptions. A class or a meeting may be missed, but most responsibilities will continue, perhaps in a less demanding way.

In the United States, we learn about this right to be excused from certain responsibilities at an early age. Children wishing to avoid a difficult situation at school, for example, understand that claiming a hard-to-diagnose stomachache may provide a legitimate excuse from the responsibility of attending school. As we mature, this knowledge of how to avoid unwanted or unpleasant situations is expanded. Findings indicate that people's prior behavior is generally the best predictor of whether this exemption will be sought, particularly if their fathers displayed such behavior (Moss, 1986).

Not at Fault.   The second dimension of the model presented by Parsons is the right not to be held responsible for continuing in the sick condition. The social group recognizes that sick people cannot become well by self-decision or by their own will. This right is clearly associated with the first dimension, that is, the exemption from usual social-role responsibilities. To avoid the accusation of malingering, the sick person must obtain social acceptance that the illness is not being prolonged unnecessarily in an attempt to avoid social obligations. This dimension also suggests that the sick individual should accept help in order to return to health and normal social responsibilities.

Research has shown that the characteristics of the individual in the sick status influence the willingness of others to accept the person's right to this dimension of the sick role. For example, Fisher, Arluke, and Levin (1985) found that young people were more likely to not blame the sick person for the condition when that person was elderly. In addition, persons holding lower prestige jobs were more likely to be allowed the dependency of the sick role than those in more responsible positions (Honig-Parnass, 1983).

Defined as Undesirable.   Third, as part of an obligation to want to get well, incumbents of the sick status are expected to define their condition as undesirable. If those in the status seem to find the excuse from responsibilities a comfortable adjustment to social demands, others will question their right to exemptions. Such people may be suspected of not being willing to seek an early enough return to normal role performance and may even have the exemption taken away from them.

Parents, for example, are often quick to sense the delight of a child who is allowed to stay home from school and be waited upon. When the sickness no longer demands time and rest for recovery, the parents may force the child to return to school. Similarly, employers initially allow their workers time to recover from sickness but, after a certain number of days, they may question the excuse from usual duties and demand proof of the illness. The rules some professors have for permitting make-up examinations is another illustration of a demand for evidence of illness. For them, it is not enough to claim the onset of flu or a long-lasting case of mononucleosis, so the student may be asked to present a note from the university health service or a private physician.

Seek Technically Competent Help.   The fourth dimension of the sick role is for the status incumbent to seek technically competent help and cooperate in the recovery process. In the United States, the help source is almost always a medical doctor. Other healers, such as the osteopathic physician or chiropractor, are alternative choices. When the sick person seeks help, it is the healer's responsibility to provide the assistance needed to return the individual to a normal routine. In return, the sick person is expected to follow the guidance given.

Evaluating the Sick-Role Model

Since its publication in 1951, Parsons's model of the sick role has received both praise and criticism. Since the model has influenced the field of medical sociology for about forty years, it is useful to review some of these evaluations. This will help us to understand some of the contributions and limitations of the concept.

Contributions to Our Understanding of Sickness.   From a sociological perspective, the major contribution of the model is that it places sickness firmly in a social context. It outlines the behavioral expectations of the individual occupying the sick status as well as reactions that can be expected from the group, it sets the stage for understanding the role of health workers, it introduces the setting of the doctor-patient relationship, and it suggests the social significance of the legitimacy of incumbency. The concept also provides a sociological context within which a wide variety of sicknesses can be viewed, and in doing so, it points to important similarities among a variety of diseases. Our attention is drawn to a common social situation for such seemingly different conditions as pneumonia and accidents. Parsons's concept indicates that medical conditions may be clinically different, but the social definitions, expectations, and reactions to them are similar. Understanding the commonality of behavioral expectations that cuts across conditions helps us understand sickness behavior in general.

As we shall see, many studies have cast doubt on the universality of Parsons's model of the sick role. But even those who comment on its limitations, who question its validity, and who have reservations about its use across all segments of society have indicated that it provides insight into the social nature of sickness (see, for example, Fisher, Arluke, and Levin, 1985; Moss, 1986; Augoustinos, 1986). There is agreement that, in many ways, the sick role provides a general model that represents what is meant socially when we think of someone as being sick.

Parsons's sick-role concept has generated a vast amount of significant research on the behavior of the sick and on societal reactions to sickness. Many sociologists empirically investigating a variety of diseases use the concept as a basic guide to the important questions to ask. Perhaps this has been its most important contribution: its guidance to researchers concerned with the social meaning of illness.

Areas in Which the Model Does Not Contribute to an Understanding of Sickness.   As noted, there are a number of criticisms of Parsons's sick-role concept. First, the model presupposes that the sick person will become a patient. It accepts a medical model that takes the illness condition as a given (Freidson, 1970; Nuttbrook, 1986; Meile, 1986). This assumption ignores research showing that many people exhibit clinical signs of disease without recognizing their symptoms as indications of physical disturbance. On a separate level, many who recognize symptoms do not seek the rights and obligations of the sick role (Verbrugge, 1985; Verbrugge and Ascione, 1987).

Many sociologists contend that the implicit insistence on the doctor-patient relationship in the model is particularly limiting. Thus, Freidson (1970) and Mayou (1984) both indicate that if we limit the sick role only to those obtaining professional help, we learn nothing about people who do not follow this particular pattern. Meile (1986) shows that most people are slow to seek a physician's care; they would not be considered sick in this model until they finally sought such care.

As suggested by many (including Gordon, 1966; Twaddle, 1969; Freidson, 1970; Kurtz and Giacopassi, 1975; Gallagher, 1976; Honig-Parnass, 1983; Fisher, Arluke, and Levin, 1985; Meile, 1986; Arluke, 1988), the model does not accurately describe responses to chronic diseases, physical impairments, and conditions that do not readily respond to treatment. The model is also inappropriate for mental illness (Greenley, 1972; Petroni, 1972; Mayou, 1984; Augoustinos, 1986).

The inapplicability of the Parsonian concept for chronic illness has been a particular target of criticism. Freidson (1970) suggests that if incumbency in the sick status depends on the extent to which recovery is possible, the model rules out all but acute illnesses. Honig-Parnass (1983) concludes that the emphasis in chronic illness is on acceptance of the impaired condition as normal, without the expectation of returning to a previous active state, or what Lau (1988) refers to as "learned helplessness." Combining many of these criticisms, Arluke (1988) suggests four ways the sick-role model does not fit the chronically ill. First, it is difficult to excuse the sufferer from normal responsibilities over a long period of time. Second, the chronically ill often see themselves, and are seen by others, as being at fault for the condition. Third, by definition, the chronically ill cannot be expected to get well. Finally, those with chronic illnesses do not, as a rule, cooperate fully in their medical regimens.

Parsons's model has also been criticized for its lack of applicability to mental illness. Augoustinos's research (1986) indicates that the sick role was adopted only by patients who perceived their problems as medical and who sought the exemptions the role allowed. Psychiatric patients oriented toward independence, on the other hand, did not accept the sick status. Mayou (1984) found that some mental patients were likely to adopt the sick status inappropriately. He also concluded that psychiatrists used the sick-role concept in ways other than those specified in Parsons's model.

Another shortcoming of Parsons's sick-role model is its neglect of the subjective aspects of illness. The concept portrays illness only in an objective sense. It separates the self-interpretations and definitions of the human player from the social role of sickness. The self-concern and, possibly, the fear of the sick person do not play a part in Parsons's model. Doehrman (1977) notes that "the psychological and social problems resulting from coronary heart disease are typically distressing and, for some patients, as debilitating as the primary illness itself," and "long lasting emotional distress, familial problems, and occupational maladjustment are observed in a significant minority of patients" (p. 199).

The dimensions Parsons presented may not even match the way in which people generally view sickness. For example, in interviews with several hundred hospital patients, Gordon (1966) focused on how perceptions of sickness matched the model's expectations. He concluded that the formulation was too simplistic to describe the actual response to sickness. Parsons's model describes only one segment of sickness behavior. According to Gordon, several roles are needed to encompass the sick condition. In particular, he distinguishes between those illnesses with serious or uncertain prognoses and those with minor and certain prognoses.

Twaddle (1969) found that research subjects (a small sample of older male patients) frequently mentioned Parsons's expectations. But rarely were all four named together. Twaddle identified at least seven potential sick-role configurations, which included such factors as interpersonal influence, well roles, and the extent and severity of the particular sickness.

Finally, Segall (1976) explored the question of how closely public expectations regarding the sick role agreed with Parsons's model. Based on a sample of hospital-ized patients, he found that the actual expectations for behavior of the sick person gave little support to the concept. Although few totally disagreed with the model's stated expectations, they did not support the total model, more from being uncertain than from actual rejection. The only clear agreement Segall found with Parsons's four dimensions was that the sick person has an obligation to get well.

Sociological reaction to the Parsonian sick-role concept shows us that a single model cannot cover such a complex phenomenon as the expected social behavior of the sick, especially in a society as diverse as ours. The model does not describe the sickness behavior of those lacking economic, social, or psychological access to the health system. Nor does it tell us anything about those who do not seek health care because of such factors as lack of information, financial constraints, fear, or because they feel it would be useless. And it does not provide insight into the behavior of those who seek help outside the recognized health system. But despite the criticisms and the limitations pointed out by many, the sick role is, in the words of Fox (1989:28), "a concept that overshadows all others in the field of medical sociology." It certainly remains the only fully elaborated statement of any role related to sickness.

Sickness as a Deviant Position

Once adopted, the behavioral expectations of the sick status allow the incumbent to behave in a manner different from what is considered normal. In sociological terms, the expected behavior of the incumbent of the sick status deviates from the expecta-tions of the "normal" (that is, the nonsick) members of society. Within this sociologi-cal context, "deviant" is a sociologically neutral term, with no judgments suggested or implied. Thus, sickness is perceived as a deviant status, and the individual plays a deviant role to deal with a particular problem. The members of the group tolerate such deviance because it is socially legitimate: It is understandable, can happen to anyone, and is eventually beneficial for the individual and society. But there are limitations. As Arluke (1988:169) comments, "The social system . . . functions smoothly only insofar as persons perform their roles adequately. Deviation from the normal performance of these roles can become a threat to the stability of society. Given the potential negative consequences of role deviance, social control mechanisms arise to minimize its occurrence."

A society in which many people played the sick role simultaneously could not function for long because this would interfere with its everyday activities. Consequently, societies develop ways to control sick-status occupancy, to guard against the use of the role for purposes other than a return to the healthy state. The implication of this statement is that some people may desire the sick status, not as a means of becoming well, but as a means of acquiring its privileges and exemptions. For example, they may find release from usual social responsibilities pleasant. The status provides a nondemanding lifestyle for some and could serve others as an acceptable excuse for failure. Parsons refers to such use of the sick status as "secondary gain," in contrast to the "primary gain" of the role, that is, recovery from illness.

Control of Entry

Given these conditions, it is logical to expect that society would develop some means of controlling entry into the sick status. Field (1953, 1957) provides an example of how the Soviet society coped with this issue. When the government followed the success of the revolution with a program of national industrialization, it faced a severe labor shortage. To alleviate this shortage, the government instituted rules controlling absence from work. Workers had to obtain certificates to authorize disease-caused excuses. The government restricted the number of certificates a clinic could issue and, in some instances, physicians were encouraged to compete to see who could issue the fewest certificates.

The closest U.S. society has ever come to a mass system of testing the right to exemption from social responsibility occurred when the military draft was operating within the selective service system. Physical examinations to determine fitness for service were routinely given. It was a special type of secondary gain for some potential draftees to feign physical or mental conditions that led to their excuse from service in the armed forces. Representatives of society asked doctors to differentiate between those who should legitimately be exempted and those who were seeking secondary gain (in this case, between legitimate and illegitimate excuse from service).

Many factories, schools, business establishments, and governmental agencies establish their own criteria for legitimate claim on the sick status. Individuals whose stay in this status is expected to be infrequent and short are given much freedom. The rules are more strictly enforced for those who appear to be abusing the privileges of the status.

On the other side of this approach, some rules test people to see if they should be forced into the sick status for the society's well-being. Current examples are obligatory testing for AIDS and for the use of certain drugs. The validity of the tests and the ethics of administering them are questioned by many, yet it seems likely that these tests will continue and force some people into the sick status.

How deviant behavior is viewed depends on several factors. Freidson (1970) constructed a typology of U.S. middle-class reactions to different types of deviance that helps us place the sick person within a specific context (see Table 4–1). He maintains that reactions to the person claiming the status depend on whether the condition is serious and whether the individual is held responsible for it. Reaction to those judged responsible is punitive; reaction to those judged not responsible results in privileges. The seriousness of the condition modifies the reaction but the key factor is responsibility.

Since different judgments can lead to radically different social responses, those with the right to assess individuals and control entry into the status have considerable power over those being judged. This social control function was discussed from the radical perspective by Waitzkin (1983), who sees it as power given to elites in western capitalistic society. Waitzkin contends that through this "blame the victim" approach, the capitalistic system places the responsibility for illness on the sick themselves. But in his view, the system creates conditions that contribute to sickness. Navarro (1986) agrees, arguing that by placing the blame on the victim, the real cause of illness—the economic system—is ignored.

Table 4–1

Types of Deviance, by Judgments of Responsibility and Seriousness

	Judgment of Responsibility	
Judgment of Seriousness	*Individual Held Responsible*	*Individual Not Held Responsible*
Minor deviation	Slight addition to normal obligations; minor or no suspension of a few privileges or a fine (for example, a parking violation)	Partial suspension of a few ordinary obligations; slight enhancement of privileges; obligation to get well (for example, a cold)
Serious deviation	Replacement of ordinary obligations by new ones; loss of privileges (for example, murder)	Release from most ordinary obligations; addition to privileges; obligation to seek help and cooperate with treatment (for example, a heart attack)

Source: Reprinted by permission from *Profession of Medicine: A Study of the Sociology of Applied Knowledge* by Eliot Freidson. Chicago: University of Chicago Press. Copyright 1988, 1970 Eliot Freidson.

FACTORS AFFECTING THE DECISION TO SEEK THE SICK STATUS

During the discussion of sickness as a social position, reference was made to entry, occupancy, and incumbency in the status. This terminology suggests that when people assume the sick position they change their social status from a nonsick to a sick one. This change does not always occur easily or automatically. Sociologists note that the most important factors guiding entry into the sick status have social, cultural, and psychological antecedents. We turn our attention to some of these.

Our primary concern is with factors that may or may not motivate the individual to seek health care. The occurrence of symptoms is not enough; discomfort does not lead to an automatic movement toward and entry into the sick status. Clinicians point out that some people suffer from nonexistent symptoms and others ignore those that physicians consider severe. Furthermore, only a small proportion of those experiencing problems actually consult a doctor. Thus an explanation of health behavior must be sought in areas that go beyond the presence of symptoms.

In their efforts to discover factors that explain help-seeking behavior, medical sociologists have considered a large and diverse number of variables. Becker (1979:253) refers to these variables as a "constellation of diverse and complex health-related attitudes and behaviors which often seem enigmatic, irrational, erroneous, and relatively immutable."

The question is, what leads to the recognition of the presence of a health problem and then leads to a particular course of behavior? After examining data from patients at Massachusetts General Hospital, Zola (1966, 1973) concluded that five factors influence a person's health behavior:

1. Interpersonal crisis. The individual experiences a crisis that calls attention to the symptoms.
2. Social interference. The symptoms may threaten and interfere with a social activity valued by the individual.
3. The presence of sanctioning. Someone advises the individual to see a physician (or may insist on it).
4. Perceived threat. The individual feels that the illness is threatening.
5. Nature and quality of symptoms. The individual is influenced by whether the present symptoms are similar to others experienced in the past.

The message in this listing suggests that health action is not influenced by physiological, anatomical, or biochemical factors, but by social and psychological factors that reflect the individual's daily life as a social being. Even after reviewing these factors, the question remains of how the person moves from noticing symptoms to seeking help. And, as a subsidiary question, one might ask what determines the kind of help sought. These questions are not easy to answer. Nevertheless, some factors do dominate the individual's decision about whether or not to take action.

The Health Belief Model

One attempt to tie together many social and psychological factors influencing sickness behavior is the health belief model. Originally developed by Rosenstock (1966) in a social-psychological attempt to explain preventive medical behavior, the model has been generalized to include an explanation of how people make decisions about their health activities (Becker, 1979). According to the model, health behavior is modified by such factors as demographic variables, health motivation, health knowledge, perceived threat of a disease, one's usual means of coping with illness problems, lay referral systems, social support and pressure, relationship to prior experience, and cues to action. These, in turn, modify the individual's interpretation of possible benefits of, and barriers to, health activities.

Janz and Becker (1984) summarize the model by classifying specific actions into four perceptions of the individual: perceived susceptibility, severity, benefits, and barriers. In a review of approximately fifty studies that have used this model to explain health action, Janz and Becker report that the model does indeed predict health behavior. At least two important messages in this model help identify behavior that leads to taking on the sick status. First, the listing of modifying factors suggests that many variables simultaneously influence the individual's decision. This flows from extremely complex sociological and psychological bases. Second, subjective judgments of the benefits to be received by health action are critical in the steps that will be taken.

Presentation of Symptoms

How symptoms become visible influences the decision to seek care. For some diseases, such as pneumonia, visibility is clear and disruptive. For some types of cancer, however, there are no clear signs. Research shows that much of the delay in seeking care for cancer occurs because many of the symptoms are not apparent (see, for example, Goldsen, Gerhardt, and Handy, 1957; Goldsen, 1963; Fink, Shapiro, and Lewis, 1968; Calnan, 1987). Even when symptoms do appear, the individual may attempt to interpret their meaning and seriousness in a way that delays treatment. Since many symptoms eventually disappear or go into remission, the individual can minimize their severity. Some people may postpone health action even after recognizing the presence of symptoms and interpreting them as severe.

The frequency with which symptoms occur also influences the tendency to seek help. Given a particular level of seriousness, the more frequently symptoms occur, the more likely the individual will seek treatment. For example, a person coughing for a brief period may self-diagnose a simple cold that does not need professional help. A person whose coughing continues for an extended period will more likely consult a physician.

Bizarre symptoms (as interpreted by the person and group) can be alarming and will most likely lead to health activity. A person with a symptom that is obvious and unpleasant in appearance will more likely seek help. But if the symptom is common and familiar and not obvious, help is less likely to be sought. Further, the visibility and perceived seriousness of symptoms and their disruptive effects on the individual's daily activities affect help-seeking behavior. Despite their medical significance, symptoms that do not interfere with activities are less likely to lead to action.

Perceptions of susceptibility to a particular condition also affect the probability of seeking care. Thus, Becker, Drachman, and Kirscht (1974) asked mothers in a clinic to name diseases their children had and asked if they felt the condition might recur. These investigators found that belief in future susceptibility, based on past experience, usually made mothers more willing to keep appointments at the clinic. It has also been found that the perception of susceptibility to chronic illness is an influential factor in the decision to seek medical care (Verbrugge and Ascione, 1987).

Sociocultural Factors

The broadest category of factors influencing health action are those grouped under the general term sociocultural. Among such factors are social class, ethnicity, attitudes toward health care, and availability of services.

One of the earliest investigations of differential perceptions of appropriate health action was carried out by Koos (1954). He reported that what might be considered health problems by many middle-class people were accepted by many lower class people as a normal part of life. A comparison of answers from middle-class and lower class respondents to a question asking which symptoms should be called to the attention of a medical doctor reveals significant differences. In a more recent report, Dutton (1986) confirms the relationship between social class and health behavior. The perceptions of appropriate or inappropriate health behavior on the part of lower class members may be part of their experiences in the so-called cycle of poverty.

Part of the effect of social class on health action reflects a difference in level of knowledge about health matters. For example, Hackett and Caseem (1976) report that blue-collar victims of a heart attack know less about its cause and meaning and are more frightened by treatment than white-collar patients. This may be, in part, because physicians tend to tell lower class patients less about their condition and its treatment than they do when the patient is closer to them in social-class position.

The perceptions and use of the health care system are strongly influenced by economic factors. The system of health care in the United States has raised financial barriers that keep many people from using services. Some suggest that with the advent of Medicare and Medicaid, the old and poor are now provided with adequate medical care, but others indicate that solutions to the economic problems of health care and financial barriers have not been instituted (Aday, Anderson, and Fleming, 1980).

Lifestyle also affects health behavior. Bruhn (1988) suggests that half of the mortality attributed to the ten leading causes of death can be traced to the lifestyle of the individual. Troyer (1988) reports a relationship between the lifestyles prescribed by conservative religious groups and health behavior. Religions providing firm directives for personal living have a significant effect on resultant health behavior.

For example, the banning of certain foods, alcohol, and tobacco provides protection against certain types of cancer.

Ethnic background and race also are related to the seeking of health care. The data usually may be interpreted as differences rooted in subcultural lifestyles, including assumptions about the meaning of health and illness (Dutton, 1986:37–38). These assumptions, in turn, affect what action is considered proper when illness occurs.

A study of cultural backgrounds and reactions to pain showed ethnic subcultural differences. In a hospital-based study, Zborowski (1952, 1969) observed that patients with Jewish and Italian backgrounds responded to pain emotionally and in an exaggerated way, patients of "Old American" background were stoical and minimized pain, and those of Irish origin often denied pain altogether. Although patients of Jewish and Italian backgrounds exhibited similar reactions to pain, their reasons were different. The patients of Jewish background took a long view toward the meaning of pain; they were concerned about its meaning for their future life, and their reactions did not subside when pain-relieving drugs were administered. The patients of Italian origin, on the other hand, were mainly concerned with the pain itself, and drugs both relieved the pain and their complaints.

Zola's (1966, 1973) research on patients attending medical clinics supports Zborowski's findings. He also notes that patients of Italian background express pain as a major part of their problem. Those of Irish descent do not; many actually denied its existence. As a corollary, those of Italian background had more varied complaints than those of Irish origin. Those in the latter ethnic group also described their symptoms specifically whereas descriptions were more general among those of Italian descent.

Dutton (1986) suggests that differential access to health care and knowledge about health problems are particularly important contributing factors. In a study focusing on differences in health facility usage between blacks and whites, Manton, Patrick, and Johnson (1987) link different usages to variations in lifestyle and risk factors, to different living conditions, to the amount of knowledge possessed concerning health problems and what to do about them, and to genetic factors.

Wells and his associates (1988) also provided data on the use of health services by Mexican Americans, who are significantly less likely than the general population to make an outpatient visit, even with other factors controlled. These investigators found the same to be true with regard to outpatient visits for mental problems. Heller and his associates (1987) reported similar differences in seeking help during psychological distress, especially when a distinction was made between those raised in Mexico and those whose childhood was spent in the United States.

Suchman (1964, 1965) maintains that a person's sociocultural networks are more important for explaining attitudes toward health services than class or ethnicity. He suggests that the more self-centered, isolated, cohesive, and locally oriented the group (a pattern he describes as parochial), the less likely are members to accept help from the medical system. Those from opposite types of networks (referred to as cosmopolitan) are more likely to seek help.

Consistent with these observations, several investigators found that much of the motivation for seeking care comes from attitudes of family members. Gorton and colleagues (1979) reported a strong intrafamilial pattern of illness reports and physician visits. Similarly, Osterweis, Bush, and Zackerman (1979) found that the family unit was the strongest determinant of the individual's attitude toward following medical regimens. Their analysis indicated that family characteristics are a better predictor of individual medical use than any set of individual characteristics.

Demographic Characteristics

Demographic characteristics such as age, sex, and education have a significant effect on patterns of health care utilization. Graham (1957) found that increasing age brought greater use of health facilities. Estes and Lee (1986) report the same pattern and attribute it to the higher incidence of chronic illnesses among the aged. These findings are confirmed by Levkoff, Cleary, and Wetle (1987), who concluded that although the middle-aged sought health care for acute illnesses more frequently, the aged suffered more from chronic conditions and were confined to bed more days per year.

Becker and Maiman (1975) report that noncompliance to medical-care regimens is associated with the extremes of age, "perhaps because the very young are more resistant to ingesting bad tasting medicine, and because geriatric patients more often experience problems of forgetfulness and neglect" (p. 20). When studying willingness to participate in screening for breast cancer, Fink, Shapiro, and Lewis (1968) found that younger women were more likely to seek an examination than older women.

Gender is another demographic variable influencing health care. Numerous studies have found that women are more likely to visit the physician than men (Graham, 1957; Blackwell, 1967), but recently this assertion has been questioned. Verbrugge (1985) reports that men are less likely than women to delay seeking care, although women take more sick days or quit work for health reasons more often. Her principle thesis is that differences in health behavior for men and women are mainly a matter of differential risks. Waldron (1988) indicates that the major gender difference in seeking health care is the type of illness, with reported higher use of physicians by women resulting from the complexity of the female reproductive system.

ESTABLISHING SICK-STATUS LEGITIMACY

In cases of obvious and severe illness, entry into the sick status may be automatic; the person has nothing to "prove" and may even enter against his or her will. But entry is not always this routine. Very often, permission to assume the sick status, the time of entry, and the length of stay all depend on decisions made by, or on behalf of, the social group. On a general level, society often gives the incumbents of certain positions responsibility for screening those seeking entry and for judging the legitimacy of their claims. When it comes to sickness in U.S. society, physicians have such a function; they are expected to screen and judge whether the conditions brought to their attention meet the requirements for entry into the sick status. The incumbents of other occupational positions who may also perform this function are nurses, members of the clergy, social workers, and even courtroom judges and the police. Sociologists refer to those who hold screening and judging statuses, those given the right to determine legitimacy, as *gatekeepers.*

The individual may have some choice in seeking the sick status, often by going to gatekeepers for assessment. For example, the child may go to the school nurse to obtain a written statement, which serves as an official school-system-authorized legitimation of the claim to occupy the sick status. The document exempts the child from many normal demands of the school day, such as gym. On the other hand, society may force the status on certain individuals without their permission. Mental illness is such a situation. Today, AIDS patients and those who use drugs are being forced into the sick status.

With some conditions, the individual's desire to claim the status is influential in determining the timing of entry. Pregnancy, for example, provides an opportunity for a woman to discontinue some usual social behavior by entering the sick status. Rosengren (1961, 1962) examined factors influencing a pregnant woman to claim the sick status and found that she exercises considerable choice in the matter. His findings show that personal instabilities or disturbances strongly influence the woman to take the status. In addition, McKinlay (1972) suggests that many of the sick-status privileges are given to the pregnant woman more or less on request.

Several other conditions, not serious as far as permanent physical disability is concerned, are also open to self-definition. Among these are the common cold and lower back pain. But if the cold becomes serious or the back problem leads to incapacitating pain, persons may be forced to enter the sick status, whether they want it or not.

Lack of agreement about whether certain conditions are sicknesses also affects the right to the sick status. Alcoholism, for example, has often been the subject of contradictory sickness perceptions. Several studies suggest that most physicians accept alcoholism as a sickness, but, in contradiction to the Parsonian sick-role model, they also hold the patient responsible for the condition. Linsky (1970) reports that in a representative sample of adults, younger and better educated respondents showed more acceptance of medical treatment for alcoholism. Despite stating that alcoholism is a sickness, only 65 percent of the respondents chose medical or psychological help as most appropriate.

Thus the alcoholic may be perceived as sick, morally wrong, and criminal all at the same time. Such differential definitions influence the type of social response. The same alcoholic may receive psychotherapy in one setting but be "dried out" in a jail cell in another. In this context, we can note that the most successful treatment developed for alcoholics is neither medical nor penal in nature. Alcoholics Anonymous provides psychological, social, and spiritual support for individuals attempting to recover from the condition.

There is more agreement about whether physical diseases are legitimate. For example, few question that those with pneumonia, heart ailments, and stomach cancer have legitimate claims to the sick status (Kurtz and Giacopassi, 1975). If a disease has an obvious physical and incapacitating feature to it, societal consensus is that the sick status is legitimate. In fact, it is socially desirable, since it is assumed that entry moves the patient toward recovery.

THE SICK STATUS AND SOCIAL CONTROL

In his discussion of the sick role, Parsons referred to sickness as a deviant position. This connotation hinges on the observation that, while in the status, incumbents are not expected to perform their usual tasks, those that keep society functioning on an everyday basis. The sick position is deviant, but it is a special type of deviance, since the person is not looked upon as responsible for the condition. Once the injury or sickness has occurred, it is recognized that the person cannot effect a cure by his or her own willpower. In a special sense, the sick person is not only entitled to help, but also must submit to being treated by others.

Zola (1972) interprets this situation as one in which those in the sick status are manipulated for the needs of society. Such manipulation is all the easier because the sick person faces complex problems of adjustment to the status. This includes possible anxiety about the future, which makes it difficult for a person to make an objective judgment about his or her situation. Further, when the individual enters the health system, which by definition has experts in the area of disease and cure, an important degree of control of his or her life is turned over to others. It is within this context that some sociologists discuss the doctor-patient relationship as an association within which the doctor exercises social control and in which the doctor may be faced with divided loyalties. According to some sociologists, the doctor functions as an agent for society, as a maintainer of the status quo, and as a defender of the present social system (Waitzkin and Waterman, 1974; Waitzkin, 1983). Others suggest that the doctor's loyalty to the patient is conditional and ambiguous because of the social-control role. When the doctor's allegiance to the patient is conditional, the interests of the social order are served. An extreme example is the case of the military psychiatrist (Daniels, 1969); for the doctor, the conflict between the interests of the patient and those of the society (in this case the military) is clear. The medical officer is always near that point where service and duty to the military become more important than service and duty to patients.

Weisner and Room (1984) point to similar role confusion for the new breed of substance-abuse counselors. The development, and recent profusion, of for-profit treatment centers for alcoholics and other drug abusers has led to new duties for the counselor. Responsibility is not solely to the patient; it is also to the institutional needs of the treatment center. The counselor may act in the interests of the treatment agency rather than in the interests of the patient. Even the confidentiality of patient information may be compromised in such a situation. Those who work in testing centers for AIDS victims may also find themselves in this role confusion: They may be required to break confidentiality and work for the society rather than protecting the interests of the client.

Those theorists of deviant behavior who follow a labeling or societal reaction approach have been most concerned about the social-control aspects of the health system. According to this approach, deviant behavior is any behavior defined or labeled as such by appropriate agents of society. Deviants are people assigned to these roles and identities by the group or its surrogates. Thus, an understanding of deviance actually lies outside the norm-violater and associated behavior; it lies in the group itself and in those processes in which policy making, social control, and labeling of deviance take place.

Applied to health and illness, the labeling approach calls attention to the possible misuse of the power held by those who define conditions as sickness for purposes of social control and to the consequences of being labeled (or diagnosed). According to this perspective, the most important factor in becoming sick is whether the individual has been labeled as sick, and interest is in why now, why this person, and why this label? These questions are most appropriate for conditions, such as alcoholism and mental illness, in which agreement about definitions is lacking. For example, one can raise the question of the extent to which long-term chronic hospitals are being used to protect the social system rather than to treat patients.

SUMMARY

To the sociologist, sickness is more than a biochemical state of the body. It is also a social and psychological condition that affects the individual and those with whom he or she interacts. This view has led sociologists to four related observations:

1. Sickness is a position or status in the group, with behavioral expectations that constitute the sick role.
2. Social factors influence the decision to seek the sick status.
3. There are socially defined rules concerning entry into the status.
4. Occupancy in the sick position means giving up some of one's authority to social-control agents.

Concerning the first point, the most significant sociological work on the sick role has been a theoretical statement by Parsons, who set forth four behavioral expectations for the incumbent of the sick status. The status incorporates two rights—excuse from normal social responsibilities and not being held at fault for the condition—and two obligations—to define the sick condition as undesirable and to seek technically competent help.

Major contributions of the concept are its firm placement of sickness in a social context and its identification of social similarities among disparate conditions. The model also has been criticized for several reasons. First, it presupposes that the sick person will become a patient. Second, it does not adequately describe chronic diseases and impaired conditions. Third, those conditions that do not respond well to treatment are not included in the model. Fourth, it ignores important subjective aspects of sickness.

The sick-role model is most appropriate as a description of the sickness behavior of middle-class people with temporary conditions who are knowledgeable about health and how to use the health system.

From Parsons's perspective, the sick status is a deviant one. The incumbent has the right to give up normal social activities. The underlying premise is that people will not linger in the status and not too many will occupy the status at the same time. Otherwise, the everyday normal routine of society would be adversely affected. To prevent overuse and abuse, social controls are developed to ensure that those who request entry have a legitimate claim on the status.

Several social factors affect a person's entry into the sick status. Among these are interpersonal crises, interference with valued social activities, the presence of sanctioning, perceived threat, the nature and quality of the symptoms, subjective judgments of benefits, how symptoms become visible and, broadly, social class, ethnic-group membership, and the sex and age of the individual.

From the societal point of view, entry into the sick status is usually not automatic. Instead, certain recognized representatives of society are responsible for screening those seeking entry and judging the legitimacy of their claims. Physicians clearly function in this gatekeeper capacity; other occupational positions that also may serve this function are nurses, clergy, social workers, courtroom judges, and police. For some minor ailments and for very short periods, individuals themselves and the parents of children are acceptable gatekeepers. For conditions such as alcoholism, societal consensus concerning the legitimacy of the condition as sickness is lacking.

The person in the sick status is under the authority of social-control agents. From this perspective, medicine is a system of social control, which raises some questions about the loyalty of the physicians and others who deal with patients. Is it to the patient or to the social system? At such times, loyalty may be divided, if not in conflict. The effects of groups defining the individual's behavior have led to recognition that the labels placed upon people are significant for understanding societal reactions and entry into the sick status.

References

Aday, Lu Ann, Ronald Anderson, and Gretchen V. Fleming. 1980. "Equity of access to medical care: A conceptual approach." *Medical Care* 19(December suppl.):4–27.

Arluke, Arnold. 1988. "The sick role concept." In *Health Behavior: Emerging Research Perspectives*, ed. D. S. Gochman, 169–188. New York: Plenum.

Augoustinos, Martha. 1986. "Psychiatric inpatients' attitudes toward mental disorder and the tendency to adopt a sick role." *Psychological Reports* 58: 495–498.

Becker, M. H. 1979. "Psychosocial aspects of health-related behavior." In *Handbook of Medical Sociology,* 3rd ed., ed. H. Freeman, S. Levine, and L. Reeder, 253–274. Englewood Cliffs, N.J.: Prentice-Hall.

Becker, M. H., R. H. Drachman, and J. P. Kirscht. 1974. "A new approach to explaining sick-role behavior in low-income populations." *American Journal of Public Health* 64:205–216.

Becker, M. H., and L. A. Maiman. 1975. "Sociobehavioral determinants of compliance with health and medical care recommendations." *Medical Care* 13:10–24.

Blackwell, Barbara L. 1967. "Upper middle class adult expectations about entering the sick role for physical and psychiatric dysfunctions." *Journal of Health and Human Behavior* 8(June):83–95.

Bruhn, John G. 1988. "Life-style and health behavior." In *Health Behavior: Emerging Research Perspectives*, ed. D. S. Gochman, 71–86. New York: Plenum.

Calnan, Michael. 1987. *Health and Illness: The Lay Perspective*. London: Tavistock.

Daniels, Arlene Kaplan. 1969. "The captive professional." *Journal of Health and Social Behavior* 10:255–265.

Doehrman, Steven R. 1977. "Psycho-social aspects of recovery from coronary heart disease: A review." *Social Science and Medicine* 11:199–218.

Dutton, Diana B. 1986. "Social class, health and illness." In *Applications of Social Science to Clinical Medicine and Health Policy*, ed. L. H. Aiken and D. Mechanic, 31–62. New Brunswick, N.J.: Rutgers University Press.

Estes, Carroll L., and Philip R. Lee. 1986. "Health problems and policy issues of old age." In *Applications of Social Science to Clinical Medicine and Health Policy*, ed. L. H. Aiken and D. Mechanic, 335–355. New Brunswick, N.J.: Rutgers University Press.

Field, Mark. 1953. "Structured strain in the role of the Soviet physician." *American Journal of Sociology* 58:493–502.

———. 1957. *Doctor and Patient in Soviet Russia*. Cambridge: Harvard University Press.

Fink, R., S. Shapiro, and J. Lewis. 1968. "The reluctant participant in a breast cancer screening program." *Public Health Reports* 83(June):479–490.

Fisher, William, Arnold Arluke, and Jack Levin. 1985. "The elderly sick role: An experimental analysis." *International Journal of Aging and Human Development* 20:161–165.

Fox, Renee C. 1989. *The Sociology of Medicine: A Participant Observer's View*. Englewood Cliffs, N.J.: Prentice-Hall.

Freidson, Eliot. 1970. *Profession of Medicine*. New York: Dodd, Mead.

Gallagher, Eugene B. 1976. "Lines of reconstruction and extension in the Parsonian sociology of illness." *Social Science and Medicine* 10 (May): 207–218.

Gochman, David S. 1988. "Health behavior: Plural perspectives." In *Health Behavior: Emerging Research Perspectives*, ed. D. Gochman, 3–17. New York: Plenum.

Goldsen, R. 1963. "Patient delay in seeking cancer diagnosis: Behavioral aspects." *Journal of Chronic Diseases* 16:427–436.

Goldsen, R., P. Gerhardt, and V. Handy. 1957. "Some factors related to patient delay in seeking diagnosis for cancer symptoms." *Cancer* 10:1–7.

Goode, Erich. 1989. *Drugs in American Society*. New York: Random House.

Gordon, Gerald. 1966. *Role Theory and Illness*. New Haven: College and University Press.

Gorton, T. Ann, Donald L. Doerfler, Barbara S. Hulka, and Herman A. Tyroler. 1979. "Intrafamilial patterns of illness reports and physician visits in a community sample." *Journal of Health and Social Behavior* 20(March):37–44.

Graham, Saxon. 1957. "Socioeconomic status, illness and the use of medical services." *Milbank Memorial Fund Quarterly* 35(January):58–66.

Greenley, James R. 1972. "Alternative views of the psychiatrist's role." *Social Problems* 20:252–262.

Hackett, Thomas P., and Ned H. Caseem. 1976. "White-collar and blue-collar responses to heart attack." *Journal of Psychosomatic Research* 20:85–95.

Heller, Peter L., David Briones, H. Paul Chalfant, Salvador Aguirre-Hochbaum, and Walter Farr. 1987. "Class, ethnicity, familism and locus of control." Paper presented at the Southern Sociological Society conference, Atlanta, Georgia, March.

Honig-Parnass, Tikvah. 1983. "The relative impact of status and health variables upon sick-role expectations." *Medical Care* 27:208–224.

Janz, Nancy K., and Marshal Becker. 1984. "The health belief model." *Health Education Quarterly* 11:1–47.

Koos, Earl L. 1954. *The Health of Regionville.* New York: Columbia University Press.

Kurtz, Richard A., and David Giacopassi. 1975. "Medical and social work students' perceptions of deviant conditions and sick-role incumbency." *Social Science and Medicine* 9:249–255.

Lau, Richard. 1988. "Beliefs about control and health behavior." In *Health Behavior: Emerging Research Perspectives,* ed. D. Gochman, 43–63. New York: Plenum

Levkoff, S. E., P. D. Cleary, and T. Wetle. 1987. "Differences in the appraisal of health between aged and middle aged adults." *Journal of Gerontology* 42:114–120.

Linsky, A. S. 1970. "The changing public views of alcoholism." *Quarterly Journal of Studies on Alcohol* 31:692–704.

McKinlay, John B. 1972. "The sick role—illness and pregnancy." *Social Science and Medicine* 6:561–572.

Manton, K. G., C. H. Patrick, and K. W. Johnson. 1987 "Health differentials of Blacks and Whites: Recent trends in mortality and morbidity." *Milbank Memorial Fund Quarterly* 65:129–199.

Mayou, Richard. 1984. "Sick role, illness behavior and coping." *British Journal of Psychiatry* 144:320–322.

Meile, Richard L. 1986. "Pathways to patienthood: Sick role and labeling perspectives." *Social Science and Medicine* 22:35–40.

Moss, R. A. 1986. "The role of learning history in current sick-role behavior and assertion." *Behavior Research and Therapy* 24:681–683.

Navarro, Vicente. 1986. *Crisis in Health and Medicine: A Social Critique.* New York: Tavistock.

Nuttbrook, Larry. 1986. "Socialization to the chronic sick role in later life." *Research on Aging* 8:368–387.

Osterweis, Marian, Patricia J. Bush, and Alan E. Zackerman. 1979. "Family context as a predictor of individual medicine use." *Social Science and Medicine* 13(May):287–292.

Parsons, Talcott. 1951. *The Social System.* Glencoe, Ill.: Free Press.

Petroni, Frank A. 1972. "Correlates of the psychiatric sick role." *Journal of Health and Social Behavior* 13:47–54.

Robinson, David. 1978. *Patients, Practitioners, and Medical Care.* 2nd ed. London: William Heinemann Medical Books.

Rosengren, William R. 1961. "Social sources of pregnancy as illness or abnormality." *Social Forces* 39(March):260–267.

———. 1962. "Social instability and attitudes toward pregnancy as a social role." *Social Problems* 9(Spring):371–378.

Rosenstock, I. M. 1966. "Why people use health services." *Milbank Memorial Fund Quarterly* 44:94–127.

Segall, Alexander. 1976. "Sociocultural variation in sick role behavioral expectations." *Social Science and Medicine* 10(January):47–52.

Suchman, Edward. 1964. "Sociomedical variations among ethnic groups." *American Journal of Sociology* 70:319–331.

———. 1965. "Social patterns of illness and medical care." *Journal of Health and Human Behavior* 6:2–16.

Troyer, Henry. 1988. "Review of cancer among 4 religious sects: Evidence that life-styles are distinctive sets of risk factors." *Social Science and Medicine* 10:1007–1017.

Twaddle, Andrew C. 1969. "Health decisions and sick role variations: An exploration." *Journal of Health and Social Behavior* 10(June):105–115.

Verbrugge, Lois M. 1985. "Gender and health: An update on hypothesis and evidence." *Journal of Health and Social Behavior* 26:156–182.

Verbrugge, Lois M., and Frank J. Ascione. 1987. "Exploring the iceberg: Common symptoms and how people care for them." *Medical Care* 25:539–560.

Waitzkin, Howard. 1983. *The Second Sickness*. New York: Basic Books.

Waitzkin, Howard, and Barbara Waterman. 1974. *The Exploitation of Illness in Capitalist Society*. Indianapolis: Bobbs-Merrill.

Waldron, Ingrid. 1988. "Gender and health related behavior." In *Health Behavior: Emerging Research Perspectives*, ed. D. Gochman, 193–208. New York: Plenum.

Weisner, Constance, and Robin Room. 1984. "Financing and ideology in alcohol treatment." *Social Problems* 32:167–185.

Wells, Kenneth B., Jacqueline Golding, Richard Hough, Audrey Burnam, and Marvin Karno. 1988. "Factors affecting the probability of use of general and medical health and social/community services for Mexican-Americans and non-Hispanic whites." *Medical Care* 26:441–452.

Zborowski, Mark. 1952. "Cultural components in response to pain." *Journal of Social Issues* 9:16–30.

———. 1969. *People in Pain*. San Francisco: Jossey-Bass.

Zola, Irving Kenneth. 1966. "Culture and symptoms: An analysis of patients' presenting complaints." *American Sociological Review* 31(October):615–630.

———. 1972. "Medicine as an institution of social control." *Sociological Review* 20(4):487–504.

———. 1973. "Pathways to the doctor—From person to patient." *Social Science and Medicine* 7(September):677-689.

5

Medical Socialization and the Medical Profession

INTRODUCTION

Every profession establishes control over entry into the programs of study that lead to official certification. This control constitutes a powerful hold on members of the profession since all must acknowledge a higher authority that grants the most essential of all professional rights: the right to practice. It also gives the higher authority the power to set and guarantee standards of practice.

In the medical profession, entry and initial practice standards are controlled through the medical school. In this context, the American Medical Association (AMA) has made medical education a top priority since the early 1900s. It established a Council for Medical Education in 1904 and, with funds obtained from the Carnegie Foundation for the Advancement of Teaching, launched a project to evaluate medical schools in the United States and Canada. The result was the 1910 Flexner Report (the study director was Abraham Flexner), which was used as a springboard for initiating reforms in medical schools. For example, the AMA based uniform standards of quality in medical schools throughout the United States on this report. This also placed the AMA firmly in control of entry into the profession and gave it a strong voice in setting the educational program that must be experienced before the right to practice is allowed.

We turn our attention now to the process established for controlling entry, that is, recruiting and training the new generation of medical doctors.

UNPLANNED SOCIALIZATION

Students acquire knowledge about the doctor's status and role many years before they enter medical school. During the normal course of events, we are all presented with some picture of the physician's activities from our earliest years. Since the doctor's role is a favorite childhood play pattern, it is practiced by many in a simplistic and idealistic form. Personal experience with physicians, statements by family and friends, and the image portrayed in the media also help to shape general notions about the doctor's role. These experiences may be what first influences a person's decision to become part of the medical profession, and they may serve the unplanned function of anticipatory socialization to the doctor's role.

Sociological studies have indicated that the decision to become a doctor occurs at an early age. For example, in a study of the medical school classes at the University of Pennsylvania, Rogoff (1957) found that most students reported thinking about becoming a doctor when they were less than fourteen years of age. Only 14 percent were eighteen or over when they first considered a career in medicine. It has recently been suggested, however, that this early choice pattern of the mid-1950s is changing. Fox (1974, 1989) notes that there are now more late deciders than previously, and Reitzes and Elkhanialy (1976) present data indicating that more students currently enrolled in medical school made a later decision to study medicine than was the case for physicians already in practice. But the decision is still an early one compared to the time of choice among many other occupations.

PLANNED SOCIALIZATION: THE MEDICAL SCHOOL EXPERIENCE

The process through which the student is formally taught the rights and duties of the doctor status is an example of planned socialization. One part of this socialization concerns the teaching of the specialized knowledge needed for practice. Also vitally important is learning how to act like a doctor, that is, learning the proper patterns of interaction, along with the proper patterns of attitudes, values, and thought (Pellegrino, 1987; Fox, 1989). Thus, through planned socialization the knowledge and skills are learned, and students are shaped into individuals "endowed with appropriate attitudes, values, and ways of thinking" (Coombs, 1978:13) for their positions in the social structure.

Coombs and Powers (1975) illustrate how necessary such socialization into the attitudes of the profession is for the medical student. They point out that a major problem for students is taking a professional stance toward death and dying. The authors suggest that the medical student enters school with attitudes typical of the public in which the doctor's role and abilities are idealized: The physician is seen as a bulwark against death and as being personally involved with the dying person. New students can be shocked when they observe the coolness of teacher-physicians in their handling of dying patients; yet this attitude is necessary if the physician is to perform effectively, and the student must acquire a professional attitude and approach toward death.

Handling death and dying is only one of many experiences for which the student's attitudes, feelings, values, and behaviors must be shaped to a professional model. Others "are the attitude-learning sequences of 'training for uncertainty' and limitation, 'training for detached concern,' and training in managing medical mistakes and medical failure" (Fox, 1989:75). Sociological interest centers on the way in which the medical school setting and structure provide the opportunity for such development, and on the kinds of attitudes and values fostered during the educational experience.

Recruitment and Social Barriers

Medical students are by no means a random sample of the population. Demographic, economic, and social characteristics play important parts in the selection process from the very beginning. Formerly, the barriers to becoming a medical student were onerous for particular groupings, and medical school classes in the United States consisted basically of white, middle-class males. But recruitment during what Funkenstein (1978) calls the "activism era" resulted in an increase in students who previously were unable to enroll. Although this has lost its edge somewhat, the proportion of minority students is significantly higher than in the past (Shea and Fullilove, 1985), and the proportion of females has increased dramatically. Thus, 5.7 percent of the students enrolled in medical school in 1979–1980 were black, a considerable increase over ten or twenty years before (Thomae-Forques and Tonesk, 1980), but this figure dropped to 5.1 percent in 1988; the total minority enrollment in

1988 was 10.6 percent (Jonas and Etzel, 1988). Only 5 percent of all medical school graduates were female in 1960, whereas the figure was close to 31 percent in 1985 (Klepke, Marder, and Silberger, 1987).

There are particular factors in the admissions process that are disadvantageous to some candidates. For example, unless the four years of college undergraduate work are specifically planned for medical school entry, minority-group students and women may not have taken the science courses that colleges of medicine would like applicants to have completed during their premedical years; such courses are usually not high on the interest list of these students. The Medical College Admissions Test (known as the MCAT by college students) stresses science and mathematics, whereas minorities and women are often steered away from such courses during their high school attendance. In addition, the indirect (such as postponed income) and direct (such as tuition) costs of a medical education are significant. Nevertheless, more than one-half of the women who applied for the entering class in 1987–1988 were admitted to medical school and they now make up 37 percent of the students (Jonas and Etzel, 1988).

Increasing acceptance in medical schools has presented problems for many women. Past research, for example, has pointed to conflicts women seem to feel about entering the medical profession (Roeske and Lake, 1977). Many report that they faced an identity crisis, feeling a need to possess masculine characteristics to make it through medical school and into the profession. From another perspective, Bourne and Wikler (1978) suggest that although discrimination against women in the medical school environment may not be overt, the structure of the school is based on the conception of a commitment to medicine congruent with the traditional roles played by males, rather than those played by females. Failure to conform to a basically male image may make the female student seem less than thoroughly dedicated to the medical profession.

Further, it is a rare person who can devote eight years to studies in institutions of higher education. For one thing, few people can afford the sizeable investment of so many adult years to schooling, years that mean a major period of postponed income. Although many medical students are married, the postponed income can delay the normal activities of family and social life. Also, tuition and other college expenses must be paid during this period. Then, many may not be able to endure, or may decide not to endure, the intellectual grind. Nevertheless, there are many more applicants to, than places in, U.S. medical schools; the recent ratio of applicants to vacancies is 1.7 to 1.0 (Jonas and Etzel, 1988).

Admission

Acceptance is the most critical factor for the student who wants to be a doctor. The data reveal that only 2.1 percent of medical students drop out or are dismissed from medical schools (this rate is much lower than that of any other course of postgraduate study; Gough and Hall, 1975). Thus, admission to a medical school is virtually tantamount to admission to the medical profession, which underscores the importance of entry control by the profession.

Medical school admissions committees use several criteria in the selection process. In the typical school, candidates are initially screened on the basis of grade-point average earned in undergraduate school and scores obtained on the MCAT. Reference letters of those who have passed this screening are then examined. In most schools, the candidates who survive these hurdles are invited for an interview by a team consisting of medical college faculty members and, sometimes, present medical students. In such an interview, the applicant's self-presentation becomes all important to the admission decision (Albrecht and Ross, 1977); interviewers are most often attempting to judge whether the candidate has personal qualities considered important in the practice of medicine.

It has been suggested that current admission criteria are biased toward a particular type of student: those who take notes well and who study and work obediently, irrespective of their interest in the material (Greer and Aronson, 1980). This tends to discriminate not only against those with a more social or humanitarian view of medicine but also against members of some minority groups. Even today, many traits sought in the medical school applicant are most likely to be found, because of their prior socialization, among white middle-class males.

Having successfully completed the admission process and having selected or been selected by a particular college of medicine, the new recruits to the medical world almost always approach the school with a mixture of enthusiasm and apprehension. Both feelings might be seen as appropriate, for the students are taking the first step into a new world—the health care institution—where they will be shaped and molded by the characteristic organization and its norms during the next four years.

The Teaching Process

Students advancing in the medical education program pass through two distinctly different phases of education: the preclinical years and the clinical years. Both the subject matter and the methods of teaching change between these two periods. In most colleges of medicine, initial contact with the teaching program, the two-year preclinical period, brings the students into situations similar to their premedical undergraduate days. For many this will necessitate an adjustment because the medical school does not live up to their expectations of learning "to doctor" at the very beginning. Thus, entering students may be disillusioned when they find they must attend lectures, take notes, and pass multiple-choice examinations in a class being taught by a professor holding a Ph.D. instead of an M.D. To many it feels like a fifth undergraduate year.

During their first two years of medical school, the students generally take their courses as a group or cohort. Students in the cohort take the same courses, share the same classroom experiences, complete the same assignments, face the same professors, and take the same examinations. These conditions often foster intimate primary-type social relationships among fellow students, who define themselves as an in-group of classmates. They also lead to a working consensus that focuses student attention on meeting the day-to-day activities required by the medical school. When this cohort is then broken into clinical-learning teams in the final two years of schooling, the intimacy among students in the smaller groups may become even stronger.

During the clinical years, the classroom-lecture method is replaced by contact with patients, usually in a teaching hospital. Students now learn by observing a faculty member-doctor dealing with patients. The teaching and learning experiences change from lecture to demonstration, from the classroom to the bedside of the patient.

In addition to accompanying the doctor on his or her daily rounds visiting the patients, the student attends sessions known as grand rounds; these are usually held weekly by several of the medical school departments before an audience of students and health professionals employed by the medical school and teaching hospital. A goal of grand rounds is to promote an open discussion of such medical aspects of the case as diagnosis, establishment of etiology, history of the illness, the patient's behavior on the ward, prognosis, and treatment decisions. Through the grand rounds of surgical, medical, psychiatric, pediatric, and other clinical departments, the student begins to witness how the techniques of medicine are applied and to learn about relationships with the incumbents of other health-relevant statuses, who are called on during the discussion to provide information deemed relevant to the case. Thus, through textbook reading, lectures, individual rounds, and grand rounds, the student is formally learning the techniques of medicine and is, at the same time, learning how to dress, speak, act, and think like a doctor.

Faculty Members

In many respects, the faculty of a medical school is not unlike the faculty of the rest of the university. Faculty members are expected to be committed to the same academic goals of teaching, research, and service. An important division exists in the medical school, however, that does not exist in the general university—that between the basic scientists and the clinicians, generally between those faculty members with a Ph.D. and those with an M.D. Often, the basic scientists are academically oriented, with a strong commitment to laboratory research; most are in departments of anatomy, biochemistry, community medicine, microbiology, pharmacology, and physiology. Most clinicians are the medically qualified physician-teachers who spend much of their time with patients as a means of teaching the practice of medicine to students; they are found in departments of medicine, surgery, pediatrics, obstetrics-gynecology, family medicine, and the other clinical departments. Many medical faculty members combine basic science and clinical orientations and often hold both the Ph.D. and M.D. At times, the difference between the "two faculties" of the medical school can lead to internal conflict, problems, and resentment, especially when differences are accentuated through differences in salary and privileges.

Student Subculture

To meet its objective of educating the next generation of physicians, the medical school has designed a formal course of educational experiences for its recruits. As in other formal institutions focusing on a particular goal, however, many informal and unplanned experiences affect the fulfillment of objectives. Many of these experiences, which occur during the students' association with their fellow students, take on particular patterns that are specific to the medical student's way of life. This way of life is interpreted by sociologists as a student subculture. From the sociological perspective, the informal spontaneous interactions might even be the most significant part of the training program for the students.

Several sociologists have studied the nature of student life in the college of medicine. Two of the earliest studies were a three-school investigation of the medical school programs of Cornell University, Western Reserve University, and the University of Pennsylvania conducted by Merton, Reader, and Kendall (1957), and a study of the University of Kansas Medical School by Becker, Geer, Hughes, and Strauss (1961). Although the two studies were independent of each other, both focused on the social transmission of the values, norms, beliefs, knowledges, and symbols of medicine to students. But they reached quite different conclusions about the life and status of the medical student.

Perhaps their major conclusions, contrasting as they are, are best summarized by the titles the authors chose for their books. The three-school study is named *The Student-Physician: Introductory Studies in the Sociology of Medical Education* (Merton, Reader, and Kendall, 1957), and the Kansas study is named *Boys in White: Student Culture in Medical School* (Becker et al., 1961). Both studies describe the college of medicine as an institution functioning within a training school atmosphere, with a focus on how, rather than why, something should be done. They also describe the schools as protectors of the basic values of effective medical care (Merton, Reader, and Kendall, 1957), suggesting that new ideas and innovations face a difficult time in this setting.

The three-school study focused on the medical school years as a time of anticipatory socialization. In a regulated curriculum, the student-physicians moved toward a time when they could assume the full responsibilities of being physicians in practice; both the technical skills and the attitudes of doctors were emphasized by the research team. Learning to be a doctor was observed as consisting of more than mastering voluminous scientific material; it was also a process of internalizing the attitudes and values of physicians. During the four-year progression, the student-physicians gradually shed the student aspect of the term and they become physicians in their own right.

Those who studied the University of Kansas school viewed medical education as a set of processes through which the material and nonmaterial aspects of medicine are kept alive and extended to a new cohort of individuals (see Hughes, 1961). They emphasize a medical student subculture that has made an adjustment to the demands of the system by "playing it cool." In this subculture, deferring to the faculty becomes routine behavior. The demands of the medical school curriculum are so intense that students find they must band together to meet the challenge. The subculture represents, first, a strategic joining of those who find themselves in what seems like an impossible situation. Once the student group is organized, however, it becomes much more general in purpose and a moderating force in the lives of the students.

Other studies of student life in medical school support the conclusions of the Kansas study. Miller (1970) found the relationship between the students and faculty to be characterized by distrust rather than by the confidence and respect expected in a relationship between colleagues or near-colleagues. One consequence of this is referred to as a "passion for anonymity," which characterizes many U.S. medical students. That is, many medical students believe they have a greater chance of making it through the program without difficulty if they remain unidentified throughout the four-year course. This suggests a medical student group separated from the faculty, making it through by developing its own structures. The students are seen as committed to the task of learning, but they become quite concerned about the most fundamental and simple objective of many college students: obtaining passing grades. This emphasis on passing courses may change a student's idealistic notions concerning medicine—for example, wanting to help people—into a more practical consideration—for example, preparing for an examination.

Coombs (1978) reports strong cohesiveness among medical students as a result of their mutual needs and problems. He notes that most students depend on one another for both academic and emotional support in this stressful situation. A feeling of togetherness helps make the educational trials and tribulations more tolerable. Following students over their four-year program, Coombs found that they developed a strong camaraderie as they worked together to accomplish student tasks. The emergent interdependence leads him to liken the students to the crew of a submarine submerged for a four-year period, making only transient contact with the surface world.

Outcomes of Socialization

The formal educational program of the medical school produces people possessing the skills necessary for the technical practice of medicine. The informal process of socialization is also significant and long-lasting, as the medical students acquire particular attitudes toward themselves, their work, and their patients.

Cynicism and Idealism.   Eron (1955) focused on the attitudes of medical students and found increasing cynicism (or loss of idealism) among students as they experience medical school socialization. (In contrast, nursing and law students exhibit a *decrease* in cynicism during their student careers.) Some observers have challenged Eron's findings and others have corroborated them; under either condition, it seems certain, as Bloom (1965) comments, that medical students do change their feelings about people as they move through the process of medical education. Whether idealists are being made into cynics, however, is not at all clear.

Becker and Geer (1958) disagree with the notion of an increasing cynicism on the part of medical students. They feel that idealism in medical school suffers much the same fate that it does anywhere: Youthful stereotypes are translated into more realistic understandings. These authors contend that a loss of idealism may be functional, as medical students will eventually have to deal with a reality that cannot be clouded by naivete. Fox (1957) agrees and describes a developmental process from a naive attitude to a more mature view of reality. Rather than the correction of stereotypes, the process she describes is a patterned experience built into educational situations that leads to attitudes well fitted to the doctor's role.

Consistent with this perspective, Coombs (1978) suggests that students enter medical school with idealistic expectations. They have come into contact with the stereotype of the physician as a type of superhero and romanticize about the medical profession. Such idealism and romanticism can be dashed quickly by the harsh realities of medical school. Disillusionment seems almost inherent in the everyday chores of attending class, taking notes, and studying for the next examination. Coombs does not find students to be generally cynical, however. Rather, he finds a continuing basic idealism among them, albeit one heavily tempered by reality.

It may be, as Light (1975) suggests, that students go through a period of suspended idealism. That is, they set idealism aside while they complete the tasks of the medical school and internalize the attitudes necessary to the practice of medicine. But when medical school is completed, the suspension can be "lifted" and a more humanistic, benevolent approach to the task of medicine can be taken. Rezler (1974) indicates that, at least for physicians in practices with a great deal of interaction with patients, cynicism soon gives way to strong idealistic feelings. After reviewing firsthand accounts of four doctors describing the medical school experience, Conrad (1988) agrees with this view. He indicates that humanistic perspectives are not taught or emphasized in medical school. Nevertheless, "there are sensitive and caring doctors practicing medicine, but I contend that these individuals had a humanistic orientation *before* they came to medical school. Somehow they were able to hold on to their values and to put their caring skills into practice against the odds of medical training" (p. 331).

Dealing with Uncertainty.   One of the skills to be acquired in the student culture is the ability to deal with the uncertainty that is an inherent part of medical practice. In a classic statement, Fox (1957) suggests that the sources of uncertainty faced by the medical student stem from the limits of medical knowledge, an inability to master all the knowledge that exists, and an inability to distinguish between these two. Light (1979), however, contends that several more sources of uncertainty must be dealt with by the student in the course of medical education and that learning to deal with the whole array of uncertainties is a necessary part of the educational experience. Medical students may not learn and perfect the technical skills to overcome these uncertainties, but they learn how to control their feelings toward them. Light (1979) states that student uncertainties also come from their relationships with the faculty, problems in reaching valid diagnoses, questions about proper treatment, and unpredictability of the patient's response. The student must learn to control each of these uncertainties.

Overall, students acquire autonomy and solve the problems of uncertainty on their own. As the responsibilities of the medical student grow, training is centered on learning to control the situation so that uncertainty can be avoided. Because the doctor must act even in the face of uncertain knowledge, learning to control the situation becomes more important as the medical student moves closer to graduation.

Recent Critiques

Both what the medical school teaches and how it is being taught have been subjects of recent criticism. Criticism of the traditional curriculum is particularly prevalent. Thus, Stemmler (1988) refers to current education as a "treadmill to professionalism" and calls for more balance in the curriculum. Petersdorf (1988) suggests that the medical school experience does not produce what should be the end product of medical education—good doctors. He lists several criticisms of the curriculum: The preclinical years require too many courses, the cases in the clinical years are poorly organized, and the fourth year of elective courses is generally a waste of time and effort. Furthermore, Petersdorf also criticizes the way in which teaching hospitals are organized and how instruction is carried out.

A prevalent observation among critics is that the medical school curriculum demands a large amount of rote memorization and only a small amount of information about the human condition of patients. The technological aspects of science, that is, instruments and machines, are emphasized, and "there is almost nothing in medical training that encourages compassion, empathy, and 'care' for patients; indeed, there is a great deal that militates against those qualities. To be a humanistic doctor in our technical world of medicine is to swim against the stream" (Conrad, 1988:329). Consequently, the medical school is "producing an elite core of highly trained medical specialists who are prepared to practice a science-based, technologically complex type of medicine" (Bloom, 1988:295) rather than doctors who understand how to treat people.

Why has academic medicine lost sight of its mission to train doctors to understand that patients are human beings with medical problems? Bloom (1988) attributes the pattern to the underlying emphasis on research and specialization, which has "overwhelmed the educational purpose of the medical school" (p. 301). He goes on to quote personal correspondence, with which he is in agreement, stating that medical education has become *a minor activity* of the medical school. This is consistent with an Association of American Medical Colleges statement that teaching medical students "often occupies last place in the competition for faculty time and attention" (AAMC, 1984:15). We turn to Bloom to put the situation in perspective: "Preparation of physicians to serve the changing health needs of the society is asserted repeatedly as the objective of medical education, but . . . this manifest ideology of humanistic medicine is little more than a screen for the research mission of the institution's social structure" (1988:295).

Bloom attributes the present pattern to a dominance of structure over ideology among medical schools, which function as large multipurpose organizations in which the research mission is the major concern. Research is what brings attention to and obtains financial support for the medical school. Furthermore, the research orientation of academic medicine has joined forces with specialty medical practice, and the two together are a strong lobbying force for research and research support (Bloom, 1988:300).

Many of those who see a misdirected course of study as the major problem have suggested a new curriculum, one that returns medical education to its patient-care orientation. Medical education reform has been attempted recently at McMaster University with its problem-based curriculum, at the University of New Mexico Medical School with the introduction of a Primary Care Curriculum, and at the Harvard University Medical School, with the New Pathway curriculum for a limited number of students. (These and several previous attempts at curriculum reform are reviewed in Kendall and Reader, 1988.) Generally, these programs focus on "problem-based learning," which attempts to return the medical student to the real world of the patient and the patient's subcultures. Each reform attempt has its enthusiasts, but the results of new curriculum approaches are not yet clear.

INTERNSHIP AND RESIDENCY

In one sense, the medical student's formal education is completed when the doctor of medicine degree is awarded after the four-year course of study. But, although no further degrees are awarded to practice medicine, at least one more step is necessary in the education of new physicians; they are "still amateurs in medicine" (Conrad, 1988:330). Since they have been functioning exclusively within the protected environment of the medical school and teaching hospital, at graduation the newly recognized medical doctors still have never practiced their profession on their own.

The next and final step necessary for practice on their own is a year of internship. During this year, the new graduates practice medicine under the supervision of doctors in hospitals with internship programs that are usually designed to present a wide range of patients and medical problems. Interns are salaried hospital employees who are often expected to be available to give service twenty-four hours a day, often on an unpredictable and grueling schedule. This experience provides the graduates with an opportunity to put their medical knowledge to use in the actual practice of the profession. The intern is not yet licensed to practice medicine; therefore, practice is limited to the internship hospital, and responsibility for the intern's actions is assumed by a supervisor, a licensed medical practitioner in the program. This is an extremely significant year of learning, "on the front line," so to speak.

The residency, which is also a learning program under the supervision of established doctors, is different from internship. It is usually a three-to-five-year specialized program in a college of medicine that is designed to prepare medical specialists. Residents have made long-term career commitments to focus and specialize their medical knowledge and practice. As specializing has become more prevalent in U.S. medicine, residencies have become more important as definers of where the doctor "fits" in the world of medicine. One sociologist makes the point in the following way: "As occupational destinations have diverged, residency has replaced medical school as the summative statement of one's professional identity. Residents learn what it is to be a physician by learning to think, act, feel like a specialist—be it a surgeon, an obstetrician-gynecologist, a psychiatrist, or an internist" (Bosk, 1986:465).

But commitment to a residency program requires still another postponement in setting up or joining a practice, which again means lost income and lost time. For this reason, and because some may not have decided which specialty is appealing, many doctors do not enter a residency program until they have been in practice for several years after graduation from medical school.

MEDICINE AS A PROFESSION

In a national opinion survey conducted over a fifteen-year period by the National Opinion Research Center, respondents were asked to indicate how much confidence they have in the leaders of various professional and industrial institutions in the United States (NORC, 1988); included in the listing were leaders in business, the judiciary, labor, education, religion, and medicine. Responses indicated that leaders in medicine were trusted more than the others mentioned in the survey. One-half of the almost 20,000 respondents indicated they had a great deal of confidence in medical leaders, and only 7 percent claimed to have hardly any trust. Few respondents expressed great confidence in the leaders of other listed occupations.

Of course, the medical profession also has its detractors. People negative toward the profession question the altruism of the doctor with an income in six figures, and television shows and cartoons sometimes make sarcastic references to the doctor's avarice. Nevertheless, the image of the steadfast, family-oriented doctor dedicated to the welfare of patients is also expressed in popular culture, particularly on television soap operas and other dramas. There is little doubt that members of the medical profession are highly respected.

The Physician as a Professional

No other occupational group in the United States has held the type of dominance and autonomy in its field that the medical profession has for the past century (Starr, 1982). For decades, the physician has had a pervasive and overpowering influence on the provision of health services in the nation. Freidson (1970a) suggests that this influence is based on an assumption that a professional has special esoteric knowledge and humanitarian intent.

The widespread acceptance of professional authority accorded the physician today is relatively recent. Until the latter part of the 1800s, few people used the services of the medical doctor, and being a physician was not necessarily a full-time occupation (Rothstein, 1972). Further, the knowledge and capability of medical practitioners in the eighteenth and nineteenth centuries varied greatly. Some country doctors did not have even a high school education; they learned to practice by being apprentices to older physicians. Even the best medical skills of the time were unsophisticated and technologically imprecise. Medical practice was largely based on cursory observation and followed two main principles: Diagnoses were based on external symptoms, and anything that changed the pathological state of the patient was defined as helping (Rothstein, 1972). In short, physicians, whatever their training, lacked medical knowledge, and their rate of success was far from satisfactory.

Another reason the professional authority of physicians was lacking in earlier centuries is that the professional elitism suggested by development of the profession was incongruous with dominant thought in U.S. society. Such authority, for example, contrasted sharply with the egalitarian views of the Jacksonian era. The profession was up against an idealistic view of U.S. society, a view that downplayed exclusive privilege (Starr, 1982). Physicians faced an uphill battle against cultural values when they sought elitist positions of power in the health care system.

Starr comments that the eventual transformation of medical authority was not an isolated event occurring only in the sphere of health care. It was related to wider shifts within the socioeconomic life of the developing society. The success of science in establishing a core of knowledge upon which the practice of medicine could be based was essential to the development of medical power as we currently know it.

Navarro (1986) has criticized this interpretation because it implies that the development of professional dominance was part of a changing consensus in cultural values. He contends that the move toward professionalism was a consequence of a changing society and was a part of the coercion and repression by the dominant elite that came to underlie a society with the capitalistic economic system.

Whatever the source, the change critical to this development was the discovery of specific causes for disease, causes that had specific remedies (Starr, 1982). The work of Pasteur and Koch in the middle of the nineteenth century paved the way for many new developments. Such advances as antiseptic medicine and diagnostic tools also were instrumental in changing the status of physicians and scientific medicine. A medical discovery of critical importance was that disease can be caused by bacilli; from this discovery developed the concept of specific causative agents for disease and the idea that some specially trained persons could identify these causes and use this information to eradicate disease. The growth of authority in medicine was related to such advances. The scientific revolution thus laid the groundwork for the medical revolution. Such scientific breakthroughs, coupled with the advances of surgery and antiseptic medicine, led to the public image that medicine could work wonders.

The Development of Professional Medicine

Nevertheless, the transformation to professional recognition did not come easily, even though the history of medicine is frequently told as an impressive string of successes that add up to an accounting of scientific achievement (Freidson, 1970b; Starr, 1982). Such accounts gloss over the many failures. The great improvements in knowledge during the scientific revolution were mostly in science per se, not in the practice of medicine (except for advances in immunization), although they did provide the basic core of knowledge from which medicine emerged as the dominant force in health care.

The development needed to confirm the profession's control of the health and illness system was a respected organization that could act as a base for authority and policies in medical practice. Fostering this development was the threat of rival healing systems, which motivated some 250 physicians to meet in Philadelphia in May 1847 to establish the American Medical Association (AMA). These rival systems, sometimes referred to as cults (Bordley and Harvey, 1976) and sects (Rothstein, 1972), ranged from the botanic system of care to homeopathy. A central concern of the fledgling AMA was legislation favorable to its type of medicine (Bordley and Harvey, 1976). This umbrella organization, which had as its goal the representation of the entire medical profession, saw this as the means through which it could eradicate abuses and establish professional standards (Freidson, 1986:77).

At first, the national association was no more successful than previous groups that had similar goals had been. As late as 1900, the AMA was still ineffectual and could not claim to truly represent the medical profession. There was little evidence that members of this new nationwide medical society had any more influence over matters relating to health and illness than did the other associations. In fact, the association experienced so much internal political strife that more scientifically oriented members left the AMA to form the Association of American Physicians.

Caught up in an increasing and improved technology and pragmatic success, however, the AMA began to extend its authority until it became the most important influence on the practice of medicine in the United States. Both the obvious advances of medical skill reported in the *Journal of the American Medical Association*, founded in 1883, and a reorganization of the association in 1901, which made local and state societies its base, were significant to the growing power of the professional organization.

The AMA reorganization brought it closer to local physicians. The new organization created a House of Delegates, a legislative body comprising representatives of state medical associations. Thus the AMA became a "confederation" of state societies made up of representatives from the county-level organizations. This new organization provided considerable strength for the state associations. This strength was important because states were making legal decisions about the practice of medicine, and the stronger state associations had more effect on the new laws. As a result of closer ties to the individual physician and proof of its ability to effect needed changes, more physicians joined the AMA and its influence grew, both within medicine and among the legislative decision makers of the larger society. Membership in the AMA was made contingent on membership in the local organization, which set its own qualifications of membership under national AMA guidance.

One AMA accomplishment was the establishment of a code of ethics, a code that hit at many disreputable practices within the profession. The AMA has always set itself at the forefront of the fight against all forms of fraudulent medical practice and quackery. The code of ethics has also always been protective of the members of the medical profession. As Starr (1982) comments, it shows a "peculiar reserve" (p. 94) toward those outside the profession.

Four general principles, formulated as early as 1934, still stand as the basic guiding philosophy of the AMA: (1) the medical profession should have total control of all aspects of medical care, medical practice, and all other matters relevant to health and illness; (2) third parties, such as governmental agencies or insurance carriers, should not be allowed to break into the basic relationship between the individual doctor and the individual patient; (3) patients should have no restrictions on choosing a physician; and, (4) wherever possible, the cost of medical care should be handled by the patient (Lasagna, 1963).

Although the AMA is still a powerful influence in the practice of medicine, its power presently seems to be diminishing, particularly among younger physicians. It currently has almost 200,000 members, a much smaller proportion of the physicians in the country than the 90 percent the association could boast of in the mid-1960s. (Twaddle and Hessler, 1987, estimate that only one-third of all doctors were members by the 1970s.) The loss of membership and power is due to several factors. Many physicians resented the use of their dues by the association leadership to wage a battle against the federal government's Medicare proposals. Others were politically too radical to go along with the consistently conservative stance of the AMA's House of Delegates (Twaddle and Hessler, 1987). Further, the growth of specializations made the AMA less representative of the interests of all physicians in the United States; in today's medicine, physicians have so many specialties and such divergent interests that no single organization can truly represent or speak for all.

PRACTICING MEDICINE

Solo Practice

Except for the small group employed full time in medical schools, working in research, or employed by industries and governmental units, most doctors are engaged in various types of private practice. In the United States, the ideal model of the physician, based on one moment in the history of the profession, remains that of the solo general practitioner—the private entrepreneur providing personalized care and taking full responsibility for individual patients. The AMA has traditionally taken this type of medical practice as symbolic of the best in patient care. In such practice, one physician is responsible for all medical problems of the patient—professional and managerial—and has complete charge insofar as the person-to-person relationship with the patient is concerned, unless a specialist is called in (McCormick, Rushing, and Davis, 1978:10).

Solo practice has several ideological compatibilities with the general value system of the U.S. culture. A central theme surrounding solo practice is independence or autonomy. At this stage of the profession's development, however, although the idea carries an aura of autonomy and personal care that is appealing to many, operating a true solo practice is extremely difficult. Among the shortcomings are isolation from professional colleagues and new medical knowledge, constant concern for the financial aspects of daily practice, financial difficulties in the early (and possibly late) stages of the medical practice, and the difficulty of controlling one's working hours. Although patients may hold on to the ideal of a solo practice, they also complain about its effect: long waits, difficulty in reaching the doctor when there is need, and lack of personal attention.

Despite these disadvantages, many physicians and patients prefer the independence that solo practice has the image of offering. In addition, many physicians and patients hold negative feelings toward such other options as group practice. Some physicians may not like sharing decision making with others or having to meet the requirements to join a group. Patients may feel their care is less personalized in other types of practice because they might not see the same physician during each illness episode (Hingson, Scotch, Corenson, and Swazey, 1981:237).

The first step for the new physician entering solo practice is to establish an office and recruit patients. It might seem to the layperson that this is a simple task. But setting up a practice can be expensive, and choosing the right location and making appropriate connections with the professional and lay community can be complex and difficult. In the usual case, after an office is opened, the new doctor must concentrate on entering into the community health network (Hall, 1948). If the doctor is from a family or friendship group in which other doctors are already in practice, the option of joining an established and functioning office may be open and attractive since so many start-up problems are solved. More often, however, the doctor must rely on such factors as friendships developed during medical school or before.

Although members of the profession may not state the point in this way, the young doctor is in competition with other physicians (and other types of healers) for patients. At the same time, the medical profession's code of ethics and the doctor's general orientation forbid behavior that may be interpreted as actively recruiting patients. In smaller communities, especially those with few doctors, the selection of a doctor is limited. Consequently, some physicians start their practice in such areas and move to larger cities after building a firm financial base and establishing a network of colleagues and facilities that might still be used in the new location. But the problem can be difficult for the doctor initiating private practice in a city with many physicians. To advertise without advertising (because of its business implications, advertising is considered unethical by many doctors and members of the public), the doctor may announce an office location and telephone number in the local newspaper—a subtle (possibly not very subtle) appeal for patients.

There are other mechanisms by which both new and established physicians can legitimately (that is, in a "nonbusiness" manner) announce initial or continuing availability. One is for the doctor to volunteer for valued community causes, perhaps by becoming a board member in a community settlement house set up for economically disadvantaged groups. Another is to participate in noncontroversial worthy-cause fund drives, such as those sponsored by the American Cancer Society or the Muscular Dystrophy Society. Participation in the settlement house or in the fund drive may be active, possibly leading to news media coverage, or it may be passive, that is, the doctor's name appears on a list as a supporter or sponsor. Still another legitimate way to place one's name before the public is to volunteer in medically relevant programs like immunization clinics or certain medically important screening programs.

A means of impressing colleagues is to publish an article in a professional journal. Participation, or even simple attendance, at medical conferences and meetings can help establish a reputation and relationships with colleagues. While all of this is occurring, the physician might attempt to avoid controversial issues that could antagonize others. For example, irrespective of their personal assessment of a political candidate or of a decision announced by a religious figure, physicians might make an effort to refrain from public statements about the person or topic. This neutral stance is not as necessary if the controversial person or topic is defined as related to the quality of medical care.

Once the practice is established, the doctor must make certain it is maintained. Whether in solo or other types of practice that give patients a choice, perhaps the best way to ensure this is to project a favorable "bedside manner." From the patient's perspective, the most attractive bedside manner seems to be a combination of calm, assured competence and an appealing personality. Physicians not presenting an image of professional confidence may find their patients switching to doctors in whom they have more faith. Those who do not have pleasant personalities also may find themselves with few patients. A screening process based on image and personality actually starts in medical school, where most students finding it difficult to relate to patients select a specialty with no direct patient contact or in which their practice will consist only of referred patients.

Other Modes of Practice

The organization of medical practice has been undergoing important changes for some time. Over the past few years, movement has been away from solo practice to some form of practice in which the doctor is in professional and financial association with other physicians. This cooperative banding together has made it possible for physicians to share the burden of work, to have more free time, to share the expense of equipment needed, to guarantee an income, and to provide more comprehensive general and special care. The simplest form of such cooperation is what Freidson (1970b) refers to as the association, in which two or more doctors share office space and other necessary facilities. Under this plan, expenses for office space, nursing care, bookkeeping, and sophisticated equipment are shared. The association solves the eternal problem of overwork and lack of time off, since the doctors can cover for one another. The association also can preserve the personal nature of the relationship between doctor and patient.

For both practical and legal reasons, many physicians have gone beyond the simple association and formed legal partnerships. In this type of organization the physicians involved are, in a legal sense, carrying on a business. Each doctor is equally liable under the law for the conduct of the business. In the true sense of the term *partnership*, both fees and overhead are shared by the partners, although they may hire some nonpartner physicians whose salaries will come out of the overhead. Such an organization of practice has much to offer both the younger and the older physician. The former, although not perhaps a full partner, is established in a practice and has access to a number of patients, thus cutting through the problem of establishing a practice and announcing his or her availability. The older doctor is helped by having the younger partner's assistance in keeping up with the patient load. In a partnership, patients need not be referred to another doctor and then, perhaps, be lost.

By far the most important development in modes of medical practice in the United States goes beyond the usual small partnership into a group practice organization consisting of several doctors. The AMA definition of *group practice* is three or more doctors sharing facilities and ancillary personnel, all within a formal agreement for the distribution of revenues. Using the AMA definition, 28.4 percent of all doctors were practicing in such a setting in 1984; if the definition used is a much looser criterion of five or more full-time doctors in association, as suggested by Freidson, the 1984 figure is 45.2 percent (both definitions are given in Andersen and Mullner, 1989:147)

A change in ideological overtones in this country has fostered the development of group practice. This change fits the complexities of modern society but departs significantly from the old-line individualistic ideology of solo practice. In recognition of the importance to many patients of a feeling of personalized care, attempts often are made to preserve the individual doctor-patient relationship, even though several physicians make common use of the equipment, facilities, and personnel of the practice under a formal agreement. The income derived from the practice is shared on the basis of whatever the members of the group have decided is equitable.

Mackintosh (1978:53) suggests six major advantages to group practice: (1) sharing the equipment, facilities, and ancillary workers reduces costs for individual group members; (2) group members can schedule a regular system of patient coverage, allowing plans to be made for vacations and weekends, or when they themselves are ill; (3) the association allows the communication of ideas and informal consultation with other physicians; (4) in multispecialty groups, patients receive greater continuity of care when specialists are needed; (5) persons skilled in administration can be hired to handle managerial details; and (6) it is a good way for practitioners to establish a fairly large practice in a short time.

Mackintosh (1978) also lists disadvantages: (1) when a mistake in diagnosis or treatment is made, especially if a malpractice suit ensues, the professional reputation of all members of the group may be damaged; (2) the members of the group may be personally incompatible; and (3) a nonmember physician may be reluctant to refer patients to the group for fear the patients will then continue to consult the group after the need for the referral has passed.

Two other organizational medical settings have attracted many doctors, and approximately 20 percent of the U.S. population has either used their services or have services available through membership. The two are Health Maintenance Organizations (HMOs) and Preferred Provider Organizations (PPOs).

HMOs, which provide comprehensive care for prepaid subscribers, had 29.2 million enrollees in 1987 (up from 21.0 million in 1985; National Center for Health Statistics, 1989). In the usual HMO, physicians are salaried employees of the organization and subscribers pay a fee that gives them access to all the personnel and resources of the organization; the medical services are usually centralized in one or two buildings. In addition, groups of physicians may contract to provide service in the HMO. A variation on this model includes private practitioners who contract individually and provide services out of their offices. Doctors may negotiate set fees with the organization and bear some financial risk if these do not cover the expenses of the HMO. The patient would use the private office of the practitioner, as in the fee-for-service situation. The appeal of such an arrangement to many doctors is some degree of freedom from the bureaucracy and a feeling of still running a solo office.

Another system of medical practice, recently devised, is the Preferred Provider Organization (PPO). In such an organization, private doctors, hospitals, and other providers of health services contract with employers and insurance companies to provide services to people who have taken out insurance policies specific to the organization. The contract calls for a fee-for-service arrangement with a substantial discount on normal fees, usually about 20 percent. As an indication of an increasing appeal of such an arrangement, the number of people covered by PPO systems in 1986 was 17.1 million, compared with 5.5 million one year earlier (Andersen and Mullner, 1989:151). The PPO is only one of the latest experiments in health care delivery; judging by the 300 percent increase in one year, it currently seems a successful one. Here, the doctors are employees of a group that has contracted with the organization and are financially dependent on the terms of the contract signed with the employer or insurance company.

Two other rapidly growing services in the private sector are the independent ambulatory care center and the outpatient surgery center. In such systems, doctors and other health personnel, sometimes including nurse practitioners, offer a walk-in outpatient service. The centers are an internal business arrangement among owners and have no official affiliation with a hospital or another group of doctors. As a means of attracting patients, they are often located in areas within easy reach, such as shopping centers, and may be open well into the evening seven days a week. Minor medical problems, emergency service (often labeled "urgent care"), and surgery that does not require an overnight stay are emphasized. These centers often advertise in the local newspaper and the yellow pages of the telephone directory, as well as on their "store front"; these advertisements often stress immediate medical attention with at least an implication of lower charges. There were approximately 3,000 ambulatory care centers and 459 outpatient surgery centers in the United States in 1985, a 30 percent and a 39 percent increase over 1984 (Andersen and Mullner, 1989:151).

A CHANGING PROFESSION

The number of sociological publications and discussions about changes in the world of medicine has increased recently, but this increase may have more to do with sociology than with the medical profession. Certainly, the profession is changing and seems to be changing at a faster pace than in the past. What probably brought the subject of change to the forefront was the 1982 publication of a book by sociologist Paul Starr entitled *The Social Transformation of American Medicine*. This book is important for understanding the history of medicine and the social changes it is experiencing in the United States. We will review Starr's presentation, since it provides insight into medicine as we now know it and as it may be in the future. We also will review the work of Eliot Freidson, who has discussed changes in the profession from a sociological point of view for many years, and who has recently brought many of his observations together in one publication.

Starr's history of the U.S. medical profession indicates that medicine was a legitimate, entrenched, and autonomous social institution by 1920. This position of professional sovereignty over all medical matters served the profession well for the next fifty years. Medicine and its practitioners flourished; not only did authority go unchallenged, it was virtually unchallengeable. Given this monopoly, change was slow. Calls for change were scrutinized by the profession itself, which screened all suggestions to make certain the monopoly was not disturbed.

Starting with the 1970s, however, changes began to encroach on this autonomous and independent position. The profession had become so inward-looking, so insular, so parochial, that it paid little attention to outside developments. As U.S. society changed, it pulled medicine along with it. A major change in society was what Starr refers to as the "reprivatization of the public household," that is, the transfer of public services to the ownership (thus control) and administration of private corporations. This had a major effect on medicine. In medical practice, more and more private practitioners were entering corporate settings, with a corresponding loss of autonomy. Corporate medicine looks upon the physician as an employee; its concern is with its shareholders rather than with the nature of medical practice, except for how it may affect the financial balance sheet and the profit line.

U.S. corporations are not alone in moving in this direction; doctors themselves have established medical corporations and are owners of corporate medicine practices. Some may remain in private practice, but Starr anticipates that the important distinction in medicine in the future will be between private practitioners, employees, managers, and owners of medical corporations. If Starr's prediction is correct, the private practitioner is vanishing in the United States.

Freidson (1986) suggests that "Medicare and Medicaid legislation was the single most important factor of change for the health care system in the past two decades" (p. 63). These programs brought the enormous cost of health care to public attention; health care costs became a subject of public consideration and debate. At the same time, such events as the cost of new technology were leading to major increases in health care costs. Furthermore, the public was becoming accustomed to open discussion of increasing health costs, along with publicity in the mass media about malpractice suits, the use of human subjects in medical research, and pollution of the environment. The proper use of life-support equipment designed to keep comatose patients functioning, organ transplants, in vitro fertilization, abortion, and other social issues of the day also were debated. These all seemed to fit together into generalized questions about the medical profession, especially questions about what authority a physician should have in such crucial matters of life and death.

Freidson (1986) indicates that public confidence in medicine has declined in the United States, but he suggests that most commentators have "grievously exaggerated the consequences of this shift in the climate and focus of public opinion about health care" (p. 65). He points out that any decline in confidence in the medical profession is part of an overall decline in the public's confidence in U.S. institutions.

Before such a discussion goes too far, it must be pointed out that "the medical profession retains its basic, legally enforced monopoly over the key functions of health care and, the consumer movement notwithstanding, retains its basic 'cultural authority' " (Freidson, 1986:70). The physician has a strategic position in the health care system, one that will not change quickly. Moreover, changes in the system probably will continue to be channeled through the medical profession, which monitors and attempts to shape events that it recognizes as affecting its vital interests.

Nevertheless, the physician's authority in the system has been questioned. Thus, at a 1986 symposium entitled "The Physician as Captain of the Ship: A Critical Reappraisal," sponsored by medical and pharmaceutical organizations, one speaker stated:

> *Twenty years ago, a single metaphor accurately captured the role that American society accorded to physicians. The physician was "captain of the ship." Physicians were in charge of the clinic, the operating room, and the health care team, responsible—and held accountable—for all that happened within the scope of their supervision. This grant of responsibility carried with it a corresponding grant of authority; like the ship's captain, the physician was answerable to no one regarding the practice of his art. . . . However compelling the metaphor, few would disagree that the mandate accorded to the medical profession by society is changing. (Churchill, 1988:xi)*

Another speaker at the symposium stated: "As far as medicine and health are concerned, most of us probably share the feeling that the ground is shifting under our feet. Things are changing. The litany is everywhere: for-profit hospitals, the senescence of the biomedical model, Diagnosis Related Groups, the malpractice crisis, and so on" (Maulitz, 1988:3).

There seems little doubt that, whatever the reasons, members of the profession agree with the general conclusions of Starr (1982) and Freidson (1986) and also see a decline in the doctor's independent authority. Control of medical practice is moving from the hands of doctors to the hands of large corporations. According to Cockerham (1989), this has not created major problems for practitioners: "Physicians have not shown strong objections to being employed by the corporations or in sending their patients to for-profit hospitals" (p. 203). Cockerham presents two major reasons for this acceptance: the surplus of doctors and the work situation of the health care corporation, which provides a security of "jobs, offices, equipment, hospital privileges, and perhaps even a salary guarantee" (p. 204). In other words, such a post could solve many of the problems physicians face in setting up a practice.

Will medicine of the future be very different than it is today? The data we discussed in the modes-of-practice section are compelling. They definitely indicate the answer is yes. The number of HMOs, PPOs, and independent medical facilities is rapidly increasing. No one can predict the innovations that are coming, but all change is toward medicine in group situations and in organized settings in which nonmedical decisions are made by managers and leaders of business rather than by physicians. Whether this will lead to "better" medicine is debatable and whether the trend is a "good" one will be decided by society's core values.

SUMMARY

Entry and initial practice standards of the medical profession are controlled through the medical school. The manifest function of the medical school is to teach students basic medical knowledge and techniques. An equally important function is socializing students to develop the proper patterns of interaction, thoughts, motivations, interests, attitudes, and values that are necessary for the graduate to play the doctor role as the profession feels it should be played. Such socialization is important to the medical profession for passing on, and thus maintaining, its traditional value patterns.

Acceptance by the medical school is the most important step in initiating a medical career. Traditionally, the admissions process and social factors have favored white, middle-class, male medical students. But recent social changes have led to increased enrollment among minority-group members and women. This is extremely significant to the career pattern because once admission has been gained, the probability that the student will graduate with a medical degree is very high.

Education in a medical school has two distinct stages: the preclinical years and the clinical years. During the preclinical stage, students often find little difference from their undergraduate years and may feel disappointed that they are not yet learning "how to be a doctor." During the initial two years, the students take courses as a cohort, usually in large class sections. During the clinical years, however, the whole pattern of education is changed to clinical-learning small groups in which students have doctor-supervised contact with patients in a teaching hospital.

Medical school is a time of intense pressure for the students. The amount of work to be done and material to be mastered goes beyond what can easily be accomplished in the time at hand. A mechanism for dealing with this pressure and work is the development of a student subculture. Several studies have called attention to this subculture and its role in helping the student cope with the many problems of medical school.

Among the effects of medical school on the student are a loss of idealism and the development of cynicism; some investigators indicate that idealism is postponed, or suspended, rather than lost. The student also is led to choose what field of medicine to pursue. Initial interest in general practice gives way to the choice of a specialty as the student progresses in the education program.

Another stage of medical education is necessary before practice is possible in the United States: the internship. During this period, the graduate doctor becomes the practicing physician. During residency, the final stage, the general doctor becomes a specialist, and a long-term career commitment is made.

Recent critiques of medical school programs have centered on both what is being taught and how it is being taught. With such pejorative descriptions of the curriculum as a "treadmill to professionalism," and references to rote memorization, the medical school is accused of producing highly trained specialists who are short in humanistic orientations toward patients. This is attributed to an underlying emphasis in the medical school on research and specialization. Several attempts at medical education reform are under way, but the results of new approaches are not yet clear.

Assessments of health care in the United States describe the physician as the dominant member of the system. National opinion survey data show that the respect of the people for physicians remains high in comparison to other occupations. But the public may be judging an image of the physician that is no longer valid. Today's doctors are unlikely to be general practitioners taking a personal and intimate interest in patients and families. They are more likely to be specialists practicing in some form of group or organized practice.

Contemporary medical practice is organized in many different ways. Although the ideal is that of the solo general practice, the complexity and expense of modern medicine has led many physicians to associate with other doctors in partnerships or in group practice. Group practice usually involves three or more doctors providing care to patients, jointly using equipment and personnel, and distributing income among themselves. It has many advantages to both patients and doctors, particularly when it is comprehensive in scope, but there are also disadvantages.

A major problem in contemporary medical care in U.S. society is cost. In response, new modes of medical practice have been devised. For example, many HMOs are now operating; they provide, on the basis of prepayment, comprehensive care for subscribers. A major advantage of the HMO is that the flat fee for future service encourages both preventive medicine and cost containment. Many people in the United States feel that some system of health insurance that provides coverage for all should be instituted at the national level.

A recent and rapidly growing service is the Preferred Provider Organization in which a group of doctors contract with employers and insurance companies to provide health care at preferred rates (usually a 20 percent discount from normal rates) on a fee-for-service agreement. Other expanding innovations are the ambulatory center and the outpatient surgery center, which provide walk-in service for minor and emergency cases.

References

Albrecht, Gary L., and Jerry Ross. 1977. "Entry into the medical profession: The first hurdle is the highest." *Sociological Symposium* 19:1–19.

Andersen, Ronald M., and Ross M. Mullner. 1989. "Trends in the organization of health services." In *Handbook of Medical Sociology*, 4th ed., ed. H. E. Freeman and S. Levine, 144–165. Englewood Cliffs, N.J.: Prentice-Hall.

Association of American Medical Colleges (AAMC). 1984. *Physicians for the Twenty-first Century: The GPEP Report.* Washington, D.C.: Author.

Becker, Howard, and Blanche Geer. 1958. "The fate of idealism in medical school." *American Sociological Review* 23(February):50–56.

Becker, Howard S., Blanche Geer, Everett C. Hughes, and Anselm L. Strauss. 1961. *Boys in White: Student Culture in Medical School.* Chicago: University of Chicago Press.

Bloom, Samuel W. 1965. "The sociology of medical education: Some comments on the state of a field." *Milbank Memorial Fund Quarterly* 43:143–184.

Bloom, Samuel W. 1988. "Structure and ideology in medical education: An analysis of resistance to change." *Journal of Health and Social Behavior* 29 (December):294–306.

Bordley, James, III, and A. M. Harvey. 1976. *Two Centuries of American Medicine.* Philadelphia: W. B. Saunders.

Bosk, Charles L. 1986. "Professional responsibility and medical error." In *Applications of Social Science to Clinical Medicine and Health Policy*, ed. L. Aiken and D. Mechanic, 460–477. New Brunswick, N.J.: Rutgers University Press.

Bourne, Patricia, and Norma Juliet Wikler. 1978. "Commitment and cultural mandate: Women in medicine." *Social Problems* 25(April):430–440.

Churchill, Larry R. 1988. "Introduction." In *The Physician as Captain of the Ship: A Critical Reappraisal*, ed. N. King, L. Churchill, and A. W. Cross, i–xx. Dordrecht, Holland: D. Reidel Publishing.

Cockerham, William C. 1989. *Medical Sociology*. 4th ed. Englewood Cliffs, N.J.: Prentice-Hall.

Conrad, Peter. 1988. "Learning to doctor: Reflections on recent accounts of the medical school years." *Journal of Health and Social Behavior* 29 (December):323–332.

Coombs, Robert H. 1978. *Mastering Medicine*. New York: Elsevier.

Coombs, Robert H., and Pauline S. Powers. 1975. "Socialization for death: The physician's role." *Urban Life: Journal of Ethnographic Research* 4(October):250–271.

Eron, Leonard D. 1955. "The effect of medical education on attitudes: A follow-up study." *Journal of Medical Education* 30, pt. 2(October):25–33.

Flexner, Abraham. 1910. *Medical Education in the United States and Canada*. New York: Carnegie Foundation for the Advancement of Teaching.

Fox, Renee C. 1957. "Training for uncertainty." In *The Student-Physician*, ed. R. Merton, G. Reader, and P. Kendall, 207–241. Cambridge: Harvard University Press.

———. 1974. "Is there a new medical student?" In *Ethics of Health Care*, ed. L. R. Tancredie, 197–220. Washington, D.C.: National Academy of Science.

———. 1989. *The Sociology of Medicine: A Participant Observer's View*. Englewood Cliffs, N.J.: Prentice-Hall.

Freidson, Eliot. 1970a. *Professional Dominance*. New York: Atherton.

———. 1970b. *Profession of Medicine*. New York: Dodd, Mead.

———. 1986. *Professional Powers: A Study of the Institutionalization of Formal Knowledge*. Chicago: The University of Chicago Press.

Funkenstein, Daniel H. 1978. *Medical Students, Medical Schools and Society During Five Eras: Factors Affecting the Career Choice of Physicians 1958–1976*. Cambridge: Ballinger Publishing.

Gough, Harrison G., and W. B. Hall. 1975. "An attempt to predict graduation from medical school." *Journal of Medical Education* 50:940–950.

Greer, David S., and S. M. Aronson. 1980. "Failure as a criterion for medical school admissions." *Journal of Medical Education* 55(7):616–618.

Hall, Oswald. 1948. "The stages of a medical career." *American Journal of Sociology* 53:327–336.

Hingson, Ralph N., A. Scotch, J. Corenson, and J. P. Swazey. 1981. *In Sickness and In Health*. St. Louis: C. V. Mosby.

Hughes, Everett C. 1961. *Students' Culture and Perspective: Lectures on Medical and General Education*. Lawrence: University of Kansas.

Jonas, Harry S., and Sylvia Etzel. 1988. "Undergraduate medical education." *Journal of the American Medical Association* 260(8):1063–1071.

Kendall, Patricia L., and George G. Reader. 1988. "Innovations in medical education of the 1950s contrasted with those of the 1970s and 1980s." *Journal of Health and Social Behavior* 29(December):279–293.

Klepke, Phillip R., William D. Marder, and Anne B. Silberger. 1987. *The Demographics of Physician Supply: Trends and Projections*. Chicago: American Medical Association Center for Health Policy Research.

Lasagna, Louis. 1963. *The Doctor's Dilemma*. New York: Colliers.

Light, Donald. 1975. "The sociological calendar: An analytic tool for fieldwork applied to medical and psychiatric training." *American Journal of Sociology* 80(March):1145–1164.

———. 1979. "Uncertainty and control in professional training." *Journal of Health and Social Behavior* 20:310–322.

McCormick, J., R. Rushing, and W. Davis. 1978. *The Management of Medical Practice*. Cambridge: Ballinger.

Mackintosh, Douglas R. 1978. *Systems of Health Care*. Boulder, Colo.: Westview Press.

Maulitz, Russell C. 1988. "The physician and authority: A historical reappraisal." In *The Physician as Captain of the Ship: A Critical Reappraisal*, ed. N. King, L. Churchill, and A. W. Cross, 3–21. Dordrecht, Holland: D. Reidel Publishing.

Merton, R. K., G. Reader, and P. Kendall, eds. 1957. *The Student-Physician*. Cambridge: Harvard University Press.

Miller, Stephen J. 1970. *Prescription for Leadership: Training for the Medical Elite*. Chicago: Aldine.

National Center for Health Statistics. 1989. *Health, United States, 1988*. DHHS Pub. No. (PHS) 89-1232. Public Health Service. Washington: U.S. Government Printing Office.

National Opinion Research Center (NORC). 1988. *General Social Survey*. Chicago: Author.

Navarro, Vicente. 1986. *Crisis, Health, and Medicine: A Social Critique*. New York: Tavistock.

Pellegrino, E. D. 1987. "Altruism, self-interest, and medical ethics." *Journal of the American Medical Association* 258(14):1939–1940.

Petersdorf, Robert G. 1988. "The scylla and charybdis of medical education." *Journal of Medical Education* 63(February):88–93.

Reitzes, Deitrich, and Hekmat Elkhanialy. 1976. "Black students in medical schools." *Journal of Medical Education* 51:1001–1005.

Rezler, Agnes G. 1974. "Attitude changes during medical school: A review of the literature." *Journal of Medical Education* 49:1023–1030.

Roeske, Nancy, and Karen Lake. 1977. "Role models for women medical students." *Journal of Medical Education* 52:459–466.

Rogoff, Natalie. 1957. "The decision to study medicine." In *The Student-Physician*, ed. R. Merton, G. Reader, and P. Kendall, 109–129. Cambridge: Harvard University Press.

Rothstein, William G. 1972. *American Physicians in the Nineteenth Century*. Boston: Little, Brown.

Shea, Steven, and Mindy Thompson Fullilove. 1985. "Entry of black and other minority students into U.S. medical schools: Historical perspective and recent trends." *New England Journal of Medicine* 313(15):933–940.

Starr, Paul. 1982. *The Social Transformation of American Medicine*. New York: Basic Books.

Stemmler, Edward J. 1988. "Medical education: Is it?" *Journal of Medical Education* 63 (February):81–87.

Thomae-Forques, M. E., and X. Tonesk. 1980. "Datagram: Enrollment in U.S. medical schools." *Journal of Medical Education* 55:1042–1044.

Twaddle, A. C., and R. M. Hessler. 1987. *A Sociology of Health*. 2nd ed. St. Louis: C. V. Mosby.

6

Physicians and Their Patients

INTRODUCTION

In 1931 Sigerist stated that the health care relationship is essentially a social one (Roemer, 1960). When Sigerist first made this statement, the nature of the relationship seemed a rather uncomplicated person-to-person association that was easy to understand. But, in the United States, changes in our insight and in both society and medicine have altered our understanding of many traditional patterns. Medicine has become more professional; it has become more modern; it has become big business. The impersonality of clinics, the automation of testing, and the practice of medicine within contexts that avoid or preclude close personal relationships between patients and doctors all have contributed to social distance within the health care system. Many patients speak with nostalgia about the past, when the doctor was a friend of the family. And many lament the passing of the close personal relationship they feel they had with the physician. If pressed for an example of the loss, the public often refers to house calls by doctors, which are almost never made in the practice of today's medicine. The failure of the modern physician to come close to the nostalgic image leaves many people angry or ambivalent about the health care system and about the doctor. This is significant to the image the public has of doctors because the major criteria used by many people to evaluate the quality of their medical care have more to do with the personal relationship between patient and physician than with the skillful application of medical knowledge.

PHYSICIAN-PATIENT INTERACTION

In view of the importance of the physician's role in U.S. society, the interaction between doctors and patients has been the subject of discussion by many social commentators and social scientists. Conclusions have not always been in agreement, but the common interest has led to important insights into the nature of the relationship. In this section we will review four sociologically oriented descriptions of doctor-patient interaction patterns; this will be followed by criticisms, critiques of the present nature of the doctor-patient interaction system, and by a discussion of ways in which the relationship is changing.

Szasz and Hollender

In an early sociologically oriented and theoretical approach to the doctor-patient relationship, Szasz and Hollender (1956), both physicians, set up a threefold typology of possible interaction: activity-passivity, guidance-cooperation, and mutual participation. The typology can be used to understand different aspects of both the doctor's role and the patient's role.

In the activity-passivity relationship, the doctor actively intervenes for a passive patient who can make no contribution to the treatment process and who is in no position to make decisions. Szasz and Hollender liken the relationship to that between a parent and an infant.

The guidance-cooperation pattern is probably the most frequent example of doctor-patient interaction and is typical of the usual medical care pattern. The patient is ill, but can still interact as a thinking and feeling individual. The patient seeks help or guidance from the physician and expects to cooperate in a medical regimen selected by the doctor. Although the physician dominates in the interaction, both parties participate and contribute to the relationship. The patient is expected to follow the physician's orders much like a child is expected to obey the instructions of parents.

The mutual participation pattern envisions equality between the physician and patient. Such a model is only possible when both parties have equal power, depend on one another, and find satisfaction in the interaction. Szasz and Hollender suggest that such a model would be best seen in cases of chronic illness when the patient is, of necessity, active in self-care. It is a cooperative relationship between adults.

Bloom

In a book focusing specifically on the doctor-patient relationship, Bloom (1963) suggests that the association can best be understood in a much wider context than as an association between two roles. The relationship takes place within a broad sociocultural matrix into which the doctor and patient carry their own reference groups. The medical profession, with its specific sets of values and norms, shapes the view of the interaction for the doctor; the family, with its values and norms, sets the framework for the patient. In addition, the doctor and patient are both influenced by the many subcultures and other groups important to them. The relationship is discussed within the sociological concept of a social system.

Bloom's model is most appropriate for the solo-practice, general practitioner doctor-patient relationship. However, the trend toward group and other forms of institutional practice makes other models seem more appropriate. The patient may now engage the services of an organization rather than of an individual, which would not seem to change the basic structure of the doctor-patient relationship. However, another circle of influence, the doctor's placement within a secondary organization, means that still another sociocultural matrix must be taken into account.

Anderson and Helm

In a description closely related to Bloom's presentation, Anderson and Helm (1979) suggest that the physician and patient engage in "reality negotiation." This process is strongly influenced by the definitions of the situation each role player brings into the relationship, definitions that may not agree. These authors state that if there is disagreement, the physician has the upper hand in the decision concerning which definition is acceptable: "In the negotiating process the physician has the setting, language, latent status, stereotypical categorization of illness, tendency toward . . . [finding illness even if it is not there], and organizational clout—all supporting his or her definition of reality over the patient's" (1979:269). The physician clearly controls the negotiation of reality.

Anderson and Helm also draw upon a metaphor used by Balint (1957:216) in which he describes the physician as having an apostolic (or missionary) function: "Every doctor has a vague, but unshakeably firm idea of how a patient ought to behave when ill. It is as if the doctor had the knowledge of what was right and wrong for the patient to expect and to endure, and further, as if he had the . . . duty to convert to his faith all the ignorant and unbelieving among his patients." If the patient does not accept the physician's diagnosis or treatment regimen, the doctor may reject or ignore the patient's point of view. More likely, however, the doctor will attempt to convert the patient to the more acceptable definition and decision. Only if this works will the physician consider the encounter successful.

Parsons

In what may be described as the most provocative, controversial, and research-generating sociological discussion of the doctor-patient relationship, Talcott Parsons (1951) discusses medical practice as an "important sub-system of modern Western society" (p. 428). This places the discussion within the broad context of a major sociological theory of social systems. In his theoretical approach to the structure of social action, Parsons indicates that the expected behavior of people in the social system is structured; that is, people's behavior is not undefined, it is patterned by particular orientations. These orientations, which vary from one status to another, are referred to as "pattern variables" (Parsons, 1951:58–67). Parsons suggests that a theoretical model of pattern variables can be used as a standardized comparative framework for understanding how the occupants of statuses are expected to interact with others. The model was thus constructed in terms of the orientations expected of role players. Parsons introduced five pattern variables and set them up as five dichotomous or twofold role-definition choices in interaction patterns. He applied his theoretical construct of pattern variables specifically to the expected value orientations of the doctor's role (Parsons, 1951:428–479).

The Five Pattern Variables

1. *Affectivity-affective neutrality.* The interaction patterns of the incumbents of some statuses are based on an affective or emotional base, whereas others are based on affectively neutral or objective grounds. In U.S. culture, the physician's application of medical knowledge to the patient is expected to be affectively neutral. Among other things, neutrality guarantees that the doctor's relationship to the patient is on a professional level. This protects both the doctor and the patient from inappropriate and potentially dangerous involvements, while permitting the physician to give appropriate attention to the technical considerations of the patient's medical problem.

Commitment to affective neutrality also prevents physician involvement in emotionally charged problems that may influence the relationship. Pain, the possibility of death, and institutionalization are examples of experiences that must be handled objectively for the physician to function effectively. If emotions were allowed to affect the relationship, they might influence the doctor's decisions concerning treatment choices. Even diagnosis could suffer, for the doctor might inadvertently seek agreeable signs and ignore the disagreeable. Decisions might be based on desires, hopes, and fears, rather than on medical knowledge.

With affective neutrality, the physician displays uninvolved professionality in an objective situation calling for the routine, nonemotional application of solid scientific knowledge. Such a matter-of-fact approach can be therapeutic, as it forces the patient and the patient's family to recognize that even an emotional situation can be approached with objectivity.

The orientation is significant in other ways. Affective neutrality provides a guarantee of noninvolvement in situations that otherwise may be defined as charged with emotion. For example, the physician must sometimes inquire into aspects of the patient's private world, asking for information about experiences that may be hidden from friends and relatives. Only if the patient perceives the physician as uninvolved emotionally will there be willingness to reveal and discuss certain of these private experiences. Related to this point, in the course of the examination the physician may have to examine and touch parts of the body that have sexual connotations. Functioning under the concept of affective neutrality, the physician's viewing and touching the body does not suggest a sexual or emotionally involved relationship.

2. *Specificity-diffuseness.* By specificity-diffuseness, Parsons means the scope or inclusiveness of an association. A diffuse relationship has a wide range of rights and duties; a specificity relationship's rights and duties are narrow in scope. This orientation may be further interpreted as the degree of involvement of one social status with another. In the model Parsons constructed, the relationship between doctor and patient is a functionally specific one that restricts the physician's access to information and activities that are relevant to the patient's condition.

Specificity thus allays possible patient anxieties about the information being given to the doctor. It is a guarantee that information sought by the physician will be significant to the patient's condition. The decision concerning what is relevant to the case rests with the physician, who is defined as the technical expert. Specificity complements affective neutrality because, together, they indicate that the patient is free to provide the physician with otherwise private information, without fear that it will be interpreted evaluatively or that it will be misused.

Some physicians, such as psychiatrists, who see most illness as a function of the psychological condition of the patient, define specificity in broader or more diffuse terms than their more body-oriented colleagues, such as surgeons, radiologists, or pathologists. Even those who take the broad position, however, agree that only questions pertinent to the condition of the patient are legitimate. Differences are about the extent of inclusiveness, not about whether limits should be set; definitions of relevancy are not hard, fast, or stable.

3. *Universalism-particularism.* Parsons used the universalism-particularism pattern variable to describe how the incumbents of one status are supposed to relate to those of another status. If a person should react to all incumbents of a status in the same way, the pattern is universalistic since individuals are seen as members of a universal class. If a person should react to each incumbent of a status in a unique way, the pattern is particularistic; the individual is expected to be treated as a special person in a social relationship.

The physician is expected to treat each person who comes for help as an incumbent of the universal status of patient. The doctor's obligation is to make certain that all incumbents of the patient status are treated alike, that each occupant is provided with the best technical care available.

From the patient's perspective, a particularistic relationship with the doctor could make the situation difficult. The patient might be willing to provide private information to an incumbent of the general status called doctor, but not to someone with whom there is a particularistic relationship. To obtain health care uncluttered by personal matters, the patient is expected to seek a physician with whom the relationship can be universalistic.

The close association of universalism-particularism with affectivity-affective neutrality is evident. By definition, the affective relationship implies a particularistic association since, in most interaction situations based on emotion, each person involved is set off as different from others. The quality of the affective-particularistic relationship is recognized in the norm that doctors are not supposed to treat close members of their own families. If the doctor is to practice medicine effectively, judgments cannot be confounded by feelings of emotion and by an implied obligation to treat someone in a way that is unrelated to the medical nature of the case. All patients should be treated alike.

4. *Ascription-achievement.* We occupy some of our statuses because of the biological and genetic characteristics with which we were born and others because of our behavior; the former are ascribed statuses and the latter are achieved. To a large extent, we have control over our occupancy of achieved statuses and no control over which ascribed statuses we occupy. We all occupy both types and are expected to play the relevant roles. In U.S. society, sex and family statuses are ascribed (other than those we enter through marriage); student and occupational statuses are achieved.

A person can become a physician in the United States only through specific education and training, so the status is clearly achieved. The technical competence of the physician is based, at least partially, on long training, exhibited success, and official certification, which indicates that achievement is essential to entering the status. In western societies, one cannot inherit the right to practice medicine; even the children of doctors must first be certified as competent, with competence demonstrated through accomplishment.

To some extent, objective criteria can be used to evaluate the role performance of people in business, for example, the profit criterion. But no such criterion exists for evaluating the role performance of doctors. Fellow doctors have developed some ways of judging each other, such as board certification and through hospital review committees but, because knowledge of actual functioning is limited, public judgments of the quality of the doctor's performance are usually based on nonprofessional criteria.

5. *Self-collectivity orientation.* The final pattern of behavioral expectations presented by Parsons classifies social relations on the basis of whether they are entered into for personal (self) benefit or for the benefit of others (the collectivity). Physicians are expected to be more interested in the welfare of their patients than in their own personal gain; their services and decisions are supposed to be rendered for the patient's good rather than for their own benefit. Thus, the doctor's role fits squarely in the collectivity orientation.

Combining collectivity with specificity and affective neutrality helps round out a total package that presents a message to the patient: "I am here for your benefit, as a professional seeking information technically relevant to the determination of your condition and its proper handling." Belief in the sincerity of the message allows the patient to feel free to share intimate information with the doctor. Affective neutrality, specificity, universality, achievement, and the collectivity approach combine into the doctor's expected value orientations that affect interaction with the patient. Consequently, occupants of the doctor status are allowed access to the body and psyche of individual patients.

Criticisms of Parsons's Model. A consistent theme affecting each dimension of Parsons's model is that the physician must have authority in the relationship, authority to be used for the patient's benefit. This portrayal of a beneficial asymmetrical power relationship has been severely criticized by several sociologists. Responding to critics, Parsons (1975) defends the relationship as he described it on the ground that their technical and scientific training puts physicians into the position of knowing what the patient needs. In Parsons's view, the doctor-patient relationship is one of demand by the patient and response by the doctor. The act of entering the doctor's office constitutes the patient's request for help. In this situation, the doctor-patient relationship is committed to active intervention on the part of the doctor and to cooperation on the part of the patient. Since the doctor must engage in specific activities designed to relieve the condition that brought the patient into the doctor's office, the association is biased in favor of intervention on the part of the physician.

Not everyone would agree that the power and authority granted the physician is for the good of the patient, or that the patient is only a passive recipient of action in the situation. What Parsons perceived as mutually advantageous has been interpreted by some sociologists as exclusively for the benefit of the physician, with the possibility that the rewards to the patient in such a structuring of the physician's role may be minimal and even dysfunctional for health and recovery. For example, the authority may impede the necessary dialogue between patient and physician, leading to obstacles in the therapeutic process.

Freidson (1970) was one of the first sociologists to challenge Parsons's formulations of both the sick role (see Chapter 4 of this book) and the pattern variable dimensions as applied to physicians. He presents four major criticisms of Parsons's model of the physician's role. First, because it focuses on the physician, the model construct essentially ignores the expectations of patients and others with whom the doctor has professional contact. Second, as they are presented, the expectations of the physician are made to seem an unalterable fact of the human condition. Third, the influence of the physician does not really come from ideal societal expectations, but from the power the position of physician has gained. Finally, the model ignores the inevitability of conflict between unequal groups in social interaction.

Starr (1982) presents similar criticisms of Parsons's model. He notes that it does not make allowances for the "obvious" ambivalence that exists in the doctor-patient relationship. Indeed, Starr suggests that physicians and patients have contradictory expectations of each other in their interaction. Parsons focuses so directly on the dominance of the physician that such contradictions are ignored.

Parsons's models of the sick role and of the pattern variables present a picture of people behaving harmoniously within a social system of consensus and cooperation. But many sociologists approach social systems, including that of doctor-patient, quite differently. They see people holding different and conflicting perspectives, implying that the doctor-patient relationship may be a clash of perspectives. In this context, the association is a transaction between the members of two social systems, between people who have different interests and who seek to advance their own interests in the relationship. In the eyes of some critics, Parsons's harmony is replaced with hostility, ambivalence, and conflict.

Freidson (1970) discusses the implications of the power acquired by the physician in our time and the effect this may have on the quality of medical care. He notes that illness has become a ubiquitous label for any kind of deviance in our time (see, for example, Chapter 10, in this book) and that authority over such a broad area of social life gives the physician considerable power. Freidson sees today's physicians as entrepreneurs seeking new conditions or behaviors to be labeled illness, over which they will then have control. In this context, the physician functions not as a morally neutral member of society, as suggested by Parsons, but as one who makes judgments about the patient. Furthermore, physicians consider it a duty to seek out illness. And, they feel it is better to diagnose suspect cases as real illness rather than to miss identifying a disease.

What the physician overlooks, according to this critique, is that labeling a person as having a disease can create a socially damaged image that may never be completely erased. A faulty diagnosis often has social and psychological as well as medical consequences. For example, a person with an incorrect diagnosis of heart disease may undergo a major change in lifestyle, with serious social and psychological readjustments for both the person labeled and many members of their social systems. The doctor may have been correct in not wanting to fail to diagnose a potentially serious physical problem, but the social and psychological repercussions of an incorrect diagnosis can be disastrous for the person.

Starr (1982) criticizes Parsons's notion of the power of the physician and its source. According to Starr, it is inappropriate to take this power as a given. The power resulted from the medical community's successful fight to obtain dominance and goes beyond the process of healing. For example, if a patient does not follow a medical regimen suggested, the patient can be "blamed" as unwilling or uncooperative, rather than attributing noncompliance to the doctor or to problems in the interaction process. This is related to the medical ideology supported by Parsons's model that physicians are basically altruistic or collectivity oriented. Such blind acceptance of physicians' selflessness ignores both the actual structure of medicine and the collegial bond between physicians. For example, it does not consider the sizeable incomes of many physicians or the considerable evidence that physicians are prone to overlook the mistakes of others in the profession.

Freidson (1970) also suggests that other factors, which he refers to as pseudoscientific elements, operate more from the ascription of authority to the physician than from solid scientific achievement. Since physicians are trained to believe in surgery as a successful means of therapy, there tends to be a bias toward operating even when the need is not fully validated. In addition, as fashions in treatment change, doctors want to seem up to date, so they may follow the methods of the leading physicians in their community, frequently without objectively comparing treatment options. Finally, physicians often feel, perhaps unrealistically, that their ideas and procedures are sound and will be successful.

RADICAL CRITIQUES OF PREVIOUS CONCEPTUALIZATIONS OF THE INTERACTION

As part of generalized critiques of the U.S. health care system, several social commentators and sociologists (Waitzkin and Waterman, 1974; Carlson, 1975; Illich, 1975; Navarro, 1976, 1980, 1986; Waitzkin, 1983) attack physicians' activities, which they feel support a health care system that exploits society and patients. Most of these critics deny that the physician, despite professional education and training, should have any special power over the patient, particularly since they feel the physician acts in the interests of the capitalistic system, rather than in the interests of the patient.

Capitalist Production and Medicine

The radical critique is aimed at the entire capitalist economic system and its social institutions, of which medicine is presented as one example. Within this context, Illich (1975) suggests that the growing power of the medical profession is a consequence of the industrialization and technical developments of capitalism, which have brought about the medicalization of society. Navarro (1980) is more directly critical: He suggests that the capitalist profit motive is the principal cause of increasing professional power.

These critiques suggest that the health problems in our society are rooted in the wider capitalistic social structure of the United States (Waitzkin, 1983). Consequently, problems of the medical care system can be solved only through a radical restructuring of our society as a whole. It also follows that little can be done to improve or correct problems in the current system so long as health care is delivered within a profit orientation; that is, the most critical change necessary for a less exploitive system is to develop a nonprofit health care system. Such a change is unlikely to occur in the United States because it means that only a complete restructuring of the society would bring about the suggested changes in the health system; only the most naively optimistic would believe that such a restructuring is possible.

Change is particularly difficult because the products of medical technology are controlled by members of the "medical-industrial complex," who determine health care distribution and use. Capitalism defines health services as commodities that can be bought and sold on the market. The radical theorists contend that the physician is drawn into the web of big business as decisions concerning delivery of medical care are taken over by corporate enterprises, which are making enormous profits (McKinlay, 1977; Waitzkin and Waterman, 1974). In one sense, they suggest that physicians function as go-betweens for the commercialization of health as a commodity and are "bought off" by sharing in the profits derived from increasing technology and costs.

According to Navarro (1980, 1986), the capitalistic ideology, which reflects general U.S. thought, is found in every aspect of the ways in which health care is delivered and medical knowledge is advanced. For example, the physician's position as an expert interacting with the nonexpert layperson provides a legitimacy to the authority to demand that the patient use more and more of the industrial health producers' output. This at least partially explains the tremendous costs of, and profits in, the health care system.

Power Relationship

Writers critical of the doctor-patient power relationship take the position that those in powerful positions manipulate the health care system to serve their own interests. A leading spokesman for this point of view is Waitzkin (1983), who maintains that the system serves the dominant elite of society. The physician is seen as a pawn in the manipulation: Power has been placed into the hands of the physician, who serves as a social control agent for those who are benefiting from the present system. Physicians are trustworthy representatives of this policy and can be counted on to make every effort to maintain the existing situation (Navarro, 1986).

Parsons's model of the physician role, with its asymmetrical power relationship between patient and physician, is viewed as a portrait that supports this exploitive situation. It presents a favorable picture of the physician as a figure of authority, without recognizing that the physician is working for the interests of established society and an increasingly expensive health care industry. For example, Waitzkin and Waterman (1974) indicate that Parsons's sick status-role model gives the medical doctor critical power as the most important gatekeeper for entry, which makes the physician a powerful agent of social control. People feeling in physical or mental distress come to the physician for certification of their illness and the right to incumbency in the sick status; the doctor has the right to grant or withhold legitimacy.

In this social control agent status, however, the physician's allegiance may not always be to the patient, or it may be conditional and ambiguous. Thus, the physician's allegiance may be to the society (as in the case of draft board doctors), to a corporation (as in the case of a company doctor), to a trial attorney, or to an insurance company, rather than to the patient. This social control aspect can cause tension between the physician and the patient. At the very least, it jeopardizes the patient's trust in the doctor.

Waitzkin and Waterman feel the role of the physician is similar to that of the judge, the police officer, and the cleric. To Parsons, this control function primarily allows a limited amount of deviance that will not unbalance the system, but to these authors, Parsons fails to see that the conditions leading the patient to consult the physician may be rooted in the system rather than in the patients. In other words, one function of the physician is to "cool out the mark," in the sense of blaming the individual for problems that, more validly, should be attributed to societal malfunctions.

Patient Exploitation

Waitzkin and Waterman (1974) view capitalism as the ideal economic system within which illness may be exploited by those in power positions. Business interests and individual physicians are concerned with their financial position. In this context, health services are goods offered for sale in the marketplace. Particularly important to financial gain is the restricted communication from the physician to the patient and the concomitant power the control of information gives to the doctor. The physician is the sole determinant of many aspects of treatment, with the patient simply assuming that questions cannot or need not be asked. The relationship is established in such a manner that the patient is led to believe that he or she is "in good hands."

This imbalance in knowledge, however, differs according to the patient's position in the social structure. Access to medical care in the United States is dictated to a great extent by the relationship of the patient to the economic system. Physicians are seen as favoring those with larger incomes who can pay for more expensive care (Waitzkin and Waterman, 1974; Navarro, 1986). Entry into the sick status can be manipulated to give special preferences to members of certain favored groups and subcultures.

A CHANGING RELATIONSHIP

By both law and custom, physicians hold authority over medical care, are protected from encroachment into the field by those whom they do not control, and have been granted a mandate that amounts to a virtual monopoly over the care of the sick. According to Jonas (1980), the medical profession dominates health care and gives the system direction, priorities, and ethical tone for four reasons:

First, there is the medical licensing system, which gives physicians control over the health care delivery system's present central functions: making diagnoses, prescribing drugs from a restricted list, and performing surgery. Second, it is the physicians of all health care workers who have the highest level of training in biomedical science, the scientific basis for our modern health care delivery system. Third, because of the peculiarity of the health services market, it is the physician who determines about two-thirds of the total expenditures in the system. Fourth, for most people, the physician is the healer, a role which is almost mystical in its importance to the public. (1980:9–10)

But society shows glimmers of a breakdown in this ready acceptance of the all-powerful medical miracle worker. Although the existence of the physician's power cannot be denied, the legitimacy of that power is increasingly being challenged. A significant, and vocal, minority of the public challenges the proposition that technical expertise or self-sacrificing labors should give doctors a monopoly over the health care system and patients.

Several explanations for this growing challenge have been offered. The most frequent explanation refers to the high cost of medical services and the suspicion that the physician may be avaricious; in essence, the collectivity orientation of physicians is being questioned. Other explanations refer not to the value positions of doctors but to structural changes that have led to the increasing bureaucratization of medicine. We have categorized value and structural explanations under three headings: changing attitudes toward the medical profession, the need for cost containment in health care, and the increasing number of physicians who are now employees of a bureaucratic organization rather than free professionals exercising autonomous power over the treatment situation.

Changing Attitudes

To this point in time, physicians have had a virtual mandate to practice their profession within the health care system as they saw fit. But in the 1970s, economic and moral difficulties within the profession contributed to the emergence of questions about this autonomy (Starr, 1982; Churchill, 1988). Doctors began to "feel the ground shifting" under their feet (Maulitz, 1988).

Haug and Sussman (1969) attribute the emergence of such questioning to broad sociocultural changes that were occurring in society as a whole. They refer to a general "revolt of the client," a "revolt" within which flames were fanned by various rights groups—civil rights, the women's movement, welfare rights, and others—and found expression as a consumer-oriented rights activity. Starr suggests the same process, placing it a few years later: "Medicine, like many other American institutions, suffered a stunning loss of confidence in the 1970s" (1982:379).

Although the general public may accept the stereotypical model of patient-physician interaction, certain segments of the population are particularly critical of the relationship. These are groups that, because of poverty, minority status, gender, or chronic ill health have had less than successful experiences with health professionals. Haug and Sussman (1969) note, for example, that some patients feel that the broadness of physician control over areas of their lives is not relevant to their therapy. Thus, consumer organizations have questioned the extent to which the health system should be allowed access to such personal information as a patient's economic affairs, including information about social security and welfare benefits.

Some who have had contact with the health system are thus becoming part of the consumer movement in the United States, perhaps not in large numbers, but in sufficient strength to make an impact on the delivery of care. Reeder (1972) summarizes the changing pattern by pointing to the new label *consumer* compared with the older label *client*. Clients, calling on any professional, are bringing problems they cannot solve to the expert. "Good" clients follow the advice given by the professional. Consumers, on the other hand, purchase goods or services and may question the quality of such purchases. If the patient is a consumer rather than a client, the whole nature of the relationship between patient and physician is changed. Just as in the marketplace, there is now room for negotiation. Each party brings resources to the "bargaining table." Physicians can claim medical knowledge as well as access to medications and other forms of treatment. But patients bring their own fund of knowledge, the right to go elsewhere for treatment if not satisfied, and the legal requirements that they must be informed about what treatments are proposed and what effects treatment might have. Together, physician as provider and patient as consumer may bargain over the way in which treatment will proceed.

How real, and how important, is such a movement? Haug and Lavin (1981) attempted to test the extent of a consumer orientation toward medicine in terms of both attitude and actual behavior. In a sample of about 500 members of the public and 100 physicians, they found about one-half of the former and more than one-half of the latter hold a consumer orientation. Having an attitude and behaving in response to it, however, are two different things. Measuring consumer behavior as willingness to challenge the physician, Haug and Lavin found that this behavior was based on the past experience of the patient. Those who had been successfully treated for serious debilitating illnesses continued to play the dependent or client role; those with poor experiences with the profession were more likely to play the consumer role and challenge the regimen ordered by the physician. About one-fourth of the physicians surveyed indicated a willingness to accommodate to such a challenge, particularly if it came from a patient with apparent knowledge of medical matters.

It seems that a consumer orientation exists, but its time as an active movement may not have come. Haug and Lavin did find, however, that the young and the better educated patients were more likely to hold such an orientation and act upon it than older, less well-educated patients. This may mean an increase in patient definition of the physician-patient encounter as one of provider-consumer over time, but it is also possible that the orientation will dissipate as the young grow older.

Cost Containment

Starr states that the 1970s opened with an ominous public declaration of a "crisis" in health care. "First and last, this was understood to be a crisis of money" (Starr, 1982:381), as the costs of medical care were "skyrocketing." Initially rooted in financial concerns, specific aspects of the care crisis were generalized as the discussion broadened to other deficiencies in the health care system. Liberal critics looking for ways to bring an agenda of health system problems before the public used the financial emphasis to highlight many other problems with the system. But the spotlight was always on costs and how to contain them.

The problem of financing health care was further emphasized when Medicare and Medicaid became law in 1965. Funding for health care was no longer simply a private matter; it became part of public policy. The budgets of state and federal agencies were affected. But, as the legislation was written, government authorities did not have the right to control costs. The funding system contained neither mechanisms for control nor incentives to be cost-effective.

This state of affairs began to change in the early 1980s (Areen, 1988). As the U.S. economy faced new needs for austerity, health care costs were identified as an area needing control (Bodenheimer, 1989). The physician now had the government as a "partner" in medicine (Maulitz, 1988) because the particular diagnosis and the course of treatment selected led to particular reimbursement amounts. Reimbursement from federal sources was being regulated by managers and economists as well as by physicians themselves. For example, Diagnostic Related Groups (DRGs) were developed to help control charges by the physician. This concept would allow only so many days of hospitalization for a diagnosis that fell into a related group. The payment for a specific DRG is calculated by a formula related to a hospital's payment system. Each case is assigned to a DRG, and service is based on the time and money provided for that diagnostic group regardless of complications.

Prospective Payment Programs (PPPs) limit the amount of money the government will pay for services. Obviously, where the federal government began, private insurance companies were sure to follow. At first, such programs were meant to simplify the process of reimbursing hospitals while controlling the number of patient days, and thus the cost, of given procedures. Medicare and Medicaid have been the largest beneficiaries of the PPPs but, as suggested, all insurance agencies stand to receive aid from this limitation on the amount paid to hospitals for services to patients.

Physicians as Employees

Madison and Konrad (1988) suggest that a revolution in medical care is occurring in U.S. society; it will change the nature of the work of physicians and their relationships to their patients. Many physicians are, in fact, no longer free practitioners—they work for corporations that manage health care (see Starr, 1982). These corporations prefer employees who will hold costs in line, irrespective of whether they are clerks or physicians.

Perhaps the prototype of the medical corporation is the Health Maintenance Organization (HMO), in which the physician occupies a main status in a prepaid vertically integrated health care facility. One feature of such prepaid plans is the increased bureaucratization of medical care; the physician is no longer a "friend of the family" but is the employee of an organization that the patient has already paid for services. The patient is thus not so much a client seeking professional advice as a consumer of the services provided by the physician-employees of the program. As indicated previously, within the consumer orientation a person is more likely to want to evaluate the worth of the service, as the purchaser of any product may question the quality of the merchandise bought.

SUMMARY

This chapter focused on sociological discussions of the interaction between doctor and patient. Four models of the doctor-patient relationship were presented, one that emphasizes types of possible interaction, another that focuses on the sociocultural context of the association, and a third that deals with the "negotiation of reality" between incumbents of the two statuses. But primary attention was given to the fourth description, the provocative and controversial model of the doctor's role orientations presented by Parsons in 1951.

Parsons's model describes the physician's orientation toward the patient as affectively neutral, concerned only with specific aspects of the medical condition, universalistic in treating all patients alike, and practiced on the basis of achieved knowledge, with all decisions made and actions taken for the good of the patient and society. Parsons views the patient-physician relationship as an action-oriented one. The physician is expected to use knowledge and skill for the good of the patient, and the patient is expected to put total trust in the physician.

Many sociologists feel that Parsons's model presents an incorrect description. Some deny the harmonious doctor-patient relationship implied by his model, claiming instead that the association should be understood as one based on conflict. In his discussion of the physician's role and the physician-patient relationship, Freidson rejects a description indicating a neat, harmonious, mutually accepted relationship in which a powerful physician dictates to a powerless patient. Instead, he sees a clash of perspectives, with each party emphasizing his or her own needs, interests, and ideas. Freidson also views the physician as an entrepreneur seeking out new conditions or behaviors that can be labeled as sickness. Starr suggests that physicians and patients have contradictory expectations of each other. He attacks Parsons's assumption of the collectivity orientation of physicians, and states that Parsons ignores both the structure of medicine and the collegial bond between doctors. Parsons fails to take account of the sizeable incomes of physicians and their willingness to overlook the mistakes of colleagues.

In a series of radical critiques, several social commentators and sociologists attack the total health care system in the United States, especially because of its capitalistic base. Radical sociologists have asked whether the physician acts more in the interest of society than of the patient, using capitalist values to determine the disposition of patient complaints. By the manipulation of communication on the basis of status characteristics, the physician exploits the patient. According to some radical theorists, physicians are being transformed into agents for promoting the increasingly expensive products of the health care industry. They are seen as pawns in the system, members of an occupation who have been given power to serve as social control agents for those who are benefiting from the present system.

But society is showing a glimmer of a breakdown in this all-encompassing power of the physician. Changing attitudes on the part of the public seem to be arising, with a new consumer attitude that changes the definition of the physician-patient relationship to one of provider-consumer. This is, perhaps, an outgrowth of the severe criticisms that have been voiced about the ever-increasing costs of health care in the United States. Initial criticism focused on costs, but as this was brought into the open as a social problem, the critique was broadened to include other problems of the health system.

The changing relationship between the physician and the patient and society is also related to important changes that are taking place in the profession itself. There is a rapidly growing number of physicians who are becoming employees of bureaucratic organizations, rather than practicing as free professionals who exercise autonomous power over the treatment situation. Some observers refer to this change as "a revolution in medical care" that is occurring in U.S. society. Many physicians now work for corporations that manage health care. As employees, they find they must give up much of the autonomy that is characteristic of private practice.

References

Anderson, W. T., and D. T. Helm. 1979. "The physician-patient encounter: A process of reality negotiation." In *Patients, Physicians, and Illness*, 3rd ed., ed. E. G. Jaco, 259–271. New York: Free Press.

Areen, Judith. 1988. "Legal intrusions on physician independence." In *The Physician as Captain of the Ship: A Critical Reappraisal*, ed. N. King, L. Churchill, and A. W. Cross, 39–65. Dordrecht, Holland: D. Reidel Publishing.

Balint, Michael. 1957. *The Doctor, His Patient and The Illness*. New York: International Universities Press.

Bloom, Samuel W. 1963. *The Doctor and His Patient*. New York: Russell Sage Foundation.

Bodenheimer, Thomas S. 1989. "The fruits of empire rot on the vine: United States health policy in the austerity era." *Social Science and Medicine* 28 (6):531–538.

Carlson, Rick J. 1975. *The End of Medicine*. New York: Wiley.

Churchill, Larry R. 1988. "Introduction." In *The Physician as Captain of the Ship: A Critical Reappraisal*, ed. N. King, L. Churchill, and A. W. Cross, i–xx. Dordrecht, Holland: D. Reidel Publishing.

Freidson, Eliot. 1970. *Profession of Medicine*. New York: Dodd, Mead.

Haug, Marie R., and Bebe Lavin. 1981. "Practitioner or patient—Who's in charge?" *Journal of Health and Social Behavior* 22(September):212–229.

Haug, Marie R., and Marvin B. Sussman. 1969. "Professional autonomy and the revolt of the client." *Social Problems* 17(Fall):153–161.

Illich, Ivan. 1975. *Medical Nemesis: The Expropriation of Health*. London: Calder and Boyces.

Jonas, Steven. 1980. "The Need for Preventive and Community Medicine Faculty in Schools of Medicine." Mimeographed. Hyattsville, Md: Office of Graduate Medical Education, Health Resources Administration, U.S. Public Health Service.

McKinlay, John B. 1977. "The business of good doctoring or doctoring as good business." *International Journal of Health Services* 7(3):459–483.

Madison, Donald L., and Thomas R. Konrad. 1988. "Large medical group-practice organizations and employed physicians: A relationship in transition." *Milbank Memorial Fund Quarterly* 66(2):240–282.

Maulitz, Russell C. 1988. "The physician and authority: A historical reappraisal." In *The Physician as Captain of the Ship: A Critical Reappraisal*, ed. N. King, L. Churchill, and A. W. Cross, 3–21. Dordrecht, Holland: D. Reidel Publishing.

Navarro, Vicente. 1976. *Medicine Under Capitalism.* New York: Prodist.

———. 1980. "Work, ideology and science: The case of medicine." *Social Science and Medicine* 14C(September):191–206.

———. 1986. *Crisis, Health, and Medicine: A Social Critique.* New York: Tavistock.

Parsons, Talcott. 1951. *The Social System.* Glencoe, Ill.: Free Press.

———. 1975. "The sick role and the role of the physician reconsidered." *Milbank Memorial Fund Quarterly/Health and Society* 53:257–277.

Reeder, Leo G. 1972. "The patient-client as consumer: Some observations on the changing professional-client relationship." *Journal of Health and Social Behavior* 13(December):406–412.

Roemer, M., ed. 1960. *Henry E. Sigerist on the Sociology of Medicine.* New York: M. D. Publications.

Starr, Paul. 1982. *The Social Transformation of American Medicine.* New York: Basic Books.

Szasz, Thomas, and Marc H. Hollender. 1956. "The basic models of the doctor-patient relationship." *Archives of Internal Medicine* 97:585–592.

Waitzkin, Howard B. 1983. *The Second Sickness.* New York: Free Press.

Waitzkin, Howard B., and Barbara Waterman. 1974. *The Exploitation of Illness in Capitalist Society.* Indianapolis: Bobbs-Merrill.

7

Nursing and Other Health Occupations

INTRODUCTION

The health care system of the United States is one of the country's most important employers. In 1987, 7.5 percent of the U.S. work force, that is, 8.5 million people, were employed in health service facilities; 4.4 million of these employees were working in hospitals and 1.3 million were on the staff of nursing and personal care facilities (National Center for Health Statistics, 1989). Data compiled in 1986 indicate that 1.6 million registered nurses and more than one-half million physicians were working in the system (Bureau of Health Professions, 1986; National Center for Health Statistics, 1989). Members of other occupations employed in the health care system are administrators, licensed practical nurses, ancillary nursing personnel, medical record administrators, pharmacists, medical technologists, dietitians, occupational therapists, physical therapists, social workers, physician assistants, doctors of osteopathy, doctors of chiropractics, dentists, and large numbers of housekeeping, laundry, dietary, and maintenance workers.

Space limitations make it impossible to discuss all health occupations, so we will discuss only nurses, physician assistants, pharmacists, social workers, physical and occupational therapists, doctors of osteopathy, doctors of chiropractics, dentists, podiatrists, optometrists, and folk practitioners. Discussion will thus center on the largest group of personnel, those in nursing service, and on two institutionalized alternatives to the medical doctor, three practitioners who maintain independence and authority in fee-for-service offices, and healers who base their practice on pseudoscientific premises.

NURSING

The wide variety of health occupations is categorized according to their extent of dependence on the physician for occupational activities. If the occupations are classified in this way, a large segment of the health care hierarchy can be visualized as a pyramid. At the top is the physician; the next layer is occupied by nurses and such other highly trained personnel as pharmacists, physical therapists, and dietitians. Below this level is an army of support workers who keep the health care system functioning.

In the hospital, the nurse manages the patient care team under the authority of the physician, who is the prime decision maker. Under the nurse's authority in this hierarchical structure come ancillary personnel who usually perform middle-ground functions of health care and employees who carry out lower level work.

Occupation or Profession?

Nurses, like the practitioners of several other health care occupations, would like to be viewed as professionals, but find it difficult to obtain this image because of the medical profession's dominance. Nevertheless, a large proportion of nurses, especially those with bachelor's degrees, consider themselves professionals. We will use the term *semiprofessional* when referring to nursing because nurses almost always work in situations in which they are subordinate to physicians and do not have full control of their work; such control is one of the elements by which professional status is usually judged.

Although nurses have some independent decision-making rights and dominance over other health workers when taking charge of bedside care, they are still carrying out the orders of the doctor. Thus, occupants of the status are simultaneously in a position of subordination and domination—subordinate to the doctor and superordinate to the other statuses of nursing service. Such a combination suggests that the term *semiprofessional* is appropriate. This is consistent with sociologist Etzioni (1969), who refers to practitioners in occupations such as social work, teaching, and nursing as semiprofessionals because, even though they bear most of the attributes of a profession, they do not possess functional autonomy.

In another view of positions in the health care system, Pavalko (1971) describes a continuum that runs from occupations to professions. At one end of the continuum, he suggests several characteristics of a professional occupational grouping: a body of theory and intellectual technique, social values and concerns, a lengthy and involved program of training, complete autonomy over work, a sense of commitment to the task, a feeling of community with others in the field, and commitment to a code of ethics. At the other end, an occupation lacks these characteristics.

Using this approach to clarify the status of nursing, Lambert and Lambert (1989) suggest that the position is mixed, having both professional and occupational characteristics. They conclude that the nurse is very near the professional end of the continuum when social values and ethics are considered and near the midpoint with respect to theory and intellectual technique, period of training, and occupational commitment. When autonomy over work and feeling of community are considered, however, nursing is placed at the occupational end of the continuum.

Iglehart (1987) also indicates that nursing has both professional and occupational characteristics. He attributes this mixed position to difficulties faced by nursing in shedding its traditional image, which places the occupation under the control of the medical profession. In another accounting of the mixture, Hardy (1987) suggests that the educational experience encourages students to think of nursing as a goal-oriented occupation in which practitioners are responsible for developing plans for individual patient care, which frees them from the medical model. But he also suggests that this has become so mechanistic it is hard to see nursing functions as professional activities, rather than simple routinized work.

To a large extent, the baccalaureate degree has provided some nurses with leverage in the development of a professional image. No regulation requires such education, and the monetary incentive to pursue a degree beyond the training necessary for certification is small; there is usually no differential between the salaries received by degree and nondegree nurses. Nevertheless, many established nurses who received their training in hospitals enter programs to obtain the bachelor's degree (Lethbridge, 1989) because they can then see themselves as more professional. Research focusing on associate-degree nurses finds that most chose this route to the occupation because it is the quickest and least expensive, but feel that they will need a baccalaureate degree to achieve their full potential as nurses (Williams, 1989).

An underlying problem is that nursing lacks a clear definition of its scope and domain. The image of the nurse as "physician's helper" is not a clear job description, yet this is what the public and many in the health occupations think of when asked for a statement of the nurse's contributions to patient care. A far more satisfactory description of nursing functions would focus on the relationship between the nurse and the patient. Following this emphasis, the unique function of the nurse becomes that of assisting people to perform activities that will eventually contribute to their physical and psychological well-being, and of caring for patients with the goal of returning them to independent functioning as soon as possible (Ellis and Hartley, 1988).

With limited exceptions, however, physicians determine the pattern of activities in the nurse's work. Pankratz and Pankratz (1974) state that this lack of autonomy and the asymmetry in the doctor-nurse relationship handicaps any attempt to develop a truly professional conception of the nursing role. All this reinforces the "physician's assistant" image, but it can also be said that nurses themselves often see their roles in this fashion. They are available to perform basic medical tasks that the doctor does not have the time or inclination to do.

The roles that have traditionally been assigned to the nurse are a major obstacle to the emergence of a clear-cut nursing role independent of the physician's domination. Many nurses feel that, by working closely with the physician, the prestige of that status will somehow be reflected on theirs. This, however, adds to the ambiguous position of the nurse.

The Development of Nursing

Early Images.   Ellis and Hartley (1988) discuss three historical images of nurses and nursing as an occupation before the nineteenth century. The first of these was the *folk image* in which nursing activity was perceived as an inborn skill and practitioners were identified with superstition and magic. Nursing was not viewed by the public as a professional occupation.

The second historical image was the *religious image*. As a specific and independent status-role, nursing can be traced back to the time of the rise of Christianity. For centuries, Catholic sisters carried the major share of the nursing workload and few secular women, other than some disreputable ones, engaged in the occupation. Conditions in hospitals in the early days were so bad it took an act of charity just to work there. Members of monastic orders (males) were also involved in nursing. Because of this religious background, nurses are still referred to as "sisters" in some countries.

In areas where the Protestant Reformation succeeded, a substitute occupation did not develop when the monastic orders were dissolved. The care of patients in the hospital was considered suitable only for women from the lower classes, and nursing took on the third historical image, that of *servant*. Much of the nurse's work, during what Ellis and Hartley (1988) refer to as "the dark ages of nursing," was performed by prostitutes and prisoners.

Transformation of Traditional Images.   Florence Nightingale, a British nurse, is credited with bringing about a major shift in the public perception of nursing, from the "dark" early images to a place of honor and service in the community. After being trained as a nurse in Germany, Nightingale returned to her native England and established a hospital for "gentlewomen," staffing it with trained young ladies from "decent" families. She maintained that nursing should be a respectable occupation for the daughters of upper and middle-class families.

When the Crimean War broke out, Nightingale organized a contingent of women who provided nursing services to soldiers. This presented an ideal opportunity to demonstrate the quality of good nursing through practical action. After facing much difficulty in receiving acceptance, she finally convinced the military authorities that the high quality nursing being offered was beneficial to the wounded. Nightingale and her fellow nurses then received much positive publicity from the press, who labeled them "angels of mercy," a major turnaround in the public's perception of nurses. When the war ended, she established a school of nursing at St. Thomas's Hospital in London, which was so successful that, in a few years, her system became the model for all such training. As Cockerham (1989:216) puts it: "Nightingale's approach to nursing training emphasized a code of behavior that idealized nurses as being responsible, clean, self-sacrificing, courageous, cool headed, hard working, obedient to the physician, and possessing the tender qualities of the mother; this idealized portrayal of nurses saw them as nothing less than 'disciplined angels.' " Cockerham goes on to note that these qualities come close to those required for a good mother or housekeeper, a drawback to nursing's attempts to achieve recognition as a profession.

Ellis and Hartley (1988) indicate that Florence Nightingale's major contribution to the changed and positive image of nursing was a strong emphasis on education. She believed that nurses should be educated in teaching hospitals. She also emphasized that the nurse was a skilled person caring for patients and should not be used for mundane and unskilled tasks such as cleaning the wards. Nightingale's image of nurses was that of intelligent women using their abilities to improve patient care by continuing with education throughout their lives.

Rosenberg (1987) reminds us that Nightingale's movement did not take place in a vacuum. The new image and specialization confronted an already established world of hospital work and well-defined authority. The new nursing was allowed to enter the entrenched situation because it promised to produce a nursing corps that was skilled and reliable and that acted with intelligence. It was recognized that this corps would improve the quality of hospital programs.

The Nightingale nurses were women. To those living in this era, women were more capable of taking on the tasks of nursing, as they were seen as more sensitive and warm and thus able to reassure patients, even as they brought greater cleanliness and order to patient care activities. As a result of such attitudes, nursing became one of the few socially acceptable occupations women from respectable backgrounds could pursue (Rosenberg, 1987).

But the woman's place was still defined by dominant males. Consequently, although the model offered by Nightingale was extremely important for public and professional acceptance, it also established nursing as a mother-surrogate role. New generations of nurses wanted professional status, but the mother-surrogate perception had to be changed because such a role was not technically specialized and allowed little room for occupational autonomy (Schulman, 1979).

Roads to Nursing

Nursing students come mainly from the lower and middle classes (Mauksch, 1972); they also tend to come from smaller cities or communities. Minorities remain underrepresented in nursing. Racial and ethnic minorities comprise approximately 20 percent of the population of the United States, but only 7.2 percent of nurses come from these groupings (Crawford and Olinger, 1988).

Although motivations for becoming a nurse vary, some generalizations can be made. Most studies conclude that those who choose nursing as a career have a strong service orientation. For example, O'Neill (1973) found that nursing students were much more concerned with helping others than were fellow students in other educational programs. Also, nursing students emphasize service over self-expression, an attitude that lessens competitiveness, individual development, and a desire for recognition (Simpson, 1979). As a result of this orientation, most have little sense of long-term career goals (such as becoming a supervisor or faculty member). Rather, they indicate a desire to develop close relationships with patients. Thus, student nurses express attitudes that fit well with the traditional image of nursing. This service orientation is crucial in determining whether given students will finish the nursing course and whether they will continue with the occupation after graduation. The development of a professional image has also been found to influence whether the nurse continues in the occupation.

Rothrock (1989) studied students specializing in surgical nursing and compared them with others, in the same curriculum, who had not received such focused education. She found that such specialized training was essential to the development of a professional image. Other researchers also found that nursing students were less likely to develop such an image when the curriculum did not emphasize clinical experience (Carroll, 1989).

Educational Programs

A major issue among nurses today concerns the nature of their education programs. Currently three different identifiable tracks lead to registered nurse certification. Each track has a different length of time for training, and each provides a different level of educational preparation. Further, each program socializes its students toward a different image of the nursing role (Iglehart, 1987).

Diploma Programs.   Hospitals were the original nursing education institutions. Graduates of hospital nursing programs are certified nurses who possess diplomas rather than educational degrees. These programs, usually three years long, emphasize a practical, doctor-association role for nurses. This is particularly significant because the graduates of diploma programs have been most prevalent in the occupation. These programs were popular, partially because the students were inexpensive and disciplined workers who provided a great deal of free work to the hospital (Rosenberg, 1987). Until 1971, more than one-half of the nurses graduating each year were products of hospital training, but such programs have declined steadily since then. Thus, 721 diploma programs existed in 1968 but only 209 remained in 1987 (Rosenfeld, 1988).

The socialization philosophy of the diploma program, which places the nurse into a subservient relationship with doctors, is usually consistent with the physician's view of nursing. The philosophy also incorporates institutional goals and needs. As a consequence, the nurses may work well for the institution, but are not likely to be involved in the fight for professional recognition. Relatively low social status is attached to this type of training within the occupation itself, and the level of career commitment among these nurses is correspondingly low.

Associate-Degree Programs.   In response to a perceived shortage of nurses, nursing education programs were started in fast-growing junior and community colleges during the 1950s. After successfully attending such a program for two years, the student receives both official certification as a registered nurse and an associate of arts degree. Simpson (1979) comments that nursing educators preferred this approach to hospital diploma programs because they were under the control of educational institutions. Some nursing leaders hoped that the associate-degree approach would replace diploma programs. Nurses in associate-degree programs were trained to give technical care, to stay close to the patient's bedside, and not move into administrative or teaching positions.

Associate-degree graduates are fast overtaking diploma-school students (Rosenfeld, 1988); they are presently the fastest growing segment of nursing education. Since 1978, 123 associate-degree programs have been approved, leading to a total number of 789 in 1987. Rather than eliminating diploma nurses, such programs have added yet one more layer of claimants to the title of registered nurse.

Baccalaureate Programs.   The increasingly important road to nursing certification is the baccalaureate degree. These degree programs grew rapidly after World War II as part of the general move to give a more professional character to nursing. It was thought that degree-program graduates would eventually replace diploma-school graduates, who were viewed as being trained but not educated.

It was also hoped by the professionally oriented that the prestige of a college degree would upgrade the status of the registered nurse. In addition, those nurses interested in upgrading the occupation saw this as a way of emphasizing the distinction between the "professional" registered nurse and nursing service personnel who lacked professionally oriented formal education.

Baccalaureate programs are becoming increasingly important to nursing service in this country. Thus, between 1980 and 1986, the number of diploma and associate-degree nurses increased by 15.4 percent, but the number with a bachelor's degree increased by 49.3 percent. The proportion of registered nurses with a bachelor's degree increased from 28.6 percent to 34.2 percent in six years (National Center for Health Statistics, 1989). With regard to baccalaureate education, Simpson (1979:93) comments, "The movement was aimed at gaining full academic status for nursing within the structure of the university so as to give nursing the freedom to develop its own programs apart from hospital administration. Leaders of the movement felt that in this way nursing education could be upgraded to prepare 'professional' nurses."

In 1988 there were 467 baccalaureate programs in the United States. The baccalaureate program usually takes four or five years, the normal time it takes to obtain any bachelor's degree with, perhaps, the addition of one more year. General education courses are added to the technical courses that comprise a large part of nursing education. The program combines the usual nurse's training and the usual educational requirements of a college undergraduate education. Graduates have been taught how to take care of patients, but they can also lay claim to the prestige of being college graduates.

Licensed Practical Nurse Programs.   Licensed practical nurses make up a level of nursing service personnel different from those already discussed. The licensed practical or vocational nurse is trained under the supervision of the registered nurse or the physician, usually for approximately ninety days. The educational level is that of a beginning junior college program or an extension of high school. The work of the licensed practical nurse is supervised by nurses. Consequently, licensed practical nurses have little prestige, and they exhibit a low commitment to the occupation.

Problems in Nursing Education.   Simpson (1979:96) summarizes the rather confused division of labor resulting from several layers of nursing service personnel:

> *A four-way differentiation internally stratifying nursing service has been occurring. Aides, orderlies and attendants are at the bottom. Practical nurses are over them and immediately under registered nurses. Baccalaureate education is adding a layer of degree-holding nurses above nondegree registered nurses. The direction of development of the baccalaureate movement has been to upgrade nursing education while holding on to the ideology and traditions of nursing, thereby ensuring an elite corps of nurses for the top positions in nursing service.*

With such a variety of training programs, it is not surprising to find that some authors refer to the situation in nursing education as chaotic (Fagin, McClure, and Schlotfeldt, 1976).

Two major reports in 1948 attempted to outline nursing's problems and to suggest solutions (Brown, 1948; Ginzburg, 1948). In general, both studies recommended that there should be only two levels of nursing: the professional nurse and the practical nurse. The basic proposal was to abolish the registered nurse category and replace it with that of professional nurse, to develop the practical nurse category, and to focus nursing education programs toward one or the other of these positions. The professional nurse would have academic and professional training suitable for administrative duties, planning, and nursing education. The practical nurse would be trained to perform duties at the patient's bedside under the direction of the physician or the professional nurse.

According to Fagin, McClure, and Schlotfeldt (1976), the nursing profession responded to these recommendations by doing almost the exact opposite. Two major steps taken from 1950 to 1970 had a significant impact on the occupation: the development of associate-degree programs and an expansion of practical nursing programs. The chaos was compounded by an expansion of university-related baccalaureate programs aimed at producing professional nurses, who were socialized to function as professionals, with expectations that other health statuses would respond in kind.

A very serious problem for the professionally oriented is that state laws permit any registered nurse, regardless of education type, to perform essentially the same kinds of tasks. Associate-degree nurses have added to the problem because they are specifically trained to take over the bedside duties of baccalaureate nurses, who could then become administrators, planners, and teachers. But the need for large numbers of trained nurses and the tendency of hospital administrators to ignore the differences among types of nurses has led to the use of the associate and the baccalaureate graduates in essentially the same way (Hogstel, 1977; Miller, 1974).

The trend toward baccalaureate education as a goal has created other problems. As Reed (1979) suggests, one is the uneven levels of baccalaureate training programs. Many universities developed rigorous and meaningful plans of education for the professional nurse, but others used this as an opportunity to add another program and more students to their programs to inflate student numbers. The quality of nurses coming from baccalaureate programs, therefore, varies considerably.

Another problem stems from the academic setting of nursing education. Theoretically, the move to the academic unit should provide nursing with more autonomy. In many settings, however, the nursing program is subsumed under another academic unit, frequently the medical school, which dominates it, putting the nursing program into a subservient position. This defeats the use of education to enhance the professional aspirations of the baccalaureate nurse. It starts nursing off in a not-so-subtle position dominated by the medical profession, which has the opposite effect of that desired by the professionally oriented nurse.

Self-Images

Nurses hold distinctly different images of their occupation. Indeed, some are diametrically opposed. For example, sociologists analyzing the work orientations of nurses in different situations several years ago concluded that there are three nursing-role self-conceptions: the *utilizer*, the *traditionalizer*, and the *professionalizer* (Habenstein and Christ, 1963).

Those who define nursing primarily as a job for pay are referred to as utilizers. Nurses subscribing to this self-image exhibit little commitment to the occupation and are likely to drop out of the occupation at some time. The traditionalizer is committed to nursing work, viewing it as a personal rather than an occupational goal; the Florence Nightingale image is glorified. The idealistic traditions of nursing probably attracted this person to the occupation. The professionalizer nurse is oriented toward the collective ideals of the occupation in its push toward professionalism. Such a nurse is working toward change in work activities. Baccalaureate nurses are most likely to see nursing in this light. Those speaking to their colleagues about professionalizing the occupation may face worse than resistance; they may face an incredulous audience that overtly agrees with the physician's image of the occupation.

Research indicates that these descriptions of nurses' self-conceptions continues (Dagenais and Meleis, 1982; Marshall, 1988). But Brotherton (1988) disagrees; her research with nurses indicates a lack of consensus about these self-concepts. She suggests that one dimension best describes the nursing role: the bureaucrat. If this is valid, it certainly provides an indication of trends in nursing and in the health care system.

Professionalization

We previously suggested that a strain toward professionalization characterizes semi-professional occupations such as nursing. But this desire for professional status is not found among all subgroupings within the occupation. Some nurses are strongly committed to gaining a more professional status, and others have little or no interest in such matters. Further, there are pushes toward and pulls away from professional status within the work setting. Herein lies several of the problems for the professionalization of the nursing occupation.

The work setting is particularly important. Most nursing takes place in the hospital or in hospital-like institutions, so nurses can rarely be independent. They are clearly dominated by physicians who control medical decisions and who have no interest in the nurse's push toward a professional status. The physicians give medical orders that must be followed; this is all that counts to the doctor.

Wolinsky (1988) calls attention to other factors that make it difficult for nurses to claim professional status. First, the nature of the socialization process nurses experience during their student years emphasizes a role of subordination to the physician. Second, the public image of the nurse is that of a helper rather than of an independent worker. Third, nursing is largely a female occupation in a society in which the clearest professional occupations, doctor and lawyer, are dominated by males. And fourth, physicians perceive nurses as helpers rather than as decision makers.

This is not to imply, however, that a more professional position is impossible for nursing. Nursing education, especially with regard to the baccalaureate program, is changing in a way that holds promise for a more professional stance for nursing in the future. In general, emphasis on the quality and quantity of education is seen as the most important indication that nursing is ready to move into the status of a profession. Nursing educators have, in fact, sought to make a distinction between the technical and the professional nurse, a distinction based largely on education. Still, these distinctions are not strongly felt in the actual practice of nursing, and the perception of nursing as a dependent occupation still plagues those nurses working for professional status (van Maanen, 1979).

Expanded Roles

Three factors encourage the nursing role to expand so it includes more responsibility and autonomy in the care of the patient, which clearly affects the move toward professional status. The first factor involves the feeling on the part of many health workers, including many physicians, that nurses have more capabilities than are being used. That is, they accept that nurses' training, particularly that received in baccalaureate degree programs, equips them to carry out more health care tasks than they are currently performing.

Second, perceived physician shortages combined with an actual maldistribution of physicians have led to the consideration of extending nursing into somewhat autonomous situations of patient care. A registered nurse practitioner status has developed. The extension of nursing services into practice also was thought to be a way to provide care for those living in rural areas and the inner city, where doctors tend to be in short supply. Nurses in practice are also seen as able to provide services for poorly served segments of the total population, for example, the elderly (Office of Technology Assessment, 1986).

Third, attempts to raise the prestige and increase the skills of nursing through education have played an important part in the movement toward professionalization. A significant trend in the occupation is the continual increase in nurse specialization, often interpreted as a move toward professional status, which has provided more opportunities for nurses to take on skilled activities. Among the nursing specialties that have become part of the position are health nurses, nurse anesthetists, community health practitioners, emergency department nurse practitioners, occupational health nurses, nurse midwives, and nurse practitioners.

The convergence of these factors established new and expanding nursing roles, which go under such titles as nurse practitioner, nurse associate, clinical nurse specialist, and nurse clinician. The use of the term *nurse practitioner* seems to have originated with a program for pediatric nurses at the University of Colorado in 1965 (Levine, 1977). It refers to nurses who carry out limited medical care activities after having completed specially designed educational courses in anatomy, physiology, and clinical applications beyond the minimum requirements for registered nurse licensing. Although educational requirements for nurses in such expanded roles vary from state to state, with length of additional training ranging from three months to two years, nurse practitioners throughout the United States generally learn the same skills. Depending upon specialization differences, the tasks learned generally include such simple primary care activities as taking medical histories, giving routine physical examinations, and ordering laboratory tests. In some medical facilities, a patient with a routine health problem may be treated by the nurse practitioner alone, although a physician is still responsible for the intervention decision and treatment regimen prescribed by the nurse.

Reviews of the work of nurse practitioners have been favorable. They are reported to assist patients with acute illnesses as effectively as physicians and to prescribe medications (with physician responsibility) accurately. Nurse practitioners have been found to have better communication skills than physicians and to spend more time with their patients. Both patients and physicians appear to be satisfied with their work. Physician acceptance depends upon the individual physician and the complexity of the task performed by the nurse practitioners (Office of Technology Assessment, 1986).

The large majority of nurses are women, which affects the acceptance of the nurse practitioner as a health professional. Horman, Campbell, and DeGregory (1987) studied stereotypes associated with gender and the degree to which the status of a health care provider would be correctly identified. They found such evaluations were based on the sex of the worker; the status of the male practitioner was correctly identified more often than that of the female worker. The researchers conclude that, in health care as in other fields, women are less likely to be seen as holding higher status than men.

The full development of such an occupational role has obstacles, however. One is the psychological barrier resulting from the traditional shape of the physician-nurse relationship. The mindset that sees the nurse in a subordinate role is as much in the perception of the nurse as it is in that of the physician, and this inhibits the development of expanded roles. There are also some tangible barriers, such as the legal practice acts for nursing (Bullough, 1976). These barriers have been torn down to some extent, however; thirty states have amended their nursing practice acts to allow an extension of nursing responsibilities, although legal restrictions are still placed upon them by some states.

The nurse practitioner position will be more successfully introduced into a health system in which the position of the physician is not threatened by the new status-role. In a study conducted by Burkett, Parken-Harris, Kuhn, and Escovitz (1978), it was found that the majority of nurse practitioners felt it was proper for them to work under the supervision of physicians; the nurses in the study also believed more tasks were appropriate for the nurse practitioner than did the physician. Nurse practitioners seem to be incorporated more easily into institutions where physicians play a minor role in administration than into solo or group practice (Zammuto et al., 1979). In any setting, the new health professionals felt they should be allowed more occupational latitude (Barr, 1979). Another solution may be acceptable to all: to recognize that the doctor is solely responsible for the medical care of the hospitalized patient—no one wants to challenge this domination—but that the professional nurse is responsible for the bedside care of the hospitalized patient, another domination no one will challenge.

OTHER HEALTH OCCUPATIONS

Physician Assistants

The physician assistant status was developed in response to a demand for health personnel with enough education and training to supplement the work of the medical doctor. Unlike nurse practitioners, physician assistants are not trained in nursing service duties. The training program specifically focuses on ways of helping physicians in their medical work. Thus, whereas the nurse practitioner position is an expansion of the nursing role, the physician assistant status constitutes a new occupation.

Physician assistants usually receive their training in two-year programs that provide both formal teaching and clinical experience. Some four-year programs have been developed in conjunction with obtaining a baccalaureate degree. Physician assistants are trained to assist physicians in such areas as diagnostics, evaluation, monitoring, counseling, and referral. But other than the generalization that they assist physicians, their specific occupational duties are unclear, which means that duties vary with the demands of the situation. Many physician assistants work with family physicians or doctors specializing in internal medicine, and many others work in the hospital (Division of Allied Health Education and Accreditation, 1989).

Physician assistants seem to be more readily accepted by physicians than are nurse practitioners, possibly because their role is that of assistant rather than independent practitioner. In one Kaiser-Permanente program it was found that the number of physician assistants used has increased, whereas the number of nurse practitioners has not (Record and Greenlick, 1975). The major factor for this pattern seems to be physician perceptions of the two statuses: Physician assistants are viewed as taking over menial work from the physician, whereas nurse practitioners are perceived as replacing the physician in certain duties.

Recent research (Ferraro and Southerland, 1989) produced mixed findings on doctor acceptance of both physician assistants and nurse practitioners. The professional dominance of the physician has an important effect on the acceptance of statuses that are defined as assistants, rather than as independent. Physician extenders are most likely to be seen as providing greater opportunity for good health care when they are located in areas where doctors are not interested in practicing, such as in the inner city and in rural areas.

Pharmacists

Approximately 161,500 pharmacists were practicing in the United States in 1986 (National Center for Health Statistics, 1989). The occupation is increasingly important, as suggested by a rise in numbers per 100,000 people in this country: This figure was 55.4 in 1970 and 67.1 in 1986. The training period for pharmacists is a minimum of five years, after which the graduate receives a baccalaureate degree. Six-year educational programs grant the student the doctor of pharmacy degree. Pharmacy training is mostly in the areas of chemistry and pharmacology, including the composition of medications and expected body reactions to their administration. Training to be a pharmacist includes one or two years of preprofessional work. Most schools of pharmacy now include courses in clinical practice in which students are brought into contact with patients, physicians, and other members of the health care team.

Pharmacists may practice in hospitals, clinics, nursing homes, pharmaceutical companies, drugstores, and academic settings; the vast majority operate or work in community pharmacies or drugstores. In these work settings, the pharmacist deals directly with consumers, but in doing so, the pharmacist is almost always following the written orders of a physician. The doctor issues orders in the form of a prescription, and the patient selects the pharmacist who will fill it. The pharmacist is clearly in an entrepreneurial role centered on pleasing customers by making their association pleasant.

Periodically, pharmacists have made overtures toward acquiring a professional image; this is often through such activities as increased emphasis on clinical pharmacy, which would give practitioners a role in therapy decision making (Birenbaum, 1982). But the occupation faces two seemingly insurmountable obstacles: the dominant position of the physician and the entrepreneurial situation within which most practice.

Social Workers

Social work is different from most of the other health occupations discussed in this chapter because most of its practitioners attend college beyond the usual four years, to obtain a master's degree. Many nurses do not hold a college degree, and almost all who have had a college education stop at the baccalaureate level; many physician assistants have only two years of training beyond the high school diploma; most pharmacists hold only a bachelor's degree; and most occupational therapists stop their formal education with their first college degree. To become a social worker in most institutions, however, a two-year study program after completing the bachelor's degree (in a few cases, one year) leads to the master of social work degree. Some bachelor's-degree-level social work programs do exist, but they have not had much influence on the general training and education programs for social work. This graduate degree status gives most social workers an edge in their claim for recognition as professionals.

Most social workers are employed by welfare agencies that have little direct relationship with the health care system. Health problems of clients may bring them in direct contact with the health system, but not as employees. Those employed in the health system, some in community hospitals and others in psychiatric settings, are known as either medical social workers or psychiatric social workers. Whenever they have contact with the health system, social workers are expected to work under the authority of the physician, which would weaken any claims to professional status despite their advanced college degrees; we consequently look upon social workers as semiprofessionals.

The occupation faces an additional problem with regard to a professional image: no clear definition of who shall be allowed to call themselves social workers. Although the National Association of Social Workers attempts to limit the title to those with the master's degree or at least the bachelor's degree, some of those hired as social workers have degrees in fields that have little or nothing to do with the actual work. Social work organizations have been requesting mandatory licensing, but only a few states have passed laws to this effect.

In the medical setting, social work is in a position similar to that of nursing. Social workers have contact with both patients and families to help bring about proper adjustment to disability, long-term illness, or other problems related to disability. Often their only association with doctors is to provide information about the family that may be relevant to the disease and its treatment. Much to their chagrin, some hospitals still use social workers mainly to do "financial planning," a euphemism for helping them collect bills.

A hospital expecting full accreditation by the American Hospital Association must have a social service department that employs qualified social workers. In larger hospitals, social workers are assigned to such specialized areas of hospital functioning as the emergency room, the pediatric unit, and intensive care unit. They are also employed by many long-term care facilities and nursing homes, and in home health care.

Heffernan, Shuttlesworth, and Ambrosino (1988) list six functions for social workers in health care. First, they provide individual counseling to families and patients. Second, they provide a bridge between the hospital and other social services in the community. Third, they can help other health care workers understand the emotional needs of the patient and family. Fourth, they represent the hospital to other community agencies. Fifth, they often set up educational programs in such areas as nutrition, family planning, and prenatal care. Finally, they contribute to health planning and social policy.

Physical Therapists and Occupational Therapists

Because both physical and occupational therapists are concerned with the rehabilitation of those injured or disabled, the two occupations are often classified together. They are, however, separate occupations. More than 30,000 physical therapists and physical therapy assistants and aides were employed in community hospitals in 1986; in the same year more than 11,000 occupational and recreational therapists held such positions (National Center for Health Statistics, 1989). Many more in these occupations are on the staffs of special hospitals, such as Veterans Administration hospitals and psychiatric facilities.

The educational program for physical therapy consists of a four-year baccalaureate degree or a master's degree for those who did not pursue the undergraduate course. Some schools offer a twelve- to sixteen-month certification program for those with the proper background. For occupational therapists, the minimal educational requirement is completion of a four-year bachelor's degree program, with options similar to those for physical therapy open to those who obtained the bachelor's degree in another field.

Physical therapists seek to restore the physical capability of those who have lost the normal use of some part of the body because of disease or injury. In the course of therapy, these health workers use such approaches as exercise, heat and cold, traction, and prosthetic devices. The aim is to improve or restore function, relieve pain, and prevent permanent disability.

Occupational therapists design a program of activities to help the patient regain functioning that has been impaired. They seek to evaluate the learning and performance capabilities of patients and then instruct them in functioning. Neither the physical therapist nor the occupational therapist is allowed to use medications without specific instructions from a doctor.

Both occupations are relative newcomers to the health care system. They have increased their scope, but they exhibit little desire to function independently from the physician. Perhaps these therapists recognize that the educational time needed to enter their occupations puts them in a disadvantaged situation relative to other health workers. Some schools, however, are beginning to think in terms of a master's degree specifically in rehabilitation, a sign that a move toward a professional claim may be made in the future.

INSTITUTIONALIZED ALTERNATIVES TO THE MEDICAL DOCTOR

In large measure, the American Medical Association was formed to gain control of care by medical practitioners, a goal that necessitated authority over all other occupations offering competing services to the public. The move toward control was generally successful and, over the years, many rival healing systems have dropped by the wayside while the practices of medical doctors have flourished. But some practitioners who based their approach on different theories of body functioning and medical care have persisted, and large numbers of the U.S. population continue to use alternatives to the medical doctor. Two that have been particularly recalcitrant in resisting the medical association and continue to attract many people are osteopathy and chiropractic. We will discuss both of these institutionalized alternatives to using the medical doctor.

Osteopaths

Osteopathy was developed by Andrew Still, a medical doctor who became disillusioned with the curative powers of available treatment options while serving as an army surgeon during the U.S. Civil War. A loss of confidence led Still to develop a new set of therapeutics that he considered more rational. This new approach to the treatment of ailments has been summarized into a basic definition of the theory of osteopathy (Stoddard, 1969:1):

> [Osteopathy is] . . . a system of healing in which chief emphasis is placed on the structural and mechanical problems of the body. The practice of osteopathy, while recognizing that human beings are complex entities influenced by a wide range of environmental and inherent factors, is concerned primarily with the mechanics of the body—how far the body is structurally normal or where it is abnormal, how that abnormality influences its health, and how to restore normal mechanics or when that is not possible how best to help the body adapt itself to its structural weakness.

This set of principles is not inconsistent with conventional medical practice, but the emphasis on structural and mechanical problems of the body means that therapy must include body manipulation and attempts to strengthen its structure. Medications and surgery are adjuncts to body manipulation.

These principles lay the foundation for a separate and distinct approach to patients and for a separate and distinct association of practitioners. This is especially so since osteopathic physicians were initially a separatist and cultist group. Emphasis on independence from the medical association led to the founding of the American Osteopathic Association, an organization completely separate from the American Medical Association.

In 1979 Wardwell classified doctors of osteopathy as "marginal practitioners" because, although they treated most health disorders, their use of body manipulation was considered an unorthodox method of healing. But lately, osteopathic practice has been moving closer and closer to the practice of traditional medicine, and many of its advocates have either abandoned or have reduced their reliance on body manipulation. As a consequence, the practice of osteopathy has moved closer to the practice of the doctor of medicine. This move toward traditional medicine continued during the past decade, and osteopathy has received more acceptance, although it is still viewed with suspicion by some medical doctors. Albrecht and Levy (1982) suggest that this new respectability for the osteopath comes from the way in which the practice of osteopathy has adapted to the medical model; it is being seen as a valid profession because it mimes the world of the medical doctor, rather than because its unique theories have achieved acceptance.

Osteopathic medicine today represents a complete therapeutic program that differs little in actual practice from that of the doctor of medicine. It has influenced traditional medicine, and in return, traditional medicine has influenced osteopathy. Thus, many medical doctors have started to pay attention to the adaptive capabilities of the body and have adopted some manipulation as part of their practice; most doctors of osteopathy now routinely use medications, surgery, and other traditional approaches. For this and other reasons, it is possible to refer realistically to the convergence of medicine and osteopathy. The best evidence occurred in the late 1950s, when licensed California osteopaths were granted medical degrees upon request. Doctors of osteopathy are now fully licensed as medical practitioners in all fifty states.

In a turnabout, opposition to a convergence between traditional medicine and osteopathy now comes more frequently from the osteopathic than from the medical association (Twaddle and Hessler, 1987). For example, the public relations department of the American Osteopathic Association advertised in professional journals with the following message: "You probably think all doctors are M. D.s. If so, you're wrong!" (American Osteopathic Association, 1986). The professional association also has established certification boards, as has traditional medicine. In the same advertisement, the association points out that 14 percent of osteopathic doctors are board certified in eighteen medical specialties, including surgery, radiology, obstetrics, pediatrics, and psychiatry. Having declared legitimacy by such references, the association also carefully points to the special approach of its practitioners by stating that focus on the body's musculoskeletal system is central to the osteopathic physician's practice.

An indication of the growing importance of osteopathic medicine can be found in increasing numbers. Thus, between 1980 and 1986 the number of active doctors of medicine in this country grew by 21.6 percent, whereas the number of doctors of osteopathy increased by 36.1 percent. In 1986 there were 21,875 osteopaths practicing medicine in the United States (National Center for Health Statistics, 1989), and these practitioners received 50 million visits by 25 million patients (American Osteopathic Association, 1986).

Chiropractors

Like osteopathy, chiropractic focuses on the musculoskeletal system, but the two differ in many important ways. The contention of chiropractic is that illness results from a lack of normal nerve functions; body manipulation and adjustment, with emphasis on the spinal column, are the suggested therapy for these abnormalities. A healthy relationship between the spinal column and the nervous system is viewed as primary for good overall health. Often, the initial consultation with a chiropractor consists of a medical history and a "spinal checkup," which may include an X-ray of the spinal column. A physical examination may include the taking of blood pressure.

The important difference between osteopathy and chiropractic is that the latter rejects many basic premises of modern medical practice. This can be a self-serving rejection because chiropractors do not have the legal right to write prescriptions, perform surgery, or carry out other functions that are routine procedures for doctors of medicine and osteopathy. Without such rights, the practice of chiropractic is limited to body manipulation, heat treatments, and recommendations to take over-the-counter medications and vitamins. If problems found are not identified as having a musculoskeletal involvement, the chiropractor is supposed to refer the patient to other health care practitioners, particularly medical doctors and doctors of osteopathy.

Unlike osteopathy, a cloud has hung over the chiropractic theory of healing since its earliest days, when it was viewed as a cult, a fad, and even a direct steal from Still's osteopathic concepts. Originated in 1895, the approach was presented by its initiator, Daniel Palmer, as a method of healing that had nothing to do with any other system or method of practice. It has faced problems of acceptance from its beginning.

Transition toward respectability came in 1974 with four significant events: (1) the last state (Louisiana) voted to license chiropractors; (2) the U.S. Office of Education gave the Chiropractic Commission on Education power to accredit chiropractic colleges; (3) Congress voted to reimburse chiropractors' fees under the Medicare program; and (4) Congress instructed the National Institutes of Health to allocate funds to study the scientific basis of chiropractic medicine (Wardwell, 1979). The transition toward respectability has not led to an endorsement of the chiropractic approach by the medical association.

Despite opposition from organized medicine, however, the use of chiropractic by the public continues to grow. It has been estimated that the nation's chiropractors, who numbered 34,500 in 1984, are visited by 19.8 million persons annually; musculoskeletal complaints and lower back pains were the major ailments leading patients to the chiropractor's office (Nyiendo and Haldeman, 1987).

Gesler (1988) examined the status of the doctor of chiropractic in the health care system, the cultural beliefs that surround the practice, and the types of patients attracted to chiropractors. Following the lead of Cowrie and Roebuck (1975), Gesler notes that the chiropractor holds a deviant status in health care. Due in great part to the negative image held by groups ranging from the American Medical Association to labor unions, chiropractors have been labeled as unorthodox, sometimes even as "quacks." Although Coulehan (1985) suggests that increased use of chiropractors indicates upward mobility, members of the occupation still tend to rank last in the healing hierarchy of professional health practitioners.

The scientific validity of chiropractic practice is not its main drawing card (Gesler, 1988). Rather, its hands-on approach to care is valued by those who use chiropractors. Rural or small towns in the United States appear to be most favorable areas for chiropractic practice. In such areas, there is a cultural congruence between chiropractic and folk attitudes and beliefs. Chiropractors often advertise for patients in newspapers, emphasizing the "helping hands" theme, spinal checkups, and their particular skills with accident victims.

Rosenthal (1981) suggests that changes in chiropractic continue in the direction of removing the stigma of marginality. Contacts between chiropractors and physicians on a professional level are increasing, with chiropractors receiving more and more referrals from medical doctors. A study of Washington physicians (Cherkin, MacCornack, and Berg, 1989) found that doctors in that state viewed chiropractors more favorably than might be expected, given the negative stance of organized medicine. Whereas two-thirds were uncomfortable about the nature of chiropractic practice, one-quarter viewed these practitioners as an excellent referral for patients with musculoskeletal problems. Only 3 percent viewed them as "quacks." More important, 57 percent of the physicians surveyed had encouraged patients to seek the help of a chiropractor for certain ailments.

LIMITED PRACTITIONERS

Health personnel who limit their practice to specific parts of the body and practice independently of the medical doctor are referred to by Wardwell (1979) as "limited practitioners." Dentists, podiatrists, and optometrists are limited practitioners.

Dentists

Of the several limited health practitioners, dentists come closest to the physician in terms of public knowledge, use, acceptance, and professional status. This is at least partially due to the educational time requirement similarity, the acknowledged high quality of dental schooling, and to the decision-making autonomy of the dental practitioner. As in medicine, the education program consists of four years of professional training after the bachelor's degree has been obtained. Although it is still possible to enter dental school after as few as two years of undergraduate study, the vast majority of dentists complete the baccalaureate degree before starting dental education.

Research indicates that, like medical students, dental students tend to come from professional or managerial homes (Fusillo and Metz, 1971); a sizeable proportion have a parent who is a dentist. Dental students are slightly poorer in undergraduate academic performance than medical students, reflecting a pattern whereby some not accepted in medical school choose dentistry instead. During their senior year as undergraduates some students apply to both medical and dental schools, with the latter viewed as a "backup" if the medical school application is not successful. Most dental students indicate they chose dentistry because the profession provides an opportunity to serve people; they also state they were motivated by the possibility of being professionally independent and of gaining monetary advantage. Some indicate they were attracted by the opportunity to work with their hands.

Dentists are viewed as professionals—as long as work is confined to that specific limited area of the body that is their province. They are usually private practitioners in fee-for-service settings in which they are autonomous and independent decision makers. They can prescribe medications that are specific to the teeth, gums, and the general mouth area.

Aspects of the occupation, however, present some difficulties for the dentist. For one, dental problems do not seem to demand attention as readily as do diseases presented to physicians, which means that the pool of patients is smaller for dentists. In addition, more dentists than are necessary to maintain a successful practice are usually available; attempts have been made to regulate the profession to limit competition. Some states use the licensing process to restrict the number entering the profession and reduce the number of competitors (Freund and Shulman, 1984). Conrad and Sheldon (1984) see competition among dentists as a means of "cost containment," but regulation of entry into the profession limits the lowering of costs.

Podiatrists

Podiatrists limit their professional attention to the examination, diagnosis, and medical and surgical treatment of the foot. The number of active licensed podiatrists in the United States in 1986 was 11,000, an increase of 54.9 percent since 1970 (Bureau of Health Professions, 1986). Practically all are self-employed, the majority in solo practice in large cities. Podiatrists meet all criteria for professional status but they are sometimes overlooked in a listing of professional health personnel, possibly because they receive almost all their patients by referral.

To be licensed as a podiatrist, one must graduate from a college of podiatric medicine and pass a state board examination; some states also require an internship. Students admitted to a school of podiatry must have completed at least two years of undergraduate college and then undertake a four-year program; many enter such schools after completing the bachelor's degree.

Although the medical profession accepts podiatrists as legitimate practitioners, physicians may be concerned about when to make referrals. There is no doubt, however, about the rights of the podiatrist to prescribe medications and to perform surgery on the foot. It is recognized that the foot and its treatment require extensive knowledge of the musculoskeletal structure and function of the foot, and podiatrists are viewed by physicians as possessing this knowledge.

Optometrists

Optometrists specialize in problems of vision; they examine the patient's eyes and the physical structures related to them to determine whether visual, muscular, neurological, or other problems are present. Much of the optometrist's professional time is spent in testing patients' eyesight, with the intent of prescribing corrective lenses or exercises to correct refraction faults. Optometrists are not allowed to use or prescribe medications or perform surgery; if these are necessary, they refer patients to medical practitioners.

In 1986, about 24,300 licensed optometrists were in active practice in the United States (National Center for Health Statistics, 1989). Most are self-employed in solo-practice offices. The training for optometry is at least two years of preprofessional training in an undergraduate college followed by four years of professional education. Schools of optometry are often associated with universities. Optometrists must pass a board examination to obtain a license.

Optometrists must be distinguished from medical doctors specializing in the diagnosis and treatment of eye diseases, who are known as ophthalmologists. Ophthalmologists can legally do everything the optometrist is allowed to do with regard to the examination and treatment of the eye, with important additions: As medical doctors, they can also prescribe medications and perform surgery.

At what might be considered the other end of a continuum, the optometrist should also be distinguished from the optician. The optician's practice is limited to fitting and adjusting corrective lenses, and only in accordance with the prescription of an optometrist or ophthalmologist. Opticians are not allowed to examine the eyes or prescribe treatment; these activities are reserved for optometrists and ophthalmologists.

Like the pharmacist, the optometrist faces difficulties with regard to professionalization because the occupation usually includes a mixture of business and service. Most optometrists not only prescribe eyeglasses, they also sell them. Indeed, it has been alleged by some that the selling of eyeglass frames and lenses constitutes the major part of the income of the typical optometrist.

QUASI-HEALERS

The healing approach of quasi-healers is based on what most people would consider nonscientific premises. Therefore, the presence of so many of these healers in the United States and their current use by so many people seems a puzzle. Tradition and subcultural commitment are undoubtedly important reasons. Another is a reaction to the approach of modern scientific practitioners, who often fail to deal successfully with all problems presented, particularly emotional problems. When they are not satisfied with scientific medicine, some people turn to the nonscientific. Thus, one of the authors of this book recently bought a copper bracelet that claims to "cure" the wearer of the pain of rheumatism; it was purchased in a pharmacy in one of the most sophisticated urban areas of the western world, on the corner of Oxford and Regent Streets in London.

Many alternative healing methods emphasize a more holistic approach to disease, placing health, illness, and means of healing in a broader perspective (McGuire, 1988). Perhaps because of the placebo effect, or because so many diseases are self-limiting, many quasi-healers have impressive track records. In addition, faith healers, Christian Science practitioners, and folk healers of all sorts seem to meet at least the emotional needs of their clients better than do modern physicians. This is especially true when scientific medicine clashes with the cultural backgrounds of clients. Each quasi-healer presents a family-oriented, intimate general practice, which often includes such unheard-of present medical doctor practices as making house calls and joining hands in prayer.

Of these various healers, folk practitioners are of most interest here because they are so immersed in the subcultural knowledges, beliefs, values, norms, and symbols of the local population. Several ethnic subcultures in the United States and certain rural groups perceive illness and healing quite differently from the main-stream culture (Hautman, 1979). Thus, the intervention of the folk practitioner often goes well beyond focus on physical ailments. Those who believe in the power of folk doctors often bring their personal, spiritual, and financial problems to the doctor-patient relationship. Further, many of these healers practice various forms of preven-tive medicine, often by focusing on the powers of people and events that are seen as causative in the disease process and by providing medals and amulets to ward off harm.

Since *curanderismo* has become increasingly important with the growth of the Hispanic background population in the United States, we focus on this one system of folk healing as an example of the quasi-healer. *Curanderismo* is a system of health beliefs and practices among people in Latin America and among Hispanic Ameri-cans, particularly in the southwestern states. By referring to the *curandero* as a non-scientific healer, we are giving way to our cultural bias toward what we consider scientific. We are tempted to see the *curandero* as superstitious and magical, but we must remember that healing theories and practices used by those from non-Anglo cultures may represent an earlier scientific position as well as a different perspective on health and illness. To the first point, the herbs used by Hispanic folk healers are often earlier forms of many medications currently prescribed by medical doctors in the United States. The practice of *curanderismo* is older than that of scientific medicine and has, over time, proved to be the only successful way to deal with certain illnesses rooted in a particular cultural base.

Hispanics have blended a number of traditions, including western medicine, into an approach to healing. For specific culturally rooted illnesses, people of this subculture will not go to any other type of practitioner because they know that others can do nothing to help overcome their problem. In part, this is because there is a different conception of what illness is and what causes it. In scientific medicine, the body is likened to a machine. Illness comes about when the machine breaks down because parts of the mechanism are traumatized or wear out, which implies a physical approach to etiology. In contrast, many folk conceptions of illness dwell upon the disturbed quality of personal relationships as the reason for a breakdown. A basic belief for *curanderismo* is that an even balance between what are defined as "hot" and "cold" substances must be maintained for good health. The healthy body is a balance or blend of these substances, and imbalance in either the hot or cold direction can lead to illness. Further, the mental-physical division common to modern medicine is not mirrored in Hispanic medical beliefs. The division is more likely to be between natural and supernatural conditions.

Curanderos are the point of first contact both for those believing themselves to have a Latino-specific condition and for those seeking help in deciding whether to take advantage of western care. In a sense, they act as a point of reference one step above a lay-referral system. But *curanderos* may be as much a barrier as a gateway to scientific medical care, because many folk practitioners do not refer the seriously ill to western doctors. From a modern medicine perspective, care for Hispanic Americans would be improved if appropriate referral patterns or linkages could be made between the folk and the modern practitioner.

SUMMARY

Dominance by the medical profession is an important factor in the organization of the U.S. health care system. Dominance does not mean the profession is alone in the provision of care, however. Far from it. The physician-patient relationship is at the center of the system, but many spokes radiate from this association. A virtual army of ancillary and support personnel is necessary to modern health care. Patients have their major contact with these personnel but most are in some way dependent on the decisions, actions, and orders of the physician.

One way of visualizing the large grouping of health care workers is by depicting it as a patient care decision-making pyramid. In this arrangement, the physician is at the top, the next layer consists of nurses, and many other patient care personnel come under the nurse's supervision. The place of nursing in this pyramid, subordinate to the physician but superordinate to so many others, provides an excellent example of the problems and struggles health care occupations face in their attempts to gain recognition as professional occupations.

A major issue among many nurses is whether the occupation is viewed as having professional status. In reviewing sociological writings about the nature of professions, we have come to agree with those who characterize the occupation as a *semiprofession* because the nurse must usually work under the orders of the physician. This lack of autonomy over work is crucial in the characterization—the recognized right of autonomous decision making is essential for professional status. In other respects, nursing exhibits professional features placing it nearer the professional end of an occupation-professional continuum, but it is not at the extreme end.

One problem nursing continually encounters in its strain toward professional recognition is that three quite different paths can be followed to gain official registration. The first and traditional road is the diploma program. Three-year programs connected with hospitals, diploma programs involve considerable practical experience. A second road, the baccalaureate degree granted by a university, is gaining prominence and numbers; this has helped nurses to strengthen their self-images as professionals. The third road, the associate-degree plan, in which a two-year degree is earned at a community or junior college, is not helping this image. The existence of three different paths to registration only confuses the situation and interferes with the bachelor's-degree nurses' attempts to bring unity to the occupation's goals and programs.

Such factors put a question mark on the conception of nursing as a profession, but some steps are being taken to achieve this image. An important one is the development of a more independent role for the nurse—the nurse practitioner. An increasing number of nurses are involved in more-or-less independent practice. But the future of this status would be threatened if predictions about an oversupply of physicians are correct. If an oversupply does occur, nurse practitioners may find they are in demand in the inner cities and rural areas, and without patients in those areas of the United States where physicians want to practice.

Other occupations in the health field face many of the same difficulties in being recognized as professions. Some, like the physician's assistant, are viewed as so physician-dependent that the very definition precludes the question of professional status. Others, although not directly defined as dependent, are still required to act only upon the orders of the physician. Thus, the pharmacist cannot provide medications without a doctor's prescription, and physical and occupational therapists cannot help a patient without a physician's request. Social workers employed in the health care system are similarly restricted in what they can do without a physician's order, although they may function independently in other contexts.

Limited practitioners are fully recognized as professionals but their autonomy is limited to specific kinds of conditions, usually associated with parts of the body. The dentist is an autonomous worker so long as treatment remains focused on the teeth, jaw, and mouth area.

Alongside the pyramid are alternatives to the medical doctor in the health care system as we portrayed it. We discussed three alternative healers; two were formerly considered marginal practitioners: the osteopath and the chiropractor. Both of these practitioners have been considered unorthodox in their approach to healing for many years, but they have moved out of the margins of practice to a more central location in the U.S. health care system. The professional practice of osteopaths is now very similar to that of the traditional physician. It is suggested, however, that osteopaths reached respectability by forsaking much of their unique approach and adopting the medical model. The chiropractor is still viewed with some concern by physicians but, again, the occupation is moving toward a more accepted place in the hierarchy of health care.

Still on the margin are folk practitioners, who function on what we consider nonscientific bases; such practitioners are still common among some subcultures in the United States. Among the important folk practitioners still common are the *curanderos*, who practice in communities populated by Hispanic Americans. For several reasons, many folk practitioners have excellent track records as healers of the sick.

References

Albrecht, Gary L., and Judith A. Levy. 1982. "The professionalization of osteopathy." *Research in the Sociology of Health Care* 2:161–205.

American Osteopathic Association. 1986. "You probably think all doctors are M. D.s. If so, you're wrong!" *Science* 234(7 November):787.

Barr, J. K. 1979. "Task performance and consensus: The health associate role." *Social Science and Medicine* 13A(1):65–71.

Birenbaum, Arnold. 1982. "Reprofessionalization in pharmacy." *Social Science and Medicine* 16:871–878.

Brotherton, Sarah E. 1988. "Nursing role orientation of three groups: From the naive to the realistic." *Journal of Nursing Education* 27(3):117–123.

Brown, E. L. 1948. *Nursing for the Future.* New York: Russell Sage Foundation.

Bullough, Bonnie. 1976. "The law and the expanding nursing role." *American Journal of Public Health* 66(3):249–254.

Bureau of Health Professions. 1986. *The Fifth Report to the President and Congress on the Status of Health Personnel in the United States.* DHHS Publication No. HRS-P-OD-86-1, March. Washington, D.C.: U.S. Government Printing Office.

Burkett, G. L., M. Parken-Harris, J. C. Kuhn, and C. H. Escovitz. 1978. "A comparative study of physicians' and nurses' conceptions of the role of the nurse practitioner." *American Journal of Public Health* 68(11):1090–1096.

Carroll, Theresa L. 1989. "Role deprivation in baccalaureate nursing students pre and post curriculum revision." *Journal of Nursing Education* 28(3):134–139.

Cherkin, D., F. A. MacCornack, and F.A. Berg. 1989. "Family physicians' views of chiropractors: Hostile or hospitable?" *American Journal of Public Health* 79(5):636–637.

Cockerham, William. 1989. *Medical Sociology.* 4th ed. Englewood Cliffs, N.J.: Prentice-Hall.

Conrad, Douglas A., and George G. Sheldon. 1984. "Competition as a means to contain dental costs." *Advances in Health Economics and Health Services Research* 5:181–211.

Coulehan, J. L. 1985. "Chiropractic and the clinical art." *Social Science and Medicine* 21:383–390.

Cowrie, J. B., and J. Roebuck. 1975. *An Ethnography of a Chiropractic Clinic.* New York: Free Press.

Crawford, Laura A., and Betty H. Olinger. 1988. "Recruitment and retention of nursing students from diverse cultural backgrounds." *Journal of Nursing Education* 27(8):379–381.

Dagenais, F., and A. I. Meleis. 1982. "Professionalism, work ethic, and empathy in nursing roles." *Western Journal of Nursing* 13(1):8–15.

Division of Allied Health Education and Accreditation. 1989. *Allied Health Education Directory.* Chicago: American Medical Association.

Ellis, Janice Rider, and Celia Love Hartley. 1988. *Nursing in Today's World: Challenges, Issues and Trends*. Philadelphia: Lippincott.

Etzioni, Amitai. 1969. *The Semi-professions and Their Organization*. New York: Free Press.

Fagin, Claire, Margaret McClure, and Rosella Schlotfeldt. 1976. "Can we bring order out of the chaos of nursing education?" *American Journal of Nursing* 79(January):98–107.

Ferraro, Kenneth F., and Tammy Southerland. 1989. "Domains of medical practice: Physicians' assessment of the role of physician extenders." *Journal of Health and Social Behavior* 30(2):192–205.

Freund, Deborah A., and Jay D. Shulman. 1984. "Regulation of the professions: Results from dentistry." *Advances in Health Economics and Health Services Research* 5:161–180.

Fusillo, Alice E., and A. S. Metz. 1971. "Social science research on the dental student." In *Social Science and Dentistry*, ed. N. D. Richards and L. K. Cohen. London: Federation Dentaire Internationale.

Gesler, Wilbert M. 1988. "The place of chiropractors in health care delivery: A case study of North Carolina." *Social Science and Medicine* 26(8):785–792.

Ginzburg, Eli. 1948. *A Program for the Nursing Profession*. New York: American Nursing Association.

Habenstein, R. W., and E. A. Christ. 1963. *Professionalizer, Traditionalizer, and Utilizer*. 2nd ed. Columbia: University of Missouri Press.

Hardy, Leslie. 1987. "The search for professionalism." *Nursing Times* 84(35):43–44.

Hautman, Mary Ann. 1979. "Folk health and illness beliefs." *Nurse Practitioner* 4(4):23, 26, 31–32.

Heffernan, Joseph, Guy Shuttlesworth, and Rosalie Ambrosino. 1988. *Social Work and Social Welfare: An Introduction*. St. Paul, Minn.: West.

Hogstel, Mildred O. 1977. "Associate degree and baccalaureate graduates: Do they function differently?" *American Journal of Nursing* 77:1598–1600.

Horman, Darla, James D. Campbell, and Jerry L. DeGregory. 1987. "Gender and the attribution of the nurse practitioner and physician status." *Medical Care* 25(9):847–855.

Iglehart, John K. 1987. "Health policy report: Problems facing the nursing profession." *New England Journal of Medicine* 317(10):646–651.

Lambert, Vickie A., and Clinton E. Lambert. 1989. "Nursing: An evolving profession." In *Perspectives in Nursing*, ed. C. E. Lambert and V. A. Lambert, 3–17. East Norwalk, Conn.: Appleton and Lange.

Lethbridge, Dona J. 1989. "Motivational orientations of registered nurse baccalaureate students in rural New England." *Journal of Nursing Education* 28 (5):203–209.

Levine, Eugene. 1977. "What do we know about nurse practitioners?" *American Journal of Nursing* 77:1799–1803.

Marshall, Floreine. 1988. "What is a nurse: Perceptions of baccalaureate nursing students." *Journal of Nursing Education* 27(4):185–186.

Mauksch, Hans. 1972. "Nursing: Churning for change." In *Handbook of Medical Sociology*, 2nd ed., ed. H. Freeman, S. Levine, and L. Reeder, 206–230. Englewood Cliffs, N.J.: Prentice-Hall.

McGuire, Meredith. 1988. *Ritual Healing in Suburban America*. New Brunswick, N.J.: Rutgers University Press.

Miller, Michael. 1974. "Work roles for the associate degree candidate." *American Journal of Nursing* 74:468–470.

National Center for Health Statistics. 1989. *Health, United States, 1988*. DHHS Pub. No. (PHS) 89-1232. Public Health Service. Washington, D.C.: U.S. Government Printing Office.

Nyiendo, Joan, and Scott Haldeman. 1987. "A prospective study of 2000 patients attending a chiropractic college teaching clinic." *Medical Care* 25(6):516–526.

Office of Technology Assessment. 1986. "Nurse practitioners, physician assistants, and certified nurse-midwives: A policy analysis." Health Technology Case Study 37. Washington, D.C.: U.S. Government Printing Office.

O'Neill, M. F. 1973. "A study of baccalaureate nursing student values." *Nursing Research* 22:437–441.

Pankratz, Loren, and Deanna Pankratz. 1974. "Nursing autonomy and patient's rights: Development of a nursing attitude scale." *Journal of Health and Social Behavior* 15(September):211–216.

Pavalko, Ron. 1971. *Sociology of Occupations and Professions.* Itasca, Ill.: F. E. Peacock.

Record, Jane C., and Merwyn R. Greenlick. 1975. "New health professions and the physician role: A hypothesis from the Kaiser experience." *Public Health Reports* 90(May/June):241–246.

Reed, Fay Carol. 1979. "Education or exploitation." *American Journal of Nursing* 79 (July):1259–1261.

Rosenberg, Charles. 1987. *The Care of Strangers: The Rise of the American Hospital System.* New York: Basic Books.

Rosenfeld, Peri. 1988. *Nursing Student Census with Policy Implications.* New York: National League for Nursing.

Rosenthal, Saul F. 1981. "Marginal or mainstream: Two studies of contemporary chiropractors." *Sociological Focus* 14:271–285.

Rothrock, Jane C. 1989. "Professional self-image: A research study of perioperative nursing students." *AORN Journal* 49(5):1419–1425.

Schulman, Sam. 1979. "Mother surrogate—After a decade." In *Patients, Physicians, and Illness*, 3rd ed., ed. E. G. Jaco, 272–280. New York: Free Press.

Simpson, Ida. 1979. *From Student to Nurse.* New York: Cambridge University Press.

Stoddard, Alan. 1969. *Manual of Osteopathic Practice.* London: Hutchinson.

Twaddle, Andrew C., and R. M. Hessler. 1987. *Sociology of Health.* 2nd ed. St. Louis: C. V. Mosby.

van Maanen, H. M. 1979. "Perspectives and problems of quality of nursing care: An overview of contributions from North America and recent developments in Europe." *Journal of Advanced Nursing* 4(July): 377–389.

Wardwell, Walter I. 1979. "Limited and marginal practitioners." In *Handbook of Medical Sociology*, 3rd ed., ed. H. E. Freeman, S. Levine, and L. G. Reeder, 230–250. Englewood Cliffs, N.J.: Prentice-Hall.

Williams, Jody K. 1989. "Why students choose ADN programs." *American Journal of Nursing* 89(3):396, 398.

Wolinsky, Frederic. 1988. *The Sociology of Health.* 2nd ed. Belmont, Calif.: Wadsworth.

Zammuto, R. F., I. R. Turner, S. Miller, I. Shannon, and J. Christian. 1979. "Effect of clinical settings on the utilization of nurse practitioners." *Nursing Research* 28(March-April):98–102.

8

Hospitals and Health Care Agencies

INTRODUCTION

Medical care is becoming increasingly costly in the United States. In 1986 national expenditures for this care comprised 10.9 percent of the gross national product, that is, $458.2 billion. This figure is double the proportion and seventeen times the amount of the gross national product spent for medical care in 1960, when the corresponding figures were 5.2 percent and $26.9 billion. The per capita amount spent in 1960 was $142; the 1986 figure of $1,837 is thirteen times higher (National Center for Health Statistics, 1989).

A significant proportion of medical care expenses is spent for hospital services; in 1986 these services accounted for 39.2 percent of all national health expenditures. This large figure reflects the hospital's place in the health care system, as it has become the hub of medical care and the center for specialized medical treatment. In many respects, during this century medical care has become "hospitalized" (Rosenberg, 1987). The office of the solo entrepreneur physician is no longer sufficient for medical practice: High-technology equipment is too expensive and too infrequently used to be maintained in the average doctor's office. As a result, the physician's care is more frequently given in the hospital, where both technical equipment and ancillary personnel are available.

DEVELOPMENT OF THE HOSPITAL

We generally believe that a hospital is a place for the care and treatment of the sick and injured. But the sick are a varied lot, and the places for their treatment are equally diverse. *Hospital* is an umbrella term covering institutions that vary in ownership, profit orientation, size, complexity, resources, structure, and type of care given. Irrespective of such differences, each has broadly similar goals and activities and each performs a similar function. But from the health care perspective there is one key element that is fundamental to the hospital: service to patients. Central to meeting its goal of patient care, the hospital provides the setting for the work and talents of many health personnel.

This concept of service has always been an essential feature of the hospital. Although the pivotal patient-care role is fairly recent in the history of medical care, as a facility committed to caring for the sick, the hospital is an old institution. Indications are that such institutions existed in Sri Lanka and India in the fifth century B.C., and both the Greek and Roman empires have left records of hospitals connected with their temples.

The theme of service gained more prominence as early Christianity emphasized concern for others, and hospitals sought to heal the soul as well as the body. Religion and the power of the Roman Catholic church's hierarchy dominated all thinking and practice in the Middle Ages. It is not surprising, therefore, that theology and church dogma influenced not only treatment but also concepts of health in the hospitals of the time. Differences between works of faith and works of healing were small in such hospitals. Reflecting the tone of religion, the basic functions of hospitals were those of charitable institutions—they cared for the poor and needy. They resembled the churches that operated them, and the atmosphere was similar to the lives of the monks who cared for the sick.

As the Renaissance brought a more secular view of the world, beliefs about medical care also changed. The service theme remained, but the extent of service offered broadened. The rise of mercantilism in the seventeenth century produced a need for able-bodied, healthy laborers for business and industry. By the eighteenth century, maintaining levels of health in the population adequate for the needs of industry became public policy. Order, efficiency, and social discipline were called for in the realm of health as well as in other areas of life (Rosen, 1963; 1979).

The Industrial Revolution and accompanying population shifts to urban areas precipitated new and threatening health problems. The squalid conditions of the growing urban areas, the crowding of individuals within such places, and the lack of adequate sanitation created serious health problems and, sometimes, crises. More rational approaches to health care became imperative.

Societal forces demanded lower sickness rates and significant advances in scientific knowledge about environmental contributions to disease; preventive measures were developed to start answering that demand. At the same time, effective treatment measures were developed. Pasteur's contributions to the germ theory of disease, coupled with Lister's application of the theory to surgery, dramatically changed the power of medicine to provide therapeutic services. Successful treatment in the hospital became more viable. Further, the work of Florence Nightingale in reforming nursing and in creating a corps of dedicated and trained personnel to care for those hospitalized provided a new positive image of the hospital as a place for cure.

Following the Civil War there was an explosive growth in number of hospitals in the United States, which accompanied the nation's increasing urbanization (Lynaugh, 1988). As the workforce moved into factories and out of workers' residences and the extended kinship network began to dissipate, a place to care for the sick outside the home became more important. At this time the hospital was still small and homelike. But improved medical competency in the institutions changed the direction in hospital care. Religious domination of the hospital began to give way to a scientifically oriented institution. The values related to service prevailed, but functions were in transition. At this time the hospital was operated by an administrator and nursing staff. The metaphor of "captain of the ship" in reference to the physician began to emerge. As doctors became more dependent upon the hospital, they sought and gained more control over its operation. This was partly because hospitals depended on the physician for patients, and administrative boards granted more authority to doctors (Lynaugh, 1988).

The status of the hospital had changed dramatically by 1920. It was no longer solely a place for the urban poor. Most middle-size cities now had a community hospital, as both physicians and patients changed their expectations of the facility. Surgery was now the key to hospital growth. As a result, the hospital became more capital-intensive, and scientific medical values began to dominate its activities and decision making (Rosenberg, 1987).

TYPES OF HOSPITALS

The variety of institutions sheltered under the one word, *hospital*, may be classified in many ways. Each is designed to care for people in ill health, but the specific nature of the output varies according to the service it renders, the cultural system in which it functions, and the social and economic systems supporting it (Ver Steeg and Croog, 1979).

In 1987, there were 6,281 hospitals with a total of more than one million patient beds in the United States (American Hospital Association, 1988). In the peak years, 1965–1975, there were more than 7,000 hospitals. Nevertheless, the number of admissions during the 1965–1975 period and during 1987 is approximately the same, reflecting a decline in the average length of hospital stay. About 33 million people were admitted to nonfederal, short-stay hospitals in 1987 in the United States (National Center for Health Statistics, 1989). The average daily census for 1987 (622,000) and average length of stay (6.3 days) were the lowest for any year since 1946.

These trends vary by type of hospital. Nongovernmental, not-for-profit hospitals increased from 2,584 in 1946 to 3,364 in 1985. The number of beds in such hospitals was 708,000 in 1985, an increase of 401,000 since 1946. The number of investor-owned (for-profit) hospitals declined in this same time period, from 1,076 in 1946 to 805 in 1985. But the number of beds in investor-owned hospitals increased from 39,000 in 1946 to 104,000 in 1985, and admissions more than doubled during this period (American Hospital Association, 1986).

General Hospitals

The term *general hospital* implies a multipurpose facility. At least at the point of intake, general hospitals offer services to patients with all kinds of diseases and health conditions. More than one-half (58.2 percent) of the general hospitals in the United States are community-owned, not-for-profit facilities (American Hospital Association, 1986). Those incorporated as not-for-profit cannot legally distribute their profits to any individual; theoretically, all excess money is put back into the hospital. Government ownership—mainly municipal or county—prevails in just over one-fourth of the hospitals (27.9 percent).

Proprietary or privately owned for-profit facilities make up the remainder of U.S. hospitals. These are distinguished from not-for-profit facilities by articles of incorporation indicating that profits can be distributed among owners or stockholders. The general feeling is that voluntary and government hospitals put the needs of patients first, whereas proprietary facilities are more interested in profits. But many people also believe that proprietary hospitals run more efficiently than not-for-profit facilities.

In his book on the transformation of the U.S. medical system, Starr (1982) suggests that an essential element in the growth of corporate medicine was the integration of the decentralized hospital system by corporations: "Unquestionably the most dramatic corporate expansion has taken place in hospital care. The free-standing general hospital, governed by its own board, administrators, and medical staff, is now giving way to larger multihospital systems run by an increasingly powerful corporate management" (p. 430). The profit motive is the stimulant. It is anticipated that the trend toward multihospital systems will accelerate, especially among for-profit corporations, leading to growth among proprietary company chains.

Proprietary hospitals are increasingly owned and managed by corporations that are run like any other business (some even have their shares listed on stock exchanges), which indicates that profit is the motive. Although not denying this, proprietary hospitals contend that they hold costs down by not giving unneeded services and can, therefore, supply higher quality service at lower cost. Not-for-profit hospital officials, however, charge that one reason for the greater profit of the for-profit hospitals is that they "skim the cream" of patients from the top of the ability-to-pay pyramid. That is, they do not accept patients unable to pay their bills, a burden the voluntary hospitals bear more often (Mackintosh, 1978). Thus, when describing one of the hospital corporate chains that follows a policy of initially treating all emergency cases, Starr (1982) comments that after emergency admission, "if a wallet biopsy—one of the procedures in which American hospitals specialize—discloses that the victims are uninsured, it transfers them to public institutions" (p. 436).

It is not surprising that corporate hospitals have been the targets of criticism. Combining the familiar commercial outlook with U.S. society's care orientation for hospitals challenges the traditional image of hospitals as places where humane service and charity are the primary raison d'etre. Perhaps the most common criticism is that the profit motive may outweigh the staff's responsibilities to patients; for example, expensive but unnecessary tests could be ordered, or some unneeded treatment could be rendered. In addition to reducing the quality of care, the for-profit facilities are criticized for neglecting patients who cannot pay for treatment (Light, 1986).

These corporations use several types of formal organization. The most highly structured arrangement is that of multihospital systems. A common form is one in which the corporation contracts to manage the hospital, reporting directly to the institution's board of trustees, which retains full legal responsibility for the facility. A more highly organized form is that in which the managing organization actually owns or leases the hospital. In some organizational forms, care is vertically integrated, that is, linkage is at different stages in the health care process (Andersen and Mullner, 1989).

Specialty Hospitals

Specialty hospitals focus their services on specific kinds of health conditions or on certain categories of patients. For example, some specialty hospitals treat only mental illness, cancer, tuberculosis, heart conditions, and broken bones. Some deal exclusively with the problems of children, some with veterans only, others with conditions and illnesses of women, and some only with those who cannot afford to pay a hospital bill.

Although the number of general hospital beds per 100,000 population in the United States increased from 1963 to 1984, the number of specialty hospital beds declined. The decrease is attributable mostly to a dramatic 36 percent decline from 1977 to 1987 in the number of psychiatric hospital beds (American Hospital Association, 1988).

The overall decline in specialty beds reflects several trends: (1) new methods of treatment have made hospitalization less necessary for some conditions; (2) new cures and treatment methods have made stays in specialty hospitals shorter; (3) new medications control symptoms that formerly led to hospitalization; (4) a number of medical personnel feel that specialty hospitals are unnecessary because general hospitals can care for most patients; (5) a social movement in the United States leans toward community residence during treatment for many people who were formerly treated in specialty hospitals, especially mental hospitals; and (6) this social movement also has led to deinstitutionalization of some who were already residents of specialty hospitals.

Psychiatric illness is the largest single condition treated in specialty hospitals. The number of such hospitals for the mentally ill increased from 1977 to 1987, from 541 to 684, but the number of beds has at the same time decreased, leading to a much smaller average capacity per facility. The decline in beds reflects the effects of medications that allow many people with mental problems to remain in the community, the social movement toward deinstitutionalization of patients already in mental hospitals, and increasing acceptance of treatment in the community.

Also notable is the decline in the number of facilities and the number of beds in tuberculosis hospitals. As of 1987 only ten hospitals focusing on this condition remained (American Hospital Association, 1988). This decline may be attributed to changed conceptions of the treatment needed for tuberculosis, along with the development of antibiotics effective in managing patients with the condition.

From 1977 to 1988 the number of hospitals for chronic diseases declined by 34.4 percent and the number of beds by 19.4 percent; such a decline reflects an increasing tendency for such conditions to be treated in general hospitals. On the other hand, the number of hospitals offering programs of rehabilitation has increased, as have hospitals for the care of alcoholism and drug abuse. Rehabilitation departments in hospitals have increased from 690 in 1977 to 2,149 in 1987.

Hospitals also have begun programs for the treatment of alcoholism and other substance abuse, with 19 percent providing such a service in 1987 compared to only 7 percent in 1977 (American Hospital Association, 1988). As Weisner and Room (1984) report, this is at least partially due to increased governmental funding of programs and the purchase of hospitals for these conditions. Because more hospital beds are available for the treatment of addictions, patients are actively recruited, sometimes within a broader definition of persons who need such specialized care, which could result in inappropriate and ineffective treatment.

THE HOSPITAL AND SOCIETY

From one perspective, the hospital is an organization with a bureaucratic authority structure that provides written rules and policies within a system of formal authority patterns. But formal organizations are not structure alone; they are more than collections of statuses, authority patterns, written policies, and organization charts. Organizations are also people interacting in a shared system of values, norms, beliefs, knowledges, and symbols; in its own way, each institution reflects the value system of society. Furthermore, specific organizations function within social systems composed of other organizations also seeking society's support.

From this perspective, the contemporary hospital's significant place in the health system cannot be taken for granted. The facility has not always been important in the maintenance of health and the healing of the sick and injured. Neither happenstance nor the overwhelming superiority of hospital care has given it the honored and powerful position it now holds. Such prominence reflects concordance with the values of the mainstream contemporary western culture.

These values support the hospital as the core facility in western scientific medicine in at least three ways. First, health is seen as a value in and of itself. Beyond the economic needs of society to maintain a sufficient number of able-bodied workers, we have come to see good health as a valued resource; its maintenance and restoration are viewed as rights of the individual. Second, the hospital is where the knowledge of science is applied, and society has faith in the power of scientific biomedical advances. Third, the belief system in the United States has a strong strain of humanitarianism and compassion built upon a commitment to the worth of individual life. As we have seen, hospitals have charitable, religious, and compassionate roots. In a way, the pragmatic efficiency of science and humanitarian values meet in the hospital. Here, the worth of the individual is supported by the wonders of science.

Overlapping Social Institutions

The hospital must accommodate society's other social institutions that share an interest in its special function. Religion, the family, and the economy, which constitute part of the U.S. way of life, are all involved in the care of the sick, and all are concerned with the health and welfare of the population.

Religion.   Religion influences the care of the sick in several ways. In contemporary society, religious organizations provide charitable services to the sick, offer explanations or justifications to sufferers concerning the meaning of afflictions, indicate proper actions for patients and their families, and may also inform hospital staff about whether the care of patients is consistent with their beliefs. In hospitals functioning under the authority of a specific denomination, particular values may be espoused and monitored. In hospitals supervised by the Catholic church, for example, religious doctrines concerning such matters as contraception and abortion set specific policies for allowable medical practices in the institution.

Similarly, particular religious doctrines affect the willingness of persons viewed as sick by medical standards to seek medical treatment. Christian Scientists and the faithful of some small sectarian groups, for example, suggest that illness is related to errors in living, sinful acts, or lack of faith. This belief may affect decisions concerning resource utilization and, if a hospital is used, it can affect the type of treatment sought.

The Family.   The family has always been intimately involved in the hospital's programs. In most societies, one function of the family is to provide physical protection and psychological comfort for its members, especially when they face physical or emotional problems. This traditionally has meant a commitment to provide constant attention to those so ill they cannot meet normal social expectations.

Despite its recognition of the family's role, however, the modern hospital subordinates the family to the position of visitor while most tasks of the physical (and perhaps psychological) care are provided by members of the hospital staff. Parsons and Fox (1952) see this treatment of the sick outside the family as positive in three respects. First, it protects the family from disruption of its normal routine by the illness. Second, by keeping patients in a closely supervised atmosphere, the hospital helps maintain the sick role as a method of social control. And third, the hospital situation facilitates the therapeutic regimen technologically and motivationally.

Litman (1966) found empirical support for these observations. Over 40 percent (42.3 percent) of a sample of midwestern U.S. families stated that they would find it extremely difficult to care for a sick person in their home. More than one-half (58.6 percent) of the sample indicated willingness to turn over the care of a sick or injured family member to the hospital, and one-third (31.8 percent) declared that they would be unable to care for a sick person at home under any circumstances.

Hospitalization does, of course, have an impact on the family, especially when the role of the wife-mother is disrupted (Litman, 1974), and the isolation of family members from the patient can add to the problems. Although the structure of the contemporary family in the United States may not make it easy to care for the sick person at home, other family members may feel guilty about abandoning the sick individual. Most families can justify these feelings with the belief that the hospital, long-term care center, or nursing home can provide much better technical care.

The perceived place of family members in the health care system differs by subculture. Hospitalization may fit the values of the U.S. middle class but not the customs of many ethnic subgroups within the society. For example, the possible separation of family members is a major reason for Hispanic Americans to shun western medical resources. For members of this subculture, good medical care can only be obtained in the home with relatives in continual attendance. For example, in the ritual to heal the Latin American folk illness *susto*, the family is expected to literally surround the ill patient while particular rites are performed. Although this obviously does not carry over totally to western illnesses, the sense of family involvement in treatment—denied in the western hospital—is sorely missed by the Hispanic American patient and family.

The Economy.   In 1986 hospital expenditures accounted for 39.2 percent of the $458.2 billion spent on health care in the United States ($179.6 billion; National Center for Health Statistics, 1989). Over one-half of these expenditures (53.9 percent) were for the salaries and benefits of more than three million full-time-equivalent employees. Other than the educational system, one would be hard-pressed to name another service system in this country that spends so much money and employs so many people.

The hospital is the major employer in many U.S. communities. Further, it provides employment for a wide range of skilled workers. It is staffed by workers of all socioeconomic levels, from unskilled housekeeping and laundry personnel, aides, and orderlies, to college-educated nurses and pharmacists. Other than the school system, the hospital may be the only employer paying salaries that reflect advanced educational achievement. It also tends to be a reliable and steady economic unit since employee strikes are rare and bankruptcies are almost unheard of. A major fringe benefit for many small communities is the hospital's attraction of doctors; some communities would be without a doctor if they did not provide a hospital.

In the eyes of the public, the hospital is a humanitarian facility, but some perceive it as an economic institution. To the business-oriented, possibly the hospital's board of trustees, the hospital is a business that must be concerned with finances and must meet its payroll. Some critics of the U.S. health system (see, for example, Ehrenreich and Ehrenreich, 1971; Krause, 1977; Navarro, 1976, 1986) have charged that the delivery of care in hospitals, and much of the formal organization of these institutions, is dominated by the economic interests of the massive health care industry rather than by the interests of the individual patient.

THE HOSPITAL AS A LARGE-SCALE SOCIAL ORGANIZATION

The hospital exhibits the social characteristics of all large-scale social organizations—a hierarchical power structure, formal norms, an emphasis on efficiency, positions that delimit each aspect of function, and occupational specialties coupled with a detailed division of labor. But hospitals, particularly community general hospitals, have special features that prevent the development of a typical bureaucratic structure.

As in other institutions, the division of labor is extensive with much specialization of function in the hospital. With work interlocked and interdependent, statuses cannot function independently. Almost everyone working in the hospital depends on others for the performance of his or her own role. But, unlike some other social organizations, hospitals depend on skills that must be motivated and coordinated rather than coerced if they are to be effective. The hospital needs smooth management and integration of skills; each part must function effectively with other parts. Health care employees and physicians must make voluntary and informal adjustments, and this cannot be accomplished by rules alone. A value structure must support the formal organization chart of the facility. Even then, several problems make it difficult for the hospital to work in the same way as other social organizations. As one sociologist stated in the title of an article, "It defies all logic—but a hospital does function" (Mauksch, 1960).

Forms of Organization

Perhaps the overriding reason the hospital has not developed a full bureaucratic form of organization is its functional domination by doctors. Within broad limits, doctors can manipulate the hospital bureaucracy to serve their own ends. The power of doctors precludes the full implementation of bureaucratic rules for several reasons. First, as professionals, physicians can essentially create their own role definitions within the facility. This generally includes the formulation of rules that allow them freedom to outline the conditions under which they work and to define the rights they expect to have extended to them. Second, vested interests within the medical profession can demand special rules that countermand some rules laid down by the hospital's formal administration.

The lack of routine in many hospital tasks also hinders typical bureaucratic functioning. The variation from time to time and case to case frustrates attempts to set down rigid rules. Thus, rather than the typical Christmas-tree-type of bureaucratic organization, the hospital's organization chart is more comb-shaped with no single line of authority from top to bottom (see Figure 8–1). The organizational plan has two divisions. A governing board appears as a single point of command or policy making over both the medical director and the hospital administrator, but the medical part and administrative part have no formal relationship. One section of the hospital is focused on the medical tasks of the institution, whereas the other focuses on administrative concerns.

Given these two sections, two almost-separate bureaucracies are functioning within one large-scale organization. From this perspective, each bureaucracy in the hospital finds it necessary to consider the other, but the focus of each is on its own long-range goals and daily requirements. Smith (1958) refers to one aspect of the separate bureaucracies as "dual lines of authority" in the hospital, which he specifies as lay-administrative and professional-medical. Fox (1989) reaffirms this duality in hospital management, referring to two bases of authority—administrative and professional.

The two lines of authority are structured quite differently. In the community hospital, all occupants of the statuses listed in Figure 8–1 are employees of the hospital; but the physician is not. The doctor has command over the resources of the hospital, but is independent of its personnel office and often has no financial connection with the facility. Doctors set their own hours within the hospital and come and go as they please. They can rebuke the staff, but independence and professional decision-making rights make them immune to reciprocation—an uncommon bureaucratic arrangement in U.S. society.

The traditional lay-administrative line is similar to the typical bureaucratic pattern of a pyramid. Authority is arranged according to a series of descending levels. Each status or position is slotted at some point in the power structure. But the medical-professional line of authority is another matter. Here the authority of the physician, especially when claiming a medical emergency, defies the implementation of bureaucratic regulations. The cultural and legal authority of physicians gives them the freedom to ignore some rules if they decide they are inappropriate.

Figure 8–1
Organization of Typical Large General Hospital

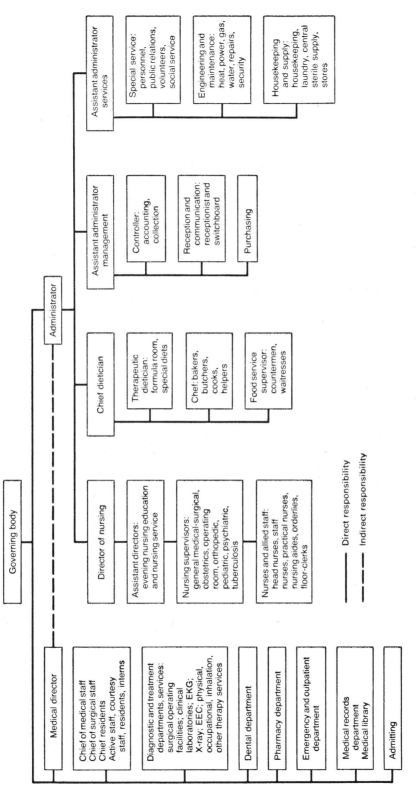

Source: U.S. Department of Labor (1967).

The two lines of authority affect the lives of all people involved with the hospital, from nurse to patient. Nurses are in a particularly vulnerable position between the bureaucratic rules of the administration and the medical orders of the physician. Frequently they must attempt to balance the demands of both. Nurses may have a particularly difficult task when physician's orders are contrary to hospital policy. In one experiment, Rank and Jacobson (1977) found that in the extreme case of a supposed overdose of a non-life-threatening medication nurses did their best to compromise medical orders, hospital policy, and their own knowledge of what was right. In the end, sixteen of eighteen nurses in the study used their own judgment and refused to give the medication.

Most other employees of the hospital—aides, orderlies, and maintenance staff—have highly routinized tasks that ordinarily could be followed without problem. But when physicians demand that rules be broken, such lower level workers are powerless to resist.

In general, the existence of these two lines of authority has been seen as a serious problem for activities within the hospital. Some sociologists, however, have suggested that it has helped upgrade the professionalism of lower level personnel (Rosengren and Lefton, 1969). Others feel that the supervision and authority of physicians are necessary if standards are to be upheld and if medical work is to be accomplished properly (Goss, 1961; Perrow, 1965).

Some investigators refer to three, rather than two, lines of authority in the hospital. The third line consists of a decision-making flow from the governing board, which is usually referred to as a board of trustees in voluntary hospitals. Supposedly, the board is the central authority for the community hospital. But, in reality, the board has limited power, especially over medical personnel. The governing board is usually composed primarily of persons who know relatively little about the daily work and needs of the hospital and who have little time to give to its activities. In general, board members are selected from the business and professional sectors of the immediate community and are chosen because of their influence in the community.

An important contribution of board members to the hospital is linkage with the community. In theory, the board protects the interests of the public while also representing the hospital to the community; this can be important public relations in both directions. The board usually remains an outside force in decision making, however, especially since members tend to view problems differently from the administration and hospital employees (Riska and Taylor, 1978).

Statuses, Roles, and People in Interaction

Organization charts, like the one presented in Figure 8–1, show formal relationships among the various statuses in a bureaucratic hierarchy. By implication, such charts also suggest some aspects of role relationships, especially those of a subordinate-superordinate nature, which set patterns of interaction along stratification lines.

Stratification Lines.   One key to understanding interaction patterns within the hospital is to recognize its rigid system of social stratification. The hospital has a definite and well-recognized hierarchy of prestige for each position held. Each status is ranked in terms of value, difficulty, and prestige, and each is differentially rewarded according to its judged value. Given the dominant structure of medical care in the United States, the prestige and presumed value and knowledge of the doctor make that position the most highly rewarded and the most powerful. From the pinnacle of physician prestige, privilege and power move down through succeedingly less esteemed and rewarded positions.

This status system is displayed in a number of ways, from the deference exhibited toward physicians to the clothes the occupants of each position wear. Aides, licensed practical nurses, and registered nurses display the prestige of their statuses within the structure through such symbols as the uniform, pins, and badges. Administrative personnel may wear business clothing with a name badge specifying their position. Physicians display their superior status by *not* wearing special clothing; their claims to status may be made by the symbolic stethoscope dangling from the neck or pocket or, more powerfully, by their self-presentation in the wards through such actions as deliberately not returning patients' charts to the nurses' station.

Fox (1989) points out that such distinctions are not solely the result of structured inequality. She compares the use of different uniforms in the hospital with such use in the military. According to her, the military distinctions serve to make action almost automatic when emergencies arise. Similarly, emergencies that arise in the hospital can be handled with dispatch because the various dress styles facilitate the reaction process of personnel to meet the situation.

One study of interaction between ward personnel in a large private general hospital (Wessen, 1958) found that the levels of personnel on the ward are represented by as many as twenty-three occupational groups. These are divided into physicians, nurses, paramedical workers, technicians (such as dietitians and physical therapists), semiskilled workers, and unskilled workers. Rigid lines were drawn between each group and social distance was generally maintained. Seating patterns in the hospital cafeteria confirmed separation by occupational status. Except for some special groups, like the surgical team, each occupational group usually had its own place in the dining room. In many hospitals, the cafeteria formally designates one area for physicians only. Although such separation is defended on pragmatic grounds, the prestige implications are obvious.

Physicians.   The physician's relationship to the community hospital bureaucracy is unusual and is not found in any other large-scale social organization in the United States. The physician is not an employee of the community hospital but can, nevertheless, assume control over the work activities of almost all the facility's employees. Under the declaration of a medical emergency, the doctor can virtually take control of decision making in the entire facility. Yet the physician is a "guest" given the right to use the hospital's services and resources. But the hospital could not function without the physician, which gives the doctor a very special and, as we have seen, powerful place within the life of the general hospital.

At the same time, the hospital is vital to the medical doctor because it serves as a convenient and specialized extension of the office. No doctor can be truly successful in the practice of medicine today without a hospital appointment. Thus, a symbiotic relationship exists between the medical doctor's needs and those of the hospital. For the newly graduated physician establishing a medical career, staff membership in a hospital is a necessary beginning step.

Some hospital personnel, especially administrators and nonmedical personnel, charge that physicians show little real concern for the fate of the hospital. Physicians are relatively uninformed about most aspects of the institution's function and organization, and they generally do not really understand the problems and needs of other personnel within the facility. This does not mean, however, that the medical staff is not interested in the fate of the hospital. Physicians give much time and expertise to the success of the hospital because without it they could not survive professionally.

An important concern for all is the quality of physician practice in the hospital. Although it is not aggressively pursued, all control comes from other physicians. A commonly used means of controlling quality is to ascertain whether surgery was necessary; committees of concerned medical staff who examine laboratory reports on tissue removed during operations have been established in hospitals. But these tissue committees are composed of other physicians, and this approach has been criticized because "members of the club" may be reluctant to criticize their fellows.

A constant question for hospitals and physicians is whether different methods of payment would affect the quality of hospital care. Approaching this question, Georgopoulos, D'Aunno, and Saavedra (1987) surveyed nine hospitals in Rochester, New York, where a prepayment system effectively froze hospital budgets for five years. Using several measures of care quality, these investigators concluded that such prepayment plans had no negative, and had some positive, effects on patient-hospital relationships. In particular, no adverse effects on physician performance quality were found; in fact, respondents felt that physicians had gained a better concept of the hospital's needs.

A serious problem remains in controlling the quality of medical practice through such self-policing techniques as tissue committees because they are, as Millman (1978) points out, "cordial affairs" in which great care is taken to see that no embarrassing charges are publicly made. The purpose of such committee meetings is to review medical cases ending in patient death to see whether the death could have been prevented. But admitting such a possibility would be very uncomfortable, so mortality conferences are treated as educational meetings, with attempts to avoid recognizing the failures of other physicians. The committees seek evidence of error while at the same time covering up any that is found.

Nurses.   Relationships between nurses of different education and levels can be a source of friction in the hospital. Ambiguities in duties, prestige differences, and role definitions create difficulties for nursing supervisors. In particular, registered nurses resent being asked to perform tasks they consider beneath them, and they are simultaneously unhappy about licensed practical nurses and nurse aides performing duties they feel are specifically theirs. A clearer definition of nursing roles is needed to reduce this friction.

Nursing has been stereotyped as a female occupation; it grew into a respectable occupation at a time in our history when women were subordinate to men, serving their needs. Women were viewed as dependent and lacking in creativity and initiative. Although the place of the nurse has changed, the status order of the hospital still reflects this subordinate role. It is clear that the gender-oriented view of nurses maintains their lower place in the stratification of the hospital. Sexism in hospital occupations, particularly as it relates to the nurse, is a vital concern for many.

Lower Level Employees.   Nurse aides, orderlies, housekeepers, janitors, cleaning workers, and maintenance workers are at the bottom of the hospital's occupational hierarchy. As Freidson (1970) notes, these are poorly paid, basically unskilled or untrained workers who perform the dirtiest jobs in the hospital. They understandably have none of the professional orientation of other occupations. In some long-term-stay hospitals, such as those for the mentally ill and the aged, these lower level workers may have more face-to-face contact with patients than do doctors and nurses; in short-term general hospitals, however, such contact is usually minimal.

Some hospitals provide training programs for their lower level workers. According to Feldman (1977), however, such programs do not accomplish what hospital administrators intend because they do not help workers communicate better nor do they motivate them with some ideal standard of work. Some programs do raise the general satisfaction level, which reduces the problem of turnover. Nevertheless, research indicates that lower level employees have very low job commitment. Turnover and absenteeism are extremely high, and most workers feel apathetic and alienated. They receive low pay and have no opportunity for advancement.

Patients.   By social definition, hospital patients are in a helpless position, one dependent on the expertise of technical personnel. Further, the patients may be anxious about the course of events and about themselves and their families. While they are meeting the needs of the patients, hospital personnel also are concerned about their own needs that stem from problems inherent in any formal organization, generally, and from the hospital, specifically.

The patient is not within the hospital stratification system, but is the prime object of those who are. When problems arise in the process of caring for patients in the aggregate, staff members work in terms of their own needs rather than those of the patients. In the process, as Freidson (1970) comments, patients are turned from human beings into clients who must take what service can be bargained for. Patients may begin to feel depersonalized as if they are objects to be handled rather than persons to be cared for. They may object to hearing themselves referred to as "the hernia in 417," a reference that comes close to meeting Goffman's (1961) conception of a nonperson.

Lorber (1975) suggests that, from the perspective of the hospital, the good patient is one who can be dealt with easily with a minimum of inconvenience. Although hospitalized patients may resent the passivity expected of them, they tend to conform because the patient role is defined by hospital personnel, they feel it is necessary to behave according to the norms of the organization, and they believe this is the best way to obtain care. This perception is accurate; hospital staff do respond better to the quiet, trouble-free patient who behaves properly, is obedient and cooperative, and is objective about his or her illness. Staff evaluations of the patient depend on perceptions of how much trouble the patient gives. Patients who complain, are emotional, and constantly seek reassurance are considered to be problems and may be referred to by the hospital staff, including doctors, by pejorative terms (Leiderman and Grisso, 1985).

Problems Created by Stratification Lines.   The rigid stratification of the hospital has several consequences: (1) communication and interaction between occupants of the various status levels are difficult, (2) informal in-groups based on hospital occupational position tend to develop, (3) overlapping areas of authority cause some workers to be unsure of their relationship with others in the hierarchy, and (4) the lines between status groups emphasize blocked mobility, which affects commitments to the hospital and its goals.

   The years of preparation needed for specialization in hospital positions blocks the advancement of individual, lower level workers. But an occupational group can try for advancement by attempting to assume the functions of the next higher status, meanwhile relegating some of the more unpleasant duties to those below. For example, nurses on the treatment team can pass the task of emptying bedpans to nurse aides. If nurses can shed the clearly nonprofessional tasks, perhaps some small movement upward in the stratification system will result. Such attempts by nurses and others have been successful in the hospital social environment.

   Blocked mobility is probably a major reason for the high worker turnover in the hospital. On-the-job training for a better position or a "battlefield promotion" in the hospital are unavailable, and advancement within rank is highly unlikely. Without leaving the system, obtaining more education, and then returning in a different status altogether, low-level employees have no way to rise above the confines of the tasks for which they were hired. Those workers not committed to the goals of the facility tend to leave and seek other work.

   With the rigid stratification and the conflicting ideologies of members of the hospital work force, it is not surprising that communication is difficult among the occupants of different statuses. Three essential elements for good communication are lacking: (1) adequate channels of interaction between all members, (2) agreement on goals and means to achieve those goals, and (3) clear role responsibilities and authority for all positions (Wessen, 1958). Given these problems, the greater the social distance between groups, the less the communication. Most communication between groups in the hospital moves downward in the stratification system, although the nurse tends to be a liaison between groups.

The Informal Organization.   Investigators of large-scale social organizations have long recognized that, although they are structured with formal rules, bureaucratic regulations can actually be an obstacle to meeting objectives; formality can also lead to the alienation of workers. Sociologists also have observed that people in bureaucratic organizations develop ways to circumvent the formal structure, either to accomplish the task better or to find some relief from the formality of organizational life. Often, informal norms arise from the needs of the members of particular groups and subgroups within the organization.

Such is the case in the hospital, which can be viewed as a network of subcultural worlds within which groups develop their own norms (Fox, 1989). As the day wears on, the rigidity of the system begins to wear thin, especially as the demands of work diminish in the late afternoon and visitors have left. By nighttime, with the patients asleep, visitors gone, and the work schedule easing, the lines often break down altogether, in the face of an informality that comes from working in the lonely hours. This pattern is not exclusive to hospitals—it is often found on night shifts in many other formal organizations.

In a classic study of hospital relations, Wilson (1954) analyzed interaction in the operating room of a general hospital. Here the work demands intricate teamwork, which may be endangered by the rigid stratification lines of the formal organization. Surgical procedures can be dramatic, full of intensity, fear, excitement, and importance. Operating rooms are physically separate from the mainstream of routine activities in the rest of the hospital, a separation that becomes symbolic for staff members, since they have their own territory. All others may be seen as outsiders, and a strong in-group feeling can develop among the members of the surgical staff. Although the authority of the surgeon is respected in the operating room, a spirit of teamwork transcends the usual occupational lines in the hospital.

The Emergency Room: Bending the Formal Rules.   Emergency room activities also encourage workers to bend some formal rules of the hospital. The emergency room can be exceptionally busy, partly because many patients in a large urban hospital are neither trauma cases nor urgent medical problems. Thus, patients may have delayed seeking routine medical care until after hours; others may not have access to other medical resources. Many people in the lower socioeconomic status groupings in large cities use the emergency room as a walk-in doctor's office (Kurtz, Chalfant, and Kaplan, 1974). Further, a number of people coming into the emergency room appear to have created their own problems, such as those in difficulty with alcohol or drugs (Roth, 1971).

Emergency room workers evaluate the validity and urgency of the problems presented. By the rules, this should be done on universalistic principles, but moral and personal standards often are used in the control of emergency room clientele. Roth (1972) cites two standards emergency room staff use to decide who should receive prompt and full care: One standard is based upon the worker's judgment of the patient's social desirability or value to society and the second on whether the worker feels that the case is appropriate to the use of the emergency room.

In the first instance, workers tend to make moral judgments that are separate from the seriousness of patients' conditions and to depart from official regulations in giving care. For example, the young patient often will receive quicker attention than the older one. Likewise, evaluations of conditions such as alcoholism or a condition presented by a prostitute may be affected more strongly by moral labeling than by medical diagnoses.

Relative to the second point, many emergency room personnel agree that no patient should be turned away without being seen by medical staff, but if the condition is not a true emergency they feel they have no obligation to provide treatment. Consequently, those coming to the emergency room with conditions not perceived as appropriate for emergency services are viewed negatively. Principally, the staff resent what they see as outpatient department cases—that is, patients who could have been treated by the outpatient department of the hospital or by a private physician. It is argued that the hospital emergency service deserves full and separate status as a department in the organizational structure of the hospital so it can continue its main function, that of providing needed emergency services (Spencer, 1972).

OTHER HEALTH CARE AGENCIES

The hospital is only one of several organizations that provide health care to members of the community. In some respects it competes with other agencies for some types of patients. For example, outpatient and home-care institutions also provide services for the sick and injured; a patient could receive health care from these institutions or from the hospital.

The Nursing Home

The nursing home, which focuses on long-term care for the aged, can be viewed as an adjunct or alternative to the hospital for particular types of patients, especially the elderly. Stroke, heart disease, rheumatoid arthritis, and senility are the major conditions treated in a nursing home (Decker, 1980); these conditions could be treated in the hospital. In some instances, health professionals and family members may disagree about which facility is most appropriate. This is particularly true when the patient is troublesome or may not be able to pay for the needed service. Hospital and nursing care administrators sometimes engage in battles over such patients. On the other hand, the organizations may agree on a working arrangement concerning transfers between them.

As chronic disease and the need to provide custodial and rehabilitative care has increased in this country, the nursing home has become the major large-scale organization for long-term health care. The number of nursing homes grew from 10,636 in 1967 to 14,250 in 1986—an increase of 34 percent. The increase in the number of beds is even greater; the one-and-one-half million beds in such homes in 1986 represents an increase of 152 percent since 1967 (Andersen and Mullner, 1989); apparently using different criteria, the National Center for Health Statistics (1989) lists the number of nursing homes with 25 or more beds in 1986 as 16,033 and the number of beds as 1.6 million.

Home Care and Hospices

A relatively new transitional form of care is found in agencies that provide programs of health care in the home. The number of such programs increased from 1,753 in 1967 to about 6,000 in 1986 (Andersen and Mullner, 1989). Most are owned by for-profit corporations or are associated with hospitals. Perhaps the most important factor leading to the increase is the trend for earlier release of patients from hospital care.

Patients are released when they still require nursing service care, but not to the extent of that offered by the hospital. This situation is found particularly among the chronically ill and the aged.

Another new form of health care agency is the hospice, which is dedicated to making the dying process more comfortable and less inhumane for all concerned. As recently as 1974 only one hospice existed in the United States; in 1986, this figure had grown to more than 1,500 facilities providing care for 140,000 people (Andersen and Mullner, 1989). In some areas of the United States, the growth of these facilities has taken on the form of a social movement, and interest in the "hospice movement" is increasing (Paradis, 1985, 1988). This has been a response by individuals who have seen a social problem in the way in which hospitals and other health care agencies care for the dying.

SUMMARY

Hospitals began as facilities to care for the poor who could not be treated at home; they were frequently little more than places to die. The medical discoveries that led to improvements in care, however, brought more and more treatment into the hospital, which now functions as an extension of the physician's office. The hospital is now the hub for all but the most routine medical care.

Hospitals vary in size, funding, types of patients, and conditions treated. But fundamental to the work of all facilities called hospitals is the treating of and caring for patients. Even as the orientations of hospitals changed from theological to scientific, concern for the patient's care and treatment remained central. The major change concerning hospitals in the United States is their recently acquired central position in the medical care delivery system.

Hospitals can be categorized in many ways; in this chapter, we focused on function. The general hospital, increasingly the dominant form, is directed to treating, to some degree, all kinds of health problems. Specialty hospitals focus on particular conditions or specific types of people. Currently, most kinds of special facilities are being deemphasized, and general hospitals are handling more and more complex treatment for most health problems and diseases.

A major transformation in hospital care has resulted from the coming of the corporation to the health care system. An increasing number of hospitals are owned and operated by corporate structures in multihospital chains. In response to this movement, both for-profit and a number of nonprofit hospitals have contracted with corporate management systems to operate their facilities.

A hospital is a social organization, a subsystem of the larger medical institution and the society. It is related to the values of society as a whole in a number of ways: Health is a central concern in and of itself; faith in science spills over into a positive assessment of scientifically oriented medicine; and the humanitarianism and compassion the hospital is expected to routinely exhibit are core values in society.

The hospital must deal with other social institutions with interests that overlap those of the medical institution, for example, the family, religion, and the economy.

As part of medical care, hospitals must deal with many health care agencies and attempt to integrate their work with other parts of the health care delivery system.

Structurally, the hospital is characterized by a high degree of division of labor and task specialization. Incumbents of each status have specific functions and particular training, making the integration of personnel essential. Although some hospitals, particularly those under government authority, are organized and function according to bureaucratic rules, most hospitals find it difficult to operate within strict hierarchical patterns.

Many observers of the hospital have commented on the dual lines of authority that exist in the facility, especially in the general hospital. Given the status of the physician as a nonemployee but as a person in authority, a medical-professional line of command has developed alongside the administrative line. Structured in different ways, the two lines are sometimes in conflict. Specifically, in whatever a physician considers a medical matter, the medical-professional line can contravene the standing orders of the lay-administrative line.

A central feature of the hospital is an extremely rigid stratification system that allocates rights and obligations to the incumbents of statuses on the basis of specialized training. Several problems arise from this rigidity: Communication and interaction are difficult between members at different levels of the status system; informal groups with their own special interests develop at each status level; overlapping areas of authority make lower level workers uncertain of their roles relative to those above them in the hierarchy; and stratification also has specific consequences for lower level workers in that there is little opportunity for upward mobility, with a consequent high rate of turnover.

Still, in special cases, such as the emergency room and the operating room, informal systems of organization counter much of the rigid stratification in the hospital as a whole. In such instances, dedication to purpose, motivation, and pride in work can be more vital than formal rules or special statuses.

Although hospitals are the hub of health care today, they are not the only institutions providing medical care. Among the other agencies offering such care are nursing homes, home health care units, and hospices that seek to provide care for terminally ill patients.

References

American Hospital Association. 1986. *Hospital Statistics, 1986.* Chicago: Author.

———. 1988. *Hospital Statistics, 1988.* Chicago: Author.

Andersen, Ronald M., and Ross M. Mullner. 1989. "Trends in the organization of health services." In *Handbook of Medical Sociology*, 4th ed., ed. H. Freeman and S. Levine, 144–165. Englewood Cliffs, N.J.: Prentice-Hall.

Decker, David L. 1980. *Social Gerontology.* Boston: Little, Brown.

Ehrenreich, John, and Barbara Ehrenreich. 1971. *The American Health Empire.* New York: Vintage.

Feldman, Daniel Charles. 1977. "Organizational socialization of hospital employees: A comparative view of occupational groups." *Medical Care* 15(10):779–813.

Fox, Renee C. 1989. *The Sociology of Medicine: A Participant Observer's View.* Englewood Cliffs, N.J.: Prentice-Hall.

Freidson, Eliot. 1970. *The Profession of Medicine.* New York: Dodd, Mead.

Georgopoulos, Basil S., Thomas A. D'Aunno, and Richard Saavedra. 1987. "Hospital-physician relations under hospital prepayment." *Medical Care* 25(8):781–795.

Goffman, Erving. 1961. *Asylums.* Garden City, N.Y.: Doubleday-Anchor.

Goss, Mary E. W. 1961. "Influences and authority among physicians." *American Sociological Review* 26:39–50.

Krause, Elliott A. 1977. *Power and Illness: The Political Sociology of Health and Medical Care.* New York: Elsevier.

Kurtz, Richard A., H. Paul Chalfant, and Kipton Kaplan. 1974. "Inner-city residents and health decision-makers: Perceptions of health problems and solutions." *American Journal of Public Health* 64(June):612–613.

Leiderman, Deborah B., and Jean-Anne Grisso. 1985. "The gomer phenomenon." *Journal of Health and Social Behavior* 26:222–231.

Light, Donald W. 1986. "Corporate medicine for profit." *Scientific American* 255(6):38–45.

Litman, Theodor J. 1966. "The family and physical rehabilitation." *Journal of Chronic Diseases* 19(February):211–217.

———. 1974. "The family as a basic unit in health and medical care: A social-behavioral overview." *Science and Medicine* 8(September): 495–519.

Lorber, Judith. 1975. "Good patients and problem patients: Conformity and deviance in a general hospital." *Journal of Health and Social Behavior* 16:213–225.

Lynaugh, Joan E. 1988. "Narrow passageways: Nurses and physicians in conflict and concert since 1875." In *The Physician as Captain of the Ship: A Critical Reappraisal*, ed. N. King, L. Churchill, and A. Cross, 23–37. Dordrecht, Holland: D. Reidel Publishing.

Mackintosh, Douglas R. 1978. *Systems of Health Care.* Boulder, Colo.: Westview Press.

Mauksch, Hans O. 1960. "It defies all logic—but a hospital does function." *Modern Hospital* 95:67–70.

Millman, Marcia. 1978. "Medical mortality review: A cordial affair." In *Dominant Issues in Medical Sociology*, ed. H. D. Schwartz and C. S. Kart, 238–244. Reading, Mass.: Addison-Wesley.

National Center for Health Statistics. 1989. *Health, United States, 1988.* DHHS Pub. No. (PHS)89-1232. Public Health Service. Washington, D.C.: U.S. Government Printing Office.

Navarro, Vicente. 1976. "Social class, political power and the state and their implications in medicine." *Social Science and Medicine* 10:437–457.

———. 1986. *Crisis, Health and Medicine: A Social Critique.* New York: Tavistock.

Paradis, Lenora Finn. 1985. *Hospice Handbook.* Rockville, Md.: Aspen Systems.

———. 1988. "An assessment of sociology's contributions to hospice: Priorities for future research." *The Hospice Journal* 4(3):57–71.

Parsons, Talcott, and Renee Fox. 1952. "Illness, therapy and the modern urban American family." *Journal of Social Issues* 8:2–3, 31–44.

Perrow, Charles. 1965. "Hospitals: Technology, structure and goals." In *Handbook of Organizations*, ed. J. March, 710–790. Chicago: Rand McNally.

Rank, S. G., and C. K. Jacobson. 1977. "Hospital nurses' compliance with medication overdose orders: A failure to replicate." *Journal of Health and Social Behavior* 18:188–193.

Riska, E., and J. A. Taylor. 1978. "Consumer attitudes toward health policies and knowledge about health legislation." *Journal of Health Politics, Policy, and Law* 3(1):112–123.

Rosen, George. 1963. "The hospital: Historical sociology of a community organization." In *The Hospital in Modern Society*, ed. E. Freidson, 1–36. New York: Free Press.

———. 1979. "The evolution of social medicine." In *Handbook of Medical Sociology*, 3rd ed., ed. H. Freeman, S. Levine, and L. Reeder, 23–50. Englewood Cliffs, N.J.: Prentice-Hall.

Rosenberg, Charles E. 1987. *The Care of Strangers: The Rise of America's Hospital System.* New York: Basic Books.

Rosengren, William R., and Mark Lefton. 1969. *Hospitals and Patients.* New York: Atherton.

Roth, Julius A. 1971. "Utilization of the hospital emergency department." *Journal of Health and Social Behavior* 12:312–320.

———. 1972. "Some contingencies of the moral evaluation and control of clientele: The case of hospital emergency service." *American Journal of Sociology* 77:839–856.

Smith, Harvey L. 1958. "Two lines of authority: The hospitals' dilemma." In *Patients, Physicians and Illness*, ed. E. G. Jaco, 468–477. New York: Free Press.

Spencer, James A. 1972. *Hospital Emergency Department.* Springfield, Ill.: Charles C. Thomas.

Starr, Paul. 1982. *The Social Transformation of American Medicine.* New York: Basic Books.

Ver Steeg, Donna F., and Sydney H. Croog. 1979. "Hospitals and related health care delivery settings." In *Handbook of Medical Sociology*, 3rd ed., ed. H. E. Freeman, S. Levine, and L. Reeder, 308–346. Englewood Cliffs, N.J.: Prentice-Hall.

Weisner, Constance, and Robin Room. 1984. "Financing and ideology in drug treatment." *Social Problems* 32 (2):167–184.

Wessen, Albert F. 1958. "Hospital ideology and communication between ward personnel." In *Patients, Physicians and Illness*, ed. E. G. Jaco, 448–468. Glencoe, Ill.: Free Press.

Wilson, Robert N. 1954. "Teamwork in the operating room." *Human Organization* 12:9–14.

9

The Health Care Systems of Six Countries

INTRODUCTION

If the health institution in any society is to function properly, it must be meaningfully related to the country's demographic characteristics. Further, since a health system is society's organized way of meeting particular needs of the population, its structure and operation must reflect the overall culture, especially the dominant values of the society. These values are generally consistent and integrated; therefore, we must expect the values influencing the nature of the health institution to be consistent with those of other social institutions. The political and economic institutions are particularly interrelated with the health system because they provide the legitimacy, authority, and financial support necessary to the health system. Finally, since the health institution often requires a major commitment of financial resources, its nature also depends on the society's ability and willingness to pay the costs of the system.

Thus, our discussion of how different societies have developed different ways of meeting the health needs of their populations will focus on the demographic makeup, the value systems, and the financial status of each country considered in this chapter. After we discuss each factor, we will examine the systems that have been devised to meet the health needs of six different societies.

INFLUENCES ON THE HEALTH CARE SYSTEM

Demographic Characteristics

Different population characteristics lead to different demands on health systems. For example, one important demographic feature affecting the nature of the health system is the rural-urban distribution of the population. In an urban society, health resources and specialists are concentrated; in a rural area, resources are spread out and generalists are usually the main health practitioners.

Another important demographic characteristic affecting the nature of the health care system is the population's age distribution. The health needs of a society with a high proportion of elderly and a low proportion of young people are very different from one with large numbers of the young and few of the elderly. Age distribution differences among developed and developing nations illustrate the point; for example, the percentage of the population under fifteen years of age is only 19.2 in the United Kingdom, compared with 48.6 in Tanzania; the percentage sixty-five years of age and over is 15.1 in the United Kingdom and 2.3 in Tanzania (see Table 9–1). If the health systems in these two countries are to meet the needs of their people, facilities for the aged and physicians knowledgeable about degenerative and chronic diseases would be provided in one and extensive pediatric services would be provided in the other.

But a caveat is necessary at this point: To understand a social institution's response to the demographic makeup of the society, one must take into account the social and cultural patterns of that society. For example, two countries with the same percentage of elderly population may need different health system responses, de-

Table 9–1

Percentages of Population under Fifteen Years Old and Over 65 Years Old in 1985 and Population Living in Urban Areas in Selected Years

	Percentage			*Percentage Living in*
Country	*Under 15*	*Over 65*	*Year*	*Urban Areas*
China	29.7	5.3	1982	20.6
Kuwait	40.0	1.3	1981	80.8*
Tanzania	48.6	2.3	1986	18.2
U.S.S.R.	25.2	9.6	1985	65.4
United Kingdom	19.2	15.1	1981	87.7
United States	21.7	11.9	1980	73.7

Sources: Age distribution data are from World Health Organization, *World Health Statistics Annual, 1988.* Geneva: Author, 1988. Percentage of the population living in urban areas data are from United Nations, *Demographic Yearbook, 1986.* New York: Author, 1988.

*Estimated from information about countries in the Arabian Gulf.

pending on the sociocultural patterns relative to older people. One country may need homes for the aged that can be occupied for a fee, whereas a society in which the normal pattern is for the elderly to live with their children would have little need for such facilities. Thus, the influence of demographic variables cannot be understood outside the context of the total sociocultural environment.

National Values: Economic Systems and Concepts of Justice

Economic Values.   Two general economic orientations, capitalism and socialism, will be discussed in terms of their influences on the shaping of health care systems. Initially, theoretical constructs or pure types of these economic systems, rather than actual capitalistic and socialistic systems, will be presented. We will discuss particular societies in terms of the two models when each is discussed separately.

In a pure capitalistic state, all health care services are provided through private channels. Services are available on a fee-for-service basis; doctors, nurses, pharmacists, clinics, and hospitals levy a charge for each service in their practice. The size of this charge is set by the private practitioner or medical facility, which takes economic market forces into account. Governmental or other organizational rules and regulations might specify and monitor quality and might use such measures as accreditation to guarantee a minimum of training and performance. But, within legal and ethical guidelines, health workers and facilities would be free to decide on the nature of their work situation, that is, fees and the work schedule.

Within governmental regulations that enforce a minimum educational or training quality and, perhaps, limit some aspects of competition, practitioners are free to practice medicine as they see fit. The government is perceived as the means to prevent unfair competitive practices from tilting success toward any individual or any system. The highest quality person or system receives the highest rewards because of superior services rendered in an open and competitive field.

A capitalist health system emphasizes private practice or corporate medicine, with the doctor's office functioning much like the office in a business. (The analogy ends abruptly when the customer or patient is brought into the picture because of privacy and ethical considerations in the doctor-patient relationship that are not present in the businessperson-customer relationship.) Although the market leads to determining fees, patients are not totally helpless if they undertake comparative shopping in the health system. And, of course, if doctors want their patients to return for more medical attention, they make certain that, within ethical limits, patients are satisfied with what they are receiving from the relationship.

In comparison, in a socialist state all health services are owned and controlled by the government. (In philosophical terms, since the government belongs to the people, the health services are also owned by the people.) In such a health system, doctors are employed by the government and draw salaries for public practice. Health costs are met by the government, which obtains its funds through a variety of means, most commonly taxation. Working conditions, such as the hours an office is open, are set by the government. Legal and ethical guidelines are established by and monitored through governmental agencies. Theoretically, fees have no bearing on the type of service rendered by the doctor, who does not feel constrained by the patient's possible return for more medical attention.

Since the government or its representatives pay practitioners' salaries, the doctor-patient relationship is not dependent on any special financial consideration. The income of the doctor may not be related to the number of patients seen, the nature of services provided, or the quality of the service. Rather, the doctor is expected to meet the needs of patients and draw a salary for doing so.

Concepts of Justice.   Concepts of justice are also significant influences on the structure and operation of health care systems in any society. We will consider two in this section: market justice and social justice. Within the theoretical concept of market justice, people who succeed or do well according to the standards of society are entitled to rewards; those who fail or do poorly are not entitled to rewards. Success is judged as a result of good performance and individual initiative, and failure is a consequence of poor performance or a lack of initiative. The point is explained by Beauchamp (1979:444–445):

> *Under the norms of market-justice people are entitled only to those valued ends such as status, income, happiness, etc., that they have acquired by fair rules of entitlement, e.g., by their own individual efforts, actions or abilities. Market-justice emphasizes individual responsibility, minimal collective action and freedom from collective obligations except to respect other persons' fundamental rights.*

Such a statement correctly suggests that economic and justice values are usually closely intertwined. Thus, the capitalistic orientation of work and success is coupled with the idea of entitlement as a reward. A commitment to a capitalistic value system also suggests a commitment to a system in which some people are successes and some are failures as a result of their own behavior.

Health resources fit well into the theoretical market-justice orientation: Medical care is one of the valued ends awarded those who have succeeded. Individual initiative is also exhibited by self-responsibility since, within this concept of justice, "the primary duty to avert disease and injury . . . rests with the individual" (Beauchamp, 1979:445). This implies that preventive medicine and public health activities are not a priority in a society committed to the market-justice value system. Rather than society devising ways to provide for each person, the individual is expected to act on the basis of self-interest; people have a right to be left alone in their pursuit of self-interest, independent of whether the aim is economic success or good health.

A pure market-justice system might be generally harmful if the government did not control some activities and their consequences. Thus, the state seeks to control such activities as reckless driving, pollution of the atmosphere, and medical practice by quacks. But individuals have a right to inhale their own cigarette smoke, consume alcohol, or not buckle seat belts in cars; they have the right to engage in self-harming activities. Generally, there is a distinction between an industry's rights to harm others and people's rights to harm themselves. The former is not allowed, the latter is.

Under the concept of social justice, on the other hand, all people are entitled to social services that fulfill basic needs. Irrespective of position, success, or any other characteristic, all people are entitled to have their needs taken care of; their humanness alone entitles them to society's resources. Thus, such key needs as health protection and medical treatment are equally available to all within the society. Also, people are expected to contribute to societal programs. It is not considered fair for people to allow society's resources to come their way automatically; rather, individuals are expected to contribute what they can to society and to take from society only what they really need. Self-interest is looked upon negatively and the collective interest is emphasized.

It is evident that both socialism and the welfare state are based on the concept of social justice, just as market justice is a conceptual base for capitalism. The major philosophical difference lies in whether people are entitled to certain aspects of society's resources by the mere fact that they are humans or because they have succeeded.

A society committed to social justice makes a strong commitment to preventive medicine, investing in programs designed to take care of the health of the people. The social-justice concept implies that the government, or some other collectivity representing the people, has wide responsibility in a health program for the entire society, possibly even employing doctors and owning hospitals. This collectivity is expected to establish health prevention and health education programs for the benefit of all.

Wealth and Industrial Development

Most medical care delivery systems require major investments in personnel and facilities. To develop some understanding of the cost of an extensive western-based health care system, for example, consider the education and training of health workers (everyone from doctors to nurse aides), the salaries and support services for faculty members of educational institutions, the costs of research, and the construction of such facilities as schools (medical, nursing, allied health, dentistry, pharmacy, and public health). Consider also the investment in hospitals, clinics, ambulances, doctors' offices, X-ray machines, and stethoscopes; in the manufacture of medications in attempts to prevent disease; in educational programs designed to help people monitor their body functions; and in the health activities of medical practitioners outside the legitimate system (folk doctors, etc.). The total financial outlay can be huge. An extensive and modern western-style health care system is a luxury that is enjoyed by only a few societies.

In many poor countries, the provision of health services to the population is a lower national priority than food production, industrialization, defense, education, and transportation. Health care also may have a relatively low priority in wealthy societies, but enough money may still be available to develop an extensive system. Consequently, even if the priority in comparatively rich societies is low and in poor countries is high, the health expenditures in the former may be far higher than in the latter.

As it develops industrially and expands its financial base, a society can devote a greater amount and share of its resources to what the population considers to be a "good life." Usually included in the population's desires is an increased commitment to the quantity and quality of the country's health care system. In this context, two basic social institutions, health and education, are interrelated in their effects on the people's way of life. As the educational level of the people improves, their demand for more and better health care increases, and as the health status of the people improves, demands for better and more accessible education increase. This interplay seems never-ending. Are there societies in the contemporary world in which the people are content with either the health care system or the educational system? Not many, which accounts for the continual call in many societies for change to improve the lot of the people.

A decline in illiteracy, an essential element in western-type social and economic development, results from expanding educational opportunities. Such a decline means the society can rely more heavily on its own people to enter and take charge of the health institution. A common goal of developing societies is to educate nationals so they can take over some of the health care system's specialized services that have been in the hands of foreigners for many years. Many health leaders in developing societies feel that if health care is to be effective and meaningful for the population, it must be practiced by natives, because only they can truly understand the culture.

THE HEALTH CARE SYSTEMS OF SIX SOCIETIES

We will now examine the health care systems of six countries selected to demonstrate both similarities and differences in health system decisions. One is in North America, two are in Europe, another is in the Middle East, one is in Asia, and the final one is in Africa. They are similar in that all have made at least some commitment to the western-style health care system, but they have adapted the system to their own cultures. The discussion of these adaptations will focus on the combinations of economic and justice values within different demographic situations, economic conditions, and degrees of industrial development.

The United States

Health care delivery in the United States is an example of a system based on capitalistic economic values and a market-justice concept. It is placed in the context of a population that is changing toward a special demographic composition in a society possessing extensive wealth within a highly developed industrial economy.

Demographic Characteristics.   A distinct and important health-system-affecting demographic trend occurring in the United States is leading to special adjustments. This is the increasing proportion of residents classified in the older or senior category. Consider the following data: White men born in 1900 had only a 39 percent chance of living to age sixty-five compared with 1985, when the proportion had almost doubled to 75 percent; among white women, the chance of living to sixty-five years of age doubled from 44 to 86 percent during the same period. The proportion among black males tripled from 19 percent to 58 percent, and the increase among black women was outstanding, from 22 percent to 75 percent (based on decennial census counts; National Center for Health Statistics, 1988). There is another way of looking at such data: The percentage of the U.S. population sixty-five years of age in 1985 was 11.9 (see Table 9–1) compared with 1950, when it was a comparatively low 8.1; in actual numbers, the increase during the thirty-five-year period was from 12,195,000 to 28,536,000 people (National Center for Health Statistics, 1988). Furthermore, within the sixty-five-and-over category, the trend is particularly strong among the older age groupings: Between 1950 and 1985 the number of people between sixty-five and seventy-four years of age approximately doubled, the number between seventy-five and eighty-four almost tripled, and the number eighty-five and over almost quintupled (National Center for Health Statistics, 1988).

The elderly use health resources at higher rates than the rest of the population, and the rate of use is increasing. In 1983 the average number of physician visits per person was 5.1, close to the 1986 figure of 5.3, but the number of visits among those sixty-five and over increased from 7.6 to 9.1 during the same period, with the bulk of the increase occurring among those seventy-five years of age and older (National Center for Health Statistics, 1988).

A meaningful and effective health care delivery system in the United States must take this demographic trend into account. The system must adjust to the rapidly increasing number of elderly and must prepare for the consequences of the trend. This helps account for some recent controversies, particularly concerning such national measures as Medicare and catastrophic illness insurance legislation. There seems little doubt that much of the continuing debate about the nature and use of the health care system will center around health care for the elderly.

National Values: Economic Systems and Concepts of Justice.   Historically, the health care system of the United States has been rooted in capitalistic and market-justice values, with emphasis on free enterprise for professional practitioners and free choice for the population. But, there is an almost grudging acceptance of a governmental role within the system because a total lack of control can lead to unfairly manipulated competition and because health care costs are so high that large numbers of individuals would be excluded if the government did not provide programs for special groups. This contradicts the market-justice value, but generally the society manages to accept both ends of the justice value system without being bothered by the contradiction.

Wealth and Industrial Development.   By most measures of societal wealth, the United States is a rich country. For example, the gross national product per capita in 1985 was $16,400, considerably higher than in four of the other countries discussed in this chapter and slightly higher than oil-rich Kuwait (see Table 9–2). Wealth in itself, however, is not necessarily associated with health care availability. Thus, despite the wealth of the United States, large segments of the population do not receive adequate care because of economic barriers. From an exclusively market-justice perspective, such a pattern is not at all controversial but is, in fact, to be expected.

Table 9–2
Gross National Product (GNP; in U.S.$) in 1985 and Health Expenditures as a Percentage of GNP in Selected Years

Country	$ GNP per Capita	Year	% GNP Spent on Health
China	310	not available	
Kuwait	14,270	1984	6.2
Tanzania	290	1982	5.4
U.S.S.R.	6,763*	1984	4.2
United Kingdom	8,390	1984	6.1
United States	16,400	1986**	10.9

Sources: GNP data are from The World Bank, *The World Bank Atlas, 1987.* Washington, D.C.: Author, 1987. Health expenditure data are from World Health Organization, *Evaluation of the Strategy for Health for All by the Year 2000* (Seventh Report on the World Health Situation), 7 volumes. Geneva: Author, 1987.

*1983 data; from Cecelia A. Albert, ed., *World Economic Data.* Santa Barbara, Calif.: ABC-Clio, Inc., 1987.

**From National Center for Health Statistics, *Health, United States, 1987.* DHHS Pub. No. (PHS)88-1232. Washington, D.C.: Public Health Service, U.S. Government Printing Office, 1988.

The high degree of industrial development in the United States is reflected in its health institution. Just as private enterprise has relied more and more on industrial specialists, the health care system has become increasingly specialized. In medical and hospital systems in particular, a specialized division of labor is routine. All aspects of the health care system emphasize technical competence with reliance (those who feel nostalgia for old-type practice say "overreliance") on specialized technical skills. Reflecting this system, almost all doctors in the United States who have been in practice for some time are specialists who rely on highly technical (and expensive) equipment.

The Health Care System. With few direct rewards for the prevention of illness, the U.S. health care system focuses on curative medicine. Some of the highest rewards, basically in the form of a sizeable income, are given to doctors with specialized training whose practice focuses on particular types of patients and medical conditions. Specialists usually charge more for their services than do general practitioners, a differential they justify by reference to their extended training and experience.

The quality of practitioners and resources are checked by a variety of independent systems. Medical specialty boards control the training and quality of those vying for membership, the American Hospital Association sets standards for the accreditation of hospitals, laboratories check specimens removed during surgery and submit their findings to tissue committees in hospitals, and a constant threat of malpractice suits influences several aspects of private practice. Licensing is a function of government (each of the fifty states grants a license to practice in that particular state only, although many states grant a license to a practitioner from another state who applies for one under an agreement of reciprocity), but the criteria reflect private organization standards, such as those suggested by state medical societies.

Over the past few years, health expenditures have increased significantly in an area that is actually inconsistent with the market-justice theme of U.S. medicine: the provision of government aid to the elderly through Medicare and the poor through Medicaid, who have faced increasing difficulty in meeting rising health care costs. These programs violate the market-justice orientation, since much like a social-justice system, the government provides financial support to special segments of the population, rather than letting the free market decide on who obtains care.

Thus, in a system based on market-justice precepts, the government has stepped into some special areas of unmet needs with a social-justice or welfare approach, which clearly violates dominant values but meets the needs of those being left out of a fee-for-service system based on free enterprise. Volumes have been written to explain the seemingly selective inconsistencies. They can be attributed to the increasing number and power of the elderly in the country, political considerations by lawmakers, the unfavorable press received by organized medicine, the fact that the consequences of a pure market-justice system violate other important values in the society, and to myriad other quite logical explanations. All these explanations are correct, and all are insufficient in themselves. For a special category of people (there are others as well), the health care system of the United States has been modified to rectify what has been defined as social injustice without disturbing other aspects of the society's market-justice orientation. Consequently, the contemporary health care delivery system of the United States is eclectic, but the overall theme in the country is still market justice.

Health Problems of the Society.   The cost of the medical system has led to major criticisms of how it functions. The increase in national health care expenditures is enormous, from $13 billion in 1950 to $458 billion in 1986 (National Center for Health Statistics, 1988). Because they account for such large proportions of the total cost, hospitals (39 percent of health expenditures) and physicians (20 percent) have borne the brunt of the criticism. Despite the huge investment in the health care system, some groups, particularly the poor and minorities, find it difficult to obtain help from the system. One could say that this is a "natural consequence" of a system based on market-justice values, but the society still views this as a problem.

Summary.   In 1969 Fry summarized the nature of the health care system in the United States with nine specific statements. Although his points were not specifically addressed in our description of the U.S. health care system, they are related to our discussion and, in revised form, can be used as a summary of this section. Fry's points are:

1. Emphasis is on free enterprise, free choice, and individual responsibility. Consequently, people are supposed to determine their own health needs, seek their own care, and pay for their care privately.
2. The U.S. health care system must be understood within traditional suspicions of, and antagonism toward, the government or the state. These attitudes are held by both the public and the medical profession.
3. Planning reflects a compromise between laissez-faire policies and national planning.
4. Payment for medical services is basically on a fee-for-service basis.
5. The accessibility and availability of medical services depend on local factors.
6. Specialization within the medical profession is emphasized.
7. Attempts have been made to ensure the quality and standards of medical care.
8. Preventive care, outside of some limited public health programs, is basically an individual responsibility, although it is part of some special insurance and employment schemes.
9. Although self-help and public involvement in medical care are encouraged, no overall organization takes leadership in these areas.

The United Kingdom

Although the mainstream cultures of the United States and the United Kingdom (consisting of England, Scotland, Wales, and Northern Ireland) are similar, there are significant differences. Demographic composition and trends are similar in the two countries, but wealth and industrial development are at different levels. A paramount and core difference is found in their health care systems, which are based on different economic values and concepts of justice.

Demographic Characteristics.   In much of the western world, the elderly are becoming a larger and more politically important societal grouping. This statement clearly applies to the United Kingdom, in which life expectancy is now seventy-four years at birth (see Table 9–3), and the proportion of the population sixty-five years of age and older is an exceedingly high 15.1 percent (see Table 9–1). To meet the needs of its people, the society must provide more services for an older population. To encourage doctor interest in providing services for the elderly, the government provides extra remuneration to general practitioners for each person sixty-five years of age and over who is registered as a patient.

   While emphasizing the elderly, we should not lose sight of the 19.2 percent of the population under fifteen years of age (see Table 9–1). But it should also be noted that those in this age grouping use the health system at much lower rates than those on the other end of the age distribution.

National Values: Economic Systems and Concepts of Justice.   The health care system of the United Kingdom is based on socialistic economic values and social justice, values that lead to attempts to remove economic factors from the health marketplace. The government has created the National Health Service (NHS), which controls almost all general and specialized health services. (Since doctor participation in the NHS is not mandatory, some private practice still exists.) As employees of

Table 9–3
Crude Birth Rate, 1980–1985, Infant Mortality Rate,
Selected Years, and Life Expectancy at Birth in 1984

Country	Crude Birth Rate	Year	Infant Mortality Rate	Life Expectancy at Birth
China	19.0	1983	39.3	69
Kuwait	35.6	1984	18.5	72
Tanzania	50.6	1983	111.9	52
U.S.S.R.	19.1	1986	25.1	67
United Kingdom	13.0	1985	9.4	74
United States	15.7	1986	10.3	76

Sources: Crude birth rate data are from World Health Organization, *World Health Statistics Annual, 1988.* Geneva: Author, 1988. Infant mortality rate data are from United Nations, *Demographic Yearbook, 1986.* New York: Author, 1988. Life expectancy at birth data are from The World Bank, *The World Bank Atlas, 1987.* Washington, D.C.: Author, 1987.

the state, health personnel receive a government salary; the doctor's remuneration is determined by the patient registration load.

Since virtually every citizen has enrolled with a general practitioner, and since almost all general practitioners participate in the system, the government has almost total responsibility for medical care. Consistent with the socialist value system, planning and control are in the hands of the government. It amounts to a socialistic employment monopoly, with almost all doctors paid by the national government. Although the maintenance of standards in such a system is a governmental responsibility, the function of standards monitoring has been given to a professional health group.

Wealth and Industrial Development.   Along with other members of the western world, the United Kingdom is classified as a developed country. Its wealth is at the higher end of the worldwide economic spectrum, although its gross national product in 1985 was only one-half of that of the United States (see Table 9–2). It is easy to take the position that a country in comparatively good economic condition should provide its population with quality health care. But, as we have seen previously, the provision of health care services does not depend on wealth alone. In the United Kingdom, however, the expectation is fulfilled. The country is wealthy enough to provide health care for all and has devised a tax-supported system that meets this goal. There are no economic barriers to obtaining general and specialized health care in the country.

The Health Care System.   In the United Kingdom, "all of the population have access to treatment by family doctors and dentists, to the dispensing of prescribed drugs, to ophthalmic services, and to community nursing and health visitor services. It is generally through their family doctor that patients are referred to secondary (hospital) care" (World Health Organization, 1987, Vol. 5:211).

The general practitioner, or family doctor, is the initial contact for almost everyone entering the health system. Each general practitioner provides primary medical care for approximately 2,500 persons, all of whom have registered as patients. In true socialistic style, the general practitioner receives payment directly from the government; the amount is based on the number of registered patients. (There are also some other special payments.) Individuals can register with a general practitioner of their choice, as long as the doctor is willing to accept them and include them as part of the patient load. Once registered, patients have only this one primary care option within the government system of free care. Medical care is also available from either a private practitioner not affiliated with the NHS or from an NHS doctor with whom the patient is not registered; in these cases, the individual must pay for the service.

General practitioners set up their own offices and hire their own staff. Many have joined together in what we refer to in the United States as group practice. According to Sidel and Sidel (1983:159), "approximately 45 percent of all general practitioners today work in groups of three or more doctors." General practitioners are not on the hospital staffs, so they cannot treat their patients there; instead, they may refer them to hospitals. Patients are then treated by hospital doctors, who are specialists. Access to government hospitals and specialist service is obtained only through referral by the patient's general practitioner. This means the doctor with whom the patient is registered takes care of routine health problems only. But, as pointed out by Sidel and Sidel (1983:144), "it has been estimated that the [general practitioner] is the only point of contact for 90 percent of the episodes of ill health for which physician help is sought in Britain."

Before this system was instituted in 1948, the key status in United Kingdom medical care delivery was the general practitioner, who functioned in an independent and private enterprise system that had many similarities to that now prevailing in the United States. The new system has attempted to preserve the traditional role of the general practitioner by building around the public's cherished values of family doctors and general practice. Thus, the NHS is rooted in the mainstream culture. The major difference to the patient in the present system is the need to register with, and consequently be virtually limited to, one general practitioner. The major difference to the doctor is that instead of receiving payment from the patient, it is received from the government; that is, instead of private enterprise, medicine is now government enterprise. But, importantly, it is government enterprise that simultaneously makes the medical system a social-justice one and provides care consistent with the values of the society. Limitation to one doctor puts obvious restrictions on free choice but, in most instances, it gives people the same type of choice they had before the NHS was instituted because most tended to use only one general practitioner before the system was devised.

As a government agency, the NHS obtains almost all of its budget from taxation. Like any other such agency, the Department of Health submits a budget, which is considered by Parliament. In 1984, 6.1 percent of the United Kingdom's gross national product was spent on health care (see Table 9–2). Although this figure is considerably lower than that for the United States, by most standards the British health care system is huge. Thus, "the United Kingdom National Health Service is the largest single employer in Europe with over one million full-time equivalent staff" (World Health Organization, 1987, Vol. 5:212).

Consistent with its level of development, the United Kingdom has experienced an increasing reliance on specialists, and the health system is no exception to this social change. Thus, doctors tend to specialize. In discussing the system, Jefferys (1975:145) states that "there is considerable evidence to suggest that in the opinion of many of those who have qualified in medicine general practice does not provide a satisfying career." In some parts of the country, general practice posts remain unfilled. This pattern of specialization is akin to the one plaguing health care in the United States, but the reasons are different. In the U.S., the problem is rooted in the commitment to a market-justice system; that is, medical specialists in the United States earn substantially more money than general practitioners. According to Jefferys, the significant factor in the United Kingdom is the lower prestige ranking for general practice compared with that for specialized practice.

Health Problems of the Society. The establishment of the NHS in 1948 represented a major shift in the perception of who is entitled to health care in the United Kingdom; the shift in values was from market to social justice. This change reflected the philosophy of a new government, which was elected with promises to introduce a modified socialistic economic system. Medicine was one of several major enterprises nationalized by the new government. The mandate to socialize medicine was particularly strong because, under the market-justice system, health care was becoming too expensive for the average family.

But the nature of a health care system operated by an elected government is subject to sudden change if political events lead to changes in who is making decisions for the country. Thus, the current British government does not hold socialistic values, and it has been returning industries to the capitalist-based private sector for several years. It is only a matter of time before the government attempts the same action in the health area; how fast it moves in this direction depends on political factors. In fact, Sidel and Sidel (1983:171) indicate that the move toward privatization of the British health service has already begun.

Summary.   For a summary of the British health system, along with further description, we once again turn to Fry (1969):

1. Within a welfare state philosophy, the government has established the National Health Service (NHS) to administer a national medical care system.
2. Medical care is provided without cost to the patient.
3. Medical and other health services are readily available and are accessible to all people.
4. First contact in the system is usually with a generalist in an office or clinic who makes a decision about whether the patient needs the services of a hospital-based specialist.
5. Although much emphasis is placed on preventive care in the society, mass screening and routine physical examinations are not strongly supported.
6. Care of patients in their homes rather than in hospitals is emphasized.
7. Overall coordinated planning has proved to be difficult, primarily because of the administrative structure of services.

The Soviet Union

Whereas the health care system in the United States evolved with little direct control from the government, and the present system in the United Kingdom is the product of the government's attempt to modify an institution whose functions were inconsistent with an emergent value system, the health care system of the Soviet Union was imposed by the government.

Demographic Characteristics.   The population of the Soviet Union is relatively young; it is growing older but, in 1985, less than 10 percent of the population was sixty-five years of age or older (see Table 9–1). Even if the number and proportion of the elderly increase significantly in the Soviet Union (this, in fact, is occurring), the need for special homes for their medical care during their nonworking years will probably not be as great as it is in the United States and the United Kingdom. This is because the nuclear family concept of the western world, in which married couples and their children are expected to live as a solitary unit, has not been adopted in the Soviet Union. Consequently, many of the elderly in the U.S.S.R. are expected to move in with their married children at the same time that the elderly in the United States and the United Kingdom are moving into homes for the aged.

One-quarter of the population of the Soviet Union is less than fifteen years of age (see Table 9–1). Given the younger population, the health care system in the Soviet Union is geared toward providing many resources for children. This is reflected in the medical school training in which one of the three specialties available to students is pediatrics.

National Values: Economic Systems and Concepts of Justice.   In its description of the health system of the Soviet Union, the World Health Organization clearly states the socialist and social-justice bases upon which it stands (1987, Vol. 5:209):

> *Under socialism, health care is no longer a matter for the individual; health has become society's property, which every citizen is required to safeguard and strengthen. The right of Soviet citizens to health care is enshrined in the Constitution, the country's fundamental law. In one way or another, more than 20 articles in the Constitution relate to protecting and improving people's health.*

Wealth and Industrial Development.   By most standards, the Soviet Union is a developed society with wealth somewhere between the western world and developing societies. A 1983 estimate placed the gross national product per capita figure at $6,763, somewhat close to the 1985 figure of $8,390 for the United Kingdom (see Table 9–2). Coupling a social welfare and socialistic orientation with the ability to pay, it may be expected that a large proportion of the financial resources of the country would be committed to the health care of its people. According to World Health Organization (1987) data, however, only 4.2 percent of this gross national product is spent on health; this is the lowest proportion among the five countries under discussion in this chapter for which data are available (see Table 9–2).

The Health Care System.   All aspects of the health system and the delivery of services are centrally organized; the service is a state enterprise, with absolutely no possibility of a private sector. All health personnel in the country are on government salary. The state-provided resources are distributed by the government, which plans health care delivery for the total population. Since this is done under socialistic and social-justice orientations, the state planners have attempted to develop a network that provides all citizens with equal access to health care resources.

The flow of care is initiated at the neighborhood level, at which general practitioners and pediatricians are available in polyclinics and outpatient units, which function as local health centers. Doctors located in large industrial plants also act as first-contact resources; Sidel and Sidel (1983) state that "today approximately 30 percent of people of working age receive their health care and medical care through a special network of health services in the industries in which they work" (p. 178). In addition, there is an extensive array of facilities for pregnant women and children under fifteen years of age. In large cities, individuals do have some way of getting around this no-choice system since they can go directly to a multidoctor clinic (called a polyclinic) without a doctor's referral. This is not the case in rural areas, where practitioners with limited health training, such as some fairly basic nursing or medical education, are used extensively. These practitioners, who are expected to handle only routine and uncomplicated health problems, are known as feldshers (basically, physicians' assistants) and midwives.

Short-term general hospitals, usually with 300 to 1,250 beds, function in defined districts. The chief physician of a district hospital is responsible for all medical services in that district, including those provided by the polyclinics. Specialized hospitals provide services regionally; normally, a patient cannot seek the services of a regional facility without referral from a district hospital.

Preventive medicine is the dominant theme of the Soviet health care system. On a national level, "a system of epidemiological surveillance is in operation throughout the country. Practical work on preventive and routine surveillance is carried out by . . . epidemiological units" (World Health Organization, 1987: Vol. 5:207). Preventive medicine is supported by trade unions and branches of the Red Cross and Red Crescent societies through the dissemination of information and health education. An overwhelming majority of infants have been fully immunized against the usual childhood diseases.

Overseeing the total medical system is the Soviet Union's Ministry of Health. In addition, each of the country's fifteen republics has its own health ministry, which is responsible for health planning and delivery within its own territory. The Ministry of Health oversees a nationwide health budget and sets health priorities in conjunction with the Central Planning Council. The Ministry is supposed to act strictly as a policy-making body, with no administrative functions.

A health inventory, which sets in motion planning for the coming period, is undertaken every five years. A national plan defining needs and the ways they are to be met is announced, and each health district is expected to make its individual plans within the defined guidelines. Representatives of the public are on various government committees charged with the responsibility of setting standards and establishing goals.

Seventy percent of the doctors in the Soviet Union are women. The income and prestige of doctors are approximately the same as those of other professional and technical occupations for which extensive education is necessary; they are similar to teachers, engineers, and scientists. Like other health occupations and other professional groupings, doctors have trade union representation designed to protect the individual physician and the overall occupation.

Health Problems of the Society.   A medical problem that dominates in the country, one for which adequate preventive measures have been sought but have not been found, is alcoholism. As stated by Holden (1981:1091), "even the most cursory discussion of health in the Soviet Union cannot ignore the scourge of alcoholism." Coupled with failure in attempts at prevention has been failure in treatment. Consequently, "the toll, socially, economically, and in terms of health, is staggering" (Holden, 1981:1092).

Another problem is the vastness of the country, the largest in land area in the world, and the large proportion of the population, one-third, who live in rural areas (see Table 9–1). The provision of adequate services to such a spread-out population leads to many problems of health care delivery. As in the United States, persuading doctors to practice in rural areas is difficult; in contrast to the United States, however, the Soviet difficulties often reflect shortages of supplies and equipment in the rural areas, rather than matters of income.

Summary. Some of the principles on which the system in the Soviet Union is based and the nature of the system were summarized by Fry (1969) as follows:

1. The entire system was initiated and is controlled by the government, which makes all health care system decisions.
2. Health resources are available to the total population, even those living in the remotest of rural areas.
3. Medical students must specialize their programs to either general medicine, pediatrics, or public health.
4. Preventive medicine is emphasized in the society and in all health programs.
5. The point of entry into the system is a neighborhood physician.
6. There is no choice of doctors; patients must use the doctor in their neighborhood.

The People's Republic of China

From the Communist takeover of the mainland in 1949 until the early 1970s, the lines of communication between China and the West were essentially closed. When the "bamboo curtain" was raised in 1971, the media started flooding the West with information about the changes in China since the Communists took control. Reports stated that the Chinese had made major progress in providing resources for the entire population, especially the poor and the peasants (Sidel and Sidel, 1982). This was particularly so for the health system. As the World Health Organization points out, "against a background of poverty—the legacy of the old China—a primary network of health services has been established in both urban and rural areas" (1987, Vol. 7:54).

The last few years of the 1960s were particularly volatile, with Mao Zedong taking leadership in bringing about change. A theme of the call for change was for a shift of human resources from the well-supplied urban area to the neglected rural area and from the rich to the poor. This shift became a priority in the Cultural Revolution that was constantly emphasized by Mao. The health care system was cited as a prime example of what had gone wrong in the country, with resources concentrated in the city and among the well-to-do.

Little was known about the Chinese system of health care until the 1970s, when western visitors, including health observers, were welcomed by the government of the People's Republic of China. What emerged from reports was a picture of a country so large in area and population, so spread out, and so rural that health care delivery faces major problems. In addition, problems were created by a determined effort on the part of political leaders to bring industrialization and a modern lifestyle to the country in a very short time.

Demographic Characteristics.   In a land area close to the size of the United States, the Chinese population now exceeds one billion people, four times the U.S. population. Meeting the needs of such a large population presents many logistic problems. The rural (see Table 9–1) and undeveloped nature of the economy means that health services must be provided over a large area where there is inadequate mechanized transportation. Under these conditions, the health care delivery system must be spread widely and be based in local neighborhoods.

Two age-related factors also affect the nature of China's health care system: In 1985 the proportion of the population sixty-five years of age or older was 5.3 percent and the proportion under fifteen years of age was 29.7 percent (see Table 9–1). This means there are more than 50 million elderly and 300 million young people in the country. Since China's family system welcomes members of the older generation, the need for such facilities as homes for the aged does not exert strong pressures on the health care system. But the need for facilities that specialize in the care of children is evident; 300 million people under fifteen years of age suggests sizeable pediatric pressures on the health system.

National Values: Economic Systems and Concepts of Justice.   China's economic system is a socialistic governmental enterprise. The prevailing value system is one of social justice, and unobstructed access to health care is considered a fundamental right of all Chinese. The government recognizes that its economic development goals cannot be accomplished without a work force free from illness. Consequently, upgrading the health institution is an integral part of the move toward industrialization and modernization that has become a theme of national activities.

Wealth and Industrial Development.   With a gross national product (GNP) figure of only $310 per capita (1985 data; see Table 9–2), China must be judged a poor country by most standards. This low figure, coupled with the rural nature of the society, is one of the reasons the health system relies heavily on local practitioners. Data on the proportion of GNP spent on the health institution are not available, but given the nature of the country's economy, it cannot be high.

The Health Care System.   Before the Cultural Revolution, the health care system basically served the upper and middle classes in the urban area. In a verbal assault on this pattern, the chief revolutionary architect of the Great Leap Forward, Mao Zedong, served notice that he wanted this situation changed. He stated in 1965: "Tell the Ministry of Public Health that it only works for fifteen percent of the total population of the country and that this fifteen percent is mainly composed of gentlemen, while the broad masses of the peasants do not get any medical treatment" (quoted in Sidel and Sidel, 1982:4). Mao followed this condemnation with a phrase that has been the cornerstone of health planning in the country ever since: "In medical and health work put the emphasis on the rural areas!" (Sidel and Sidel, 1982:4). This is realistic because approximately 80 percent of the population resides in rural areas (see Table 9–1); these 800 million people are the "broad masses of peasants" referred to by Mao Zedong.

From a sociological perspective, the social characteristic that stands out in China today is rapid socioeconomic change. As two observers of the society recently put it, "The China that we visited in 1971 and 1972 was a society in the process of reorganizing its social institutions in the wake of the most turbulent years of the Cultural Revolution" (Sidel and Sidel, 1982:3). Almost twenty years later, as this chapter is being written, the change continues unabated. In the health care institution, for example, revolutionary changes in resources and delivery have occurred. In the narrow two-year period of 1978 to 1980, it was reported that the number of traditional Chinese medical personnel increased slightly (6.7 percent), whereas the number of "higher level" medical personnel (including western doctors) increased significantly. The number of western doctors in China in the two years increased from 358,500 to 447,300, the number of pharmacologists went up from 16,700 to 25,200, and the number of laboratory doctors rose from 7,000 to 14,800 (Sidel and Sidel, 1982:208f).

These numbers reflect what is taking place socially: western-style medicine is not supplanting the old system, but is being integrated into traditional medicine. Thus, in 1983, twenty-four colleges of traditional Chinese medicine had an enrollment of 25,000 students; further, the number of hospitals for traditional medicine increased from 171 to 1,009 and the number of beds increased from 210,000 to 310,000 between 1976 and 1983 (World Health Organization, 1987, Vol. 7). In addition, at least twenty-seven institutes integrate traditional Chinese and western medicine (World Health Organization, 1987, Vol. 7, points out that the data are incomplete).

One should not confuse the traditional medicine of China with irrational and superstitious folk approaches. Rather,

> *By virtue of its rich and ancient theoretical base, Chinese traditional medicine, which incorporates both diagnosis and therapy, differs from many other current systems of folk medicine, which are based purely on empirical observations, and differs from systems based on magic, witchcraft, and spiritualism. Diagnostic methods in Chinese medicine include observing and questioning the patient, limited physical examination, and detailed and prolonged pulse-taking. Therapy uses such techniques as medicinal herbs, acupuncture, moxibustion (the application of heat to sites on the skin),*

> *breathing and gymnastic exercises, and flexible splinting. (Sidel and Sidel, 1982:20)*

When health resources were being extended to the rural areas, a great deal of medical care was provided by practitioners known as "barefoot doctors." Barefoot doctors are generally peasants selected by fellow members of the agricultural commune who continue to work on the farm, but after limited training they take the responsibility for preventive medicine and some aspects of primary care in the local neighborhood. (Actually, barefoot doctors often wear shoes, but the colloquial name aptly portrays their position and function.) Their income is determined in essentially the same manner as other agricultural workers. For many of the 800 million people living in rural areas, the barefoot doctor is the only medical practitioner ever seen. From a sociological perspective, a strength of these practitioners is their within-the-culture socialization experience; given the homogeneity of peasant neighborhoods, the barefoot doctor should have little difficulty understanding the local sociocultural ways of thinking and acting.

Barefoot doctors are products of the initial governmental program devised to meet the priority of providing medical care in rural areas. These practitioners assume responsibility for such health-maintaining preventive medicine activities as environmental sanitation, health education, and immunization, and also provide primary medical care. In the treatment area, barefoot doctors rarely go beyond first aid and the treatment of minor diseases. According to Sidel and Sidel (1982), "barefoot doctors were encouraged to use a wide range of both traditional Chinese and Western medicines, and some had become skilled enough to perform limited forms of major surgery" (p. 39). Initial training of the barefoot doctor was for three to six months, often in a hospital, and many took further training. But concurrent with the upgrading of the health system has come a decline in the number of barefoot doctors.

Although the number has declined, there seems to be no governmental plan to eliminate barefoot doctors. On the contrary, the government is attempting to continue with these peasant physicians while upgrading their training with formal education programs. This is followed by examination and licensing, under close supervision by local departments of public health. Today, these practitioners take formal training for a minimum of six months; many have taken courses in specific areas of western medicine such as minor surgery. Consequently, the first point of contact in the health care system for many people in the rural areas is still the barefoot doctor.

In the urban areas, somewhat equivalent to the barefoot doctor, Red Cross Health Workers practice under the supervision of doctors in the local hospital; they were formerly known as "street doctors." The Red Cross Health Workers also focus on health promotion and disease prevention. Doctors functioning in similar capacities in factories are known as "worker doctors."

Programs to eliminate infectious diseases have been quite successful; rates have declined rapidly, especially in response to programs designed to eliminate flies, mosquitoes, rats, grain-eating sparrows, and bedbugs. Meanwhile, people are encouraged to build sanitary facilities in their neighborhoods. In the area of chronic disease, the central government initiated a campaign against the "harmful effects" of smoking (even though the estimated tobacco output in the country in 1978 was close to one million tons).

Health Problems of the Society.   Size-of-population pressures have led the government into family limitation programs. For many years, the government attempted to take a hard line against even moderately sized families, with strong efforts to convince couples that one child per family is enough. Since 1979, couples who have one child and pledge to have no others receive monetary, health care, housing, food, and work assignment benefits, and those who have three or more children lose a variety of benefits. Late marriage is promoted, contraceptives are available free of charge, sterilization is easily available to both men and women, and abortion procedures during the first trimester of pregnancy are provided by the government at no cost. As a consequence of these actions, and extensive "educational campaigns," the birth rate has been dropping rapidly. As stated by Greenhalgh and Bongaarts (1987), "since China first adopted strong birth control policies in the early 1970s, there has been a dramatic fall in Chinese fertility" (p. 1167). The present crude birth rate of 19.0 is approaching the rate of industrialized countries (see Table 9–3).

One should not conclude from these programs that the government provides little in the way of child care resources. On the contrary, China's constitution makes special mention of the protection of "mother and child." Thus, there is a national attempt to reduce the infant mortality rate, which is still much higher than in the West (see Table 9–3) but, as would be expected from the drop in infectious disease rates, is dropping rapidly. In addition, 2,500 specially designated maternal-infant care facilities have been opened, and special maternal and child care workers have been trained for preventive and therapeutic work (Sidel and Sidel, 1982).

Summary.   The following statements and principles summarize many of the points we made about the health care system of the People's Republic of China:

1. The health care system is designed by the government and reflects the dominant political and economic ideologies of the country, which are socialistic with state control of all resources. The philosophy of social justice prevails.
2. Treatment and basic preventive medicine strategies are intertwined, with prevention taking first priority; throughout the country, special emphasis is placed on health promotion and disease prevention.
3. The number of western-style physicians in the country is increasing rapidly. At the same time, the government's policy is to strengthen local traditional medicine. The upgrading of local health practitioners is strongly emphasized.
4. Attempts are being made to integrate traditional medicine with western medicine, thus preserving what are seen as the assets of both. Traditional medicine in China incorporates both diagnosis and therapy and uses acupuncture, medicinal herbs, the selective application of heat, special exercises, and flexible splinting.

5. The government continually calls for upgrading the health resources and personnel in the rural area.

Kuwait

To say that Kuwait is experiencing rapid social changes is to make a major understatement. Few other countries in the world have experienced a more than 800 percent increase in population during the past thirty years (in 1956, when the first census in the country was conducted, the population was 206,473; in a 1985 census, the count was 1.7 million), have maintained a population in which less than half of the residents are natives (in 1985, the percentage who are Kuwaiti citizens was 40.0), and have maintained high birth rates and low death rates. A snapshot of the country today reveals the effect of such change; the most prominent feature of the landscape is the building crane (visitors who expect oil well derricks will be disappointed—the oil industry in Kuwait is an underground one), as apartment houses, villas, hotels, shopping centers, government buildings, mosques, office buildings, roads, hospitals, and clinics are all under construction in a small country with little arable land.

Demographic Characteristics.   Demographers have observed that periods of economic prosperity are often also periods of increased birth rates. Perhaps as one of the many effects of Kuwait's prosperity, the crude birth rate in the country was a high 35.6 per 1,000 population in the 1980–1985 period compared with a western world rate of about 10 to 15 (see Table 9–3). But even this high figure understates the point since the rate among Kuwaitis is double that of non-Kuwaitis in the country. Thus, in 1983 the non-Kuwaiti rate was 24.7 and the Kuwaiti rate was 47.3 (Ministry of Planning, 1985).

A high birth rate (see Table 9–1) coupled with a fairly low infant mortality rate (see Table 9–3) leads to a large percentage of the total population in the childhood ages. (Table 9–1 shows that 40.0 percent of Kuwait's population in 1985 was less than fifteen years of age.) In the ordinary situation, such a high proportion of the population in an age group that must be economically supported would lead to major economic problems for the society. But this is not the case in Kuwait, where the social-justice value system is joined to a very strong financial base.

Care of the elderly is not a problem, neither from a demographic nor a sociocultural perspective. From the demographic perspective, in 1985 an exceedingly low percentage of Kuwait's population was sixty-five years of age or older (see Table 9–1). This percentage will undoubtedly increase rapidly since the life expectancy at birth figure is now comparable to that of the West (see Table 9–3). From the sociocultural perspective, many Kuwaitis follow the extended family pattern of parents and grandparents either living with their children or living in contiguous houses, which assures their care.

With more than 80 percent of its population living in cities, Kuwait is one of the most highly urbanized countries in the world (see Table 9–1). The 20 percent not in the cities are mostly nomadic and seminomadic Bedouins. Over the past few years, many Bedouins have been moving into the city, often to housing constructed by the government, and sometimes only for several months of the year.

National Values: Economic Systems and Concepts of Justice.   The orienting structure on which the Kuwaiti health care system is built is a welfare value system with a social-justice base. National values lead to the viewpoint that the government should share its wealth with the people; one means is to provide the population with free essential services. At the same time, the economic value system of the country is committed to capitalism, with the government's oil policy the finest example of this orientation.

Kuwait's enormous wealth is the underpinning for a social-justice health care delivery system in a country that holds capitalistic economic values. This is not a common combination in the world: The capitalistic economic orientation is usually joined with a market-justice value system, and the socialistic economic system is usually coupled with a social-justice value system. Since health care systems are expensive, Kuwait can continue to combine the capitalistic economic approach with a social-justice value as long as the oil is shipped out and the money keeps coming in.

Wealth and Industrial Development.   The backdrop to rapid change in the country was the discovery and production of oil. As the price of oil skyrocketed (especially since 1973) and as production increased, Kuwait's economy boomed and the country's income rose in a steep line. From an economy that plodded its way toward meeting some of the simple needs of its nomadic people, the economy rapidly expanded and Kuwait became a financial power in the world.

Dividing the huge income of the country by its small number of people became a worldwide game, and reports were issued that the per capita income of the country was the highest in the world; in 1985 the figure was $14,270 (see Table 9–2). But such data are misleading. People were not earning this money; the government and some oil companies were. Individuals do not own Kuwait's oil; the government does (the companies' shares have been bought by the government). The government did develop means for distributing part of the enormous income among many Kuwaitis in the country, but the tremendous inpouring of money went to the government itself. Further, when the price of oil declined, less money came in; but judged by the standards of most countries, the amount was still huge.

The Health Care System.   Delivery of medical care is centered in neighborhood primary care clinics that focus on patients with general and uncomplicated conditions; those with special and complex problems are referred to a multispecialty, multidoctor polyclinic or a hospital. If a special type of treatment is not available in the country, the government pays for Kuwaitis to go to another country for treatment (a favorite place is England). Foreigners are expected to go back to their own countries at their own expense for specialized care unavailable in Kuwait.

The Kuwaiti health care system response to the high birth rate and the resulting large number of children in the country has been a division of the typical local neighborhood primary care clinic into three departments: adult male, adult female, and maternal-child health. Many clinic doctors whose total patient load is children do not have the specialized training that would qualify them as pediatricians.

Health Problems of the Society.   In many ways, Kuwait was unprepared for modern development, especially in such areas as the health system. For example, in 1985 only 21 percent of the doctors were Kuwaiti (Ministry of Public Health, 1985); approximately half of the physicians in the country were Egyptian. In response, medical, nursing, and allied health colleges have been established; student admission preference is given to Kuwaitis (85 percent of new students in the medical school must be Kuwaitis).

Almost all doctors speak Arabic (the official language of the country) and all speak English; doctors communicate with patients in these languages. But this is not so among the nurses, who may be from Sri Lanka, the Philippines, Korea, or other nonArab countries. One can justifiably ask how nurses can offer the emotional support for which many want to be known when they cannot converse with patients in the language of the people.

Such problems should be solved over time, but the time dimension may be long and difficult because value changes are needed. Newly established nursing and allied health programs in the country have failed to attract many Kuwaiti students, partially because the prestige of such occupations is low in Kuwait and little is being accomplished to change the image. The medical profession is more appealing, but it takes nine years from the time of enrollment (at age eighteen) until the time of practice. In addition, the entering classes of sixty students in the newly established medical school, of which at least fifty-one are supposed to be Kuwaiti, are decreased through attrition; often, non-Kuwaiti students replace Kuwaitis who have dropped out of the program. The country is facing some serious problems in its health care program.

Nevertheless, the self-image of the country, or at least of those who write in the name of the government, is a self-satisfied one. As stated in a report of the Kuwait Ministry of Planning, "in terms of its range and quality, the medical and health services of Kuwait can be favourably compared to those of any other country in the world" (Ministry of Planning, 1985:328).

Summary.   This brings us to the principles upon which Kuwait's health care system is based and some features of the system:

1. The health care system has been devised by, and is financially supported by, the government. Health care is available essentially free of charge to all residents (both citizens and foreigners) of the country; some procedures and hospital costs must be paid for by residents, often at token amounts.
2. All health care system decisions are made by the government and are administered through the Ministry of Public Health.
3. Fee-for-service practice by doctors and private hospitals is tolerated but frowned upon.

4. If there are not enough health personnel in the country (especially doctors and nurses), they are recruited from other countries.

Tanzania

Although some of their basic social-justice values are similar, the economy and developmental experiences of Tanzania are quite different from those of Kuwait. Whereas Kuwait vies with some other oil producers in the world for highest per capita income, Tanzania is near the bottom of this economic scale. This financially poor condition dominates life in Tanzania and, naturally, also dominates the nature of its health care system.

Demographic Characteristics.   Tanzania's population exhibits patterns associated with undeveloped and economically poor countries. It is more rural (81.8 percent) than the other five countries discussed in this chapter, has the highest percentage of population under fifteen years of age (48.6 percent), the highest crude birth rate (50.6 per 1,000), the highest infant mortality rate (111.9), and the lowest life expectancy at birth (52). See Tables 9–1 and 9–3.

National Values: Economic Systems and Concepts of Justice.   It was within this difficult context that former President Nyeyre of Tanzania announced a welfare, social-justice, socialistic value system and governmental policy for the society in a speech in the town of Arusha (the statement is known as the Arusha Declaration). This statement and some other aspects of the society provide the basis for a series of principles on which the Tanzanian health care system is based:

1. All the country's resources are mobilized to eliminate poverty, ignorance, and disease.
2. Self-help programs are emphasized; villagers are expected to band together to help meet the community's needs. In some cases, the government provides materials and equipment, if the villagers provide the labor.
3. Health care resources are planned to be available to all members of the society.
4. The country's development is along agricultural rather than industrial lines; for example, health services are designed for a rural population.
5. As much as possible, services are controlled by the people. As a corollary, emphasis is on educating local villagers to staff the health services with primary health workers.
6. Capitalism and market justice are frowned upon.

Wealth and Industrial Development.   Tanzania is one of the poorer developing countries. Its per capita gross national product in 1985 was $290; expenditure on its health system is a low 5.4 percent of the low overall gross national product of the country (see Table 9–2).

Since health services are free in Tanzania, it would seem that no economic barriers to using the western-style system exist. But this supposition is based on western standards. As Chagula and Tarimo (1975:151) state, "economic factors may often determine whether a patient comes to a hospital or not—for instance, bus or railway fares can be beyond the means of the average peasant."

The Health Care System.   Djukanovic, Kalimo, and Omari (1975:61) point out that "the most important institutions in Tanzania's rural health services is the rural health center," and Chagula and Tarimo (1975:150) state that "the district hospital and the various health centers and dispensaries in a district constitute the basic health units." These points are made in the context of a society in which people are being encouraged to move to larger villages (but not to the city) where self-help programs are established. It is within these villages that the self-help programs in health, education, farming, and other important aspects of life are felt to have the most potential for success. In all areas of service, the government attempts to minimize the types of problems inherent in sparsely populated rural areas.

Village health posts, often constructed by the villagers themselves, are the main point of entry into the total health care system for many people (World Health Organization, 1987, Vol. 2). A next step toward more extensive and more specialized treatment is the rural health dispensary. In neither of these facilities is there patient contact with a doctor; such contact is much further along in the health care delivery system. The village health post may not have anyone with formal health training, but the dispensary may be staffed by a rural medical aide, a maternal and child health aide, a health auxiliary, and one or two supporting staff. Next in line are rural health centers, each with fourteen beds; six beds are devoted to maternity patients. A typical center maintains a staff of seven to nine medical auxiliaries, a nurse, two medical aides, and a health auxiliary. Each center acts as a central unit for four or five dispensaries in the area. Finally, a series of district and regional hospitals are further up the line in personnel and facilities.

The remote rural areas are not completely without contact with doctors; mobile health services visit the rural areas periodically to provide curative and preventive services. Emphasis in the preventive area is on health education, the control of communicable diseases, the improvement of environmental sanitation, and maternal and child health services. But the heart of the health care delivery system is the rural health center or dispensary; in 1980, 93 percent of the people lived within 10 kilometers (6.2 miles) of such facilities (World Health Organization, 1987:224, Vol. 2). Only one-quarter of Tanzania's population lives this close to a hospital.

Attempts are being made to educate health personnel from among the village dwellers themselves; focus in their training is on providing the country with primary care workers. "Village medical helpers are selected by fellow villagers, when they leave primary school after 7 years of education, to undergo 3–6 months' training at a district hospital. Their training enables them (1) to treat minor ailments, (2) to provide first-aid treatment for the more serious diseases, and (3) to help villagers in the prevention of common diseases" (Chagula and Tarimo, 1975:158). Their village supports them and the government provides equipment and supplies.

There are similarities to the barefoot doctors of China, with the exception that the village medical workers are full-time practitioners. More highly educated is the rural medical aide or medical assistant, who has had at least three years of medical training after completing primary education. Some medical assistants with practical experience of at least four years can enroll in an eighteen-month training course to become assistant medical officers who, in terms of education and training, fall between the medical assistant and the physician.

Health Problems of the Society.   For Tanzania, cultural change has been slow, despite attempts by planners to speed it along. Thus, despite the self-help programs oriented to bringing western-style medicine to the country, a large number of traditional healers still practice in Tanzania. As Chagula and Tarimo (1975:162) state, "These indigenous systems of medicine are not yet integrated into the organized health services. There is no registration of traditional practitioners and the only requirements demanded of practitioners over the years have been: they must have a bona fide practice, the practitioner must be recognized by the community to which he belongs as being fully trained for such practice, the practice must be among the community to which he belongs and the practice must not be dangerous."

The economy of the country is based on an attempt to become self-sufficient in agriculture. Village residential patterns are very common; those who work the land live in the village and travel out to the family plot. Many families are failing to meet the self-sufficiency goal. Poverty and illiteracy are such that the men continually migrate to the city in an attempt to find work. Since the city is not prepared to handle the influx of unskilled labor, there is much male unemployment, and those who cannot find jobs may gather on the outskirts of the city in the crowded and unhygienic conditions usually found in shantytowns.

Summary.   The World Health Organization (1987, Vol. 2:224) points out that "the major objective of the health policy [in Tanzania] has been to provide comprehensive basic health services to all the people freely and as close as possible to where they live." This policy has been partly realized in this rural developing society in which poverty is a fact of daily life. The nature of the Tanzanian health care institution can be summarized as follows:

1. The health system is based on socialistic, social-justice, self-reliance values.
2. Village health posts are the main point of entry into the system for many people. These posts provide limited and general treatment and are important referral centers. Attempts are being made to educate village dwellers in primary care.
3. For those areas far from these posts, mobile health services visit periodically.
4. A large number of traditional healers still practice, mostly in the more rural areas.

SUMMARY

The health care systems developed by six societies to meet their own particular health needs were discussed. To understand the health system of any society, it is necessary to understand some of the broad patterns that dominate in the culture as a whole. Five patterns are considered:

1. *Economic values.* Two economic systems that reflect different economic values were discussed: capitalism and socialism. In a pure capitalistic system, all health services are offered on a fee-for-service basis. In a pure socialistic state, all health services are provided by the government.

2. *Concepts of justice.* Two concepts of justice that affect the health system were discussed: market justice and social justice. Under the values and norms of market justice, people are entitled to medical care on the basis of their economic success. Under the values and norms of social justice, all people are equally entitled to all health services.

3. *Demographic makeup.* The health needs of a society are influenced by population composition. It is evident, for example, that a society with a large proportion of its population in the elderly age categories will need a different system of services than one with many young people.

4. *Wealth.* Since medical care systems are very expensive and command a significant commitment of a society's resources, wealthy and poor societies offer different health programs to their people. The influence of wealth, however, must be interpreted within the context of the societal value system and established priorities.

5. *Degree of industrial development.* Industrial development is accomplished by major social changes that influence the health system. Frequently, changes are in the educational and health systems, which often become interrelated priorities for the society.

Within these dimensions, the health care systems of six societies that have made at least some commitment to the western health pattern are examined. The systems examined are those of:

1. The United States—a system based on capitalism and market justice, with an aging population in a society of extensive wealth and a high degree of industrial development.

2. The United Kingdom—currently a capitalistic and market-justice society with a health care system left over from previously held socialistic and social-justice values with an aging population, extensive wealth, and advanced industrial development.

3. The Soviet Union—a socialistic and social-justice society with a relatively young population, which may be classified as a developed society with some wealth.

4. The People's Republic of China—a rural society undergoing rapid industrialization and modernization in a system of socialism and social justice.

5. Kuwait—a society based on capitalistic economic values but on a welfare system with social-justice underpinnings, with a very young population, rapid development, and enormous wealth.

6. Tanzania—a very poor country with almost no industrial development and an extremely young population, with a health care system based on socialistic and social-justice value systems.

References

Albert, Cecelia A., ed. 1987. *World Economic Data*. Santa Barbara, Calif.: ABC-Clio.

Beauchamp, Dan E. 1979. "Public health as social justice." In *Patients, Physicians, and Illness*, 3rd ed., ed. E. G. Jaco, 443–457. New York: Free Press.

Chagula, W. A., and E. Tarimo. 1975. "Meeting basic health needs in Tanzania." In *Health by the People*, ed. Kenneth W. Newell, 145–168. Geneva: World Health Organization.

Djukanovic, V., E. Kalimo, and I. M. Omari. 1975. "United Republic of Tanzania: An innovative approach to the development of health services." In *Alternative Approaches to Meeting Basic Health Needs in Developing Countries*, ed. V. Djukanovic and E. P. Mach, 57–62. Geneva: World Health Organization.

Fry, John. 1969. *Medicine in Three Societies*. Aylesbury Bucks: Chiltern House, MTP.

Greenhalgh, Susan, and John Bongaarts. 1987. "Fertility policy in China: Future options." *Science* 234 (6 March):1167–1172.

Holden, Constance. 1981. "Health care in the Soviet Union." *Science* 213(4 September): 1090–1092.

Jefferys, Margot. 1975. "The doctor's dilemma—A sociological viewpoint." In *A Sociology of Medical Practice*, ed. Caroline Cox and Adrianne Mead, 145–154. London: Collier-Macmillan.

Ministry of Planning, State of Kuwait. 1985. *Annual Statistical Abstract, 1985*. Kuwait: Author.

Ministry of Public Health, State of Kuwait. 1985. *Health Statistics*. Kuwait: Author.

National Center for Health Statistics. 1988. *Health, United States, 1987*. DHHS Pub. No. (PHS)88-1232. Public Health Service. Washington, D.C.: U.S. Government Printing Office.

Sidel, Ruth, and Victor W. Sidel. 1982. *The Health of China*. Boston: Beacon Press.

Sidel, Victor W., and Ruth Sidel. 1983. *A Healthy State*. New York: Pantheon Books.

United Nations. 1988. *Demographic Yearbook, 1986*. New York: Author.

World Bank. 1987. *The World Bank Atlas, 1987*. Washington, D.C.: Author.

World Health Organization. 1987. *Evaluation of the Strategy for Health for All by the Year 2000* (Seventh Report on the World Health Situation). 7 vols. Geneva: Author.

———. 1988. *World Health Statistics Annual, 1988*. Geneva: Author.

10

The Medicalization of Deviance

INTRODUCTION

Definitions of many specific social conditions are changing in the United States and, as a consequence, attitudes toward several deviant behaviors are also changing. Thus, conditions that were once defined as immoral or criminal are now being defined as diseases. Such a redefinition has important consequences both for the individual and for society. For example, if a criminal behavior is redefined as a medical condition, the authority for its treatment shifts to the health and medical institution from legal and religious institutions. We refer to this change in perception, evaluation, and treatment as the *medicalization of deviance*.

By using this phrase, we hope to convey the idea that some activities and conditions once perceived as socially deviant are increasingly being perceived as medical conditions. As a consequence of changing societal definitions, several of yesterday's crimes and immoralities are today's sicknesses, and we ask whether some of today's crimes and immoralities may be tomorrow's illnesses. The effect is that doctors and other health personnel are gaining control over an increasingly large area of behaviors and conditions, as they are being looked to as the experts on more and more types of problems.

THE DEVELOPMENT OF MEDICALIZATION VIEWS

Although the trend toward the medicalization of deviant behavior has been building for a long time, possibly since the sixteenth century, it has gained momentum in the past few decades. Conrad and Schneider (1980a) contend that there has been a transformation in the way in which deviance is defined, which has led to a medical-scientific definition. Pitts (1968), who seems to have been the first sociologist to use the phrase "medicalization of deviance," suggests that the perception developed from the diffusion and growing acceptance of Freudian thought in U.S. society. Following Freud, more kinds of deviant behavior are redefined as illness as a result of a growing belief that such behavior is caused by unconscious sources over which the individual has no control. Within this belief system, the person acting in a deviant manner is viewed as needing psychological understanding and help instead of the punishment meted out in the past. Former punishment patterns are interpreted as having dealt only with symptoms and may even have made the deviant worse. The person who has behaved in a deviant manner needs the care of a physician, possibly in a hospital, rather than a guard in a prison. Thus, the change is from punishment to therapy.

It is probably not coincidental that the social sciences have had their most significant growth at the same time as an increasing number of deviant conditions have become medicalized. It is a chicken-or-egg kind of question when one asks which is influencing the other but, no matter what position is taken, there is little doubt that an alliance has been formed between the social sciences and certain branches of medicine and that each has used the other to its own advantage. Sociologists, in particular, have lent considerable support to the medicalization trend.

The support is not surprising. After all, a basic contribution of sociologists to the belief and knowledge systems of society is that human beings have no complex innate or inborn behavior patterns (there is some controversy over this position) and that people's behavior as adults is strongly influenced by their psychological and social experiences, particularly during the early years of socialization. If we are malleable, then some individuals must deviate as a consequence of their particular shaping by, and experiences in, social groups. Thus, social scientists added justification to the medicalization trend, and those impressed by the trend contributed to the growth of the social sciences. Whatever the reasons for the change, deviant behaviors that were once thought to call for intervention by clergymen and courtroom judges are increasingly being reinterpreted as needing the attention of physicians instead, and "what was once regarded as a reprehensible act against society and met with punishment is now seen as requiring treatment" (Hawkins and Tiedeman, 1975:148). Treatment becomes the preferred societal response.

Zola (1972) suggests that medicalization is part of a larger process of social change that can be termed the *bureaucratization of society*, which has led to increasing emphasis on objective and rational decision making throughout the social system. An important consequence of this emphasis is societal reliance on the so-called expert. This is particularly advantageous for those in the health field, which seems to be a breeding ground for occupational groups that declare their expertise and assume the professional label to affirm their point. The combination of expertise and professionalism also defines areas of authority. Through medicalization, the medical profession has demanded and received authority in more areas. To the point, Freidson (1970) and Conrad and Schneider (1980b) note that the medicalization process is strengthening medical professional control because people are increasingly expected to rely on doctors as technical experts for an evaluation of their behavior.

In the past, the legal system was the social-control agent that dealt with such behavior. But it is under attack for its lack of success in rehabilitating offenders. At the same time, the medical system is viewed as being highly successful in its intervention. The advances implied by such dramatic treatment strategies as heart transplants and polio vaccinations have a spillover effect in other areas of life. The logic is simple: If the medical approach is so successful in the physical aspects of life, perhaps it can be successful in the social and psychological aspects as well. As Bernstein and Lennard (1973:16) write:

> *The theory used to recruit physicians and deploy chemical technology in the war against social deviance, crime, misbehavior, alcoholism, mental illness, drug addiction, overanxiety, overweight, overindulgence, overactivity, underactivity, insomnia, overpopulation, sadness, rage, and bizarre ideas, derives from the determination that these conditions are analogous to medical problems and therefore can be solved through medical means. Once a human problem is identified as a disease, the stage is set for mobilizing the technological apparatus for discovering its cure.*

Illich (1975) sounds a strong negative note about the social change. In a provocative and controversial book, he refers to "clinical iatrogenesis," a process in which medical problems are inadvertently caused by the doctor or by complications of the treatment. He also writes of "social iatrogenesis," the process in which placement in the sick status causes unintended negative consequences. Through the "medicalization of life," an inappropriate category of people has been given dominance over the lives of others, and the populace is being weakened through therapeutic side effects.

Among medical specialties, the field of psychiatry has probably been more affected than others by the medicalization-of-deviance trend. Two types of medicalization experiences are simultaneously taking place within the field of psychiatry. In one, old conditions were renamed when Freud provided a medical definition for social behaviors previously considered socially deviant. For example, he substituted the name *conversion hysteria* for *malingering* and then declared that such hysteria is a mental illness (Szasz, 1974). In the other type of medicalization, specific deviant behaviors are continually being moved out of the jurisdiction of the police, courts, and lawyers and into territory viewed as belonging to the psychiatrist. Examples of current conditions undergoing such medicalization (or, perhaps more properly, "psychiatricization") are alcoholism, drug addiction, unmarried pregnancy, failure in school, divorce (Hawkins and Tiedeman, 1975), transsexualism (Billings and Urban, 1982), personality disorder (Ausubel, 1961), obesity (Kolata, 1985), conversion to deviant sects (Robbins and Anthony, 1982), and even sin itself (McCormick, 1989).

Perhaps to maintain their sphere of influence and territory, or perhaps because they have been convinced of a more effective intervention strategy, aspects of the medical approach have been adopted by some nonmedical groups that deal with deviants. Thus, several traditional social-control agencies have incorporated elements of the medical, especially the psychiatric, model in their response to what they define as social problems. An example is the religious and legal systems that have formally instituted programs designed to incorporate the psychiatric frame of reference in their approaches by having practitioners take courses and attend workshops in psychotherapy; the curricula in some theological seminaries devote as much as one-third of their courses to pastoral counseling and related subjects. In addition, the school system might require that the school nurse take courses in the emotional problems of children, to help control the behavior of students who exhibit violent and hyperactive behavior.

FACTORS NECESSARY FOR MEDICALIZATION

Conrad (1976) suggests that several specific social factors precede and support the medicalization process. Five of these are viewed as antecedent to the process and two as contingent to it. We will discuss all seven.

Antecedent Social Variables

The first antecedent factor proposed by Conrad (1976) is that some segment of society must define the condition or behavior both as deviant and as a problem. There is an abundance of sociological and anthropological literature making the point that deviance and problems are socially defined and thus vary by place and time. What is and is not considered deviant is thus a matter of social definition. Social recognition, therefore, defines the condition as a problem calling for action. Those holding this perception must feel that something should be done about it, or they may attempt to convince others that some action is necessary.

The second antecedent factor is that the social activity that has traditionally been used to manage the behavior is defined as inefficient or currently unacceptable. An incredible array of methods has been devised to control behavior defined as deviant. For example, the pilgrims placed wayward members of their band in stocks or the pillory, assuming that public ridicule would contain their behavior and that of others who witnessed the shame. Religious groups have devised an almost unlimited series of punishments to control deviance under the general rubric of penance, sometimes controlled by the individual and sometimes by others. During this century in the United States, the prison has become an institution for the control of deviant behavior, under an assumption that punishment by imprisonment will deter crime. At other times in our society, and in other societies, those who have been judged guilty of theft have been imprisoned for life or had their hands cut off, and some people have been stoned to death for adultery.

Whatever the punishment, before a condition can be medicalized, there must be a serious questioning of the old or traditional ways of controlling the behavior. In U.S. society, the best example is continual attacks on the penal system, with critics of its ineffectiveness charging that punishment by imprisonment is not having a significant effect on criminals or the crime rate. The conclusion appears to be that punishment in prisons is more effective in turning out more competent criminals than in rehabilitating them.

Third, for medicalization to take place, medical means viewed as effective in controlling the particular deviance must be available. In western societies, the primary source of medical care is the physician. Therefore, any condition that is a candidate for medicalization must relate in some way to techniques of medicine that reasonably can be used to deal with the problem. Consequently, expansion of psychotherapeutic techniques and therapies into general medicine opens the door for many more medicalized conditions.

Fourth, Conrad states that if medicalization is to occur, knowledge of the causes of the behavior or condition must be unclear or ambiguous, although an organic cause must be hypothesized. Some sociologists feel that such a limitation is unnecessary. Even when a psychogenic or mental cause is claimed for a condition, medicalization can and does occur. An organic cause may constantly be sought, but even if it is not found, medicalization is not precluded. Mental illnesses are examples of medicalized conditions for which no organic cause is known, even though massive research attempts have been made to find one.

Conrad's final antecedent for medicalization is that some segment of the medical profession must be willing to accept and claim the deviant behavior as being within its jurisdiction. But consensus does not have to be complete. Alcoholism illustrates this point. Alcohol abuse can be conceptualized in almost any of the ways in which deviance has been viewed: as sin, crime, or illness. The American Psychiatric Association and the American Medical Association both designate alcoholism as a disease, but while its definition may be accepted within psychiatry, some doctors in other specialties still question whether it is a suitable definition (Fingarette, 1989).

Contingent Social Variables

Conrad also suggests that two circumstances increase the likelihood that medicalization will occur. First, it is most likely if members of the medical system feel they will benefit. For example, the availability of funding for research or programming in an area can bring about increased interest by the medical profession. When the public becomes interested in a condition and the amount of money to support efforts in the area increases, the readiness of members of the medical system to define the problem as a medical one becomes greater. Thus, the establishment of the National Institute on Alcohol and Alcohol Abuse has spurred medical interest in that problem, with medical professionals insisting on the priority of their approach in research and treatment. The National Institute on Drug Abuse, with its grant and project money, has spurred greater interest on the part of the medical community for dealing with problems relating to drug abuse. This is particularly true when quick and easy means of dealing with a problem medically can be used (such as methadone treatment for drug abuse), which increases the patient load (or recruits new patients) but does not appreciably increase the workload.

Second, the greater the acceptance of the scientific explanation, the more likely it is that the condition will be medicalized. Since U.S. society is committed to scientific explanations, it follows that it will encourage medicalization. Therefore, scientific explanations—for example, those based on nutritional enzymatic approaches—promote the medicalization of alcoholism.

Stages in the Medicalization Process

In a further elaboration, Conrad and Schneider (1980a) propose a sequential model for the development of medicalization. The first step occurs when the conduct observed is defined by others as deviant. Alcoholism and mental illness, for example, had long been seen as undesirable (even sinful) before they were defined as medical. In the second stage, the medical profession proclaims that it has discovered a medical cause or new diagnosis for the behavior.

The key stage of the process is reached when those with vested interests in the condition and entrepreneurs of medicine proclaim that the behavior should be placed within the medical system. Nonmedical and ancillary agencies (for example, Alcoholics Anonymous and the health industry in general) may make statements of support. Another stage legitimizes the medical definition and secures the claim. Generally, this means obtaining the state's official recognition, through law, that the medical profession has jurisdiction over the condition. This recognition eliminates competitive claims.

Finally, when the deviance definition is put into the form of law or becomes part of standard diagnoses included in such official publications as the *Diagnostic and Statistical Manual of the American Psychiatric Association*, it can be assumed that it is now an institutionalized part of the culture. Not everyone will agree with the changed definition; public opinion tends to lag behind the professional and legal redefinition of the problem and may challenge the medicalized perception at some other time. Nevertheless, the institutionalization in laws and codifications strongly supports the medical profession's jurisdiction over the condition.

Having discussed the stages through which medicalization develops, Conrad and Schneider present some qualifications concerning the process. First, they point out that the medicalization process is not necessarily one-directional. Deviance definitions may move back and forth between the concepts of morality and sickness.

Second, it is probable that an important reason for the medicalization movement has been to avoid criminal definitions of the behavior. To those leading the movement to medicalize behavior, the punishments meted out to criminals are too harsh. The medical designation, on the other hand, promotes treatments or, at the very least, eliminates legal punitive action.

Third, Conrad and Schneider suggest that medicalization is not medical imperialism. They note that, in almost all instances, those involved in the movement to redefine deviance constitute only a small number of people within the medical profession. Most medical practitioners pay little attention to the issues involved.

Fourth, deviant behavior usually is given a medical designation through the conception of compulsion or compulsive behavior, which means that those exhibiting the deviance could not help themselves. Attributing compulsivity to the behavior avoids the need to find an organic cause.

Fifth, the authors hold that the battle for a medicalized definition of a condition is political rather than medical-scientific. Political organization, for example, won the battle for medicalizing mental illness and alcoholism and has kept opiate addiction defined as criminal.

MEDICALIZATION AND THE SICK ROLE

If a condition is reinterpreted as a sickness rather than a crime or an immorality, this description should move it closer to conditions that have been traditionally accepted as sicknesses. Thus, from Parsons's (1951) sick-status perspective, perceptions of the medicalized condition should move it closer to each of the four dimensions constituting the model of the sick role. Such a view of the alcoholic, for example, would hold that a person with this condition should be excused from usual social behaviors, should be viewed as not responsible for having the condition, must want to become nonalcoholic, and must seek technically competent help to bring about recovery.

All four dimensions are important in the shift from deviance to sickness, but the most important is the second one: the right to be viewed as not responsible for the continued presence of the condition. Only if the person's continued deviance is involuntary are the rights of the sick role legitimate. If the individual continues with the condition on purpose, that person is viewed as trying to avoid social responsibilities and suffers the stigma of being viewed as a malingerer.

At this point, the medicalization of deviance concept identifies some extremely important changes in social perceptions. People purposively continuing with the condition are considered immoral because they have made a decision to avoid social obligations; society cannot depend on such people, and the blame is theirs. But if they are not at fault for their condition, the social view changes from immorality to understandable behavior—it can happen to any of us, and we can sympathize with and even pity those afflicted. Even strictly medical conditions resulting from what is interpreted as an individual's irresponsible behavior, however, are looked down on by medical personnel (Freidson, 1970:233):

> *I might point out that some of what are* medically *labeled as illness fall into the column in which the individual is held responsible for the deviance imputed to him—that is, they become like crimes. In our present-day society, for example, lay and professional reactions toward venereal diseases tend to reflect preoccupation with the way the infection was obtained—a way for which they hold the sufferer responsible. Such preoccupation is not found in the case of infections more innocently arrived at (as from the legendary toilet seat). In another context, it was observed that medical personnel withheld respect, and even care from people who attempted suicide, or were victims of brawls, or of accidents thought to occur by reason of drunkenness or carelessness.*

Running through this social change, then, are some subtle but important messages. For example, part of the change is a shift in definition and judgment concerning the reasons for social failure. "If the failure is seen as willful, the behavior tends to be defined as crime; if it is seen as unmotivated, the behavior tends to be defined as an illness" (Twaddle, 1973:754). This is a highly significant change in perception, because "the approved societal response is to punish the criminal to alter his motivation toward conformity, but to provide therapy for the sick to alter the conditions which prevent his conformity to social norms" (Twaddle, 1973:755). Further, in an interesting commentary, Light (1989) states that, in a sense, this concept "stands Parsons on his head" because rather than illness being defined as deviance, deviance is defined as illness.

SPECIFIC CONDITIONS AND MEDICALIZATION: SOME EXAMPLES

The process of medicalization has affected many conditions. We will focus on four: mental illness, alcoholism, mental retardation, and homosexuality. Medicalization is at a different stage of development for each.

Mental Illness

That broad class of seemingly unrelated disordered behaviors to which we now give the name *mental illness* was probably the first of all conditions to experience medicalization. Its very name, mental *illness*, indicates that this condition is probably completely medicalized.

The concept of mental illness has been traced back to the sixteenth century. At that time, the cause of strange psychological behavior was often explained as possession by the devil (Sarbin, 1969). This explanation was explored during the Inquisition and was part of its excess. During that time, the accepted diagnosis was witchcraft (Szasz, 1970, 1974), and the accepted treatment was burning or drowning.

A new spirit of understanding and appreciation followed during the Renaissance. Part of this spirit led to a new attitude toward the disordered or strange behavior previously seen as demonic possession or witchcraft. During this period, a nun, Teresa of Avila, seems to have originated the idea that such behavior was not sinful or demon-induced but was more like a sickness. She contended that nuns placed under her care for acting strangely were not doing so because of possession but because it was as if they were sick. By employing the simile "as if sick," she implied that the behavior was medical rather than moral or religious deviance and that it should be dealt with by physicians.

Historically, the most influential person to popularize this view was Freud. According to Szasz (1974), Freud routinely assumed illness in his patients by asking the "wrong question." He asked, "What kind of disease does the patient have?" instead of asking whether the patient had a disease at all. With the dissemination and acceptance of this view, mental illness completed the transition to medicalization.

If this definition of behavior as illness is extended to other areas, almost any type of social and psychological disorder may be medicalized. In the contemporary United States, for example, some people believe that criminal behavior, especially behavior violating society's most sacred norms, is an indication of illness. Mass murderers are an example. Apparently, if the crime is vicious enough, it is no longer judged to be crime in the old volitional sense; rather, the perpetrator of a hideous crime "must be mentally incompetent," "must be insane," must be judged and treated by psychiatrists instead of by juries and jailers. For example, when an Indiana mother murdered her five children, there was never any question of her ending up in prison. Her behavior was so strange, it so violated basic expectations, it was so strongly at odds with the value system, that it could not be explained by society's usual interpretations of behavior. Instead, the behavior was immediately seen to result from a condition over which she had no control, and she was taken to the regional state mental hospital for treatment, rather than to prison.

Obviously, knowledge of societal reactions to deviant behavior can be used to advantage by some people. Hawkins and Tiedeman (1975) provide a particularly good example. They cite the case of a man who was arrested for armed robbery when he was in his teens. His lawyer suggested that he choose between a prison term and time in the mental hospital. Choosing the latter, he spent a great deal of his time reading books about psychiatric ailments. After his discharge from the mental hospital, he resumed his career of armed robbery and was subsequently arrested many times for that crime, pleading not guilty by reason of insanity each time. This person never spent a single day in prison. Instead, he would be committed to a mental hospital, from which he would usually escape and resume his career.

Some in society, however, do not completely accept the definition of mental illness as a sick condition. For example, patients in mental hospitals may be subjected to definitions that blame them for being there. This is partly because there is concern that those who claim to be sick by reason of mental illness may be faking (malingering) so they can gain some imagined advantage from being defined as sick. Nevertheless, more than most other such deviants, those termed mentally ill tend to be more readily seen as suffering from true sickness.

Mental Retardation

Like mental illness, mental retardation has come to be viewed by the medical profession and the lay public as a medical condition. Retardation would seem to be thoroughly medicalized, but many psychologists and educators disagree with the appropriateness of this definition. These critics suggest that a developmental orientation is the valid and far more meaningful approach.

Objections to the medical view are based on two observations. For one, only a small percentage of retarded people exhibit any retardation-associated organic problems. In 1962, the President's Panel on Mental Retardation stated that organic signs are found among only 15 to 25 percent of the retarded, and recent authors take positions close to the lower end of this range (Kurtz, 1977). Second, many objecting to the medical view feel uncomfortable with such terms as treatment and cure, pointing out that they have little meaning for many retarded people. Nevertheless, the image of the retarded individual as sick is accepted by the medical profession and is the most common general public perception.

Given the small proportion of retarded people who exhibit organic problems, one wonders why the medical view seems so acceptable to so many. There are several reasons. First, those retarded people who have organic problems are the most noticeable, with their physical problems readily apparent; the other 75 to 85 percent are not physically distinguishable from the rest of society. Second, the easiest explanation for a person's retardation is physical problems. ("We cannot see or measure the organic problem, but this does not mean it doesn't exist.") Attributing the condition to an unobservable aspect of the person seems adequate to some people.

Third, when a child is not developing correctly, the usual reaction of parents and school systems is to ask a doctor to explain what is wrong. In response, the medically oriented have established diagnostic and evaluation clinics, usually headed by physicians. This, in itself, defines the condition as a medical one.

How justified is the medical view of the retarded? Parsons's sick-role model works best when acute physical conditions that respond to medical intervention are considered. Mental retardation is a chronic condition, not always physical, and the retardation does not usually respond to medical treatment. But something may be learned by applying the sick-role dimensions to the mentally retarded because this may clarify some aspects of how retarded people are viewed in society.

There is little doubt that the retarded are excused from many of the usual social expectations. But, according to those who do not accept the medical view of retardation, this has been carried too far. The developmentally oriented hold that society has been excusing the retarded from normal activities instead of attempting to develop their potential; thus, the potential of retarded people is being ignored because of the medical model. Some people feel that the retarded are often given a blanket excuse from responsibilities, which is tantamount to a directive to them to act as if they are retarded. Further, those who reject the medical model for the retarded indicate that the model has thus incorrectly and unfairly helped to stereotype the retarded as people without abilities, and it orders those who have been labeled to play the retarded role.

The excuse-from-fault dimension seems to apply well here; no one accuses retarded people of bringing the condition on themselves or of attempting to maintain the condition. Especially from the medical perspective, no one is to blame for the condition—an important attitude for many parents who may otherwise feel they were somehow responsible for their child's condition.

We have little information about whether the retarded want to get well. Instead of attempting to collect such information, we tend to assume that many do not have the mental capacity to think about and make decisions about their condition. It may be too much of a generalization, but it seems justified to state that many mentally retarded people would eliminate their condition if this were possible. It is difficult to think in these terms, however, since we tend to think of the retarded as children for whom we have to make decisions.

Relative to cooperating with technically competent help, the retarded are often placed in programs, and there is an assumption of cooperation. This is how we expect retarded people to behave. Given an image of the retarded as constant children and a professional attitude of "we know what is best," few retarded people are ever asked about their desires and their willingness to cooperate. But how much of their behavior is due to the retardation and how much is due to playing the retarded role they have learned is an open question.

Alcoholism

At one time in the United States, alcoholism was clearly viewed as a sin and crime. Redemption was thus left to religious and legal agents, and both atonement and criminal penalties were attached to manifestations of the condition. Elements of these views still remain, but the perception of the alcoholic as someone with a disease also has won acceptance, and it is not uncommon to hear alcoholism referred to as a disease. Thus, society simultaneously holds several views of the condition, some contradictory; all have significant effects on those being labeled.

The classical disease conception of alcoholism was first proposed in the 1930s by two reformed drinkers, and the new image was influenced by the beliefs of a religious group known as the Oxford Movement (Rudy, 1986). In the course of the disease, those afflicted inevitably progress from social drinking to heavy drinking, despite suffering a series of abnormal reactions when drinking. Blackouts—temporary spells of amnesia—may be one of the first such reactions. If the alcoholic continues drinking, the result will be premature death. The progression is unaffected by characteristics of the individual (Fingarette, 1989). This view of the condition is common (Caetano, 1987; Crawford, 1987).

From the perspective of this discussion, alcoholism is in transition to a medicalized definition, and the process is by no means complete. Since all key professional groups that might possibly be expected to have a voice in labeling alcoholism have stated officially that it is a disease (Caetano, 1987; Crawford, 1987), this should be the end of the matter; generally, a disease is what the medical and other professional groups define as a disease. But there is a difference between word and deed. The same professionals who label the condition a disease are often reluctant to treat alcoholics who may have come to their offices or clinics.

It would be informative to view alcoholism in terms of the sociological construct of Parsons's (1951) sick-role model. First of all, some people fear that the alcoholic is using the condition to avoid social responsibilities. Also, a remnant of the idea remains that since the alcoholic did not have to drink in the first place and should be able to stop at will, the fault lies with the alcoholic, who is held responsible for acquiring the condition. In addition, some alcoholics do not consider the condition undesirable, and those with the condition are not known for their cooperation with technically competent help in the attempt to change their situations.

This view of the alcoholic in terms of Parsons's sick-role dimensions received some confirmation in a study of social workers' attitudes by Chalfant and Kurtz (1971). They report that only 16 percent of the sample accepted alcoholics as legitimate incumbents of the sick status, and one-fourth presented a confused picture. (They accepted alcoholics as legitimate for some of the dimensions of the sick role but not for others.) The other respondents (59 percent of the sample) took positions indicating they did not feel alcoholics were legitimate incumbents of the sick status.

In further analysis, these investigators found that alcoholics judged acceptable in the sick status also possessed what members of the social worker sample considered positive personal behavior traits, suggesting that sample members allowed notions of social desirability to affect their judgments of the alcoholic and the sick role (Chalfant and Kurtz, 1972, 1978). This was also reflected in respondents' specific judgments relative to the sick role, since most of them clearly and emphatically rejected alcoholics who refused to cooperate with treatment. When alcoholics were described as highly motivated to recover and were self- rather than court-referred, the acceptance level among social workers increased markedly.

Once medicalized, some conditions permanently maintain the disease perception, with only occasional questions about the applicability of the image. Mental illness is an example. But alcoholism is different because of continual debate about the correct definition. Some, such as Vaillant (1983), have even questioned the symptomology. His study of alcoholics indicates that not all heavy drinkers lose control. Further, among those who do, some resume moderate drinking without treatment. In a more general attack on the disease conception, Fingarette (1989) asserts that considerable scientific evidence runs contrary to the traditional disease model. He contends that the medicalization of all heavy drinkers as alcoholics has led to inappropriate treatment of their condition.

In 1988, the U.S. Supreme Court was drawn into the controversy, and its ruling affirmed that the correct, or at least legally correct, definition of alcoholism is the confused one. In a question about whether alcoholism per se is a legitimate disability, the ruling of the court upheld a Veterans Administration classification of alcoholism into two types: "primary alcoholism," which by definition *is not* accompanied by any disability-causing disorder, and "secondary alcoholism," which by definition *is* accompanied by a physical or psychiatric disorder. The Veterans Administration does not consider primary alcoholism to be a legitimate disability, whereas secondary alcoholism is; this indicates that it is the presence or absence of another disorder that defines whether or not alcoholism is a disability. Most important to the total perception of the condition, primary alcoholism is classified as being a result of "willful misconduct."

Following this overall line of reasoning, alcoholics are responsible for their alcoholism, but not for the medical disability problems that may accompany their condition. This definition falls short of stating that alcoholism is not a disease, but its placing of blame on the individual has many important implications in this direction. To add to the confusion, if the nondiseased alcoholic can find a way "to acquire" another condition to accompany the alcoholism, the definition will change from primary (caused by willful misconduct) to secondary (unwillingly contracted) alcoholism.

The confusion surrounding alcoholism confirms its transitional status in the medicalization process. It seems probable that alcoholics will continue to fall somewhere between willful and unwillful deviance for some time, suffering a great deal of confusion and lack of understanding along the way.

Homosexuality

From the standpoint of medicalization, homosexuality is particularly interesting because it experienced medicalization at one point, only to be redefined at a later point as not being a medical problem after all. Bullough (1977) presents a thorough discussion of this transformation. He points out that, at the turn of the century, western attitudes toward homosexuality were about the same as they had been for 2,000 years, basically reflecting early Christian attitudes toward deviant sexual behavior. Up to the time homosexuality was medicalized, it was considered a sin and a crime. When the transition in perception occurred, a confused new perception emerged, one that added a disease definition to that of crime (Szasz, 1970). Such confusion within society could not last; homosexuality had to be a crime, or it had to be a disease.

If homosexuality were to be defined as a disease, physicians would have to provide the official diagnosis and would have to accept treatment responsibility for the condition. Given its initial tie-in to mental illness, it was natural for psychiatrists to perform these functions. Homosexuality was therefore added to the American Psychiatric Association's *Manual on Terminology and Classification*, and psychotherapy was suggested as the proper treatment.

But the classification of homosexual activity as disease violates some important values of U.S. culture, particularly those that give people the freedom to act as they see fit in private, as long as their actions do not harm or interfere with the rights of others. The values hold that what mature adults do in private is their own business, not society's, and especially not the government's. The British hold similar values; in 1957, a British royal commission recommended "that homosexual behavior between consenting adults in private be no longer a criminal offense" (Committee on Homosexual Offences and Prostitution, 1957:115). Note the careful wording, which limits the recommendation to adults, consent, and private, which in combination also reflect aspects of the U.S. value system.

The message of the British commission had an impact on psychiatrists in the United States. These doctors already had rejected the crime definition accepted previously and were heralding the disease definition that removed blame from the individual. But the British statement went beyond a rejection of the crime label and substitution of the disease label by removing both. To many psychiatrists, this approach was the most sensible way to clarify a confused situation.

Having only recently medicalized homosexuality, a group of psychiatrists set a goal of demedicalizing the condition. This was finally accomplished when the American Psychiatric Association removed homosexuality from its listing in the *Manual on Terminology and Classification*. Socially acceptable definitions of homosexuality have thus changed from sin, to crime, to crime and disease, and to nondeviance, which implies that the currently acceptable definition is normal behavior.

In an interesting twist to this definitional transition, one psychologist states that "far from being sick, gays often function better than nongays" (Freedman, 1975:28). This author argues that to be a liberated gay rather than a straight heterosexual can mean being honest, feeling free from some of society's stifling restrictions, being open to a varied sex life, and experiencing a more intense quest for identity, purpose, and meaning in life. According to Freedman, this freedom from societal restrictions makes the homosexual psychologically healthier than the heterosexual. Based on the history of perceptions of homosexuality in the United States, it is clear that this view faces considerable public resistance.

This shift in public attitude, in which professionals and the public of the 1960s and 1970s moved toward accepting, or at least not as strongly rejecting, "alternative lifestyles" was to change abruptly in the 1980s. A precipitating factor sent the definition into an altogether different direction, one that had been more or less discarded some time ago. This factor was the appearance of the acquired immune deficiency syndrome (AIDS). The syndrome was first found among homosexuals, and AIDS was immediately associated with their sex practices. AIDS was first named, inaccurately, GRID (Gay Related Immune Deficiency Syndrome), reflecting the feeling that it was mainly connected with the gay community, and it was referred to as a "gay plague" (Conrad, 1986). Although we have since come to recognize that AIDS is far from confined to the gay community, the link between the condition and the sexual practice brought back the strongly negative feelings about homosexuality that had long been part of U.S. culture. The condition was looked upon by some people as "punishment" (or God's retribution) for behaving in such an immoral or sinful manner. AIDS has brought on a reaction toward homosexuals that has essentially reversed the trends toward acceptance.

WOMEN AND MEDICALIZATION

Medicalization is not limited to conditions perceived as abnormal, immoral, criminal, or otherwise deviant. For example, a goal of the women's movement in the United States is to gain freedom from problems associated with natural physiological processes that prevent women from participating in a normal life and career pattern. Examples are menstruation, pregnancy, and childbirth. The attempt to be free from problems associated with such normal processes, along with cultural values of female physical appearance, have made women a particular target in the expansion of medicine into areas that have nothing to do with deviance (Riessman, 1983). Thus, the medical profession has medicalized aspects of women's *natural* physiological functions and anatomical structure. Several normal female conditions have been given medical definitions, and physicians are now thought by many people to be needed at almost every stage of a woman's life cycle. But the cross-cultural observations of anthropology suggest that a medical definition of such normal functions is not necessary.

As their problems became medicalized, women found they were placing themselves with increasing frequency under the control of doctors, almost always male obstetrician-gynecologists. Women soon found that the freedom from one set of problems meant the development of a new set, as they became more dependent on doctors who assumed control over their normal biological events. When this was recognized, feminists rebelled against this control.

We should recognize, with Riessman (1983), that women have not been passive recipients in the medicalization of their conditions; the expanding use of medical definitions for female conditions relied on action and support from women as well as physicians. In some cases, women eagerly invited and welcomed the changes necessary for medicalization to occur. Riessman (1983), among others, also contends that the defining of women's normal biological experiences as medical problems is rooted in class interests. From the perspective of the profession, the beliefs and special interests of physicians seeking to establish their authority over all medical care were enhanced. Further, physicians eagerly sought and accepted a whole new class of conditions that generated new markets for their services. These benefits for physicians combined with the desires of upper- and middle-class women, who supported the medicalization process because they were convinced it was part of the liberation process. The good "fit" between the needs of these groups promoted women's normal life events as sickness.

Riessman further suggests that women's lives have been medicalized to a larger extent than men's. The key difference is that medical expansion has focused on women's *normal* biological life-cycle experiences; men's biological experiences do not come under medical scrutiny unless they are *abnormal*. As a consequence, a medical specialty focusing on the woman's reproductive system is flourishing, while little is known medically about such normal male biological experiences as hormonal cycles and the male climacteric because these are largely neglected by medicine.

In the conclusion of her discussion of women and medicalization, Riessman (1983) indicates that, for certain conditions, *de*medicalization would serve the interests of women best. Among her suggestions for such a reinterpretation or demedicalization of normal conditions are routine childbirth, menopause, and excess weight. For the remaining medicalized female conditions, those that truly need the attention of the medical profession, she suggests that the challenge is to differentiate between treatments that are beneficial and those that are harmful or useless.

In another discussion of how women have been affected by medicalization, Ruzek (1986:184) discusses some of the harm the process has caused women, as "doctors, health policy-makers, and bio-medical researchers as well as lawmakers, predominantly male, were viewed [by feminists] as acting in men's rather than women's 'best interests.'" Some treatments that became routine medical practice were lucrative for the profession but unsafe for women. Thus, alarming evidence that some oral contraceptives have serious side effects has been found; some intrauterine devices declared safe and effective had never been tested by the federal regulatory body; standard hospital childbirth procedures have been criticized as being organized more for the convenience of the institution and staff than for the health and well-being of mothers and babies; evidence of unnecessary Caesarean sections, hysterectomies, and radical mastectomies is growing and, in some cases, lower socioeconomic status women have been sterilized without their knowledge and consent.

Ruzek (1986) suggests several responses to the harmful consequences of medicalization. For one, she feels that women should develop self-determination in making health care decisions. The key is knowledge. Medical knowledge about their bodies would allow women, instead of health professionals, to make crucial decisions about their normal biological functions and the need for professional care. For another, she points to women-controlled health services developed as alternatives to the gynecological care offered in the traditional medical system; when such services have been developed in the United States they have been successful, but few presently exist. Within this context, another suggested possibility is a reorientation of conventional health care providers away from the rational and objective outlook to a philosophy that recognizes the human quality of medicine. Such alternatives to the present medical system would stimulate the demedicalization process. To this end, Ruzek feels that women should take an active interest in influencing public policy on matters affecting their health.

MEDICALIZATION AND
SOCIAL CONTROL

Accompanying the changes in perceptions that are the essence of medicalization have been changes in strategies designed to intervene and cure the conditions that are inconsistent with society's values or violate social norms. Criminals are punished by society because they have willfully engaged in antisocial behavior. The sick person receives therapy because it is assumed that he or she wants to conform to the norms but some condition prevents correct behavior. The social response is quite different in the two cases: the willful violator must be punished, whereas the person who wants to conform must be helped to do so.

The individual being judged might have some control over the particular label that will be used to identify the deviant behavior. If the label suggests willful violation, the deviant person will be punished; if it suggests nonwillful violation, the deviant will be given therapy. Under an assumption that therapy is better than punishment, an individual would stand to gain by the second label, which defines the condition as accidental, rather than deliberate (Lorber, 1967). Thus, a person may choose to plead insanity, asking for a nondeliberate definition, rather than choosing to plead guilty or not guilty of committing a crime, implying intention. Cases in which the individual can manipulate the group definition are not all that common. Instead, it is the society that frequently manipulates the individual, through social-control systems.

Social-Control Systems

The medicalization-of-deviance trend and the consequent changes in strategies of intervention may be broadly interpreted within the historical context of sociocultural change. We start with the observation that within western societies currently, the four broad institutions of social control are represented by the religious, social welfare, legal, and health systems. Each system maintains and upholds social order by intervening with those who have deviated from acceptable behavior. The religious system singles out and punishes those who have sinned against the Judeo-Christian ethic, the social welfare system attempts to help those who have not successfully adjusted to the social institutions, the legal system acts to control those who have violated formal rules and regulations, and the health system is oriented toward the cure and rehabilitation of those who, through no fault of their own, cannot carry out normal role performance. In each case, attempts are being made to maintain the status quo; that is, social order is being maintained.

Also in each case, changing the individual to fit the system is emphasized. In this context, the clergy, social workers, judges, and doctors share the function of societal surrogate charged with the responsibility of helping a maladjusted person make socially acceptable adjustments. During the process, the society prefers to deny that people intentionally violate the values and norms, since this would imply a failure of the socialization process. At the same time, there would be an implied criticism of the society if it were identified as the etiological source of deviance. As a result, if the four social-control systems compete for power, the health system will always hold the edge in the struggle. Medical explanations of deviance take the blame away from both the individual and the society. This, of course, enhances the medicalization of even more conditions.

Implications of Medicalization

It may be, then, that the spread of medicalization is based not on the medical profession's demonstrated success in handling behavior, but on its political ability to gain an illness label for an increasing number of actions. Freidson (1970) put that point rather dramatically in referring to the way in which the physician acts as an "entrepreneur" who promotes sickness labels and seeks out illness. What Freud did for mental illness is extended to all illness, with the creation of new rules and the definition of new types of deviance bringing more conditions under the jurisdiction of the physician. This constitutes another aspect of the "medicalization of life" (Illich, 1975).

There is a further implication to the success of the medical profession in obtaining legitimacy for increasing medicalization. The representatives of other social-control systems have not remained on the sidelines, passively watching the health system expand at their expense (Chalfant, 1977). Two options are open to the losers: fight or join. Only the legal system has employed the first tactic success-fully—through malpractice suits—and all social-control systems have adopted the second. An emergent therapeutic philosophy rooted in the psychiatric approach now dominates the religious, welfare, and legal systems (Hawkins and Tiedeman, 1975). Therefore, doctors, pastors, social workers, and judges attempt to define deviant behavior as medical conditions and the public willingly accepts the definitions provided by professionals.

CONCLUSIONS

If the trend toward the medicalization of deviance continues, there will be some important consequences for society, especially for health professionals and deviants. For example, with an ever-increasing number of conditions defined as illnesses, we would logically expect a major expansion in demands on a doctor's time. If this expansion occurs, many physicians will have cause for concern; they may find themselves ill-prepared to make meaningful contributions to newly legitimized psychological and social problems that seem far removed from broken bones, patho-gens, and malfunctioning organs. They may feel unable to take on the responsibility for some of the redefined illnesses. Further, such health resources as hospitals and doctor's offices may become overcrowded with medicalized deviants, leaving less room for traditional patients.

Within the medical profession, receptivity to social change will be somewhat dependent on medical specialty. Psychiatrists, for example, would probably welcome the opportunity to expand their domain. Orthopedic surgeons, however, would probably not care one way or the other. More than any other of the specialists, psychiatrists search for behavior that can be medicalized.

Perhaps medicalization will not affect professionals as much as it will those who have been labeled deviant, who may be seen as the "benefactors" of changing images. From the individual's standpoint, it is probably better to be considered sick rather than immoral or criminal. More than that, it may be better to be treated by medical personnel than by jailers, although this point is open to debate. And if the medical emphasis does lead to the cure of unwanted conditions, medicalization could be quite beneficial.

But beware; medicalization could have negative effects on society and on the individual whose label has been changed. For example, those whose conditions have been reclassified may be denied their civil rights. Unlike the prisoner or the accused, the patient has little defense against arbitrary decisions by a person acting in an official medical capacity. Legal trials for those being involuntarily committed to mental hospitals are comparatively recent, and the right to have a lawyer present is still not always clear to the patient. Further, institutionalization may last a lifetime for a patient, whereas the prisoner is given a definite term to serve, with time off for good behavior and a chance for parole. Perhaps the possibility of such societal reactions is behind the cautions expressed by the National Research Council Committee on AIDS Research and the Behavioral, Social, and Statistical Sciences, which, after calling for research focusing on people's sexual behavior, states: "Yet the committee would point out that there are risks in a strategy of proceeding from an interest in disease to research on the 'facts' of sexual conduct. These risks involve the possibility that concerns about disease will reinforce the tradition of treating some aspects of sexual conduct as social or medical 'problems' " (Turner, Miller, and Moses, 1989:78).

In addition, a corollary of medicalization is an expanding use of medications to control deviant behavior. Such medications are not used for curative purposes; they are used to control symptoms only. Theoretically, while symptoms are under control, the therapist will be working with the deviant toward cure. But this is not commonly how things work. Instead, medicalized deviants are put on tranquilizers or antidepressants or methadone or Antabuse or Ritalin and, since they are no longer behaving in a deviant way, they are ignored. In this manner, the medicalization of deviance social change is contributing to an overmedicated U.S. society, and it perpetuates a symptom-control orientation instead of a curative one.

Perhaps negatively by implication, the question can be raised whether medicalization reduces or increases the stigma associated with being a deviant. Here we refer to a change in name from criminal to mentally ill. Any diagnosis is a social label; the question is whether someone is better off with one label than the other. We pose this as a question without providing an answer. It remains for each reader to answer the question of whether a person in the United States is better off with the label of former convict or with the label of former mental patient.

Medicalization can be used to control behavior for political purposes. During the college student unrest of the 1960s, for example, the vice-president of the United States suggested that campus radicals were not really bad but were mentally ill, and that they should be sent to mental hospitals for treatment. This is similar to the previous Soviet government reaction to some dissidents, who were considered mentally ill if they defied the system, which justified their hospitalization in mental institutions.

The dangers involved in the medicalization process have led to some rather strong cautions. Thus, Shah (1975:504) states, "By blurring and obscuring the fundamentally moral and public policy issues intrinsically imbedded in the balancing of competing societal interests and values and turning them into mental health questions, it has been possible to justify societal practices that infringe grievously upon the rights and liberties of the mentally ill."

In line with this argument, Szasz (1974:53) asks, "Whose agent is the therapist?" and suggests that the therapist may represent the employer (for example, a business, the state, the military) rather than the patient. Following up on the point, he states, "I am opposed, on moral and political grounds, to all psychiatric interventions which are involuntary; and, on personal grounds, to all such interventions which curtail the client's autonomy" (1974:261).

Zola (1972) discusses the U.S. military's use of medicalized deviance definitions. He points to the case of the redefinition of alcoholism by the armed services. Until 1971, the status of alcoholism as a disease had been unrecognized by the services but, in that year, it was officially designated an illness. An advancement in the humanitarian treatment of members of the armed forces? Perhaps. But given an unpopular war, with much resistance to service, it was also a way of keeping soldiers or recruits in the armed forces. Since alcoholism was a disease and therefore treatable, it no longer disqualified the individual for service, and many who, in the past, would have been discharged were returned to the ranks.

The medicalization of deviance thus presents a mixed bag. That its nature and consequences are controversial is to be expected. A discussion of what the change means to society and the individual takes one far afield, but such is the nature of social systems. This chapter is an attempt to present a statement on the nature of the change, along with a discussion of some of its consequences.

References

Ausubel, David P. 1961. "Personality disorder *is* disease." *American Psychologist* 16(February):69–74.

Bernstein, Arnold, and Henry L. Lennard. 1973. "Drugs, doctors, and junkies." *Transaction* 10(May–June):14–25.

Billings, Dwight B., and Thomas Urban. 1982. "The socio-medical construction of transsexualism: An interpretation and critique." *Social Problems* 29(3):266–282.

Bullough, Vern L. 1977. "Challenges to societal attitude toward homosexuality in the late nineteenth and early twentieth centuries." *Social Science Quarterly* 58(June):29–44.

Caetano, Raul. 1987. "Public opinions about alcoholism and its treatment." *Journal of Alcohol Studies* 48:153–160.

Chalfant, H. Paul. 1977. "Professionalization and the medicalization of deviance: The case of probation officers." *Offender Rehabilitation* 2 (Fall):77–85.

Chalfant, H. Paul, and Richard A. Kurtz. 1971. "Alcoholics and the sick role: Assessments by social workers." *Journal of Health and Social Behavior* 12(October):66–72.

————. 1972. "Factors affecting social workers' judgments of alcoholics." *Journal of Health and Social Behavior* 13(December):331–336.

————. 1978. "The alcoholic and the sick role (comment on Segall)." *Journal of Health and Social Behavior* 19(March):118–119.

Committee on Homosexual Offenses and Prostitution. 1957. *Report*. London: Her Majesty's Stationery Office.

Conrad, Peter. 1976. "Towards a theory of the medicalization of deviance." Paper presented at the conference of the Society for the Study of Social Problems, New York, New York, August.

————. 1986. "The social meaning of AIDS." *Social Policy* (Summer):51–56.

Conrad, Peter, and J. W. Schneider. 1980a. *Deviance and Medicalization: From Badness to Sickness*. St. Louis: C. V. Mosby.

————. 1980b. "Looking at levels of medicalization: A comment on Strong's critique of the thesis of medical imperialism." *Social Science and Medicine* 14a:75–79.

Crawford, Alex. 1987. "Attitudes about alcoholism: A general view." *Drug and Alcohol Dependence* 19:279–291.

Fingarette, Herbert. 1989. *Heavy Drinking: The Myth of Alcoholism as a Disease*. Berkeley: University of California Press.

Freedman, Mark. 1975. "Far from illness, homosexuals may be healthier than straights." *Psychology Today* 8:28–32.

Freidson, Eliot. 1970. *Profession of Medicine*. New York: Dodd, Mead.

Hawkins, Richard, and Gary Tiedeman. 1975. *The Creation of Deviance*. Columbus, Ohio: Charles E. Merrill.

Illich, Ivan. 1975. *Medical Nemesis: The Expropriation of Illness*. London: Marion Boyars.

Kolata, Gina. 1985. "Obesity declared a disease." *Science* 227(1 March):1019–1020.

Kurtz, Richard A. 1977. *Social Aspects of Mental Retardation*. Lexington, Mass.: Lexington Books, D. C. Heath.

Light, Donald W. 1989. "Social control and the American health care system." In *Handbook of Medical Sociology*, 4th ed., ed. H. E. Freeman and S. Levine, 456–474. Englewood Cliffs, N. J.: Prentice-Hall.

Lorber, Judith. 1967. "Deviance as performance: The case of illness." *Social Problems* 14(Winter):302–310.

McCormick, Patrick. 1989. *Sin as Addiction*. Ramsey, N. J.: Paulist Press.

Parsons, Talcott. 1951. *The Social System*. Glencoe, Ill.: Free Press.

Pitts, Jesse R. 1968. "Social control: The concept." *International Encyclopedia of the Social Sciences*, vol. 14, pp. 381–396. New York: Macmillan and Free Press.

President's Panel on Mental Retardation. 1962. *A Proposed Program for National Action to Combat Mental Retardation*. Washington, D.C.: U.S. Government Printing Office.

Riessman, Catherine Kohler. 1983. "Women and medicalization: A new perspective." *Social Policy* 14(Summer):3–18.

Robbins, Thomas, and Dick Anthony. 1982. "Deprogramming, brainwashing and the medicalization of deviant religious groups." *Social Problems* 29(3):283–297.

Rudy, David R. 1986. *Becoming Alcoholic*. Carbondale: Southern Illinois University Press.

Ruzek, Sheryl. 1986. "Feminist visions of health: An international perspective." In *What Is Feminism*, ed. A. Oakley and J. Mitchell, 184–207. New York: Pantheon Books.

Sarbin, Theodore R. 1969. "The scientific status of the mental illness metaphor." In *Changing Perspectives on Mental Illness*, ed. S. C. Plog and R. B. Edgerton, 9–31. New York: Holt, Rinehart and Winston.

Shah, Saleem A. 1975. "Dangerousness and civil commitment of the mentally ill: Some public policy considerations." *American Journal of Psychiatry* 132(May):501–505.

Szasz, Thomas S. 1970. *The Manufacture of Madness.* New York: Harper & Row.

———. 1974. *The Myth of Mental Illness.* Rev. ed. New York: Harper & Row.

Turner, Charles F., Heather G. Miller, and Lincoln E. Moses, eds. 1989. *AIDS: Sexual Behavior and Intravenous Drug Use.* Washington, D.C.: National Academy Press.

Twaddle, Andrew C. 1973. "Illness and deviance." *Social Science and Medicine* 7(October):751–762.

Vaillant, George E. 1983. *The Natural History of Alcoholism.* Cambridge, Mass.: Harvard University Press.

Zola, Irving Kenneth. 1972. "Medicine as an institution of social control." *Sociological Review* 20(4):487–504.

11

Biomedical Innovation: Cultural Lag and Value Conflicts

INTRODUCTION

In his classical sociological work, Robin Williams (1970) discusses fifteen core values that set a cultural base for the way of life in the United States. In this chapter we will focus on five of these values, selecting for discussion three that specifically support scientific progress and two that honor activities that focus on the development of solutions to society's problems. The five are:

1. Efficiency and practicality.
2. Progress.
3. Science and rationality.
4. Achievement-success.
5. Activity-work.

Robertson (1987) also discusses the fifteen core values, including the five that are relevant to scientific innovations. He states that the *efficiency and practicality* value indicates that people in the United States believe that all problems have solutions (as hard as it may be for U.S. students to understand, not all societies do), the *progress* value suggests that Americans look to the future with a conviction that things can and should get better, and the *science and rationality* value points to an American belief in a scientific and rational approach to the world, with the use of applied science to gain mastery over nature (p. 65). Discussing how the *achievement-success* value sets a base for activity in U.S. society, Robertson states that "great value is placed on the achievement of power, wealth, and prestige," and in describing the function of the *activity-work* value he indicates that "regular, disciplined work is highly valued for its own sake" (Robertson, 1987:64).

Since sickness can prevent behavior that fulfills the achievement-success and activity-work values, activities that restore the normal abilities of unhealthy people are judged positively. This provides one of the bases of support for science and scientific innovation in U.S. society. Consequently, the five values may be interpreted within a medical sociology context as exhibiting a consistent negative attitude toward sickness and a positive assessment of activities designed to restore the sick to a healthy state.

A corollary to this complex of values is a commitment to the discovery and development of procedures that deter disease, save lives, and improve the quality of life, especially if the development is a "scientific breakthrough" and if the achievement seems dramatic. This is why those who have developed effective procedures that fit this pattern, people like Jonas Salk and Michael DeBakey, have taken on the aura of heroes. Glamor is associated with the part of medical science that leads to dramatic biomedical innovation, and a spillover recognition may be attached to the application of such innovations. The scientist or practitioner or both may be honored for accomplishments that prevent disease and that restore the unhealthy to a healthy state.

Members of the medical profession are the most obvious users of newly developed biomedical procedures and are, therefore, the beneficiaries of society's recognition and positive evaluation. The resulting image has contributed in a major way to the dominance of the medical profession in the system of health care. In their practical approach to healing the sick, members of the medical profession continually make use of technical and scientific progress, new products, and different applications for health-restoring procedures.

It should be recognized, however, that those who practice in the health occupations function as technicians; they are the appliers, not the developers, of scientific knowledge. The usual U.S. doctor has a practice devoted to applying the findings of science, to the relief of symptoms, and to helping bring patients back to normal functioning within the curative orientation of the society, rather than to developing biomedical innovations. Those who technically apply the findings of medical science should not be confused with those who are discovering and developing knowledge in medical science. Most medically qualified people engaging in scientific studies to develop and discover medical knowledge are employed by universities, the government, and private companies—they are not practitioners.

Innovations have a significant effect on crucial aspects of a physician's practice, however, and have changed important aspects of the doctor's role. Thus, recent biomedical innovations have taken physicians out of their patients' homes and even out of their own offices by making the hospital the more logical place to carry out many therapeutic procedures. Innovations have also added some emotionally charged value problems to professional decision making. The remainder of this chapter will focus on some of these biomedical innovations, and on value problems they have created for the doctor, the patient, the patient's family, and for society as a whole.

LIFE-SUPPORT SYSTEMS AND CONCEPTS OF DEATH

Artificial Life-Support Systems

Personnel in hospitals today routinely use artificial life-support machines to maintain the body functioning of patients who no longer have the biological ability to maintain their lives on their own. After respiration has ceased for between five and eight minutes, the individual's brain stops functioning; from a medical point of view, "death of the brain" has occurred. But artificial respiration machines could reestablish the rest of the patient's biological processes and keep them going indefinitely. The patient lying in the hospital bed looks "normal"—the chest moves as in normal respiration, there is a pulse, and the body remains warm, but the brain has ceased to function. Is this brain-dead patient whose physiological processes are totally dependent on the respirator alive or dead? The answer to this question has profound implications for those providing the answer and, of course, for the patient.

A New Concept of Death

With the introduction of artificial life-support systems, the good old simple days, when a stethoscope on the chest and an ear to the mouth resulted in a doctor's pronouncement of life or death, have essentially passed. New concepts and definitions of death have become necessary. The agreed-upon new concept defines death by using brain function as the criterion. Almost all states have now enacted statutes that use as the definition of death the "irreversible cessation of total brain function." Among those states that still rely on heart and respiratory failure for their definitions, most at least suggest in their statutes or through their courts that the brain death definition is an acceptable alternative.

The use of life-support machines created the need for a new definition of death. Doctors, philosophers, ethicists, members of the clergy, legislators, social commentators, and members of the public grappled with the meanings and implications of different definitions during the 1950s and 1960s. Questions about the meaning of life, the difference between the concept of death and the criteria of death, the exact moment that death occurs, the appropriate use of life-support systems, the life-related meaning of a coma, the definition of irreversibility or permanency, and many others were debated. Finally, in 1968 a group of doctors from the Harvard Medical School published "a definition of irreversible coma" in the *Journal of the American Medical Association*, and discussion of this document has led to whatever consensus there is today.

The Harvard Medical School definition focuses on "those comatose individuals who have no discernible central nervous system activity" (Harvard Medical School Ad Hoc Committee, 1968:85; original in italics). Patients who are in "irreversible coma," who have "no discernible central nervous system activity," are considered dead. If these patients are then hooked into life-support machines that keep the body functioning, this has nothing to do with their irreversible coma or central nervous system activity. The committee presented four criteria designed to diagnose a "*permanently* nonfunctioning brain" that has no possibility of regaining function. To determine "permanency," the four criteria are to be used twice, approximately twenty-four hours apart. The criteria for ascertaining whether a person has died are:

1. Unreceptivity and unresponsivity. Even if painful stimuli are administered, there is no reaction.
2. No movement or breathing for at least one hour.
3. No reflexes; for example, the pupil of the eye is dilated and fixed.
4. A flat or isoelectric electroencephalogram.

After discussion, this listing was accepted by many health professionals for determining when death had occurred. Its acceptance was further reinforced seven years later when the House of Delegates of the American Bar Association suggested the following statement as a model statute: "For all legal purposes, a human body, with irreversible cessation of total brain function, according to usual and customary standards of medical practice, shall be considered dead" (American Bar Association, 1976:301). Forty-eight states now have laws or court decisions that recognize brain death.

The acceptance of such new ideas and concepts can be a slow and sometimes confused process. Thus, the first state statute recognizing a brain-based definition of death was enacted by the Kansas legislature in 1970. But instead of accepting the Harvard Medical School criteria outright, the legislature adopted two separate definitions of death at the same time, without indicating whether or how they should be related to one another. In one paragraph, the definition refers to the absence of spontaneous cardiac and respiratory functions, which is based on traditional heart-lung function criteria. In another paragraph, the definition refers to an absence of spontaneous brain functions, which is based on the new brain-death criterion. Here we have both the old and the new separately stated in one statute; the practicing doctor in Kansas (and several other states that enacted statutes based on the Kansas model) is apparently given the option to use either definition.

Value Problems

The new definition raises important value questions about patients attached to artificial respiration machines, whose body processes depend solely on the machine. Thus, if the machine is turned off or, as it is commonly referred to by the public, if "the plug is pulled," breathing and circulation will stop permanently. This is because the machine-dependent patient is brain dead and respiration is being maintained artificially. Under these conditions, if someone unplugs the brain-dead patient from the machine, causing all body processes to cease, has this person committed homicide?

Decisions to stop so-called "heroic measures" to continue the lives of some patients have been made for most of the history of scientifically based medicine, but they were quietly kept within the confines of professional medicine. These actions became subjects for open public discussion only recently, with the growing availability and use of life-support machines (Culliton, 1976). As these artificial life-support machines became part of the hospital's routine equipment, lawyers and others began to question the conditions of their use. As the new definition solved problems of the definition of death, the new machines created problems concerning their proper use. Such developments have switched the question from, "Is a person dead?" to "Should the person be allowed to die?" Stickel (1979:194) comments on these questions: "It is the second question . . . that presents difficult dilemmas to all concerned—to patients and their families, to physicians and others comprising the health care team, and to framers of institutionalized and public policies."

The change from the first to the second question is a change from the objective to the subjective, from fact to judgment, from a medical issue to an ethical decision. In the first, the doctor's clinical judgment is usually accepted as supreme, and the physician stands alone as the final professional arbiter; in the second, the doctor's judgment is no better than anyone else's, and the physician holds but one opinion among many. Frequently, however, patients and their families turn to the doctor for guidance when faced with the decision about whether to withdraw life-support efforts, which places the doctor in a difficult position.

In some medical facilities, health workers have decided that when questions about withdrawal of support are raised, the total health care team, rather than any one individual, should provide the answer. In Boston, two hospitals connected with the

Harvard Medical School independently formulated policies spelling out circumstances that would make it acceptable to withdraw artificial life-support activities. In Massachusetts General Hospital, the doctor and hospital staff play the most influential role in the decision, although the final decision to withdraw support cannot be made without the family's consent; in Beth Israel Hospital, the patient and family have the most important influence on the decision made. In both cases, however, the final decision that leads to pulling the plug of the life-support system being used with a patient in irreversible coma rests with the family.

If it is agreed by the health professions that a person has no chance of regaining cognitive and sapient life, the consensus is that it is not improper to withhold or withdraw artificial life-support efforts. In other words, most professionals agree that if damage to the brain is so severe that the person could not become a knowledgeable, functioning human being again, the recommendation to pull the plug can be ethically correct. Thus, the person's humanness is the most important criterion. This is consistent with Fletcher's (1972) attempt to list "indicators of humanhood," in which he states that cerebration (thinking) is the cardinal measure of humanness. Within this perspective, the criterion for brain death is not that the brain has stopped functioning; the primary criterion is the judgment that the person can never recover and again function as a human being. In decisions to withdraw artificial support mechanisms, the doctor is expected to provide information about whether restoration of humanness is possible—that is, whether the patient can ever again function as a cognitive human being.

The reader should note that throughout this discussion focus has been on allowing the dying to die, rather than on inducing death, as is done in euthanasia (mercy killing), which is a fundamentally different concept. Euthanasia is not concerned with those who are dying but, rather, with those who are alive and biologically capable of life on their own. But these individuals are experiencing pain or other suffering so severe that it is considered merciful by some to *induce* death. Semantics are very important here: In the artificial life-support situation, the withdrawal of treatment results in the *natural death* of the patient. This is a critical way of interpreting the situation, for it relieves the decision maker from possible accusations of murder and from guilt feelings that could result from inducing death. It removes the onus of responsibility for a death from the shoulders of the doctor, and it helps keep the role of the doctor clear—that is, to be devoted to the saving, rather than the taking, of life.

ORGAN TRANSPLANTS

Brain Death and Organ Transplants

Definition of Death.   The permanently nonfunctioning brain criterion for the definition of death draws a distinction between the death of the brain and the death of the body. Several extraordinary implications flow from this distinction, one of which is directly tied to another value-laden biomedical innovation: the transplantation of an organ from a person whose brain is dead but whose body is still functioning to a person whose brain and body are functioning normally with the exception of the malfunctioning organ. This statement sounds like doubletalk, but it is consistent with the acceptance of the brain-death concept.

Whether the brain-death definition was a response to a need created by the development of transplantation techniques is a matter of ethical sensitivity in some professional medicine circles. The link has been publicly stated, has been denied, and has led to value conflicts. Thus, when a member of the clergy stated in testimony before the President's Commission for the Study of Ethical Problems in Medicine and Biomedical and Behavioral Research that "brain death statutes would seem to exist for essentially one reason only: to permit aggressive action on a body that would, but for that status, be considered alive" (Father Paul Quay, quoted in Sun, 1980:669), several physicians in attendance defensively responded that very few brain-death cases are involved in organ transplants. But the Harvard Medical School Ad Hoc Committee (1968:85), which had earlier produced the generally accepted statement on brain death, seemed to have taken the connection between the two for granted in its statement that "there are two reasons why there is need for a definition: (1) Improvements in resuscitative and supportive measures have led to increased efforts to save those who are desperately injured. . . . (2) Obsolete criteria for the definition of death can lead to controversy in obtaining organs for transplantation."

Whether the connection is there or not, it is clear that the brain-death definition does present the opportunity for obtaining still-functioning organs for transplantation. If the traditional definition of death, that is, irreversible cessation of spontaneous respiration and circulation, was not changed, the organs of the cadaver could not be kept "alive" and would therefore be unsuitable for transplanting. This is because "the suitability of organs for transplantation diminishes rapidly once the donor's respiration and circulation stop. . . . Thus, it became important for physicians to be able to determine when the brains of mechanically-supported patients irretrievably ceased functioning" (President's Commission for the Study of Ethical Problems in Medicine and Biomedical and Behavioral Research, 1981:23).

The Search for Norms.   How ethical is it to declare a person dead while maintaining artificial life-support systems to keep the body functioning until the organs can be removed for transplantation? Or, on the other side, how ethical is it to deny a patient who is dying because of a malfunctioning organ the opportunity for a life-saving transplantation when the organs of cadavers can be kept functioning through artificial support? Either of these questions can be answered in either direction. U.S. society has been searching for the proper norms in response to these value-confused situations.

Social norms are slowly emerging to handle these difficult decisions. One that received surprisingly quick acceptance is the Uniform Anatomical Gift Act, which allows the postmortem donation (with no mention of brain death) of an individual's tissue, organs, and whole body; the donor and two witnesses sign a wallet-sized consent card that is carried by the donor at all times so consent does not have to be sought under emotional and hurried conditions. The act was ratified by all fifty state legislatures between 1967 and 1970. However, this approach has not appreciably increased the number of donors since many people do not carry the consent card. In recognition of the act, in forty-two states drivers can sign a form or check a box printed on the back of their driver's licenses to indicate that they wish to donate their organs. But only a fraction of the drivers have signed this form. And even for those who sign, relatives are still asked to make the final decision. Thus, even given clear intent, irrespective of the consent card, most doctors still insist on family consent before accepting a patient as a donor.

A far more aggressive approach by several western countries is the enactment of so-called "presumed consent" laws, which reverse the consent-giving process. Such laws state that unless people explicitly state that they do not want their organs donated, permission for the procedure is assumed to have been given. Such laws have already been enacted in Austria, Czechoslovakia, Denmark, France, Israel, Italy, Norway, Poland, Spain, Sweden, and Switzerland. Whether this approach would be ethically acceptable in the United States is unknown, but apparently it is not.

Still, the shortage of cadaver organs available for transplantation in the United States is a problem. In response, several health organizations have pushed the use of the donor card and have suggested changes in social norms to make it easier for all cadavers to be donors. For example, some states allow the removal of organs for transplantation without prior permission from the individual or family if there is not enough time to seek consent, such as after an accident. And, in what may be an indicator of future norms in U.S. society, California's Diligent Search Act states that if a careful search fails to reveal the identity of a brain-dead individual, organ removal can proceed legally without the person's or family's consent. It is clear that society is searching for acceptable social norms. Once again, a biomedical innovation has created new situations needing new value decisions and stated norms.

Nevertheless, since the first successful kidney transplants in the 1950s, transplantation has become a routine procedure in the United States. The procedure has been extended to the heart, lungs, and pancreas. In addition, the increased experience of surgeons, refinements in surgical techniques, improvements in tissue typing and matching, more careful selection of candidates, and the development of effective immunosuppressant medications have led to major increases in long-term survival rates (House and Thompson, 1988). Given the presently positive and ever-improving track record, transplantation is clearly part of modern medicine.

Heart Transplants and Value Problems

The first human heart transplant was carried out in South Africa in 1967; it received extensive attention worldwide, reflecting a race among medical teams in several countries to report the first successful transplant of this nature. The procedure was successfully carried out in the United States the next year. Since 1968 the number of heart transplants has been increasing steadily; in 1988 1,647 of these procedures were performed in the United States.

Development of Criteria.   Heart transplants are reserved for patients who are beyond help from any other type of treatment, that is, those who would die without a new organ. For the recipient it is a life-or-death situation. But a serious shortage of donor hearts raises important ethical questions, particularly concerning how recipients are to be selected. As the basic ethical question was so bluntly put by anthropologist Margaret Mead, "If two people need a heart, who is going to get it? This hasn't a thing to do with hearts" (quoted in Vaux, 1969:202). Mead was correct; the life-or-death decision must be answered on the basis of subjective considerations. In the situation of a shortage, why should one person in need be selected instead of another? Stanford University Medical Center, which has a very active heart transplant unit, was one of the first to develop a listing of criteria for recipients. The criteria adopted in the 1970s were that a heart transplant recipient should have:

> *A stable, rewarding family and/or vocational environment to return to posttransplant;*
>
> *A spouse, family member, or companion able and willing to make a long-term commitment to provide emotional support before and after the transplant;*
>
> *Financial resources to support travel to and from the transplant center accompanied by a family member for final evaluation; living expenses near the center before, during, and after the transplant (a period of up to 10 months); and all pretransplant medical care, which can run more than $8,000. Contraindications at Stanford are a history of alcoholism, job instability, antisocial behavior, or psychiatric illness. (Knox, 1980a:572)*

From a sociological perspective, these criteria are a middle-class statement of social desirability or social worth. Since they are value judgments, each criterion can be supported or rejected by deciding that other patient characteristics are more valuable and important. Given the Stanford criteria, deviants, the poor, and the mentally ill in need do not stand a chance of receiving new hearts.

Other Problems.   There are other ethical questions. Thus, even at the present stage of knowledge and techniques, 20 percent of those receiving new hearts will probably live less than a year. Is this record of survival worth an intensive commitment of society's resources? Any answer to this question is debatable. For example, the trustees of Massachusetts General Hospital answered this question negatively after they found that "each heart transplant would consume the resources of six to eight routine open-heart surgery cases" (Knox, 1980b:574). This decision brings the point home: When resources are scarce, any decision in favor of a procedure must necessarily involve a trade-off with other procedures. In the area of values, in the area of ethics, there are no right or wrong decisions; there are only *different* decisions.

There are also financial problems, since transplantation procedures are expensive for the patient. Thus, the average cost of a heart transplant in 1989 was around $140,000. Further, this is only the initial expense since costs during the first posttransplant year are an additional $20,000 and each year following the transplant medications cost about $6,000. But, we are in the area of values once again—is it possible to place a monetary value on a human life?

A major problem facing transplant teams is the shortage of organs. But given the U.S. commitment to a value system that emphasizes the solving of problems, coupled with a positive assessment of developing medical innovations focusing on restoring the sick to a healthy state, it is inevitable that a medical solution will be sought for this problem. For example, a mechanical replacement heart has been developed and has been used on humans. The recipient of the first permanent artificial heart lived for 112 days after implantation. Despite high hopes, however, experiences with the artificial heart have not been altogether satisfactory. These artificial organs depend on an outside source for power, which has led to serious medical problems because the necessary hose and cable attachments encourage infection. In addition, the need for the patient to be no further away from the pumping machine than the length of these attachments means that his or her quality of life is seriously impaired. The value question may be asked whether this type of life is worth living.

However, a possible use for the artificial heart is as a temporary measure to keep the patient alive until a donor heart is found. Unfortunately, this measure has a built-in fallacy: Given the shortage of donor organs, keeping patients alive until "their turn" comes for a transplant means the creation of a forever-increasing size of the pool of waiting recipients. Increasing demand without increasing supply seems an odd way to solve problems. Is this what society wants?

A totally self-contained implantable mechanism is under development, but it must await further accomplishments in the growing technology of miniaturization. Meanwhile, presently in the development stage is a so-called "plastic heart" (constructed of polyurethane plastic and aluminum), actually a pump that can be implanted next to the natural organ, with the ability to automatically assist the biological heart to pump blood more efficiently when it is not functioning well.

Further refinement of the artificial heart also has become embroiled in politics. In 1988, the National Institutes of Health (NIH) decided to stop funding research on the latest version of the artificial heart and to swing its support instead to research on the development of the implantable pump (Booth, 1988). Withdrawal of financial support for artificial heart research would not end all activity in the development of a mechanical heart, but it would slow it down considerably. But NIH apparently did not consider the political implications of its decision. Two United States Senators, one from Utah, where one of the best known artificial heart medical teams in the country is at the state university, and the other from Massachusetts, in which one of the companies that would have lost funding if the NIH decision stood, drafted legislation in Congress that would have seriously threatened the funding of other, nonrelated activities of NIH if the funds for artificial heart research were withdrawn. The money was restored by NIH. As stated by Culliton (1988:283): "The NIH's struggle for freedom from political interference has been going on for years. For its side, NIH has the power of scientific reasoning; Congress has plain power. It is not a level playing field." Thus, U.S. society supports research leading to biomedical innovation, but from a medical-need point of view, priorities are not always rationally established.

The Diseased Kidney: Dialysis and Transplants

Dialysis. The development of the artificial kidney machine is another biomedical innovation success story but, like other innovations, it also raises many value questions. Through a procedure known as hemodialysis, or simply dialysis, the artificial kidney does for the body what the diseased kidney can no longer do. Dialysis helps patients whose malfunctioning kidneys no longer remove waste products from their blood. A patient is attached to the artificial kidney machine for six to ten hours two or three times a week. At this time the patient's blood flows through tubes into the dialysis machine, where it is purified and is then returned to the body. Dialysis is not therapeutic, and the patient's general symptoms are not alleviated; it is a life-supporting procedure rather than a curative one. The currently accepted practice in the United States is to have the procedure performed in a dialysis center (compared with other countries, such as the United Kingdom, where most patients are on dialysis at home).

Transplants. Once a person is on the dialysis machine, the only hope of getting off it is through a kidney transplant. Getting off is a logical goal since it frees the individual from dependence on the machine and, after the initial cost of approximately $32,000 for a transplant, yearly follow-up costs are only about one-third of the cost of continuing dialysis. Some of the same types of problems as those mentioned in the discussion of heart transplants are also present in kidney transplants. But kidney transplants also raise a series of fundamentally different problems because every person has two kidneys, and it has been determined that only one is needed for normal functioning. Unlike heart transplants, a live donor can give up one normal kidney to someone who has two that failed, and both the donor and recipient can then function normally. Cadavers are possible donors of two kidneys, but the death of the donor, which is necessary for heart transplants, is not a requirement for kidney transplants.

The "Gift of Life." In any type of organ transplant, the body's immune system will attempt to reject the donor organ. Therefore, part of the transplant procedure and the follow-up regimen consists of the administration of drugs to repress the recipient's immune system. Highly successful immunosuppressive drugs have been developed that alter the donor organ to reduce the possibility of rejection; but, even with these drugs, the receptivity is frequently much more successful when donor and recipient are biologically related. Because of genetic similarities, identical twins are the best pairing, and siblings are the next best.

Consequently, pressures may be applied to a healthy person to give up one kidney to make life more comfortable for a person, always a relative, with failed kidneys. But it is not that simple for the donor. The surgery is uncomfortable, and the donor then has only one kidney left, which could, theoretically, fail some day. Because of pressures, an overt statement of consent may be given, with a sotto voce feeling of being "forced" into the situation. The pressures are described by Fox

(1970:414): "Unwillingness, inability, or refusal to donate a kidney to a close relative dying of renal disease sociologically and psychologically implies not only abandoning him to his fate, but also repudiating him and the family bond that links one to him."

The long-term social and psychological meaning of what Simmons, Klein, and Simmons (1977) call the "gift of life" must also be considered. In Fox and Swazey's (1978) study of dialysis patients and kidney transplants, the gift relationships of donors, recipients, and significant others involved in the decision making are discussed. Interest in the social and psychological consequences of the relationship leads these investigators to the conclusion that the resulting emotional and moral commitment to one another can become so strong that they describe this "gift of life" as the "tyranny of the gift."

Value Problems. Doctors also face many social and psychological problems when asking someone to donate a kidney to a relative. According to Simmons, Klein, and Simmons (1977), asking a relative to donate a kidney is stressful for the doctor because it is contrary to medical norms and role expectations. The doctor's orientation is to help cure patients. But in this situation the doctor is asking a person to assume a surgical risk with no physical benefit. With whose interest should the doctor be most concerned, the recipient or the donor? If the doctor's commitment is to the patient, should pressures be put on the potential donor? How can the physician protect the interests of both? During the years of experience with these and related questions, the only agreed-on norm has been that of informed consent. But several procedures are common in many transplantation units in the United States. Among these are:

- Examination of a prospective donor by a psychiatric review board, with the intent of rejecting those who exhibit strong ambivalence, anxiety, and a decision based on undue family pressure.
- A policy of making it very difficult for the donor to volunteer (through such actions as initial rejection, or attempts to talk the person out of volunteering, or accepting only those who volunteer several times).
- Accepting only those donors whose spouses also agree to the procedure.
- Physician avoidance of the prospective donor, at least during the beginning phases of decision making.
- Immediate release of any prospective donor who, during the course of preparatory actions, indicates a desire to change the decision.
- Providing a fake medical excuse for those relatives who change their minds during the preparation stages.
- Separating the medical care of recipients and donors to the extent that they have different doctors and follow two different paths through the medical care system.
- Imposing age restrictions, mostly by setting a policy that young (often, under sixteen years of age) donors will not be accepted and that donors less than majority age must obtain court consent.

As in the case of heart transplants, biomedical innovations to treat kidney failure have moved much faster than society's ability to decide on acceptable social norms. Simmons and Simmons (1972) make this point by referring to a "lag in medical organization and communication" (p. 363), a "lag in allocation of financial resources" (p. 364), and "lags in the normative and the legal systems" (p. 367). Machines that can keep organs functioning when the brain has ceased to function, machines that mimic a normal kidney's functions, highly successful transplantation techniques, and means to suppress a recipient's immune system and to reduce the rejection of organs have all placed society, specifically doctors, in difficult situations. There is a cultural lag in the development of acceptable social norms.

Final Comments on Organ Transplants and Values

Extension and Experimentation. In 1988 there were 199 kidney, 123 heart, 59 liver, 45 pancreas, and 43 heart-lung transplant centers in the United States (United Network for Organ Sharing, 1988). The number of centers and the number of transplants have been increasing each year, and the survival rates of recipients are constantly being improved. The number and survival rate for specific transplantation procedures in the U.S. in 1986 (United Network for Organ Sharing, 1988) were:

Transplanted Organ	*Total Transplants*	*Percentage Surviving One Year or More*
Kidney	8,976	90
Heart	1,368	80
Liver	924	65–70
Pancreas	140	40
Heart-lung	50	75

Despite these sizeable numbers, organ transplantation is still viewed as an innovative procedure in the United States. Two major reasons for this view are that transplantation surgeons continually attempt to extend the procedure to other organs and other parts of the body, and much organ transplantation experimentation is still going on. Extension of the procedure and the nature of the experimentation keep transplantation in the news, especially because society has not yet reached consensus on acceptable values and norms concerning many aspects of the procedure. As a consequence of extension and experimentation, value disagreements concerning transplantation are continually subjects of debate.

To illustrate the first point, extension of the procedure, the conference program of the 12th International Congress of the Transplantation Society provides clues to the current state of transplantation. The published proceedings of the congress were divided into several clinical transplantation sections covering the following organs and procedures (Transplantation Society, 1989):

- Kidney
- Heart, heart-lung, and lung
- Liver
- Pancreatic islet
- Pancreatic organ
- Bone marrow
- Cornea
- Small intestine
- Central nervous system and peripheral nerve
- Limb
- Urinary bladder

The first seven transplantations are now considered routine by surgeons. The final four are being performed on laboratory animals but are still in the experimental stage for humans. Nevertheless, their inclusion in the listing illustrates a point: We have become so accustomed to medical success that almost everyone feels it is only a matter of time before the four join the ranks of routine procedures. What is next for the transplantation surgeons after these are successful? The answer to this question is limited only by our imaginations.

Relative to the second point, experimentation, the media periodically report on an organ transplant innovation that simultaneously taxes our imagination and jars our values. Such an event took place in 1984, when surgeons placed the heart of a baboon into an infant born with a heart defect. (Transplants between different species are known as xenographs.) The storm of controversy following this procedure did not disappear when "Baby Fae" died twenty days later. Animal-rights activists were outraged, ignoring the argument that humans routinely slaughter animals for food. The more philosophically inclined were concerned that some sacred line between humans and animals had been violated. (This was not the first case of a human receiving an animal organ, however; in 1963 chimpanzee kidneys were transplanted into six human patients, one of whom lived for nine months afterward.) Such experimentation was halted because of controversy, both because at the time it did not seem very productive and because new immunosuppressive drugs, especially cyclosporin, meant that many more nonrelative organs became available. Some people objected on the grounds that the placing of a foreign object inside a human being somehow makes us "less special" creatures of God or nature. (This view is also held by some people who object to the use of artificial hearts.)

Those who encourage continued use of animal organs point to the possibility of eliminating the long waiting lists for transplantable human organs; in mid-1988, 13,022 people were waiting for a kidney transplant, 888 for a heart, 480 for a liver, 173 for a heart-lung, and 151 for a pancreas (United Network for Organ Sharing, 1988). Proponents suggested that using animal organs was a rational way to provide all in need with a replacement heart, perhaps with two new kidneys, a new liver, or a pancreas. Since doctors have been using xenograph procedures by implanting pig's valves in human hearts for years (perhaps unknown to many recipients), many saw xenographs as a logical extension of an existing program. The suggested next plausible and rational step was to raise animals for their transplantable organs, especially those close to the human biological makeup such as baboons and chimpanzees, and to "harvest" their organs for human use.

But does this fit well with U.S. society's value system? Is this reasonable human and humane thinking or is it a ghoulish approach to life, albeit nonhuman life? To complicate matters, chimpanzees are on the endangered species list—does this excuse them from being part of the harvest? Since we slaughter pigs for food anyway, should the scientific effort be concentrated on them, so the claim can be made that their organs are "throwaways?" Is it that no one cares about pigs, but monkeys and apes are too "humanlike," too much "like us," to use in this way?

Are there right and wrong answers to these questions?

Personal and societal values were further jolted when the same hospital in which Baby Fae received the baboon heart announced in 1987 that, complying with a parental request, it would keep an infant expected to be born anencephalic (that is, with most of its brain missing) functioning through artificial support systems so its organs could be "harvested" for transplantation to other newborn babies. (The hospital placed a seven-day limit on the organ donations.) Most of the approximately 3,500 anencephalic children born each year in the United States die within a month of birth. Does keeping a newborn baby functioning to harvest organs differ from keeping an adult on the machine for the same reason?

This case carries concepts of death and organ donation several steps beyond the brain-death value consensus that was already reached, since the brain of the anencephalic infant, even if not complete, has been declared nonfunctioning, which is far removed from being declared dead. U.S. society is not quite ready to react unemotionally to this new development, which has far-reaching implications. It suggests that even a non-brain-dead human, but one practically certain to die quite soon, should be placed on artificial support systems for organ donations. The word "harvest" has taken on a new value connotation.

This experience paved the way for still another innovation, one that presents further challenges to the value system of the United States. The innovation begins innocently enough with the practical idea that, for some medical conditions, it is possible to transfer cells from one part of an individual's body to another, a procedure that would eliminate the problems of both availability and immune-system rejection. Although still experimental, this procedure yielded promising results in treating Parkinson's disease, a neurological ailment that affects more than one million people in the United States, most of whom are over the age of sixty. Parkinson's disease is presently treated with medications, but these lose their effectiveness over the course of treatment. In the new technique, part of the patient's adrenal gland is implanted onto the brain; the newly grafted cells repair specific neurological defects (Lewin, 1987a, 1987b). Such a biomedical innovation fits well with the U.S. value system since there seems little basis to question the morality of a procedure in which people volunteer to help themselves.

But acceptance and value-system consistency were short-lived, for it has been found that cells transplanted from miscarried or aborted fetuses repair neurological damage even better than a person's own cells. The virtue of fetal cells is that they reproduce much more rapidly than those of an adult. Further, and very importantly, if the fetal cells are less than fourteen weeks old, they have not yet acquired the immune-system rejection capability of older cells. In fact, in addition to their use in Parkinson's disease, fetal cells have been suggested as logical choices for implantation in patients suffering from stroke, spinal nerve injuries, and epilepsy.

The ethical problems are pronounced. How should society's value system react to this new biomedical innovation? Acceptable answers to the question remain to be formulated. And, whenever an answer to this troubling question is forthcoming, we can rest assured that another ethical and value-laden question will follow, and not very far behind.

The Allocation of Organs.   Given the severe shortage of organs for transplantation, it was inevitable that disagreements would emerge about the fairest way to allocate these scarce resources. Organ allocation became a national concern, especially when a study of the demographic characteristics of recipients concluded that "there is inequality in renal transplantation, based on age, race, and sex" (Kjellstrand, 1988:1307). Specific data revealed that among patients on long-term dialysis "a nonwhite man between 21 and 45 years of age has less than half the chance of receiving a transplant as a white man of the same age. . . . A nonwhite woman between 21 and 45 years of age has only a two-thirds chance of receiving a transplant as a white woman of the same age. Women aged 46 to 60 years, independent of race, have only half the chance of receiving a transplant as men the same age" (Kjellstrand, 1988:1306).

Congressional hearings in 1983 produced financial support for establishing a national organ procurement and distribution network. The United Network for Organ Sharing (UNOS), a not-for-profit, tax-exempt corporation was created the next year "to establish a national Organ Procurement and Tranplantation Network . . . to improve the effectiveness of organ procurement, distribution, and transplantation systems" (this statement is part of the Articles of Incorporation, 1984). As a first approach to allocation, UNOS adopted a University of Pittsburgh point system devised for kidney transplants. In this system, "credits were acquired for time waiting, quality of antigen match, degree of immunologic sensitization, medical urgency, and logistical considerations of getting the donor organ and the recipient together within the time limitations of safe organ preservation" (Starzl, Shapiro, and Teperman, 1989:3433). The Board of Directors of UNOS also established a national kidney transplant registry. With some modification, mostly by giving greater weight to medical urgency, the same point system was adopted for heart and liver transplants.

Thus, a national system of mostly medical considerations was established for transplant recipients, in contrast to the criteria established by individual institutions, some of which were accused of bias in their selection of organ recipients. The point system was adopted in an effort to make the selection process objective, to free it from value judgments. But this did not prove to be the case. Value disagreements and vested interests immediately set in: Starzl and his colleagues state that "far from settling disputes about kidney allocation, the point system has created a battleground for vested interests and viewpoints of great range and complexity" (Starzl, Shapiro, and Teperman, 1989:3433).

This experience demonstrates that any objective listing of criteria for organ eligibility must be based on subjectively selected premises; priorities are always based on value judgments. For example, should selection elements be drawn from a medical orientation or from perspectives reflecting social, demographic, economic, or religious views? Should the criteria be selected by surgeons or by politicians, judges, ethicists, philosophers, geneticists, or sociologists? Should the selection be made within doctors' offices, in hospitals, or in transplant centers? The use of value judgments in answering these questions is unavoidable. As ethicist Caplan (1989:3386) puts it, "Whether we like it or not, values determine who gets a transplant. The only question is which values will govern decisions at each stage in the allocation process and who will have input into determining the nature of those values."

Such questions reflect the diversity of values in a pluralistic society. Their presence and range do not apply exclusively to medical matters; relevant questions of this type apply to all of society's desired and limited resources. The allocation of medical resources is but one example of the many value decisions that must constantly be made. The consequences of decisions in the medical area, however, are often more vital and emotional than in many other areas, because lives can hang on the decisions reached.

GENETIC ENGINEERING

One of the most promising, and most controversial, biomedical innovations that has caught the imagination of both the scientific and financial communities in the United States is genetic engineering. Through genetic engineering, the basic structure of genes is manipulated, modified, and duplicated, to change it from what is considered an undesirable state. In addition, genes can be transferred from one life form to another and genes can be created to develop new life forms that can accomplish goals that present life does not.

Recombinant DNA

The basic genetic engineering process, which is known as recombinant DNA or gene splicing, is a product of the 1970s. (DNA is deoxyribonucleic acid, the basic genetic material in the cell.) The refinement of recombinant techniques has opened possibilities for engineering changes in plants, animals, and humans. In addition, the possibilities of the process as an economic investment have been the subject of everyday dealings in U.S. stock markets, since the process has promise for revolutionizing the quality and production of agricultural fertilizer, medications, chemicals, oil, and food.

Through the basic genetic engineering technique, an undesirable section from a ring of DNA is cut out and is replaced with a section containing characteristics considered desirable. This changed or recombined gene is then in a position to carry out the normal biological processes of division and duplication, but now with the changed characteristics. Since normal cell division includes the engineered DNA ring, the biomedical scientist has developed what seems like a self-perpetuating and never-ending production line of plasmids containing the desired characteristics.

When the recombinant DNA technique was initiated in the United States, its implications were the focus of debate about the consequences of creating new forms of life, such as genes with characteristics never before encountered. There were fears of a biological disaster if a newly created life form that our biological systems were not prepared to handle was let out of the laboratory and invaded the human body. In response to growing fears, the National Institutes of Health, the basic funding source for spliced-genes research, declared a moratorium on recombinant DNA research to provide time to consider the dangers to society. This moratorium was suspended when guidelines were developed to control investigations deemed dangerous. These guidelines, set in 1976, limited recombinant DNA research to laboratories that followed an elaborate series of strict safety precautions. After several years of experience, however, practically all genetic engineering research has now been declared safe enough to be conducted under the usual safety measures prevailing in scientific laboratories. Many scientists feel the initial response that brought strict controls was an emotional overreaction to a new and strange area of research.

Commercial Possibilities

After the safety problem was "solved," a new one arose, this time in reaction to the potential commercial gain from gene splicing. From the financial standpoint, it was necessary to stimulate research in the area. In a society committed to capitalist values, the financial rewards of accomplishments had to be protected. The discussion centered on one question which, when answered, could also resolve several subsidiary, economically inspired questions: Can new life forms be made the property of the inventor through the patent system? If not, all investigators would share alike; if yes, the patent holder would hold exclusive rights of use for seventeen years and could reap enormous profits. In 1980 this issue was decided by the highest court in the country: The United States Supreme Court ruled that new forms of life created in the laboratory *can* be patented.

The Supreme Court ruling, in conjunction with such decisions as one in 1985 by the U.S. Patent and Trademark Office indicating that genetically engineered plants, seeds, and tissue can also be patented, led to the establishment of an industry that focuses on genetic engineering. Some giant corporations, mostly pharmaceutical and chemical-fertilizer companies, established genetic engineering divisions, and smaller companies were started in efforts to create patentable new life forms with commercial possibilities. Among the animals that have been engineered are cows that give more milk, disease-resistant rats, sheep that produce milk carrying a blood-clotting element that is vital for hemophiliacs, and mice that produce milk containing a protein that is helpful to heart attack victims. And one of the largest U.S. pharmaceutical companies claims that one million people are now using its recently introduced recombinant DNA insulin derived from human cells, which eliminates many of the problems encountered in using insulin derived from cows or pigs.

Public interest in genetic engineering companies was demonstrated by the reception of one such company, which made an initial offering of common stock to the public in 1980. In the first six months of 1980, the company had earned only $81,000; nevertheless, the one million shares offered at $35 each were quickly bid up to $89. Several other small genetic engineering companies quickly made plans for public offerings of their stock.

Problems in Academia

A mixture of biomedical innovation and commercialism is an inevitable consequence in a capitalist society, in which new products are evaluated in terms of their profit potential. Consequently, private enterprise has always been a lure for the scientist working in a new area of research. Sometimes the potential for rewards is particularly bright, which can lead to a flow of researchers from their positions in academic institutions to private laboratories where the financial rewards are greater.

Like many others in a capitalistic system, academic scientists would like to identify the next IBM, Xerox, or Polaroid among the fledgling companies seeking personnel. This has led to value problems in academia. For example, the scientist in an academic laboratory may focus on old and new life forms to expand the knowledge base, whereas the scientist in a private laboratory may focus on those forms that have the greatest profit potential, irrespective of the knowledge base. Although one situation does not necessarily preclude the other, the scientist caught between the two may face conflicts of interest and value problems. Such value problems were raised recently when some academics questioned the ethics of a scientist who, when he left his university academic position to join a genetic engineering company, took with him material being used in the university laboratory.

Ethical issues took an interesting turn in 1980 when the president of Harvard proposed that the university establish and hold an interest in a private gene-splicing company. The proposal was made when a Harvard biologist offered the university a chance to join him in establishing the company. Although universities are often involved with commercial enterprises, the gene-splicing company would be unique because Harvard would be going into business with a member of its faculty. The proposal became an issue of lively debate within Harvard's academic community. Faculty opinion was divided, but leaned away from the university's direct involvement in a commercial enterprise of this type. Issues such as a possible compromise of academic freedom; the effect of the enterprise on basic personnel decisions such as recruitment, promotion, and tenure; influences on research directions; and questions about faculty members' objectivity and impartiality were raised and discussed. Finally, the president withdrew the proposal. Once again, a biomedical innovation led to value conflicts.

Two footnotes to this incident, both suggesting second thoughts, are necessary. First, in 1988 the U.S. Patent and Trademark Office granted the first patent ever issued on animals; "it went to Harvard University for genetically altered mammals that can be used to detect cancer-causing substances" (Wheeler, 1988:1). The financial potential of such a patent is huge. Second, in 1987 Harvard's managing board voted to create a new $30 million fund designed to raise money to be used for commercializing discoveries made by medical school faculty members; 10 percent of the fund's profits go to the university. Perhaps as a reaction to the former controversy, however, the program contains several safeguards designed to protect academic integrity (Marshall, 1988). It should be noted that Harvard is only joining several other well-known universities that permit or encourage collaboration between their faculty and private enterprise, including Columbia University, Massachusetts Institute of Technology, and Stanford University.

Genetic Therapy

Geneticists have found that genes are not continuous strands, but are in pieces or fragments with extra DNA in between. This finding led to the hypothesis that each gene fragment, referred to as a minigene, comes from a particular part of a protein and can be rearranged into different combinations. If this is so, it may be possible to treat defective minigenes by rearranging abnormally combined proteins into a normal arrangement, with natural-division reproduction then occurring among the now-normal genes. The advantages of correcting a genetic fault early in the cell-division process are obvious. This suggests the concept of gene therapy, especially since geneticists will some day identify each of the approximately 100,000 genes in human cells and will, therefore, have the capability of altering virtually any defective gene in the body.

Such therapy has already been attempted on human beings, although the reaction from fellow scientists was generally negative because many feel scientific knowledge has not advanced far enough to make this type of experimentation with humans safe. Here we can see another side of the value problems raised by biomedical innovations. Scientists themselves are setting limits beyond which they feel it would not at present be ethical to proceed in experimentation on human subjects. Meanwhile, the process is becoming routine for use with rats, mice, pigs, cows, goats, and sheep.

Value Problems

Publicity concerning genetic engineering has so far been on the side of the scientists, as the public marvels at what is being done and as many people speculate about financially lucrative possibilities. General value conflicts have not arisen, but this is not so for all segments of the population. As we have seen, the profit potential of genetic engineering has caused problems within the academic community. In addition, some questions are bound to lead to different value decisions. For example, do patients own their tissue in an economic sense, as they own material possessions? On a practical level, should a patient whose tissue leads to a money-making genetically engineered product receive a share of the financial rewards (Sun, 1985:789)? The California Court of Appeals answered this question affirmatively in 1988 when it ruled that "if research reveals that a patient's tissues may yield products of commercial value, the donor has a right to some compensation unless he specifically relinquishes any financial interest" (Crawford, 1988:653). Such innovations are being challenged on a specific issue level; to this point, general value questions concerning genetic engineering research have remained in the background.

One reason general value problems were avoided was the control over research exercised by the National Institutes of Health, which followed the moratorium on genetic engineering research with guidelines for investigators. This is consistent with policies governing all federally supported research in which humans are used as experimental subjects. It is now standard operating procedure for academic scientists planning research involving human subjects to have their study protocols evaluated by a committee established to protect the people being used as subjects. Such committees were set up in the 1960s when the U.S. Department of Health, Education, and Welfare (HEW) and the Public Health Service (PHS) required a review of the research protocols that were submitted for support. This review was to be carried out by academic peers and representatives from the general public before the funding decision was made. Within HEW and PHS guidelines, all universities requesting federal funds for research projects had to establish an Institutional Review Board focusing on human subjects' informed consent and right to withdrawal, with guarantees of the confidentiality of all information obtained, details about the safety of the study, and consideration of the potential benefits of the research. Over the years, most research units in academia have extended the scope of the board's authority to all research, irrespective of whether federal funding was requested.

Thus, both scientists and the public were provided with a mechanism to protect the rights of human subjects and to set ethical limits on experimental procedures (Gray, Cooke, and Tannenbaum, 1978). Fox recognizes this as a "relatively new social invention" that helps close the cultural lag gap. As she puts it, "it is an organized, now federally mandated social control mechanism, an 'ethical filter,' whose primary purpose is to safeguard the rights and welfare of human subjects" (Fox, 1989:246).

There is an undercurrent of fear among some people, however, that the scientist working in this area is walking a thin line. It is possible that despite the precautions being observed, some day a new life form that is undesirable and over which we have little or no control will escape from a laboratory. Such an event could initiate an emotional value debate in our society. But for the time being, at least, the cultural lag between innovations and social norms has been considerably narrowed.

What of the Future?

Genetic engineering is an innovation still in its infancy. The question of what lies ahead can only be answered by extrapolating from present developments and directions. In June 1989 the scientific journal *Science* concentrated on this question by presenting several articles concerning the latest developments in the genetic engineering of humans, animals, and plants. The editor of the journal set the theme for the special issue by making the startling statement that genetic engineering accomplishments "have [already] *accelerated evolution* for the benefit of humans by deliberate selection of techniques to improve livestock, crops, and other life forms" (Koshland, 1989:1233; italics added). Such an acceleration has long-term consequences; the modified path of evolution constitutes a new baseline for future developments.

Plants and animals have already been genetically changed by scientists, but our interest here is in human gene therapy, which is far more controversial. In human gene therapy, tools are being developed to first detect mutations in genes (Marx, 1989a) and then to repair them, or to replace those deemed defective with healthy genes. As stated by Friedmann (1989:1275), "recent results with several target organs and gene transfer techniques have led to broad medical and scientific acceptance of the feasibility of this 'gene therapy' concept for disorders of the bone marrow, liver, and central nervous system; some kinds of cancer; and deficiencies of circulating enzymes, hormones, and coagulation factors." A particular gene can be targeted for removal and can be replaced in the living cell by another gene, perhaps even an artificially created one that functions normally (Capecchi, 1989). As Koshland (1989:1233) puts it, this process "can reverse history in ending the progress of a deficient gene." So, not only have we already "accelerated evolution," but we can also "reverse history" by deflecting it from a direction we consider undesirable.

The necessary refinement consists of identifying and isolating the particular gene that must be treated or replaced. The technology in this area is moving ahead rapidly, as indicated in the statement by Marx (1989a:737): "For the first time, researchers are developing the ability to detect even the smallest mutations caused in human genes by chemicals or radiation." Recent successes have been reported for a virtual "who's who" of seemingly intractable and little understood diseases such as Alzheimer's disease (Barnes, 1987; Marx, 1988), cancer (Kolata, 1987; Culliton, 1989), cystic fibrosis (Marx, 1989b), and muscular dystrophy (Kolata, 1985). As the genetic involvement of more and more diseases is found, the list will be extended.

But even here value problems have arisen since not all members of society agree that genetic engineering research should continue. Thus, although recent successes have stilled some of the controversy, in 1983 "the leaders of virtually every major church group in the United States . . . signed a resolution calling for a ban on genetic engineering of human reproductive cells" (Norman, 1983). A major general objection of these religious leaders was that the concept of genetic engineering technology raises the possibility of altering the human species. Among the sentiments expressed is the possibility that humans may lose their genetic diversity. A spokesman for the group argued that "once we decide to begin the process of human genetic engineering, there is no logical place to stop. If diabetes, sickle cell anemia, and cancer are to be cured by altering the genetic makeup of an individual, why not proceed to other 'disorders': myopia, color blindness, left handedness. Indeed, what is to preclude a society from deciding that a certain skin color is a disorder?" (this statement is attributed to author-activist Jeremy Rivkin, in Norman, 1983:1360). Value disagreements seem inherent in genetic-engineering research.

In 1989 the NIH launched an estimated $3 billion, several-year project aimed at mapping all human chromosomes and deciphering the complete genetic instructions of the body. Further, genetic engineers have enthusiastically endorsed a proposal based on new information about how to manipulate DNA that could lead to the mapping of all the genetic material in human cells within the next five years (Roberts, 1989). If accomplished, this would be the major breakthrough genetic engineers are waiting for. But not everyone agrees that this ambitious goal can be achieved, even within our lifetime. Thus, Hood (1988:1843) states that "it will take at least hundreds of years to decipher the multitude of messages contained in the human genome." But if it can be achieved, virtually all inherited disorders could be subject to the genetic engineer's skills.

DIAGNOSTIC SCREENING AND VALUE PROBLEMS

Prenatal Screening

Prenatal diagnostic screening procedures are used to obtain information about the fetus well before birth. If abnormalities are found, several means are available for correcting the problem, or a decision may be made to terminate the pregnancy. The present standard technique used for prenatal diagnosis is amniocentesis, a procedure in which a sample of fluid is taken from the pregnant woman's amniotic sac; laboratory examination of this fluid yields important information about the fetus. Despite increasing medical acceptance of this procedure, attempts to develop safer and less invasive techniques for prenatal diagnosis are continually under way. Among these is ultrasonography, which has been used to screen for problems of the fetus at an early stage of pregnancy. In still another technique, a fiberoptic endoscope (called a fetoscope) is used to make direct observations of the fetus within the uterus. Another direction is continual work on developing indirect fetal diagnostic procedures by examining certain characteristics of the parents; the most promising of these are an extension of DNA techniques to diagnose potential genetic defects of the fetus by analyzing a sample of the parents' blood (Caskey, 1987; Landegren, Kaiser, Caskey, and Hood, 1988).

Abortion and Screening

By their very nature, prenatal diagnosis procedures raise important and highly charged value issues. For example, value issues are inherent in the decision of many health facilities and doctors to perform prenatal diagnostic procedures only if the parents sign a prescreening agreement that they agree to abortion if certain abnormalities are found. The reasoning of these facilities and doctors is based on such factors as the potential quality of life of the child and parents, the proper use of scarce resources, and the knowledge that even safe prenatal screening methods involve some degree of risk.

But there are important limitations to the information yielded by prenatal screening techniques. For example, amniocentesis reveals with certainty whether the newborn child will be afflicted with several abnormal conditions, such as Down's syndrome. If the child has this syndrome, he or she will be mentally retarded. But the chromosomal analysis cannot provide information about the *degree* of mental retardation. Thus, parents can be told with certainty that their child will be born with Down's syndrome, but they cannot be told whether the accompanying mental retardation will be mild, moderate, severe, or profound. And it is precisely this bit of information, that is, knowledge about severity, that may be the critical factor influencing the decisions of many parents.

Progress in genetic engineering may some day make this type of problem nonexistent, since a combination of amniocentesis and genetic engineering has the potential of creating a revolution in the identification and treatment of genetic defects. Thus, recombinant techniques may make it possible to change or replace any defective gene soon after conception, so the chromosome at fault can be modified during gestation, and the child will be born with normal genetic makeup. But this type of reasoning projects us far into the future.

Even today's knowledge and technology are adequate for completely eradicating some of the maladies associated with genetic disorders. To eradicate Down's syndrome, for example, an effective screening program that makes amniocentesis routine for all pregnancies would be necessary, and abortion would have to be accepted in society. But, given the pluralism of values in U.S. society, neither a screening program nor consensus on abortion is possible. Even when screening programs are offered to people at risk, many do not take advantage of the offer. The techniques exist, but the value consensus on utilization does not.

Screening for Sexually Transmitted Diseases

Screening for sexually transmitted diseases has been in effect for many years in several states, where couples planning marriage must have their blood tested for syphilis and other diseases before a license is granted. The recent advent of AIDS has led to suggestions that screening for HIV (the virus that causes AIDS) should be added to already established premarital screening programs. But as it turns out, this suggestion came just when many states are removing premarital blood-testing regulations from their marriage requirements. Since 1980 more than twenty states have removed the requirement; fewer than one-half of the states now have such regulations on their books. Two main reasons are usually advanced for the removal: Such testing is now considered an inefficient and costly means of case detection, and premarital sexual values and norms have changed over the years, so marriage is not the precursor to sexual activity that it was when such screening was originally imposed (Institute of Medicine, 1988). Given this trend, the suggestion to include HIV testing of prospective marital partners has not made much headway.

But AIDS has so frightened society that screening measures for some special groups of people, such as "captured" groups, have been suggested. For example, in 1987 the president recommended that all immigrants and federal prisoners be routinely tested for HIV infection, and that voluntary testing should be carried out among patients in federal and Veterans Administration hospitals. In addition, since 1985 the United States Army has tested 800,000 army personnel and more than 1.4 million applicants for military service for HIV infection (Barnes, 1987). Given the ethical and other problems that arise from mandatory screening, however, especially for low-risk groups, many professionals are recommending against such programs. Thus, the Institute of Medicine Committee for the Oversight of AIDS Activities states that "mandatory screening programs, especially those aimed at low-risk groups, are likely to be ineffective, counterproductive, and distracting. [A screening program] may divert resources from more worthwhile educational and voluntary programs, identify too few individuals at risk, and produce many false-positive test results; it may also have untoward social consequences that would outweigh any possible benefits" (Institute of Medicine, 1988:75). The committee recommends, instead, the mandatory screening not of people, but of the blood used for transfusions and of tissue and organs used in transplants.

A far more controversial suggestion has come from social scientists who want to monitor the AIDS epidemic in the United States. The suggestion comes from recognition that there has not been a major study of the sexual behavior of Americans since the Kinsey studies in the late 1930s and early 1940s (Kinsey, Pomeroy, and Martin, 1948; Kinsey, Pomeroy, Martin, and Gebhard, 1953). These studies are so out of date and have such serious methodological flaws in the research design that it is statistically inappropriate to generalize from the data. Nevertheless, some government departments have found it necessary to rely on the Kinsey data for estimates of the extent of homosexual behavior, and thus the extent of HIV infection among males, because this is all that is available. But valid and reliable data are vitally needed to understand and control the epidemic's spread (Turner, Miller, and Moses, 1989:9). This has led to a recommendation for a large-scale interview-survey of the sexual practices of Americans, which will provide the information needed to more accurately estimate the prevalence of HIV infection and AIDS. Supported by the federal government's National Institute of Child Health and Human Development and conducted through the nonprofit National Opinion Research Center, the suggested study would consist of one-hour interviews with a representative sample of some 20,000 Americans. The intention was to include questions about homosexual experiences and specific types of sexual acts (Booth, 1989:304).

Not surprisingly, the suggested survey did not survive the value-based congressional debate. The House of Representatives removed the $11 million designated for the survey from the proposed Public Health Service budget (one Representative stated in a letter to *Science* that "the survey seems more apropos for the pages of a pornographic magazine . . . than as something to be passed off as a scientific study" [Dannemeyer, 1989:1530]). Irrespective of their potential contributions to society, screening programs face difficulties when they deal with value-laden politically, socially, and personally sensitive issues.

ARTIFICIALLY INDUCED PREGNANCY

Having children is a dream of many couples in the United States; if this dream cannot be fulfilled through normal means, biomedical innovations present the possibility of pregnancy through artificial means. According to the U.S. Office of Technology Assessment (OTA), thousands of women unable to conceive by normal means are undergoing procedures designed to induce pregnancy artificially. The OTA estimates that each year 65,000 children are born as a result of artificial insemination (the result of 172,000 women attempting the procedure), 600 babies are born by in vitro fertilization, and about 100 are born to surrogate mothers (reported in Byrne, 1988). The popular press has estimated that one married couple in twelve is infertile and would like to have children.

Artificial Insemination

If medical examinations of the couple indicate that the infertility can be corrected through chemical means, fertility drugs may accomplish the task. For example, drugs have been developed that stimulate the ovaries to increase the number of eggs available for fertilization, and chemical ways of increasing the count and motility of sperm are available. If medications fail, artificial insemination is the traditional initial-attempt procedure for infertile couples attempting pregnancy. In this procedure, sperm from either the regular sexual partner or a sperm bank are deposited into the woman's vagina at the time the medical data indicate that conception has the best chance of occurring. Little controversy surrounds a couple's decision to attempt artificial insemination. But if this does not lead to pregnancy, more controversial measures are available.

Surrogate Motherhood

On the face of it, surrogate motherhood seems an easy way out for some infertile couples who want children. If the problem can be solved by using the male partner's sperm to impregnate another woman (for ethical reasons, say by artificial insemination) willing to carry the fetus until birth, after nine months the infertile couple will have achieved the goal. But, how does a couple recruit the surrogate mother? This question has led to considerable controversy and to many value disagreements.

In perhaps the most public case of this nature, which came to be known as the case of Baby M, in 1988 the New Jersey Supreme Court voided a contract signed by an infertile married couple and a woman who agreed to artificial insemination and to carry the child until birth for a $10,000 fee. The Chief Justice of the court stated that payment for surrogate motherhood is "illegal, perhaps criminal, and potentially degrading to women," and added emotionally that "there are, in civilized society, some things that money cannot buy." Apparently, the financial payment was most troublesome to the value system since the court also stated that unpaid surrogate motherhood per se was not illegal. It added the stipulation that the surrogate mother must have the right to change her mind about giving up the child after birth. Norms on this procedure are still developing—five states have declared mother surrogate contracts unenforceable, and one has declared the procedure a crime.

In Vitro Fertilization

In vitro fertilization (IVF) is used in cases in which the woman's fallopian tubes do not function correctly, making pregnancy impossible or very difficult. In this procedure, eggs from the potential mother are removed and are fertilized by the potential father's sperm in the laboratory, where early development of the embryos can be monitored and regulated in the controlled environment of an incubator. One of the fertilized eggs or embryos can then be implanted through the cervix in the mother's uterus, or it can be frozen in liquid nitrogen for future implantation. If the implantation is successful, the remaining embryos can be saved for future use or they can be destroyed. In 1983 it was estimated that 440,000 infertile couples in the United States are potential candidates for this procedure (Grobstein, Flower, and Mendeloff, 1983).

The world's first successful IVF, or "test-tube baby" as it is referred to in the popular press, was reported by a medical team in England in 1978. More than a decade of attempts were made by the team before this first success. Even today, success rates are low; egg recovery and fertilization do not present a problem, but the rate of successful embryo transfer to the mother is only 15 percent (Norman, 1988). Nevertheless, about 170 medical teams are offering the technique in the United States.

We start our discussion of the controversies surrounding this procedure with its cost, which is around $4,000 for each attempt; several states have mandated that all or part of the bill must be met by insurance companies (Raymond, 1988). Some would-be parents have had several tries, each at $4,000. Despite the costs, centers report long waiting lists with as much as a ten-year backlog of applicants, and some candidates for the procedure have their names on several different waiting lists (Kolata, 1983). To add to the cost problem, private for-profit centers that offer the procedure are a growing industry (Kolata, 1983), and the commercial orientations of some can be questioned.

The entire IVF concept has been challenged by some religious groups and right-to-life advocates, who object to a technique that leads to the destruction of some embryos (for example, if a couple has had success with one of its several fertilized eggs). This brings to the front a basic value-steeped question that also figures prominently in the abortion debate: At what point in human development does life begin? No matter how this question is answered, the implications are profound. For example, a married couple from Los Angeles unsuccessfully underwent IVF in Australia and left two frozen fertilized eggs there when they returned to the United States. Two years later the couple died in an accident, leaving a substantial inheritance and no will. There was some question of whether the embryos were still viable since the longest reported viability of a cryogenically preserved embryo that was later successfully implanted is twenty-eight months. But, if they were, should the embryos be implanted in someone (the fertility center was deluged by volunteers) and, if the implant were successful, would the resulting offspring have inheritance rights? After much debate, it was finally decided in Australia that the embryos could be offered to other childless couples in that country; in the United States, the Los Angeles Superior Court ruled that the executors of the estate had no jurisdiction over the fate of the embryos and that, if children were born of an implantation, they would not be considered heirs.

In another case, a Tennessee Circuit Court judge ruled that seven frozen embryos were human beings and, in the ruling, referred to the seven as children. The case initiated with a married couple for whom eggs from the wife were in vitro fertilized by semen from the husband, resulting in seven embryos that were then frozen. Before any attempt at implantation, the marriage disintegrated and divorce proceedings were initiated. A custody battle for the fertilized eggs developed, each party claiming they had the right to the embryos. The husband wanted the eggs to be destroyed, stating that their use could force him into unwanted fatherhood, but the wife wanted them kept in storage because they were potential lives that she might want to use or donate to someone else who wanted to use them for the same purpose.

It is clear that society must develop guidelines to solve the value problems emerging from the IVF procedure and, if possible, to anticipate future problems. Society is being forced to face these problems at the moment, and the courts are being asked to provide answers to moral questions. It is also clear that many of the problems emerging as fallouts of biomedical innovations are interrelated.

ACUPUNCTURE: AN INNOVATION THAT HAS NOT BEEN ACCEPTED

We should not assume that all biomedical innovations are acceptable to the public or to the medical-scientific community in the United States. Innovations are most easily accepted if they have a futuristic, almost science-fiction characteristic and if they are in the forefront of scientific advances. Commercial potential also helps. The absence of these characteristics explains the failure of acupuncture (the use of thin filiform needles inserted into parts of the body) to win acceptance in the United States. Despite its use both as an anesthetic and treatment procedure by more than one-quarter of the world's population (it is part of the medical practice of Austria, China, Denmark, Finland, Germany, Ghana, Japan, Kuwait, Malaysia, Nigeria, Pakistan, and Sri Lanka), and despite recent favorable descriptions of the procedure (for example, West, 1989), acupuncture has been all but ignored in the United States (World Health Organization, 1980). Acupuncture has not received what may be termed a fair trial, but perhaps a beginning has been made. There may be as many as 5,000 nonmedical and 1,000 medical acupuncturists in the United States, and roughly twenty states license practitioners (West, 1989).

Acupuncture has had a very difficult time being accepted in U.S. society. The reasons for its failure are not complex. First, acupuncture is a very old approach; the Chinese have found stone needles that may have been used for such clinical treatment during the Neolithic period, and written records on the treatment go back to around 400 B.C. This procedure clearly does not fit in with the conception of modern medicine in the United States. Second, the procedure lacks glamor; the word *acupuncture* does not bring forth an image of a white-coated scientist peering through instruments at microscopic organisms responding to laser beams. Third, there has been no major advocate of the procedure, who, at the very least, has called for the translation of the literature into English, who has pushed for legislation to control the practice of the unscrupulous, who could act as a bridge between practitioners in other countries and the United States, and who has demanded clinical trials and laboratory experiments. Fourth, the public seems pleased with the quality of western medicine and sees little use for a new approach that challenges the scientific base of the current scene. Fifth, the commercial potentials from acupuncture do not seem substantial. Sixth, it is "foreign." Seventh, irrespective of whether acupuncture actually works, it does not currently fit in well with the scientific knowledge system of the United States.

CONCLUSIONS

During the past thirty years, a number of biomedical innovations have changed how we think about death, birth, and what we should do with our lives between these two events. Many of the innovations were not anticipated and, as a consequence, society has had to adjust to situations and confront value-based questions that would have made no sense just a few years ago. Some of the innovations that have led to problems were discussed in this chapter, within the sociological concept of the cultural lag. Thus, we have faced questions about the use and misuse of artificial life-support machines, the prolonging of life so human organs can be harvested, the creation of new life forms, and the fertilization of human eggs outside the mother's reproductive system. One biomedical advance after another has led to ethical, moral, value, and legal questions; how these questions were answered has depended on who was asked to respond.

Given U.S. society's commitments to scientific innovation and problem solving, we have learned to live with constant change and its accompanying value disagreements. This is a "fact of life" of culture in the United States. Since such commitments are essential parts of the value system, future changes will probably be as rapid as they were during the past three decades. And since many of the changes are related, the pace of change in the future could be even faster than in the past.

We seem to be on the threshold of an explosion in biological knowledge and innovation; biology appears to be on the verge of a major expansion of activities such as that experienced by chemistry and physics a few years ago. As sociologists, we can only monotonously provide such general predictions as more cultural lag and increased value conflicts. As Wade (1980:288) aptly states in an essay warning against predictions for the 1980s, "Prediction, according to the delicate Chinese proverb, is very difficult—especially with regard to the future." But the proverb notwithstanding, it seems safe to predict more of the same.

References

American Bar Association. 1976. "Report of the Committee on Medicine and Law." *Forum* 11:300–301.

Barnes, Deborah M. 1987. "New questions about AIDS test accuracy." *Science* 238 (13 November):884–885.

Booth, William. 1988. "A change of heart." *Science* 240(20 May):976.

———. 1989. "Asking America about its sex life." *Science* 243(20 January):304.

Byrne, Gregory. 1988. "Artificial insemination report prompts call for regulation." *Science* 241(19 August):895.

Capecchi, Mario R. 1989. "Altering the genome by homologous recombination." *Science* 244 (16 June):1288–1292.

Caplan, A. L. 1989. "Problems in the policies and criteria used to allocate organs for transplantation in the United States." *Transplantation Proceedings* 21(3):3381–3387.

Caskey, C. Thomas. 1987. "Disease diagnosis by recombinant DNA methods." *Science* 236 (5 June):1223–1229.

Crawford, Mark. 1988. "Court rules cells are the patient's property." *Science* 241 (5 August):653–654.

Culliton, Barbara J. 1976. "Helping the dying die: Two Harvard hospitals go public with policies." *Science* 193(17 September):1105–1106.

———. 1988. "Politics of the heart." *Science* 241(15 July):283.

———. 1989. "Fighting cancer with designer cells." *Science* 244(23 June):1430–1433.

Dannemeyer, William E. 1989. Letter to the editor. *Science* 244(30 June):1530.

Fletcher, Joseph. 1972. "Indicators of humanhood: A tentative profile of man." *Hastings Center Report* 2(November):1–4.

Fox, Renee C. 1970. "A sociological perspective on organ transplantation and hemodialysis." *Annals of the New York Academy of Science* 169:406–428.

———. 1989. *The Sociology of Medicine: A Participant Observer's View.* Englewood Cliffs, N.J.: Prentice-Hall.

Fox, Renee C., and Judith P. Swazey. 1978. *The Courage to Fail.* 2nd ed. Chicago: University of Chicago Press.

Friedmann, Theodore. 1989. "Progress toward human gene therapy." *Science* 244(16 June):1275–1281.

Gray, Bradford H., Robert A. Cooke, and Arnold S. Tannenbaum. 1978. "Research involving human subjects." *Science* 201(22 September):1094–1101.

Grobstein, Clifford, Michael Flower, and John Mendeloff. 1983. "External human fertilization: An evaluation of policy." *Science* 222(14 October):127–133.

Harvard Medical School Ad Hoc Committee. 1968. "A definition of irreversible coma." *Journal of the American Medical Association* 205(August):85–88.

Hood, Leroy. 1988. "Biotechnology and medicine of the future." *Journal of the American Medical Association* 259(12):1837–1844.

House, Robert M., and Troy L. Thompson II. 1988. "Psychiatric aspects of organ transplantation." *Journal of the American Medical Association* 260(4):535–539.

Institute of Medicine. 1988. *Confronting AIDS: Update 1988.* Washington, D.C.: National Academy Press.

Kinsey, A. C., W. B. Pomeroy, and C. E. Martin. 1948. *Sexual Behavior in the Human Male.* Philadelphia: Saunders.

Kinsey, A. C., W. B. Pomeroy, C. E. Martin, and P. H. Gebhard. 1953. *Sexual Behavior in the Human Female.* Philadelphia: Saunders.

Kjellstrand, Carl M. 1988. "Age, sex, and race inequality in renal transplantation." *Archives of Internal Medicine* 148(June):1305–1309.

Knox, Richard A. 1980a. "Heart transplants: To pay or not to pay." *Science* 209(1 August):570–572, 575.

———. 1980b. "Mass. General: No heart transplants here." *Science* 209 (1 August):574.

Kolata, Gina Bari. 1983. "In vitro fertilization goes commercial." *Science* 221(16 September):1160–1161.

———. 1985. "Closing in on the muscular dystrophy gene." *Science* 230 (18 October):307–308.

————. 1987. "Human cancer gene sequenced." *Science* 235(13 March):1323.

Koshland, Daniel E., Jr. 1989. "The engineering of species." *Science* 244(16 June):1233.

Landegren, Ulf, Robert Kaiser, C. Thomas Caskey, and Leroy Hood. 1988. "DNA diagnostics—molecular techniques and automation." *Science* 242(14 October):229–237.

Lewin, Roger. 1987a. "Brain grafts benefit Parkinson's patients." *Science* 236 (10 April):149.

————. 1987b. "Dramatic results with brain grafts." *Science* 237(17 July):245–247.

Marshall, Eliot. 1988. "Harvard tiptoes into the market." *Science* 241(23 September):1595.

Marx, Jean L. 1988. "Evidence uncovered for a second Alzheimer's gene." *Science* 241(16 September):1432–1433.

————. 1989a. "Detecting mutations in human genes." *Science* 243(10 February):737–738.

————. 1989b. "The cystic fibrosis gene is found." *Science* 245(1 September):923–925.

Norman, Colin. 1983. "Clerics urge ban on altering germline cells." *Science* 220 (24 June):1360–1361.

————. 1988. "IVF research moratorium to end?" *Science* 241(22 July):405–406.

President's Commission for the Study of Ethical Problems in Medicine and Biomedical and Behavioral Research. 1981. *Defining Death.* Washington, D.C.: U.S. Government Printing Office.

Raymond, Chris Anne. 1988. "In vitro fertilization faces 'R & R': (More) research and regulation." *Journal of the American Medical Association* 260(9):1191–1192.

Roberts, Leslie. 1989. "New game plan for genome mapping." *Science* 245(29 September):1438–1440.

Robertson, Ian. 1987. *Sociology.* 3d ed. New York: Worth.

Simmons, Roberta G., and Richard L. Simmons. 1972. "Sociological and psychological aspects of transplantation." In *Transplantation,* ed. J. S. Najarian and R. L. Simmons, 361–387. Philadelphia: Lea and Febiger.

Simmons, Roberta G., Susan D. Klein, and Richard L. Simmons. 1977. *Gift of Life: The Social and Psychological Impact of Organ Transplantation.* New York: Wiley.

Starzl, T. E., R. Shapiro, and L. Teperman. 1989. "The point system for organ distribution." *Transplantation Proceedings* 21(3):3432–3436.

Stickel, Delford L. 1979. "The brain death criterion of human death." *Ethics in Science and Medicine* 6:177–197.

Sun, Marjorie. 1980. "Panel asks 'when is a person dead?'" *Science* 209(8 August): 669–670.

————. 1985. "Ownership of cells raises sticky issues." *Science* 230(15 November):789.

Transplantation Society. 1989. *Proceedings, 12th International Congress of the Transplantation Society,* August 14–19, 1988, Sydney, Australia. Books I, II, III. Norwalk, Conn.: Appleton and Lange.

Turner, Charles F., Heather G. Miller, and Lincoln E. Moses, eds. 1989. *AIDS: Sexual Behavior and Intravenous Drug Use.* Washington, D.C.: National Academy Press.

United Network for Organ Sharing. 1988. "Facts About Transplantation in the United States." (mimeographed).

Vaux, Kenneth. 1969. "A year of heart transplants: An ethical valuation." *Postgraduate Medicine* 45(January):201–205.

Wade, Nicholas. 1980. "For the 1980s, beware all expert predictions." *Science* 207 (18 January):287–288.

West, Susan. 1989. "Journey to Guangzhou." *Hippocrates* 3(2):82–86.

Wheeler, David L. 1988. "Harvard U. receives first U.S. patent issued on animals." *The Chronicle of Higher Education* 34(32):1,8.

Williams, Robin M., Jr. 1970. *American Society.* New York: Alfred A. Knopf.

World Health Organization (WHO). 1980. "Use of acupuncture in modern health care." *WHO Chronicle* 34 (July-August):294–301.

12

The U.S. Health Care System as a Social Problem

INTRODUCTION

A social problem is a negatively evaluated social condition or situation about which a significant grouping of people feels something should be done through collective action. A social history of the United States could be written by tracing the rise and fall of interest in particular social problems. Such a history would note society's continually changing values, norms, beliefs, knowledges, and symbols that identified conditions and situations judged to be social problems at particular times.

Social scientists such as Wimberley (1980) and Starr (1982) suggest that some people have attempted to define the health care system in the United States as a social problem since the early 1900s. Until then, the health care system did not relate to the entire society because many people assumed the services were for the well to do, which severely limited their coverage of the population. As the U.S. middle class became more economically and politically important, this assumption was increasingly questioned; people with new values and beliefs viewed a high-quality health care system as part of the good life all people should share. When the system was redefined as a resource for the society as a whole, the way in which it was meeting the needs of the people was criticized, and the U.S. health care system was on track to being defined as a social problem.

Starr's (1982) social history indicates that several attempts were made to bring the health care system into line with the needs of the people. But the criticisms that were voiced led to only minor modifications; the disparity between the overall needs of the society and the services offered continued. A significant grouping of people was not yet supporting major changes. It is only since the 1950s that influential groups joined in the chorus of dissatisfaction about how the system was working. Finally, in the late 1980s, the business community complained about rising health care costs for employees; both independently and in response to complaints, the medical profession began to understand that the system had to be changed, which brought the health care system before society as a social problem. Thus, after many years, significant social groupings joined the public in identifying the health care system as a social problem.

Before discussing the points of criticism, we will review the social context within which the U.S. health care system has been identified as a social problem. The bases of the system, which flow from the mainstream culture, will be presented and discussed.

THE BASES OF THE U.S. HEALTH CARE SYSTEM

Value Systems: Economic and Justice

Financial and employment figures indicate that health care strongly influences the nation's economy, including the gross national product, consumer price index, and employment rate. The health care system is thus one industry among many in the U.S. economy. It shares many attributes of such others as the defense, automobile, and entertainment industries. It functions like a massive industrial complex within a capitalistic economic system.

Given the historical development of the system, there are some humanitarian underpinnings, but the driving force of the U.S. health care system is to make a profit or, for some of its resources, to not experience a loss. Those who criticize the system because it lacks compassion miss the basic orientation of those who make decisions within it: The orientation is not to provide services for those in need, but to provide services to those in need who can pay for them. Pharmaceutical companies and hospitals, for example, are in business to provide care for those in need who can pay for goods and services. Justification for this orientation is deceptively simple: If free products and services were provided in a capitalistic economy, the result would be a financial disaster; with all outgo and no income, the pharmaceutical companies and hospitals would be bankrupt.

A Network of Independent Practitioners

The health care system of the United States is not a unified institution. It is made up of independent practitioners and facilities functioning in a loose network within which services are provided. Since there is specialization of function, and since each unit depends on others for referrals, the services are somewhat interdependent. But they still function as independent agents and agencies, especially in decision making. This pattern is a consequence of uncoordinated solo practitioners and individual facilities. It is little wonder that this network of services has been described as an "underpreventive, overspecialized, poorly coordinated, unaccountable and inaccessible" health care system (Weiner, 1987:426).

Protectionism

McKinlay (1988) likens the health care system to a professional sports game. The final decisions concerning the structure of the team and the game are made by financial interests in health care, the "owners of the park." The "players" in the game, however, are highly skilled professionals whose concerns and interests must be considered, particularly because they have the power to exert considerable influence on the play.

Within this context, physicians have been preoccupied with seeing that the rules of the game protect them. The "professional project" (Light and Levine, 1988) that characterized medicine in its climb to dominance was aimed at developing a single, autonomous profession that would control medical services while eliminating competition from others. It worked. With the consent of the "owners of the park," the medical profession constructed an organized monopolistic empire dedicated to protecting its turf.

An example of how this protection has worked can be found in the profession's reactions to the idea of compulsory national health insurance. Such insurance was first instituted in Germany in 1883 and it spread from there to other European nations. But it was rejected by the medical profession in the United States. Even though health insurance promised to increase the use of physicians' services and help pay patient bills, the American Medical Association (AMA) preferred to maintain control by restricting the supply of doctors. In the profession's judgment, health care insurance should be voluntary and left to the private system. Furthermore, the AMA insisted that any insurance plan must accept the monopoly of physicians over the care of patients. Given the power of the profession, when insurance that paid for doctors' services did come about, it came on the AMA's terms. The result was Blue Shield, a private voluntary approach that provided no control over the use of services or the amount of money that could be charged for services. The physician determined the need and set the price, and the insurance program paid the bills. The system was indeed protected, at least for a time.

EMERGENT PROBLEMS

The U.S. health care system grew without specific direction. It responded to demands piecemeal, while practitioners and facilities established themselves and then protected their gains. The system was splintered, almost searching for leadership. In these circumstances, physicians had something on their side that other professional groups did not: a powerful organization. Filling the leadership vacuum, the American Medical Association took charge by becoming the watchdog over the entire health system, which it easily dominated. It played this role by consistently protecting the position of the medical profession. To protect its increasingly dominant position, the AMA, to a major extent, became a veto group; the leaders of the profession knew far more about what they did *not* want in health delivery than what they did. Consequently, the AMA always reacted negatively to suggestions to change health care delivery, for fear that any suggested plan would have unforeseen consequences that might affect the profession negatively. In short, doctors were "on the top," and organized medicine was making certain this position was maintained.

This was not health system planning; it was, if anything, *anti*planning. This approach, or this lack of an approach, inevitably led to several major problems within the system, which we will now discuss under three headings: (1) problems of universal access—more and more people lack access to health resources; (2) constantly escalating health care costs—health expenditures have risen to what many leaders consider intolerable levels; and (3) concerns about the maintenance of quality—whether the present system will lower the quality of the care. These three problems are interrelated; some specific points can be discussed under all three headings. For presentation purposes, however, we will discuss the points individually.

Problems of Universal Access

No matter how developed technical medical skills may be, they are of no importance to society if they are not available to those who need them. Given the lack of planning, it is not surprising that services are not rationally distributed relative to the needs of the people.

Maldistribution of Services.   A shortage of physicians in rural areas is particularly serious, and there is no reason to expect that this aspect of maldistribution will change (Dettlebach, 1988). Some investigators contend that an oversupply of physicians in the United States will lead to a "trickle down" to rural areas, but data analysis indicates that this is not occurring (Fruen and Cantwell, 1982; Budetti, 1984). Given the comparative sparseness of the rural area, it is logical to expect that general or primary care physicians would gravitate there, but this is not occurring either (Nichols and Silverstein, 1987; Rabinowitz, 1988).

Within cities, physicians are concentrated in certain neighborhoods or, to put it more bluntly, they are concentrated *outside* certain neighborhoods. A major factor in the shortage of health care in poorer areas is the closing or relocation of hospitals that have traditionally served the poor and minorities in the inner city. There are several explanations for this phenomenon (Rice, 1987). As a hospital's service area becomes increasingly populated by minority groups, the facility faces more demand to deliver free care, which leads to major economic problems. For this and other reasons, inner-city hospitals tend to relocate in the more affluent suburbs. Thus, hospital care becomes inaccessible for many inner-city residents.

Closure and relocation is particularly common among for-profit hospitals. For practical purposes, publicly funded facilities such as Cook County Hospital in Chicago become the only source of care for inner-city residents. Nutter (1987) describes Cook County Hospital as deteriorated and overcrowded. The outpatient department has close to 2,000 patient visits per day, and the hospital is so severely overcrowded that nonemergencies must wait months for care.

Another aspect of maldistribution concerns specialization among doctors. The reward system of U.S. medicine—in terms of prestige, income, and lifestyle—makes specialty practice more appealing than general medicine. The medical profession in this country is becoming increasingly specialized. Thus, of the 255,027 physicians providing patient care in the United States in 1970, 19.9 percent (50,816) were in general and family practice. By 1986 the total number of doctors providing patient care had risen by more than 70 percent to 436,877, but the number in general and family practice increased by only 2,806 doctors to 53,622 and the proportion fell to 12.3 percent (National Center for Health Statistics, 1989). The number of primary care physicians in the nation is only 5.3 per 10,000 population, so many people find it difficult to obtain care at that entry point to the medical system. In sum, there are many medical doctors but there is a shortage of the kind needed.

Unequally Served Groups.   In discussions of the state of health and health care among the "underserved," McGinnis (1986) and Freeman (1989) note that a disparity between the health status of blacks and whites continues. For example, blacks have a higher incidence rate of cancer; only 38 percent of blacks survive beyond five years after diagnosis, whereas 50 percent of whites do. Cardiovascular disease also affects blacks and whites disproportionately; nearly twice as many black males suffer stroke deaths as do white males; and black women are at high risk for coronary heart disease, possibly because of the greater incidence of obesity among this group. Another health problem for blacks is chemical dependency. Mortality rates involving cirrhosis of the liver are twice as high among blacks as among whites, an indication of differences in alcohol-abuse behavior.

Another measure of disparity in health care is the nature of services hospitals provide. A review of patient experiences in a national sample of hospitals showed that nonwhite pneumonia patients were given fewer services in the hospital than their general health characteristics warranted; their hospital stays were also longer (Yergan, Flood, LoGerfo, and Diehr, 1987). These investigators suggest that some of the differences might be due to the hospitals where services were received, but their overall conclusion is that the race of the patient makes a difference in the type and amount of care received.

Death and illness surrounding birth also affect whites and nonwhites differently. In 1986 the percentage of live-born infants weighing less than 2,500 grams, usually designated "low-birth-weight babies," was more than twice as high among black infants (12.5) as among white infants (5.6). In addition, the percentage of birth weights of less than 1,500 grams was 2.66 among blacks and 0.93 among whites (National Center for Health Statistics, 1989). Low birth weight, particularly the lowest birth weights, is associated with a multitude of physical problems and with mental retardation.

Pregnant members of minority groups are less likely to have prenatal care. In 1986 only 57 percent of Puerto Rican, 59 percent of Mexican, and 61 percent of black women in the United States sought such care during their first trimester of pregnancy. By comparison, 79 percent of white women sought prenatal care. After examining the black neonatal mortality rates, Joyce (1987) suggests that the relatively high birth rates among black adolescents and unmarried women, combined with inadequate access to medical services, are primary reasons for the higher mortality rates among black infants.

Because of different lifestyles, the poor and members of deprived minority groups need health care services more frequently than members of other groups, but they are least able to afford them. Furthermore, the quality of the medical resources they use leaves much to be desired. But the conclusion should not be drawn that the only obstacle to good quality care faced by members of minority or poverty groups is financial. The roots of the problem are much deeper. In addition to serious economic barriers are deep-seated social, cultural, and psychological factors involved in obtaining health care. To a large degree, the reason the health system does not reach the poor is that it was not designed to do so in the first place (Strauss, 1967). The system is based on a market-justice, fee-for-service orientation; it is designed to benefit particular social groups while excluding others.

The aged constitute a demographic-social category with particular problems that lead to special demands on the health care system. Many of the problems for the health care system are a function of social change and medical progress, which led to major decreases in the incidence of life-threatening infectious diseases. Therefore, an ever-increasing number of people live to ages during which chronic diseases are prevalent. Some of these are degenerative diseases for which there is no cure; for these, medical intervention cannot go beyond relieving discomfort.

Logic, personal experience, and available data all indicate that the aged need health resource services at a higher rate than younger people. The average number of physician contacts in 1987 was 6.4 among those between forty-five and sixty-four years of age and 8.9 among those sixty-five and over. The hospital admissions rate of those sixty-five years of age and over was almost double the rate of the population aged forty-five to sixty-four, and the average length of stay was 8.3 days among the aged compared with 6.9 days among those between forty-five and sixty-four years of age.

Constantly Escalating Health Care Costs

In the judgment of many people, rapidly escalating costs, which have repercussions throughout the system and society, constitute the most serious problem of health care in the United States today. Fuchs (1990) shows that expenditures for health care have increased at a higher rate than expenditures for the rest of the economy since at least 1947. Prices have followed precisely the same pattern. In 1970, health care costs accounted for 7.4 percent of the gross national product; in 1980 they were 9.1 percent, and in 1986 they had risen to 10.9 percent. Some people expect them to reach 15 or 20 percent within a few decades. "There is also widespread concern that the 'spurt' of health care [costs] . . . shows little sign of abatement. Moreover, because the health sector is so large in absolute terms (about $600 billion in 1989), its rapid growth has a particularly traumatic effect on other sectors that compete with it for private and public spending" (Fuchs, 1990:534).

Figures published by government sources indicate that the United States spends a higher proportion of its gross national product on health care than any other industrialized country in the world. National health expenditures rose to about $600 billion in 1989 (Fuchs, 1990) from $248.1 billion in 1980 and $75.0 billion in 1970 (National Center for Health Statistics, 1989). The largest proportion, 39.2 percent in 1986, was spent for the services of hospitals. The cost of an inpatient day rose from $83 in 1971 to $499 in 1986, and the average cost for each inpatient stay increased from $667 in 1971 to $3,530 in 1986. Few families can afford such an outlay of money, especially if the person receiving care is also the major wage earner of the family.

When we look at the underlying reasons for the rapid rise in health care costs, we find that we have trapped ourselves in a system within which very little can be done. Many factors caused this increase; some are unrelated, but they converged into constantly escalating costs. All exerted pressure on an upward spiral for the cost of health care in the United States.

The following factors have contributed to the rapid rise in health care costs in the United States:

1. When legislation establishing Medicare for the elderly and Medicaid for the poor was passed by Congress in 1965, millions of people, many with serious and expensive health problems, were brought into the health care system. This humanitarian departure from a market-justice orientation was expensive in its own right, but Congress also failed to introduce cost-control measures that, in retrospect, seem essential. When doctors and hospitals raised their fees in response to the sudden increase in demands on their time and efforts, the government paid without serious question. From a cost perspective, the error was not in bringing the needy into the system; it was in not controlling the providers' reactions to what they considered a windfall.

2. A similar noncalculation (we use this term purposively, in contrast to the term *mis*calculation) occurred when the government decided to help those suffering from renal failure. When Congress enacted legislation in 1973 extending federal coverage of kidney dialysis and transplants to all in need, irrespective of economic position or insurance coverage, it opened the financial floodgates and the total cost skyrocketed. Furthermore, the nature of the program encourages dialysis in health facilities instead of at home, where the same procedure would be far less costly.

3. Increases in the wages of hospital workers' and doctors' fees have been continuing and major. Doctors' incomes, particularly, are rising rapidly: In 1986 fees for physician's services totaled more than $92 billion, compared with $14 billion in 1970.

4. Short-term general hospitals have a surplus of beds. The government has called for cuts in the number of such beds, but hospitals, which seem dedicated to maintaining their present positions irrespective of cost, have resisted strongly. These excess beds are a drain on the budgets of many hospitals and on the consumers of health care.

5. The U.S. public's reliance on specialists, whose fees are invariably higher than those of primary care physicians, means that the cost of seeing a doctor is high. The government has tried to convince medical schools to create incentives for students to become primary care doctors instead of specialists, but with limited success.

6. The U.S. population's love affair with high technology is at its height in the area of medical scientific instrumentation. Costs here include the latest in technical equipment and the high-priced expert who comes with it. Public response to scientific-sounding innovations is to put pressure on health providers to acquire the equipment and technique. Health resources may purchase such expensive equipment for its prestige value or because other health facilities have acquired it rather than to fill a real need. In addition, the lack of planning and a lack of cooperation among facilities can lead to purchases of expensive equipment by two or more different facilities that should be sharing instead of duplicating. Once the new equipment is in place, the tendency is to use it to help recover the capital cost.

7. The use of expensive procedures that have not been adequately evaluated continues. The life-saving value of treatment in coronary care units, which costs hundreds of dollars a day, is finally being questioned, but such units are already in place and have been functioning for some time. Also questioned are coronary bypass operations and radical mastectomies. And, despite a long-standing debate about the value of a tonsillectomy for a healthy child, close to one million are still being performed annually.

8. Insurance programs designed to ease the financial burden on the individual also lead to higher costs. The patient who knows that the insurance policy will cover the cost of a procedure may insist on it no matter what the price, since it is "free."

9. The progressive increase in the number and size of malpractice claims brought against doctors and medical facilities has led to two very expensive reactions: a marked increase in malpractice insurance premiums and defensive medicine, that is, "overcompleteness" of medical tests ordered by doctors. Although the cost of medical malpractice insurance seems to have stabilized in about 1987 (Holthaus, 1987), it remains high. Reynolds, Rizzo, and Gonzalez (1987) estimate the total cost at about $13 billion per year, 15 percent of U.S. spending for physician care. Defensive medicine costs may be extremely high, and the practice undoubtedly raises such other costs as the purchase of new equipment, doctors' fees, and insurance premiums.

10. Related to almost all of these factors is the doctor's increasing use of the hospital as an adjunct to office practice. The hospital has taken on the function of a center for technical equipment and of the area in which the specialist can carry out technical procedures under controlled conditions. At current hospital costs, this is expensive.

11. Demographic trends and advances in our knowledge of disease etiology and treatment have led to more people living to older ages, when illness is likely to last longer and be more expensive. The approximately 12 percent of the U.S. population that is over sixty-five years of age accounts for 36 percent of the nation's health bill (Mathiessen, 1989); what will health expenditures be like when this population figure swells to 20 percent, as predicted for the year 2000? The data also reveal that "almost 30% of all Medicare expenditures are devoted to the 6% of enrollees who are in the last year of life" (Fuchs, 1990). Adding years to the life of a person also adds to the time period during which other diseases can be contracted. Further, it is the nature of some curative procedures that the individual is made less resistant to other diseases. Perhaps the most common example of this is the use of antibiotics, which control one condition while making the individual more susceptible to others.

12. New and expensive diseases connected with aging have been identified; some have commanded a major research and treatment effort. An example is Alzheimer's disease, a particularly debilitating and costly condition. Hay and Ernst (1987) estimate that a patient afflicted with this condition spends $18,517 in the first year for treatment and care, with an additional expense of $17,643 each subsequent year. Depending on the patient's age at onset, the condition can cost up to a half million dollars.

New diseases are not found only among the elderly. Acquired immune deficiency syndrome (AIDS) can cost society an enormous amount of money as well as a high mortality rate among young men who should be initiating careers that would make important contributions to society. The federal government has been increasing its spending on AIDS research and other programs rapidly. In 1989 this figure was about $1.6 billion. The total financial outlay for AIDS cannot be predicted accurately, but there is no doubt that it will be extremely high.

Maintenance of Quality

Many of those concerned with the health system feel that problems of universal access and escalating costs are adversely affecting the quality of care being offered. For example, many patients who must interpret their health problems as financial burdens obtain their primary medical care in the outpatient departments and the emergency rooms of public hospitals. These resources are not designed for such services; the orientations of personnel are different, and the specialized equipment of the unit is not suited for routine medical problems. Further, the overcrowding typical of outpatient and emergency units negates the possibility of establishing the doctor-patient relationship that society feels is necessary for good medical care. Most health practitioners would agree that the quality of care suffers under these circumstances.

Problems of access and cost also lead many people to defer care. As Enthoven and Kronick (1989a:30) point out, "the deferment of care for conditions such as hypertension and diabetes adds to health risks and can cause much more expensive emergencies later. The lack of prenatal care can lead to very costly premature delivery and the birth of children with handicaps." For diseases such as certain types of cancer, the consequences of postponed entry into the system can be deadly.

Himmelstein and Woolhandler (1989:107) point out that "there is ample evidence that removing financial barriers to health care encourages timely care and improves health." These advocates of a universal national health program indicate that, after Canada instituted such a program, visits to physicians increased among patients with serious symptoms. Perhaps as a consequence, mortality rates in Canada fell to figures below those of the United States. When financial burdens are imposed, the evidence indicates a rise in some medical problems. For example, a one-year study of 164 medically indigent adults concluded that after California cut its Medicaid program, both access to care and the general health status of these patients worsened; comparison with a matched group of 94 patients in the same medical practice who did not experience termination of benefits revealed that their access to care and health status did not change (Lurie et al., 1986).

Several groups or coalitions throughout the United States feel that knowing more about the quality of health care is a priority (Droste, 1988). Too often, however, health care is viewed as so specialized and technical that only the structure of delivery can be assessed, rather than such matters as the personal relationship of physician and patient. But there is much disagreement about this point. For example,

Donabedian (1988) stresses that the quality of the provider-patient relationship is crucial to the outcome of care.

One obstacle to adequate assessment is that the medical profession insists it is the only agent capable of judging the quality of personal health care (Payne et al., 1976). Further, attempts to make such assessments are defined by some in the profession as an infringement on the rights of the practitioner (Morehead, 1989).

Financial considerations also seem to affect the type of service received by patients. Socioeconomic status, for example, influences the decision to perform some surgical procedures. Caesarean sections are a case in point. In an examination of nearly 250,000 births in Los Angeles County, California, Gould, Davey, and Stafford (1989) found a direct relationship between higher rates of Caesarean sections and socioeconomic status. Those women residing in census tracts with a median family income greater than $30,000 gave birth through Caesarean section 22.9 percent of the time, whereas women from census tracts where the median income was less than $11,000 had a rate of 13.2 percent. The decision to perform this procedure also seems to be influenced by ethnicity. The highest percentage of Caesarean sections were performed on non-Hispanic white women (20.6) and the lowest on Mexican-American women (13.9).

EFFECTS ON THE STATUS OF THE PHYSICIAN

By the mid-1900s virtually all aspects of the health care system were dominated by the medical profession. But increasing societal concern with access, costs, and quality have been accompanied by major changes in the system. Perhaps the major change has been in the doctor's status, which has affected how physicians view their profession and their role within it. Much of the emerging view has been negative, as was recently demonstrated in a Gallup Poll of practicing doctors. Almost 40 percent of the respondents stated that they are seriously questioning their decision to go to medical school (Altman and Rosenthal, 1990). Thus, added to the other problems within the health care system is the potential for alienated healers at its most important point of entry.

In the world of medical care, increasing bureaucratization, changes in organization, and shifts in financial arrangements have helped shake a taken-for-granted and comfortable status quo that in the past was rarely questioned. Suddenly, members of the profession found their authority being questioned. Social change has caught up with the medical profession. We will discuss some trends that have led to significant changes in the profession of medicine.

Professional Dominance

Parsons (1951) viewed the doctor-patient relationship as one of simple trust on the part of the patient, a trust earned and buttressed by the service or collectivity orientation of the doctor. Freidson (1970, 1984) questions this view. He describes the relationship as one of competition and conflict, with the incumbents of the two statuses holding different perspectives and interests. If we accept Parsons's description, we conclude that the physician's dominance is immutable; if we follow Freidson, we expect to see patient challenges to the physician's authority. In one, the patient is completely subordinated; in the other, dominance is challenged. Recent changes in society and in the medical profession suggest that Parsons's observations were correct until around 1950 and that Freidson's conclusions are accurate for the 1990s.

Light and Levine (1988) suggest that several trends in society have strongly affected the traditional view of physicians. First, *deprofessionalization* carries with it the idea of a consumer revolt in an increasingly educated society. Second, *proletarianization* emphasizes the inevitable expansion of capitalistic economic principles to health care. Third, *corporatization* sees professional work swallowed up in the needs of for-profit corporations.

Deprofessionalization (Public Acquisition of Medical Knowledge).   The essence of professional privilege is the contention that its members possess special esoteric knowledge. As this knowledge becomes less special and mysterious, the authority of the professional is eroded. Such erosion is occurring in the doctor-patient association. Because medical knowledge is now widely disseminated throughout society, patients are no longer willing to give blind obedience to their physicians. An educated public can now better evaluate the advice given and decide whether to follow it.

As part of an information-distribution explosion occurring in the United States, many of the startling advances in medical science and technology are no longer a mystery to the general public. The mass media reports medical developments in local newspapers and popular magazines, so the public is increasingly informed. Given the time lag between scientific meeting presentations and professional publication, the mass media may present these developments several months before they are published in scientific journals. Many people are therefore knowledgeable about what medicine can do and may, in fact, have such knowledge before the individual practitioner. The profession is no longer as esoteric because the public has gained current medical knowledge from television, magazines, radio, and newspapers.

Related to these points, Haug (1988) views increasing computer technology as the greatest threat to the professional status of individual physicians. Computer use diminishes the once sacred importance of clinical knowledge and experience. Currently available to the public are computer software programs that can be used to assess medical conditions, reach diagnoses, and consider possible treatment regimens. To a degree, the physician's rights of diagnosis and devising a medical regimen can be bypassed by the public.

Professionalism is furthered diminished by increasing specialization (McKinlay and Stoeckle, 1988). Specialization circumscribes the practitioner's scope of care, limiting it to certain diseases, parts of the body, or procedures. Also, specialists can break down aspects of their work into simpler parts that can be performed by other, less skilled health workers to whom they delegate tasks. This has led to paraprofessionals who can make some medical decisions without direct supervision by the doctor.

Proletarianization (Increasing Control by Outside Nonprofessional Forces).
Some authors suggest that many physicians are dissatisfied because they are being controlled by nonprofessional outside forces (Block, 1988; Scovern, 1988). Agreeing with this point, McKinlay (1988) attributes the dissatisfaction to major transformations in the health care system. He summarizes six of the current changes:

1. The increasing importance of financial concerns, which leads to the view of medical care as a business proposition.
2. An increase in government regulation of health care.
3. Technological changes that lead to the use of new types of equipment, such as computers, which require new types of health care workers.
4. New medical administrators for whom the financial bottom line is all important.
5. A more knowledgeable public.
6. Increasing evidence that the role of medical care in improving the population's health is marginal.

These trends have led to increasing dissatisfaction among physicians about their work situation, especially as independent practitioners. They complain about bureaucratic encroachments, governmental interference, and the expense of malpractice insurance, and they experience increasing difficulty in facing such immense problems by themselves. In one reaction, many physicians have banded together in a form of self-protection, such as in group practice or health maintenance organizations (HMOs).

The growth of group practice and the spread of HMOs introduce a new element into the organization of practice—the salaried professional. It has been estimated that almost 60 percent of physicians are now in group practice, HMOs, or similar non-solo-practice settings (Emmons, 1987). The increasing number of those who are "workers" in the sense of being salaried dramatically affects the status of physicians. Among other things, it weakens their political power and has even led to open discussion of unionization within the medical profession (McKinlay and Stoeckle, 1988). This situation reinforces the trend away from freedom of practice for members of the medical profession.

Corporatization (the Provision of Health Care in Profit-Oriented Situations).
The network of private corporations now engaged in the business of supplying health care to patients for a profit is growing. Especially over the past few years, many multinational corporations with highly diverse activities have become involved in the profitable business of health care in the United States (McKinlay and Stoeckle, 1988), and large corporations have expanded into health care. These profit-oriented companies market medications and medical equipment, but more than this, they are selling health care itself.

The increased use of technology affects corporatization. Computers not only stand between the patient and the physician, they can also be used in the corporation to monitor the physician's performance and bring sanctions to bear if that perform-ance is not up to some preset standard, such as the amount of time spent with patients. In effect, the physician becomes an employee who responds to the needs of the corporation, perhaps more than to the needs of the patient. The work becomes standardized and prescribed, and the doctor's professional independence can be threatened by company policy.

Relman (1980) discusses several problems in treating medical care as if it were another market commodity in what he refers to as "the new medical-industrial complex." First, it is difficult for the public to view health care as a market commod-ity because many people see such care as a right. Second, in many ways, such as paying the cost of research, health care is supported by government funds, which means the government indirectly provides financial subsidies to profit-motivated corporations. Third, the consumers of health care are not shoppers like those who purchase such commodities as groceries. A majority seek a service paid for by insurance companies; often, the consumers of health care are not concerned about the price someone else is paying. Finally, the amount of care delivered in the health system depends not on what the consumer wants to buy, but on the judgment of the seller—the physician. This can place the doctor in a conflict-of-interest situation.

Another problem in for-profit corporations managing health care concerns access to care. As Schlesinger et al. (1987) point out, many low-income sick have relied on an "implicit social contract" between the hospital and society. In return for public confidence, the health care system provides free or low-cost service to the needy. But this is not profitable. The implicit contract is broken.

Assessment.   Sociologists disagree about whether the trends discussed in this sec-tion mean that professional dominance has been lost. In part, the disagreement is caused by different points of focus. Thus, Haug (1988) and McKinlay (1988) focus on the individual practitioner and conclude that some dominance has been lost. Their case is strong, particularly when the past is compared with the present. Freidson (1987) argues that the core of dominance lies in the profession's control of the health care system, especially control of the process that allows individuals to legally practice. In this case, the profession is still dominant; it still has the power to control its future according to its own ideals and ideas.

A major difficulty in making such assessments is the public's unrealistic and naive expectations of medical achievement. During the past hundred years, medicine was glorified as scientific advances were emphasized. Unfairly or not, medical doctors were often portrayed as heroes winning the battle against disease. Members of the medical profession were honored for eradicating infectious disease, for bio-medical innovations that prolong human life, and for developing such dramatic procedures as transplanting parts of the body.

Lately, the medical profession has been pushed off its pedestal. The health care system and the medical profession in the United States have been criticized during the past decade. But the negative evaluation has mostly been of the system and profession as generalities, rather than of specific practitioners. Thus, people criticize the medical profession and the health care system but "have faith" in their individual doctors.

POLICY CONSIDERATIONS FOR CHANGING THE SYSTEM

Often, the identification of a social problem is a simple matter—just make a case that a particular condition or situation should be negatively evaluated, and the deed is done. The next step, deciding what to do about the problem, is usually a much more complex matter that can lead to a multitude of suggestions and countersuggestions. Such is the area of policy considerations. Determining priorities for appropriate changes in the U.S. health care system raises many issues in which value conflicts abound, vested interests are strong, and all solutions seem inadequate to cover the breadth and width of difficulties.

To indicate the breadth of difficulties, Longest (1979) suggests that five major issues revolving around questions of costs, entitlement, technology, decision making, and structure are involved in any approach to the problem. These are, how should society:

- Establish means for determining limits on expenses for health care services?
- Guarantee minimum health care services that are available to all citizens?
- Establish methods to evaluate the development and use of new medical technologies?
- Increase the decision-making capability of individuals who are not providers of health care services in matters concerning the appropriate allocation, distribution, and use of these services?
- Exert substantial pressures to reorganize and restructure the system to make health care, education, financing, and delivery more effective and economical?

This complex array of issues clearly demands some policy action to meet what is often referred to as a "crisis" in health care. But what direction should policy take? Should the system be preserved and strengthened, thus supporting its private enterprise, market-justice underpinnings? Or should the whole system be dismantled and turned over to public ownership?

Whatever the questions and whatever the proposed answers, the system is so well entrenched and resistant to change, so filled with vested interests, that serious problems lie ahead for any and all health care policy makers. Most suggestions take one of two approaches to solving the problems of the health care system: changing the cost structure or changing the way in which health care is delivered.

Changing the Cost Structure

Initiating the attack on the problem of cost has two advantages: (1) many policy makers feel that continual increases in the cost of health care make this the most urgent problem, and (2) changes in the method of payment for care may be the quickest way to influence the entire system.

Some policy suggestions stress developing better and more inclusive insurance programs that leave the status of the medical care bureaucracy essentially untouched. Blue Cross plans for hospital care and Blue Shield plans for medical care are the prototypes of such an approach, and they set a base for imitators. In essence, such schemes preserve the present health care delivery system as it is, faults and all, and simply fund it. Since many private insurance plans support the role physicians currently play in determining health care and are, therefore, interested in catering to the desires of the medical profession, this is a common approach.

But the system of health insurance has several problems. It became increasingly expensive because insurance companies were afraid to attack those who were making decisions that affected reimbursement for the insurance company itself. Consequently, they often permitted hospitals and doctors to charge more for their services; they grumbled, but felt they could not refuse to pay the bill. In response to increasingly high bills, many companies decided on the worst possible solution to their problem: They raised premium costs. This approach is apparently now reaching its limit. The solution of constantly increasing the cost for the insurance has become a problem in itself. The other option is to cut back on coverage, placing the consumer in double jeopardy, with a simultaneous increase in cost and decrease in what is covered.

The continual failure of private insurance to cover all health costs was acknowledged in the enactment of the federal Medicare and Medicaid programs in 1965. Although some politicians and pressure groups had been trying to have some form of national health insurance enacted since the early years of this century, it was not until the private system could no longer deal with insuring such segments of the population as the elderly and the poor that the government entered the picture directly. The burdens on the system, perhaps created by the behavior of the private carriers, were too heavy, and an impressive group of former opponents of any federal funding came rushing to the side of Medicare with a last minute amendment that also brought federal government payments for medical care to the poor through the Medicaid program.

Blue Cross and Blue Shield, sometimes referred to sarcastically as the "Medicaid of the middle class," had failed in a number of ways. Once seen as a great medical reform, its subscription charges were raised so often that it was priced beyond the reach of many people. Meeting the costs of insuring the elderly was transferred to the government with glee. By this time, however, even middle-income people found it difficult to meet insurance premium payments and health bills.

Medicare and Medicaid have many of the same problems. Both were designed to handle the serious economic problems caused by ill health, but soaring costs forced a curtailment in coverage while costs continued to rise. The programs have suffered the same problems as private insurance; the only difference is that the carrier is the government.

Belatedly recognizing that the system of reimbursement for care that had already been given was an important factor in spiraling costs, the government and private insurers attempted to gain more control over benefit payments on a prospective basis. The best known program is the use of diagnostic-related groups (DRGs).

In this program, medical conditions are classified within payment groups. When patients are admitted to the hospital they are classified by diagnosis and are assigned a preset number of days of care. Medicare or an insurance program will pay for only that many days of care. If the patient can be released in fewer days, the hospital receives the same amount of reimbursement; if care extends beyond the specified number of days, there is no additional reimbursement.

A primary concern for hospitals is that the burden for reducing costs by limiting stays is put only on them. Nevertheless, most hospitals are still dependent on the decisions of physicians, and they continue to respect the individual practitioner's decisions about the patient's treatment and length of stay (Weiner et al., 1987).

If hospital costs are to be affected significantly, the pattern of procedures ordered by physicians will need to be changed. Research indicates that such changes are most likely to come about if the way physicians are paid is changed. Hillman, Pauly, and Kerstein (1989) found, for instance, that payment based on a set sum for each patient and by salaries were the most efficient means of controlling some costs.

Changing the Way Health Care Is Delivered

If it is impossible to restructure the health care system through cost control, perhaps the feasible approach is to change the way care is delivered. Two approaches to restructuring are being attempted in the U.S. system. One is the Health Maintenance Organization (HMO) and the other is the Preferred Provider Organization (PPO). Both approaches promise the delivery of care outside the fee-for-service scheme, although they leave many aspects of the system unchanged.

Care-for-a-Fee Systems.   An HMO is a prepayment system. It offers members comprehensive health services in return for the advance payment of a fixed fee, thus eliminating the traditional fee-for-service arrangement. The Health Maintenance Organization Act of 1973 provided federal financial assistance to medical groupings that wanted to participate. Several arguments were presented to justify spending federal funds in this manner. It was felt that HMOs would reduce the pressure on overcrowded hospitals and would lower the cost of conventional medical care. Also, the elimination of a fee each time the patient visited the doctor would encourage individuals to take a more preventive attitude toward their health.

Since 1980, Preferred Provider Organizations have become another alternative among health service organizations (Hester, Wouters, and Wright, 1987). Service is available to members for a set fee that is lower than the usual market price. The goal of a PPO is to sign up a large number of doctors (the "preferred providers") who will accept a standard fee that is lower than the market price; the large number provides patients with a wide choice of doctors from an extensive listing. In the usual HMO, the patient is limited to one organization of medical practitioners and one hospital; the PPO patient has far more choices among health resources.

Both HMOs and PPOs still require payment, however, and that cost may be more than many people can afford. An even more comprehensive change in the system may be called for, such as some form of a national health care program.

National Health Insurance Plans.   In terms of a national health insurance program, two interesting, and perhaps related, observations can be made: (1) the United States is the only developed nation in the western world that does not have a universal program of health insurance, and (2) the United States spends a higher proportion of its gross national product on health than any other developed country.

The lack of a national health insurance program has not gone unnoticed by politicians. Such programs have been under discussion for many years, but attempts to introduce them in the United States have had limited success. A basic value problem dominates in all cases. Insurance programs run by the government do not fit well with the U.S. commitment to a free-enterprise, market-justice system. And lobbies working in the congress are organized around the principle that when people drift from such "cherished truths," they must be helped back to the "fundamental" values, to the U.S. market-justice way of life. Consequently, one after another of these programs have been defeated in the political arena. When some semblance of a program has somehow made it through, the health interests have attempted, often successfully, to turn it to their own benefit. This is the constant frustration faced by those who have offered national health insurance programs in the United States. Each proposed plan has failed to win final support by the political powers.

Radical critics contend that some insoluble problems are inherent in any health insurance system. They argue that strengthening health care insurance only evades the real problems, which center on the organization of the health care system. They suggest that the proposed insurance schemes will continue to funnel money into the hands of those presently benefiting from the health care delivery system in the United States. A national health insurance program would only cloud the problems of the system and the needed reforms by deluding us into thinking we have solved basic problems. Radicals believe that insurance systems fail because they are unlikely to meet the real health needs of people, they provide insufficient incentives to motivate a needed reorganization of the medical system, and they do not face the fundamental questions about the health needs of the society.

Many of the problems in the United States involve philosophical issues such as whether health care is a right of all, and how much power should be given to health care consumers in the decision-making processes. It extends to the adequacy and functioning of a health delivery system that has been characterized as a mosaic of fragmented parts. From the sociological perspective, the question extends even further because each part of the social system is intertwined. To fully understand the directions policy might take, one must consider the large U.S. institutions, the norms and values of various segments of the society, and the roles and role relationships that structure people's understanding of health and health action.

The root of the problem is that a system already exists, one that is consistent with prevailing market-justice concepts but is also abusing its recipients through self-serving decisions. And, many vested interests oppose change because things are going so well for them as they are. These special-interest groups have become very powerful and can influence legislation. When the government attempted to resolve problems arising from the lack of planning and control in the past, these interests brought pressure on the legislative process, and they worded their arguments to always sound consistent with the national value system. The members of society are caught in a series of contradictions; the values essential to the development of the present system are in conflict. Among these are market justice, free enterprise, the control of abuse, and the rights of people to have some access to health care. The dilemma is major.

SUGGESTED PLANS OF ACTION

The U.S. health care institution has grown without a master plan. Its growth within capitalistic and market-justice values meant that priority was given to its profit-making potential. This description sounds familiar—it sounds like the growth of the automobile or oil industry. But there was an important difference during the health system's development: Monopoly and dominance meant that even the inefficient could survive and flourish. Furthermore, the lack of competition meant that basic capitalistic principles could be ignored, and the market price for services could be set and maintained by the providers.

The overall result has been an enormously expensive health care system that has priced itself beyond the reach of the people it is supposed to serve. The automobile or oil industries could not survive under these conditions—they would have to make adjustments, to make certain they are meeting the desires of their clientele. But once the health system became entrenched in society, and once it was recognized as offering an essential service unobtainable elsewhere, the system was beyond bankruptcy, perhaps beyond change.

Consequently, the health care system is beginning to be described as a social problem, sometimes in very strong terms. Thus, in the *New England Journal of Medicine*, Himmelstein and Woolhandler (1989:102) declare:

> *Our health care system is failing. It denies access to many in need and is expensive, inefficient, and increasingly bureaucratic. The pressures of cost control, competition, and profit threaten the traditional tenets of medical practice. For patients, the misfortune of illness is often amplified by the fear of financial ruin. For physicians, the gratifications of healing often give way to anger and alienation.*

In the same journal, Enthoven and Kronick (1989a:29) state:

> *America's health care economy is a paradox of excess and deprivation. We spend more than 11 percent of the gross national product on health care, yet roughly 35 million Americans have no financial protection from medical expenses. To an increasing degree, the present financing system is inflationary, unfair, and wasteful.*

It is agreed that new means must be developed by both the health care industry and individuals to protect the virtues of the system while protecting themselves from extreme costs. Given the entrenched position of providers and facilities that do not want to endanger their positions, however, suggested changes would be supported only if they did not change the health industry.

If the system is not to be changed, it is up to individuals to protect themselves from the financial disaster of serious illness. Two sources that are capable of providing such protection are the government and private insurance. To this point, the government has selected special groups of people who are at high ill-health risk, such as the aged and the poor, for its survival programs. Private insurance has also been selective. It has provided coverage for large numbers of employed people at one time, thus assuring that the healthy as well as the unhealthy are included in their clientele. At the same time, private insurance companies have found a means to guarantee the payment of the subscription costs, by contracting with the business establishment to pay the costs of employee health care premiums. This, incidentally, has made employee and family health insurance one of the most important fringe benefits of employment.

But the programs developed by these two sources have not solved all problems. Not everyone in the United States is aged or poor; some people are unemployed and some work in companies that do not provide health fringe benefits. Therefore, large numbers of people are still not covered by government benefits or insurance company policies and cannot afford the costs of health care. To add to the problem, the two means selected to extend coverage and to meet the bills of those who could not afford care had the unintended consequence of fueling the rise in health care costs. For some time, the government paid the ever-increasing charges of providers and facilities without question, and individuals with private health insurance demanded whatever the health system had to offer. The "solutions" exacerbated the problem— the old saying about the cure being worse than the disease suddenly made sense.

The stage has thus been set for the classic response to a negatively evaluated social situation about which a significant grouping of people feels that something should be done through collective action. The health care system in the United States is being defined as a social problem. Four significant groups are voicing dissatisfaction with the system and are defining the problem for society: the government, the leaders of industry, labor unions, and leaders in the medical profession. The government's concern comes from the large amount of health expenditures in the federal budget. U.S. industry is concerned with the constantly rising cost of its health care fringe benefits. For example, the Chrysler Corporation spends $5,300 for health care per employee annually (reported in Himmelstein and Woolhandler, 1989), and costs keep going up. Corporate America's concern was expressed in the title of the cover story in an issue of *Business Week* magazine (1989): "Ouch! The Squeeze on Your Health Benefits." Labor's reaction to a 1989 plan of three regional telephone companies to shift some of the cost of their health insurance programs to employees demonstrates the union position: It made this one of the grievances in strike actions. The medical profession itself is calling for a solution to the social problem; this is best demonstrated by an editorial in the *New England Journal of Medicine* declaring in its title "Universal Health Insurance: Its Time Has Come" (Relman, 1989).

This powerful combination of definers makes it certain that society is on the verge of a debate about appropriate solutions to the social problem of the U.S. health

[margin handwritten note: gov. does not cover everyone]

care system. Two general approaches to solving the problem have been advanced: rationing health care and instituting a system of universal national health insurance.

Rationing Health Care

Rationing implies setting priorities that will be used to select who will receive health care and, by implication, who will not. Someone or some body of people is given the responsibility of deciding either on the allocation of resources or on the characteristics of individuals to receive a benefit. An example of the first responsibility is whether society should offer heart transplants as a treatment alternative. An example of the second is whether people of a certain type, possibly over a certain age, should be beneficiaries of available transplants. In either case, a value decision has to be made.

Such decisions are constantly being made in the health system, whether we recognize them or not. Society has reacted to the first responsibility by encouraging and supporting biomedical innovations. The U.S. population is committed to technological advances and marvels at what scientific medicine can achieve. The priority question is answered by providing major support for research that continually expands the frontiers of biomedical knowledge. Once this global decision is made, "objective" criteria, such as peer review, can be used to make the decision about which research projects to fund. This is a most acceptable approach, particularly because it suggests that values have been removed from decision making.

The second responsibility is much more difficult because there is no way to make value decisions appear neutral. Here the decisions affect which categories of people will receive the benefits of the system. In many ways, the health care system is devised so this decision is presently being made on the basis of socioeconomic status. To a large extent, the benefits of the system are for those who can pay, either by themselves or through insurance programs. The remainder are denied access. Understanding this, society has devised ways, like Medicaid, to attempt to rectify this situation so ability to pay is not the primary priority factor in obtaining health care.

But there are trends in the other direction. Thus, in response to financial priorities, the Oregon legislature decided in 1987 that the state would no longer pay for organ transplants for patients under the Medicaid program; instead, the funds would be used to support the state's program of prenatal services. (Arizona and Virginia have also taken this action.) This decision has led to major value conflicts and the ensuing debate has been acrimonious; as a result, part of the plan has been put on hold (Morell, 1990). This highlights the value problems of rationing. In a situation of "one financial pie," any decision concerning the slicing and giving of one piece affects the size and distribution of all other pieces.

Given demographic trends, feelings toward one's parents, and the political strength of the aged in U.S. society, the value debate is apt to be sharpest when recommendations are made to ration health care to the elderly. Such a suggestion has been made in a controversial book by Callahan (1987), who advocates setting limits on life-extending care for the elderly. In a telling statement, Callahan suggests that "we should decide whether it will be good for the bonds between generations to treat the health 'needs' of the elderly as morally identical to those of the young, as if death and decline were the equal enemy of both" (p. 219ff). He calls for "a willingness to ask . . . how we might creatively and honorably accept aging and death when we become old, not always struggle to overcome them" (p. 24).

As suggested by Callahan, many serious value problems arise. In the arena of values, answers are neither right nor wrong—only different. As Aaron and Schwartz (1990:422) point out, "concern for fundamental values such as age, visibility of an illness, and aggregate costs of treatment will inevitably shape our decisions on resource allocation." These decisions will, of course, be value based.

Universal National Health Insurance

The second approach, a universal system of national health insurance, has been advocated in the United States for some time. Many people consider universal coverage the fairest approach because all people, irrespective of their characteristics, are included under its provisions. This solves the problem of individual discrimination that is inherent in value-based rationing. Thus, advocates of the universal system are calling for the abandonment of the concept of rationing health care.

all are insured

unlike

value-base rating

Such an approach is far more acceptable to politicians because those who depend on votes usually try to project an image of fairness to all constituents. Since politicians will be the ultimate decision makers in the development of any health plan for the country, if one is eventually adopted the universal approach will undoubtedly be taken. The politicians must make certain they support a program of national health insurance, however, rather than a plan that can be accused of being "socialized medicine." Government employment of practitioners and ownership of health facilities is certain to be rejected in a society that emphasizes its capitalistic roots. This is well understood by vested interests in the health arena, which use the value term "socialism" as an effective weapon against suggested plans with which they do not agree.

The groundwork is presently being laid for the debate about a universal national health insurance program. Significant groupings in U.S. society have already started discussing suggested solutions to the social problem of the health care system. Solutions are being presented in the professional literature (see, for example, Enthoven and Kronick, 1989a, 1989b; Himmelstein and Woolhandler, 1989; and Russell, 1989), and the idea of a universal national health insurance plan for the United States is being supported by significant definers of values for the professional community (Relman, 1989).

CONCLUSIONS

We have used the final section of this book to review the problems of the health care system in the United States and to speculate about its future. Our discussion recognizes three aspects of the system that will influence it under any conditions. First is the power and pervasiveness of the free-enterprise, market-justice value system. Second, the health institution is represented in the highest national decision-making bodies by powerful vested-interest groups that have developed efficient means for monitoring legislation affecting their interests. These vested interests function as veto or supporting groups. Third, those who are entrenched in the system have become quite proficient in the art of finesse. Past experience has shown that each time a new program that the entrenched interests disagreed with has been instituted, in actual functioning these interests have turned it around, transforming it into one with which they agreed and from which they benefited.

With our knowledge of relevant values, vested interests, and the desire for the status quo on the part of many self-serving groups, we predict that any new health care programs instituted in the United States will not make major changes by bringing an entirely new health system to the people. Rather, tinkering with the present system will continue. Any changes will be consistent with the market-justice value and will support the groupings that now control the health care delivery system.

References

Altman, Lawrence K., and Elisabeth Rosenthal. 1990. "Changes in medicine bring pain to healing profession." *New York Times* 139(February 18), 1, 20–21.

Aaron, Henry, and William B. Schwartz. 1990. "Rationing health care: The choice before us." *Science* 247(26 January):418–422.

Block, R. S. 1988. "The pressure to keep prices high at a walk-in clinic." *New England Journal of Medicine* 319(12):785–787.

Budetti, P. P. 1984. "The 'trickle-down' theory—is this any way to make policy?" *American Journal of Public Health* 74:1302–1304.

Business Week. 1989. "Ouch! The squeeze on your health benefits." November 20, 110–118.

Callahan, Daniel. 1987. *Setting Limits: Medical Goals in an Aging Society.* New York: Simon & Schuster.

Dettlebach, Mark S. 1988. "Rural areas still need physicians." *Journal of the American Medical Association* 260(December 2):3214–3215.

Donabedian, Avedis. 1988. "The quality of care: How can it be assessed?" *Journal of the American Medical Association* 260(September 23/30):1743–1748.

Droste, Therese. 1988. "Quality is still the top concern of coalitions." *Hospitals* 62 (February 5):60.

Emmons, D. N. 1987. *Changing Dimensions of Medical Practice Arrangements.* Chicago: American Medical Association.

Enthoven, Alain, and Richard Kronick. 1989a. "A consumer-choice health plan for the 1990s." Part 1. *New England Journal of Medicine* 320(1):29–37.

———. 1989b. "A consumer-choice health plan for the 1990s." Part 2. *New England Journal of Medicine* 320(2):94–101.

Freeman, Harold P. 1989. "Cancer in the economically disadvantaged." *Cancer* 64(July 1, Supplement):324–334.

Freidson, Eliot. 1970. *Professional Dominance.* New York: Dodd Mead.

———. 1984. "The changing nature of professional control." *Annual Review of Sociology* 10:1–20.

———. 1987. "The future of the professions." *Journal of Dental Education* 53:140–144.

Fruen, M. A., and J. R. Cantwell. 1982. "Geographic distribution of physicians: Past trends and future influences." *Inquiry* 19:44–50.

Fuchs, Victor C. 1990. "The health sector's share of the gross national product." *Science* 247(2 February):534–538.

Gould, Jeffrey B., Becky Davey, and Randall S. Stafford. 1989. "Socioeconomic differences in rates of cesarean section." *New England Journal of Medicine* 321(4):233–239.

Haug, Marie. 1988. "A re-examination of the hypothesis of physician deprofessionalization." *The Milbank Memorial Fund Quarterly* 66(Supplement 2):48–56.

Hay, Joel, and Richard L. Ernst. 1987. "The economic costs of Alzheimer's disease." *American Journal of Public Health* 77(9):1169–1175.

Hester, James A., Annemarie Wouters, and Norman Wright. 1987. "Evaluation of a Preferred Provider Organization." *The Milbank Memorial Fund Quarterly* 65(4):575–613.

Hillman, Alan L., Mark V. Pauly, and Joseph J. Kerstein. 1989. "How do financial incentives affect physicians' clinical decisions and the financial performance of health maintenance organizations?" *New England Journal of Medicine* 321(2):86–92.

Himmelstein, David U., and Steffie Woolhandler. 1989. "A national health program for the United States: A physician's proposal." *New England Journal of Medicine* 320(2):102–108.

Holthaus, D. 1987. "Medical malpractice premiums stabilized." *Hospitals* 61(24):26.

Joyce, Theodore. 1987. "The demand for health inputs and their impact on the black neonatal mortality rate in the U.S." *Social Science and Medicine* 24(110):911–918.

Light, Donald, and Sol Levine. 1988. "The changing character of the medical profession: A theoretical overview." *The Milbank Memorial Fund Quarterly* 66(Supplement 2):10–32.

Longest, Beaufort B., Jr. 1979. "The U.S. health care system." In *Health, Illness and Medicine*, ed. G. L. Albrecht and P. C. Higgins, 341–369. Chicago: Rand McNally.

Lurie, N., N. B. Ward, M. F. Shapiro, C. Gallego, R. Vaghaiwalla, and R. H. Brook. 1986. "Termination of Medi-Cal benefits: A follow-up study one year later." *New England Journal of Medicine* 314(19):1266–1268.

McGinnis, J. Michael. 1986. "The 1985 Mary E. Switzer lecture: Reaching the underserved." *Journal of Allied Health* 15(4):293–304.

McKinlay, John B. 1988. "Introduction." *The Milbank Memorial Fund Quarterly* 66(Supplement 2):1–9.

McKinlay, John B., and John Stoeckle. 1988. "Corporatization and the social transformation of doctoring." *International Journal of Health Services* 18(2):191–205.

Mathiessen, Constance. 1989. "Unsurance." *Hippocrates* 3(November-December):36–46.

Morehead, Mildred A. 1989. "Assessing quality of care: Another step forward." *American Journal of Public Health* 79(4):415–416.

Morell, Virginia. 1990. "Oregon puts bold health plan on ice." *Science* 249(3 August):468–471.

National Center for Health Statistics. 1989. *Health, United States, 1988*. DHSS Pub. No. (PHS)89-1232. Public Health Service. Washington, D.C.: U.S. Government Printing Office.

Nichols, Andrew W., and Gail Silverstein. 1987. "Financing medical care for the underserved in an era of federal retrenchment: The Health Service District." *Public Health Reports* 102(6):686–691.

Nutter, Donald O. 1987. "Medical indigency and the public health care crisis." *New England Journal of Medicine* 316(18):1156–1158.

Parsons, Talcott. 1951. *The Social System*. Glencoe, Ill.: Free Press.

Payne, C., T. F. Lyons, L. Dwarshius, M. Kolton, and W. Morriss. 1976. *Quality of Medical Care*. Chicago: Hospital Research and Educational Trust.

Rabinowitz, Howard K. 1988. "Evaluation of a selective medical school admissions policy to increase the number of family physicians in rural and underserved areas." *New England Journal of Medicine* 319(8):480–486.

Relman, Arnold S. 1980. "The new medical-industrial complex." *New England Journal of Medicine* 303(17):963–970.

———. 1989. "Universal health insurance: Its time has come." Editorial. *New England Journal of Medicine* 320(2):117–118.

Reynolds, Roger A., John A. Rizzo, and Martin L. Gonzalez. 1987. "The cost of medical professional liability." *Journal of the American Medical Association* 257(20):2776–2781.

Rice, M. F. 1987. "Inner-city hospital closures/relocations: Race, income status, and legal issues." *Social Science and Medicine* 24(11):889–896.

Russell, Louise B. 1989. "Some of the tough decisions required by a national health plan." *Science* 246(17 November):892–896.

Schlesinger, Mark, Judy Bentkover, David Blumenthal, Robert Muascchio, and Janet Willer. 1987. "The privatization of health care and physicians' perceptions of access to hospital services." *The Milbank Memorial Fund Quarterly* 65(1):25–47.

Scovern, H. 1988. "Hired help: A physician's experience in a for-profit staff-model." *New England Journal of Medicine* 319(12):787–790.

Starr, Paul. 1982. *The Social Transformation of American Medicine.* New York: Basic Books.

Strauss, Anselm. 1967. "Medical ghettos." *Transaction* 4(May):7–15,62.

Weiner, Jonathan P. 1987. "Primary care delivery in the United States and four northwest European countries: Comparing the 'corporatized' with the 'socialized'." *The Milbank Memorial Fund Quarterly* 65(3):426–461.

Weiner, Sanford L., James H. Maxwell, Harvey M. Sapolsky, Daniel L. Dunn, and William C. Hsiao. 1987. "Economic incentives and organizational realities: Managing hospitals under DRGs." *The Milbank Memorial Fund Quarterly* 65(4):463–487.

Wimberley, Terry. 1980. "Toward national health insurance in the United States: An historical outline 1910–1979." *Social Science and Medicine* 14C:13–25.

Yergan, John, Ann Barry Flood, James P. LoGerfo, and Paula Diehr. 1987. "Relationship between patient race and the intensity of hospital services." *Medical Care* 25(7):592–602.

Name Index

A

Aaron, Henry, 282
Aday, Lu Ann, 78
Aiken, Linda H., 3
Albert, Cecelia A., 186
Albrecht, Gary L., 92, 146
Altman, Lawrence K., 271
Ambrosino, Rosalie, 144
American Bar Association, 233
American Hospital Association, 160, 162, 187
American Osteopathic Association, 146–147
Amini, H., 49
Andersen, Ronald M., 78, 105–106, 161,
    174, 175
Anderson, W. T., 115–116
Anthony, Dick, 211
Areen, Judith, 126
Arluke, Arnold, 70–72, 74
Aronson, S. M., 92
Ascione, Frank J., 36, 68, 72, 78
Association of American Medical Colleges
    (AAMC), 97
Augoustinos, Martha, 71–72
Ausubel, David P., 211

B

Balint, Michael, 116
Barnes, Deborah M., 57– 59, 251, 253
Barr, J. K., 141

Beauchamp, Dan E., 182–183
Becker, Howard, 94–95
Becker, M. H., 76–78, 80
Belloc, N. B., 41
Berg, F. A., 148
Bernstein, Arnold, 210
Billings, Dwight B., 211
Birenbaum, Arnold, 143
Blackwell, Barbara L., 80
Block, R. S., 273
Bloom, Samuel W., 95, 97, 115
Blount, J. H., 51–52
Bodenheimer, Thomas S., 126
Bongaarts, John, 199
Booth, William, 54, 62, 239, 254
Bordley, James, III, 101
Bosk, Charles L., 98
Bourne, Patricia, 91
Brandt, Allan M., 62
Breslow, L., 41
Brotherton, Sarah E., 139
Brown, E. L., 137
Bruhn, John G., 78
Budetti, P. P., 265
Bullough, Bonnie, 141
Bullough, Vern L., 220
Bureau of Health Professions, 131, 149
Burgess, Ernest W., 33
Burkett, G. L., 141
Bush, Patricia J., 80
Business Week, 280
Byrne, Gregory, 57–59, 62, 255

287

Subject Index

A

Abortion
    China, People's Republic of, 199
    liberalization of laws, 51
    religious influence in hospitals, 163
    screening and, 252–253
Acquired immune deficiency syndrome (AIDS),
    52–59
    clinical definition problems, 52–53
    confidentiality and, 82
    data problems, 52–54, 58–59
    distribution, 54–55
    drug use and, 25
    economic cost, 41, 62, 270
    emotional reaction and value conflicts, 53
    gender differences, 53–55
    HIV and, 53–54, 56–59
    homosexual behavior and, 25, 53–56, 59,
        221–222
    incubation period, 52, 56–58
    mortality, 55, 270
    opportunistic infections, 53
    prevalence increasing, 25, 54–56
    preventive medicine and, 58–59, 62
    public health alarm, 54
    screening, testing, 58–59, 75, 253–254
    sick status and, 81
    transmission, 53–54
    years of potential economically productive
        life lost and, 41
Acupuncture, 257–258

Alcoholism
    Alcoholics Anonymous, 81
    data problems, 32
    epidemiological inclusion, 27
    hospital programs for, 162
    labeling and, 83
    lifestyle and, 40–41
    medicalization and, 218–220
    sick role and, 219
    sick-status definition problems, 81
    Soviet Union and, 195
    treatment and, 81
    unclear incidence and prevalence, 31
    venereal disease and, 51
American Medical Association (AMA)
    code of ethics establishment, 101
    definition of group practice, 105
    education and, 89
    establishment, 101
    general principles, 101–102
    maintaining control, 264
    Medicare and, 102
    power diminishing, 102
    as a veto group, 264

B

Biomedical innovations, 231–258
    capitalism and, 247–248
    effect on physicians' practice, 232
    future of, 250–252, 258

About the Authors

Since receiving his doctorate from Michigan State University in 1959, Richard A. Kurtz has spent more than half his academic career in health and medical settings: three years were spent in the Nebraska State Health Department, four in the University of Nebraska College of Medicine, and eleven in the Kuwait University Faculty of Medicine. While in the Department of Sociology at the University of Notre Dame between 1966 and 1976, he was heavily involved in the medical sociology and the preprofessional (premedical) programs. He has published in several medical sociology journals and has authored two books on mental retardation.

H. Paul Chalfant is Professor of Sociology at Texas Tech University. After receiving his doctorate from the University of Notre Dame in 1970, he taught at Valparaiso University. He has published numerous articles in the area of medical sociology in such journals as the *Journal of Health and Social Behavior, Social Science and Medicine, The American Journal of Psychiatry, The British Journal of Medical Psychology,* and *Health and Illness.* He is also co-author of a text in the sociology of religion and an introductory textbook.